Crafting Constitutional Democracies

Crafting Constitutional Democracies

The Politics of Institutional Design

EDWARD SCHNEIER

ROWMAN & LITTLEFIELD PUBLISHERS, INC.
Lanham • Boulder • New York • Toronto • Oxford

ROWMAN & LITTLEFIELD PUBLISHERS, INC.

Published in the United States of America
by Rowman & Littlefield Publishers, Inc.
A wholly owned subsidiary of The Rowman & Littlefield Publishing Group, Inc.
4501 Forbes Boulevard, Suite 200, Lanham, Maryland 20706
www.rowmanlittlefield.com

P.O. Box 317, Oxford OX2 9RU, UK

British Library Cataloguing in Publication Information Available

Library of Congress Cataloging-in-Publication Data
Schneier, Edward V.
   Crafting constitutional democracies : the politics of institutional design / Edward
   Schneier.
     p. cm.
   Includes bibliographical references and index.
   ISBN-13: 978-0-7425-3073-7 (cloth : alk. paper)
   ISBN-10: 0-7425-3073-6 (cloth : alk. paper)
   ISBN-13: 978-0-7425-3074-4 (pbk. : alk. paper)
   ISBN-10: 0-7425-3074-4 (pbk. : alk. paper)
     1. Comparative government. 2. Constitutional history. 3. Democracy. I. Title.

   JF51.S33 2006
   321.8—dc22

                                                                    2005055197

Printed in the United States of America

⊖™ The paper used in this publication meets the minimum requirements of American
National Standard for Information Sciences—Permanence of Paper for Printed Library
Materials, ANSI/NISO Z39.48-1992.

Contents

Preface

On the Establishment and Survival of Constitutional Democracies

The fragmentation of the old Soviet Union ushered in a wave of constitutional change comparable to, if not exceeding in scope, the generation of change that followed World War II and the subsequent dissolution of Europe's colonial system. In just over a decade, dozens of new regimes have been constituted, not just in Eastern Europe and the former Soviet republics, but in places as diverse as the Philippines and South Africa, Croatia, and Haiti. Few governments have undergone more rapid changes than that of Indonesia. When I arrived in Jakarta 2001 as a Fulbright scholar, I had not anticipated just how timely the topic of my lecture series on constitutional democracy at the *Institut Ilmu Permerentahan* (IIP or Institute for the Study of Government) would be. During my tenure in Jakarta I participated in a series of workshops on amending the 1945 constitution. The level of insight was extraordinarily high, and media coverage of the issues of constitutional change more than comparable to that in my home state of New York when it confronted the possibility of a constitutional convention in 1998. Background materials on other democracies, however, were difficult to find in Indonesia. With the help of the IIP, I was able to have my lectures translated into Indonesian and published in summary form.[1] Returning to the United States as the Charles Evans Hughes Professor of Jurisprudence at Colgate University, it occurred to me that my lectures on constitutional democracy could serve as a suitable introduction to a course on U.S. democracy in comparative perspective. Hence this short book.

Although my Fulbright experience was the catalyst, the origins of this book date to a National Endowment for the Humanities Institute on constitutional democracy organized by Walter Murphy at Princeton University in 1996. Though formally retired, Murphy brought to the seminar the same combination of enthusiasm and intellectual rigor that he had shown many years before when we were colleagues in Princeton's Department of Politics. The endowment had, moreover, filled the seminar it with a diverse and interesting collection of political scientists and legal scholars from around the world. Without them this book never would have come into being. "In the past," as Julio Faundez has pointed out, "constitution making was generally regarded as an issue that only specialist lawyers and a select group of politicians could understand."[2] The world's most recent round of constitution-making has been characterized by far more widespread participation and awareness. The purpose of this short volume is to raise the kinds of issues that need to be addressed in countries like Indonesia that are in the process of reform. My hope, at the same time, is that it will raise the consciousness of citizens of more firmly established democracies concerning the questions that should be thought about from time to time in all countries.

Until the past decade or so, the study of constitutions by students of political science had become almost "quaint." Given widespread evasions of high-sounding texts, it was easy to consign constitutionalism to the status of symbolism and to focus instead on political "realities." Even in democracies, the dominant paradigm suggested that constitutional variables were of relatively trivial explanatory power: "Hence, it is not surprising that modern political scientists who are committed to discovering laws and regularities derived from actual social behavior should find the notion of constitutionalism both narrow and misleading."[3] The serious study of constitutions was left, virtually by default, to constitutional lawyers, the kinds of social scientists for whom—as an old joke goes—one piece of evidence is a case study, two are data. While I don't pretend that this is an empirically rigorous study, the growing number of scholars who take constitutions seriously has made it possible systematically and profitably to study them from a broadly comparative perspective. The growing body of evidence from countries that have made the transition to seemingly stable democracy has helped produce a whole new body of literature on democratic transitions that takes constitutional structures seriously. As Di Palma puts it,

> [T]ransitions such as Spain's revealed the essential reason for the experts' wavering between noncommital and pessimistic assessments. In effect, we suffered from blind spots. We were inadequately prepared for the intervening role of political actors; inadequately prepared to perceive the extent to which innovative political action can contribute to democratic evolution; inadequately prepared, in sum, to entertain and give account of the notion that democracies can be made (or unmade) in the act of making them.[4]

Comparative studies are by nature biased: we participate in one culture and observe others. But as a scholar who devoted most of his academic and political life to the politics of the U.S. Congress and my own state of New York, the especial delight I derived from my first Fulbright in Iceland (in 1989) and Indonesia was not so much how my U.S. training informed my understanding of these diverse systems, but how many of my observations there made me rethink what I thought I knew about America. I have read the *Federalist Papers* at least a dozen times, but never with more insight than when I read them in the context of what I was seeing in Jakarta. The United States was, to use Seymour Martin Lipset's felicitous phrase, the "first new nation," and it continues to serve as a paradigm for transitional regimes. If its constitution is not readily exportable, and if it is not so perfect a document as to be exempt from critical inquiry, it is without question the world's most thoroughly studied, parsed, and examined.

Returning to Indonesia in 2002 to testify before a legislative commission on constitutional amendments, I became part of a growth industry of scholars who travel the world proffering "wisdom" on how to constitute governments. Neither I, nor most of my fellow "experts," would argue that there is one best form of government, or that culture does not count. But an underlying assumption of any such study is clearly in conflict with an approach to comparative politics that begins with the premise that one must be thoroughly grounded in the culture of a society, that the study of, say, China begins with Ming dynasty vases. The premise that constitutional systems can usefully be compared, and that such comparisons can be made by people who know next to nothing about Chinese vases or Indonesian shadow plays is not without problems. While it is possible for comparative studies to draw upon the works of those scholars of particular systems who do know the language and culture, the possibility error is fairly high. But so are the possible rewards. Most fruitfully, the combined wisdom of scholars examining world governments can be used to make increasingly accurate "if this, then this" contingency statements that indicate the likely results of including particular rules in a constitution. That, in short, is what this book is about.

Writing from the perspective of Canada, Peter Russell has argued that, "The American constitutional style has been the most pervasive form of constitutionalism in the modern world."[5] True enough. It is also manifestly true— particularly in Latin America—that we have made some colossal failures in attempts to export our system of government (or, for that matter, the British model). Those failures, as well as some stories of success, will receive considerable attention in this book. And experiences such as those we are currently witnessing in Iraq underline its importance. It is, moreover, increasingly common, and increasingly possible, for political scientists to compare constitutional systems in ways that integrate both institutional analysis and contextual variables. The data universe now includes hundreds of constitutional systems that have functioned, or are still functioning, for long enough both to provide comparative insight. I have not read more than a score of these constitutions. One soon finds such a chore to be of diminishing utility and even faster diminishing fascination. Nor do I have substantial knowledge of the intricacies of more than a handful of national and subnational political systems. But the richness of the literature on comparative constitutional systems is large and rapidly growing. And it is not just parsimony that suggests a heavy reliance on secondary sources. I think that Edward McWhinney has been proven wrong when he suggested, some twenty years ago, the possibility that "the very notion of a constitutional system is inherently ethnocentric and western in character."[6] Since McWhinney wrote, the non-western experience with constitutional democracy has grown dramatically, and with it a non-western scholarship that is equally impressive. It is to this growing literature that I owe my primary debt.

Certain other obligations need also be acknowledged. The International Institute for Democracy and Electoral Assistance, its Jakarta office in particular, has both enabled me to stay abreast of developments there and provide me with numerous background papers and documents.[7] My former colleagues at City College, in particular Vince Boudreau, Joyce Gelb, Dinni Gordon, and John Harbeson have been generous with their suggestions, as have Reuven Hazen, David Olson, Werner Patzelt, David Pond, and Drago Zajc of the Research Committee of Legislative Specialists. Thanks to Renée Legatt and Anna Schwartz of Rowman & Littlefield for their patience and help, to my old friend Ellen Boneparth, to Asri Hadi, and above all to my wife Margrit for her careful reading of the manuscript, her Swiss efficiency, and loving support.

Notes

1. Edward Schneier, "The Problem of Constitutional Reform in Indonesia," *Jurnal Ilmu Pemerintahan (Journal of the Study of Government)* 15 (Spring 2002), 3-22.

2. Julio Faundez, "Constitutionalism: A Timely Revival," in *Constitutionalism and Democracy: Transitions in the Contemporary World*, ed. Douglas Greenberg et al. (New York: Oxford University Press, 1990), 356.

3. Faundez, "Constitutionalism," 354.

4. Giuseppe Di Palma, *To Craft Democracies: An Essay on Democratic Transitions* (Berkeley: University of California Press, 1990), 8.

5. Peter H. Russell, *Constitutional Odyssey: Can Canadians Become a Sovereign People?* (Toronto: University of Toronto Press, 2nd ed., 1993), 8.

6. Edward McWhinney, *Constitution-Making: Principles, Process, Practice* (Toronto: University of Toronto Press, 1981), 207.

7. Through IDEA I was able to return to Indonesia in 2005 to prepare a case study of the Constitution Building Process for a forthcoming comparative study of eighteen countries. It is available on the IDEA website.

Chapter 1

Constitutions, Democracy, and Good Government

In 1997, Indonesian General Soeharto was in firm control of the government of the world's fourth largest country. With the economy growing at an impressive rate, no foreign threats, and few political rivals, Soeharto had run the country for thirty-two years. At age seventy-seven he showed no signs of relinquishing either political power or the substantial wealth his family had acquired during his rule. Speculation on who might take over should he die or retire centered on his family.

Throughout his years in power, Soeharto operated within the context of the seemingly democratic constitution adopted in 1945 as part of the nation's fight for independence. The legislature met regularly throughout the Soeharto years, and the president himself ran for re-election every five years, usually winning more than ninety percent of the vote. The body that formally elected the president and approved the members of his cabinet consisted of 425 directly elected representatives, seventy-five appointed from the military, and 500 representatives of regional governments and so-called functional groups. In 1998, the system began to unravel as economic reversals sent the nation into turmoil. Student demonstrations of unprecedented size drew increasing support from workers and professionals, and when four students at the normally conservative Trisakti University were killed by the army, the crisis spread. The army itself began to waver, and the press began openly to question the president's competence and integrity. Even the upper house of the legislature—with more than half its members having been appointed by Soeharto—pushed for him to resign, and in May 1998 he did.

There is an old proverb, common in Asia, that you should never wish for anything too much because you might get it. In a way, this saying applies to those in Indonesia who worked for its democratization. Having suddenly and unexpectedly been released from three decades of one-man rule, with what would it be replaced? How could this diverse country of more than 13,000 islands stretched across nearly 3,000 miles of the Pacific and Indian oceans, govern itself? And if the old constitution needed to be revised, could it be done in such a way that a future Soeharto could not subvert its meaning if not its actual words? The United States faced a similar question in 1787. Having won its independence a decade earlier, the thirteen former colonies seemed increasingly unable to manage their affairs. When a group of delegates met in 1787 to discuss these problems, few expected more than minor changes in the badly flawed Articles of Confederation. Instead the delegates decided to meet the next year in Philadelphia and draft an entirely new Constitution. As much as student demonstrations in Indonesia made it clear that change was needed, Shays Rebellion, an agrarian protest movement in Massachusetts, convinced many U.S. founders that drastic steps were called for. The question for them, as for today's leaders in Indonesia, was one of how to construct a government for a large and diverse nation that allowed the majority to govern without intruding on the rights of minorities. What kinds of institutions make for good government (however that term is defined) and need to be considered in designing a government?

Questions such as these have recently intruded themselves on the United States in the wake of a seemingly easy military victory in Iraq. As the Iraqis work to establish a new constitutional order, they and their U.S. supporters are debating some of the most basic questions about the foundations of regimes. Indonesians and Iraqis have access to the examples of literally hundreds of world constitutions. In the decade between 1989 and 1999 alone, fifty-six percent of the 188 member states of the United Nations significantly revised their constitutions; more than seventy adopted completely new documents.[1] The American founders had fewer cases to learn from, but they did have the thirteen charters of the former colonies, their own experiences with the Articles of Confederation, the government of Great Britain, and their reading of history. There is much to be learned from others, but every country must adapt this wisdom to its own situation. Our goal is to retrace the paths of founders around the world to see what kinds of problems they have faced in common, and how they have learned from each other.

What Constitutions Do

Constitutions, as a rule, have two closely related functions: they *constitute* governments or define their institutions, and they *constrain* or restrict the scope of their powers. However it accomplishes it, a constitutional government is one that imposes limits, both procedural or substantive, on government. Simply put, constitutional government is limited government. Although we usually think of this in terms of constitutional democracy, where the limits are on majority rule, historically the limits have generally come first with majority rule following. The Magna Carta, a great symbol of the emergence of constitutional democracy, was a royal edict and not an act of parliament. It specified not a means of conveying power to the people but rather a set of limitations and constraints on royal prerogatives. The American constitution, for all its rhetorical flourishes, enfranchised no one and was virtually silent on the issue of slavery. While it stands as a watershed document in the evolution of constitutionalism, it placed the actual right to vote in a handful of male, largely white property owners. "We the people," in 1789, actually meant fewer than five percent of the new nation's adult population.[2]

While most constitutions "constitute" governments and describe processes of decision making, constitutionalism is as much about substance as procedure. Constitutions tell us not just *how* states can act, but about what they can, cannot, should and should not, do. Constitutionalism "presumes," as Walter Murphy says,

> that "out there" lurk discoverable standards to judge whether public policies infringe on human dignity. The legitimacy of a policy depends not simply on the authenticity of decision-makers' credentials, but also on substantive criteria. Even with the enthusiastic urging of a massive majority whose representatives have meticulously observed proper processes, government may not trample on fundamental rights.[3]

Just what rights are "fundamental" is a matter of ongoing debate; but while it is possible for a country like Great Britain to manifest a continuing concern with human rights in the absence of a formal, written constitution, every written constitution in the world has something to say about rights.

Constitutions and Rights

The most widely-recognized expressions of constitutional rights are found in sections like the U.S. Bill of Rights that specifically limit government powers, prohibiting, for example, laws that restrict freedom of speech, religion, or the press. Somewhat less common are constitutional mandates that protect citizens against private threats to freedom. Article 33 of the Indonesian constitution, which mandates state ownership of businesses crucial to the public welfare, is a controversial but not unusual example of a limit on the market rather than the government. Most U.S. states mandate public education and my own state of New York provides for the support of the poor. It also prohibits racial, ethnic, and religious discrimination, not just by government agencies but in the private sector as well. The 1997 Philippine Constitution, like many newer constitutions in the world, goes to considerable length in detailing some forty-one guaranteed rights. In many of these cases, the protected freedoms attempt not just to limit abuses of power but to express more positive ideals of both politics and economics. As such, they are intended to limit and direct the powers not just of kings and oligarchies, but of markets and majorities as well.

Most twentieth century constitutions, and particularly those adapted in the past twenty years, have tended to stress these so-called positive rights. Where the classic Bill of Rights erected walls between citizens and the government and focused on the kinds of things the government could not do, modern constitutions—both around the world and in the U.S. states—have been far more concerned with the things governments can do to protect their citizens from private injustice and to provide the material preconditions of greater freedom. Whether such "rights" are legally enforceable is another question; and indeed the issue of enforceability lurks silently behind the bold rhetoric of all bills of rights.

In the final analysis no constitution is self-enforcing. In a key flag salute case decided by the U.S. Supreme Court in 1943, Justice Jackson argued that,

> The very purpose of a Bill of Rights was to withdraw certain subjects from the vicissitudes of political controversy, to place them beyond the reach of majorities and officials and to establish them as legal principles to be applied by the courts. One's right to life, liberty, and property, to free speech, a free press, freedom of worship and assembly, and other fundamental rights may not be submitted to vote: they depend on the outcome of no elections.[4]

The idea that there are such immutable, fixed rights in a constitution is fundamental to the theory of constitutional democracy. Whether it is true in fact is another question. Indeed Justice Jackson's eloquent and oft-quoted words were written in a case in which the Supreme Court was *reversing* its earlier holding on the same issue, and in which three justices still disagreed with Jackson's position.

With whatever vigor they are enforced, however, the essence of constitutionalism remains the transfer of power from a governing order to a set of rules: if democracy is about the rule of the people, constitutionalism is about the rule of law. At the core of most constitutions are clauses that in one way or another prohibit arbitrary acts. Kings, legislators, magistrates, and police officers are required to play by the rules of the game basically to allow individuals to live ordered lives.

Constitutions and Modernity

The ideals of fixed rights and the rule of law have as their underlying rationale the attempt to make relations between citizens and states abstract and impersonal, to treat each individual, legally at least, like every other. This aspect of constitutionalism has its roots in the rationalistic traditions of the enlightenment: it substitutes rules governing relationships among strangers for the bonds of community which tend to decline in the face of growing complexity. Through such rules, it facilitates our ability to function in a world in which daily interactions are increasingly with people we have never met. In much the same way that a market system replaces interpersonal bargaining with a fixed monetary system, constitutionalism replaces face-to-face justice with uniform laws of interaction. In a market system, the price of goods is fixed: what you pay for a pound of rice is roughly what I pay. In a constitutional system what you pay for stealing that pound of rice—three months in jail let's say—is the same that I pay for the same crime.

Because it displaces personal interactions with abstractions, because it constrains arbitrary action in favor of impersonal rules, a constitution is a symbol and instrument of modernity. In his analysis of the decline of royal authority in Japan, Russia, Britain, and Western Europe, Reinhard Bendix traces remarkably similar patterns of change. In each society, the state developed under a monarchy in which

> a king governed his country like a giant household. There was little distinction between public revenue and income derived from the royal domains, though with the expansion of government an increasing proportion of revenue was derived from taxation. Members of the royal family participated in affairs of state as a matter of hereditary right. Rights were recognized as valid because they were old, not because they had been enacted by higher authority. In this way, property ownership, social status, and participation in public affairs were closely linked.[5]

The challenge to this fusion of family, property, and authority was often violent and usually commemorated in a document like the Magna Carta that codified and depersonalized rights and obligations. The "delegitimization of kingship has varied from country to country," as did the timing of the demise of the traditional social order; but, "That breakup became irreversible when even the head of the household lost his preeminent civil status, as social and economic dependents (like wives, children above minimum age, and servants) acquired a civil status of their own. Constituted authority came to be legitimatized by appeals to history, nature, and reason rather than to the symbolic inviolability of the king's authority."[6] Although Bendix does not explore the implications of these transitions for constitutional democracy, his analysis highlights the disconnect between tradition-based societies and the constitutional state. The idea that law can be depersonalized, a key prerequisite to codification, is so widely accepted today that it hardly occurs to us just how "modern" this separation is. Even today, as Bendix concludes, the transition is by no means complete. In the new states, he argues,

> Where poverty prevails and governments are weak, people find what security they can in the protection which kinship affords them, for language, religion, and group identity are transmitted through the family and thus given at birth. Where opportunities are scarce, claims based on such affinities are often effective. All modern states have developed in competition with these communal affinities, for the state directs our attention to the nonfamilial and, in that sense, impersonal exercise of authority.[7]

The transition to constitutionalism is far more disruptive of established practices than it is in more economically developed societies where a more complicated division of labor has already eroded the ties of family and clan. This is one of the factors underlying the argument—which will recur with some regularity in subsequent chapters—that some countries are not yet "ready" for constitutional democracy.

The problem applies with particular force to an ideocracy that has an absolutist or frozen perception of the world. A society preoccupied with a single vision of what is right—whether taken from holy scriptures or Karl Marx—does not fit well with the democratic vision of open debate and respect for differences. What is essential to constitutional democracy, "is the absence of either ideological or institutional monopoly: no one doctrine is elevated to sacredness and uniquely linked to the social order. Positions of power are rotated like all others and do not attract incommensurate or even particularly great rewards."[8] These are not easy standards to meet. Even in established democracies, there are subcultures that crave the security of fixed systems of belief. The wish for kings is found lurking closer to the surface of more constitutional democracies than we like to admit. And the yearning for a more personalized, less abstract system of law is very much a part of politics in virtually all modern states.

Constitutionalism and the Rule of Law

Patriotic speeches in the United States talk of putting "the rule of law above the rule of men." In our courtrooms, statues of justice show her blindfolded, unable to see those accused of crimes, and thus unable to be swayed by their personal characteristics. Leaving aside for the moment the question of whether justice can ever be truly blind, this kind of abstract justice is not without shortcomings. Indeed the Anglo-American jury system—conceived and implemented at a time when most people lived in very small, stable communities—was for most times and places quite personal. Most jurors, in most towns knew the defendant, knew about the crime, and had probably made up their minds before the trial began. Increasingly, however, knowledge of the crime, the victim, or the defendant has become grounds for dismissal of a potential juror. Objectivity has become the hallmark of justice, or almost.

A current controversy in the United States illustrates one of the key problems associated with the idea of the rule of law. Beyond the trial stage, the criminal justice system starts with the notion that punishment should be handed out according to the seriousness of the crime, not to the status of the individual. Murder is murder, rape is rape, and the penalties given to convicted murderers and rapists should be the same whether the criminals are white or black, rich or poor, handsome or ugly. Such is the ideal. But what about the mentally retarded or the very young? Should a ten-year old, who barely understands that a gun fired in real life is not the same as one fired on television, be held to the same standard as an adult? Is it right to put to death for murder people of such limited intelligence that they do not understand what they have done? This issue is very much alive, and very hotly debated in the United States today where the State of Texas recently executed a man with the mental capacity of an eight-year old, and the Supreme Court more recently decided that such uses of capital punishment were unconstitutional. Many states protect the feeble-minded from such punishment, and youthful offenders are generally defined and treated differently from adults, though the age limits for defining "youth" vary enormously from one state to another. The argument underlying the system in Texas is that the law punishes the crime not the criminal. If this argument is by not universally accepted, it is not illogical.

The system in most continental European countries tends to take the status of the offender into account. Trials are far more personalized than in the United States. But the law itself, in Europe as in the American states, still has universal applicability as its goal. If it can be subjective in application, it should be objective and neutral in its crafting and enforcement. The law is the law in constitutional governments, even if, as Anatole France pointedly remarked, it equally punishes the rich and poor for sleeping on park benches.

Constitutions cannot guarantee equality any more than market systems guarantee riches; but what virtually every constitution attempts in some way to do is to limit the ability of the privileged either to use state power to extend their privileges or to put themselves beyond the law. That most constitutions fail to some degree in this endeavor is testimony to the universal cultural, economic and political power of privilege; but it is the very essence of constitutionalism to make the effort and to some degree succeed. Constitutionalism, as Daniel Lev has written in discussing Indonesia and Malaysia,

> implies that the political process, with or without a written constitution, is more or less oriented to public rules and institutions intended to contain the exercise of political authority. At the core of constitutionalism is legal process. The point should not be exaggerated beyond the capacity of any state to represent the genre. For the centrality of law and legal process does not mean that nothing else counts. The influence of economic interests, elite leverage, and popular values all matter in every society, contrary governing principles notwithstanding. But constitutional regimes necessarily foster a common appreciation of, or orientation to, legal rules and the general principles that underlay them.[9]

Clearly, the question of whether a system is constitutional is partly one of degree. Precious few societies have ever been governed entirely in the absence of fixed rules, and none are run strictly according to the book. The places in which societies fit along this continuum occupy a broad spectrum, and the differences between them are important; but the attempt to draw a line that demarcates the boundaries between systems that qualify and systems that do not is a difficult enterprise at best. Nino uses the term "thickening" to describe what he sees as increasingly more complicated variations of the theme of limited government. The very "thinnest concept of constitutionalism," he writes, "is associated with the basic idea of the *rule of law*. . . . A slightly thicker concept," in Nino's classification, "is more specific about the way in which governmental bodies are constrained by legal rules, requiring a constitution, though not necessarily a written one. Whatever its content, this constitution is entrenched, since its reform and abrogation are more difficult than ordinary laws, and it is held to be supreme with regard to ordinary laws."[10]

The concept thickens further in Nino's construct, when the laws are equally applied; when they are enforced by an independent judiciary; and when "the constitution recognizes individual rights that cannot be encroached upon by any organ of the state."[11] Most complicated, and in a sense complete, in this formulation, are systems which add democracy to the mix, particularly those that include elaborate systems of checks and balances that place institutional restraints on the exercise of arbitrary power. The mixes of institutional forms, social forces, and constitutional types are numerous and complex. Different systems protect (or fail to protect) rights in different ways. Whether it is possible, as Nino sought, to provide "a chart for sorting out conflicting claims based on a plurality of dimensions of constitutionalism,"[12] the inter-relationships are illuminating.

How Constitutions Protect Rights

Most constitutions, as we have argued, "constitute," that is, they provide the rules of the game by which decisions are made. And the general direction of these rules is to limit or complicate the exercise of state power. Few constitutions, however, are content to rely on procedural rules alone to protect human rights. Although the original draft of the Constitution of the United States contained no bill of rights, many states made inclusion of such a list a condition of ratification, and their adoption was one of the first acts of the first Congress. Despite the plausible argument, raised by many of the founders, that no listing of protected rights was necessary against a government with no power to invade them, most constitution writers have quite deliberately set certain rights beyond the realm of ordinary politics.

In Western political thought, one could argue that such declarations of right are fundamental to most theories of governance. Higher law justifications were commonly employed to support limits on the powers of kings. Early Christian thought in particular, emphasized the notion of "two swords," the secular sword of the state and the sacred realm of the Church. This notion of separate spheres of sovereignty crept into democratic theory under the banner of natural rights, the notion that there are human attributes that in some sense or another transcend civil society. Jefferson's ringing phrase in the American Declaration of Independence that "all men are created equal, and that they are endowed by their Creator with certain inalienable rights, and that among these are life, liberty, and the pursuit of happiness" have resonated around the world. You won't find these noble words in our Constitution and they have no force of law, but the idea that a constitution should immunize some part of the private sphere from public power is found in most constitutions and tends to be justified in similar terms.

A second category of rights protected, particularly in democracies, are those that we might call functional rights, rights that sustain the system itself and that bridge the line of substantive and procedural rights. The right to vote is in this sense fundamental to a democracy, as is free speech and some right of association. As Sunstein notes, "Constitutional protection of these rights is not at odds with the commitment to self-government but instead a logical part of it."[13] Robert Dahl's listing of institutional guarantees that must be in place to give democracy a reasonable chance of working are, with some variations, widely accepted. They include, (1) freedom to organize; (2) freedom of expression; (3) the right to vote, (4) to run for public office, and (5) to campaign and compete for voter support; (6) access to alternative sources of information about significant issues; (7) free and fair elections; and (8) the functioning of institutions, such as parties and interest groups, to link government policies to public preferences.[14]

While other students of democracy might juggle the specifics of a list of this kind, Dahl's categories nicely sum up the tests, and most modern constitutions, in fact, accord them specific recognition. While the Constitution of the United States does not specifically protect those that pertain to elections, state guarantees and subsequent laws have made this a trivial point, and I think it reasonable to suggest that a constitutional democracy is in no small part defined by the degree to which it protects these rights.

Democratic constitutions protect rights both by limiting the government's formal authority to abridge them, and giving teeth to these limitations through institutional checks and balances that constrain the exercise of power. Good government limits the ability of majorities to limit the rights of others, but it also empowers those same majorities to mobilize, to choose new leaders to act in the public interest. Dahl suggests that there are two other claims to substantive interests of this kind that can also plausibly be associated with constitutional democracy. First are those rights that are "external" to democracy but necessary. By "external," Dahl explains, "I mean that it is not part of the conception of the process itself, yet it is essential to the functioning of the process. For example, from Aristotle onward political theorists have recognized that the functioning of democratic processes will be impaired if citizens are vastly unequal in economic means or in other crucial resources."[15]

While this right is nowhere to be found in the American Constitution, and has few adherents in contemporary Washington, it has emerged with sufficient frequency in American politics—perhaps most glowingly articulated in Franklin Roosevelt's four freedoms—as to have almost quasi-constitutional status. A second, equally interesting set of claims that Dahl suggests for consideration as substantive rights derive from what he calls the "Idea of Intrinsic Equality." Since democracy pre-supposes political equality, it is logical—if not necessary—that it endorse legal equality as well: "Thus a fair trial in criminal cases is not an element of the democratic process, and arguably is not necessary to it, but it is clearly necessary for equal consideration."[16]

Finally, some democracies put certain issues off limits because they are deemed so potentially disruptive as to be dangerous to the system itself. The question of language in Canada is a good example, as is that of religious freedom in America. It is not so much that Canada is not, in essence, a country with a large English-speaking majority, or that the United States is not fundamentally Protestant; but that the minorities of those who are, on the one hand French or on the other non-Protestant are large enough that the attempt to impose a state language or religion might threaten the unity of the system as a whole. In the United States, we have a federal system in which considerable powers are exercised by fifty distinct and semi-sovereign governments like my own state of New York which has an annual budget that, if it were a nation, would rank among the world's top ten. Although the states exercise considerable power, they are also significantly constrained. Under the so-called commerce clause, for example, no state can erect barriers, such as tariffs or taxes, to trade with other states or limit the free movement of citizens from one state to another. Here, "what appears to be a relinquishment of state sovereignty very likely furthers the interest of all states concerned."[17]

Although most world constitutions contain bills of rights or other sections that set such areas aside from government control, in times of crisis, they have proven to be of little value. "Mere parchment barriers," as James Madison wrote in defending the American constitution he helped draft, provide little real protection for liberty. Where then can such protection be found? The ultimate defenses are, of course, in the people. But part of the case I try to make in this book is that constitutions have consequences that do protect rights and that do affect political outcomes. What Madison and the drafters of the American Constitution counted on more than "parchment barriers" were structures of decision making that continue to make compromise a cornerstone of American politics. By confusing power and the lines of authority, the Constitution, paradoxically, protects freedom.

The two primary functions of constitutions, we suggested at the outset, were to *constitute* and to *constrain* governments. Here we can see that these two functions are, as a rule, joined at the hip. Whatever formal rights a constitutional system proclaims, whatever limits it places on government or private acts impinging on those rights, they are only as likely to be as effective as politics makes them. Constitutional structures are themselves written in parchment; but as Madison also recognized they can come to have symbolic value and more. As Murphy puts it,

> If these institutional webs formed merely "parchment barriers," they would be important only to students of rhetoric. To think that words can constrain power seems foolish. Yet a political chemistry may turn sheets of paper into hoops of steel. First, by prescribing institutional structures and fracturing power among different offices a document can push officials, as Madison recognized, to link their own interests with those of their office and jealously guard those interests against putative incursions by other officials. Further, by drawing vague divisions

of authority, a document can make it likely that no set of officials can do much that is politically important without arousing the territorial imperative of other officials. Thus a constitutional text can disperse power and protect liberty by pitting ambition against ambition and power against power.[18]

While the American Constitution dispersed power through a formal separation of powers between legislative, executive, and judicial branches; and a relatively clear division of powers between the national and state governments, the issue for constitution-makers is less one of structure than principle. The structural key to constitutional democracy is the notion of checks and balances: the idea that power is best constrained, not by abstract limits, but by countervailing power. Bills of rights are aspirational; constitutions are political, and it is structures rather than strictures that are the ultimate guardians of rights.

Of Time, Place, and Constitutional Democracy

Most world constitutions have been relatively short-lived. Looking mostly at more developed nations, Donald Lutz calculated an average age of fifty-two years per constitution.[19] Giovanni Sartori estimates that, "Of the 170 or so written documents called constitutions in today's world, more than half have been written since 1974."[20] Even in the United States, which, as a nation, has the world's oldest written constitution in continuous use, the average life of the individual state constitutions is seventy-seven years, and there are only nineteen states that have never torn up their old charters and started again.[21] Old constitutions, such as that of the United States or the State of Vermont (1793), are clearly rather exceptional, and—when you think about it—that should come as no surprise. "Each generation," Thomas Jefferson wrote in a famous letter to Madison, has "a right to choose for itself a form of government it believes most promotive of its own happiness."[22] At certain set periods of time—at one point Jefferson specified twenty years—all constitutive laws and institutional arrangements should be scrapped and rebuilt by a new generation.[23] Madison's answer began with the problem of defining which generation was binding which. Generations, he pointed out, instead of marching in parade-like cohorts tend rather to blend into one another. But Madison was more concerned with what he considered the positive role that a well-constructed constitution could play in furthering democratic government. Not only would frequent changes "deprive the government of that veneration which time bestows on everything," but they could lead to situations in which the legal vacuum created by each transition would confound the questions of constitutional structures with those more ephemeral issues of the day.[24] Jefferson's plan for frequent constituent assemblies would make the system "too subject to the casualty and consequences of an interregnum."[25]

The question of how easily a constitution should be changed is the subject of a later chapter; but the issue of mutability addressed in the Jefferson-Madison correspondence is obviously central to the very idea of constitutional democracy. The world outlier on this issue is Great Britain which has no formal constitution and can thus be changed at any time by simple majority vote of parliament. Together with three of its former colonies and—for most issues—Israel, the United Kingdom is the only world democracy that does not require some kind of special majority or procedure for changing the rules of the game.

The three most common reasons for changing constitutions are changing circumstances, newly discovered flaws in the original document, or shifts in political power. While Jefferson's notion of periodic change was justified in terms of changing circumstances, in practice the three rationales are not always so easy to distinguish. Gradually changing circumstances and minor flaws can usually be dealt with either by bending the interpretation of the original document or through formal amendment. Major shifts in power, however, can be quite tricky as constitutions often bias outcomes. The American constitution "survived" its postponement of the issue of slavery only through civil war and a series of amendments that dramatically changed its system of federalism. But many constitutions become so out of sync with political reality as to render them either farcical or expendable. Constitutions, moreover, can be abrogated—with or without the help of charismatic leaders—by general shifts in public sentiment. In the real world, the balance between the inspiring and generally complementary forces of constitutionalism and democracy are manifest in such periods of social upheaval, and they may result in formal amendment, abrogation of the existing constitution, ignoring it, or through some process of formal amendment.

If we move beyond the technical question of how such changes take place, those of us who believe in both constitutionalism and democracy are discomforted by the Jefferson-Madison debate. Somewhere, I remember a question, attributed to President Andrew Jackson, "What's a constitution among friends?," and it is a question that I suspect has been raised, more obliquely perhaps, by every one of his successors. What, indeed, is a constitution among friends? Is the concept of *constitutional democracy* an oxymoron? To what extent are the notions of fixed rules and limitations on government power compatible with those of popular sovereignty?

The Democratization of the World

The answers to questions such as these are not simply theoretical, and are increasingly germane in every corner of the world. A quarter of a century ago, it was fashionable in political science to question whether any but a handful of economically developed, largely western nations were capable of sustaining democratic government. Reversions to dictatorship in many parts of Latin America and Africa, the persistence of repressive regimes along the southern and eastern rims of Europe and throughout most of Asia, led to a focus on the shortcomings of democracy rather than its possibilities. Even in older, established democracies, some experts wrote of a "crisis of democracy," featuring the breakdown of social discipline, declining trust in government, an inability to cope with major issues, and a generally bleak future for citizen control.[26] When this dark assessment appeared in 1975, only about forty—fewer than a third of the independent countries in the world— could be described as democracies. Within five years, that number was over fifty, and included both Spain and Portugal, Europe's two longest-enduring non-democratic states. Ten years later still, Samuel Huntington, one of the co-authors of the 1975 book heralding the crisis of democracy, was describing a "third wave" of democratization, rivaling in force the first wave of the nineteenth century and the postcolonial decades of the period following World War II.[27] Unlike the second wave, which saw numerous transitions back through democracy to dictatorship, this third wave has neither crested nor receded. Some of the "transitions" in the former Soviet Union have proven cosmetic at best, and many of the new democracies are fragile indeed, but as shown in Table 1.1, democracy remains a growth product.

In George Orwell's *Animal Farm,* all animals were equal; but some, as the ruling pigs pointed out, were more equal than others. In the countries counted as democracies in Table 1.1 some are similarly more democratic than others. In fact, many observers would agree with Diamond's argument that the positive developments of increasing democratization in the formal sense "have been counterbalanced and in many countries even outweighed by conditions that render electoral democracy increasingly illiberal, unaccountable, and afflicted."[28] The figures recorded in Table 1.1, though they distinguish between countries that are "partly free" from those considered "free," cannot capture these nuances. The spread of democracy that the figures suggest is real, what they portend is more controversial. They only partially reflect the empty formalism of systems that use the trappings of democratic procedures to mask a reality of subtle oppression. They do not reflect, in any sense, what many observers feel are real slippages in the quality of democratic society in many of the world's most established free societies not excepting the United States. Voter turnout in some of these countries has declined to new lows, as has "popular confidence in the performance of representative institutions," and support for the basic institutions of constitutional democracy.[29] Democratic forms are increasingly ubiquitous, democratic polities maybe less so.

Because institutions are the tangible building blocks of democratization, they have been the primary focus of most students of comparative politics and will be central to much of what follows in this book. The notion, however, that democracy is only about methods of governing is over simple in its tendency to ignore the creative process by which participation in the community is an end as well.

The distinction between democratic institutions and democratic politics parallels the distinction between formal or procedural democracy and substantive democracy, originally introduced by de Tocqueville. Formal democracy refers to the institutions, procedures or routines of democratic systems. Substantive democracy refers to the redistribution of power—the degree to which citizens can participate in the decisions which affect their lives.[30]

Table 1.1. Electoral Democracies, 1972-2002.

Year	Independent Countries	Free Democracies		Partly Free Democracies		Neither Free Nor Democratic	
		N	%	N	%	N	%
1972	127	36	28%	32	25%	59	46%
1977	137	38	28%	42	33%	57	45%
1982	144	48	33%	42	29%	54	38%
1987	141	46	33%	50	35%	45	32%
1992	168	68	40%	63	38%	37	22%
1997	172	73	42%	48	28%	51	30%
2002	193	88	46%	56	29%	49	25%

Source: These numbers are derived from the annual Freedom House Country Ratings of Independent Countries, published every year since 1972 by Freedom House and available at www.freedomhouse.org/research. Figures for 2002-2003 are found in the Spring 2003 issue of the *Journal of Democracy*, 106-7.

Constitutions, Democracy, and Good Government

It is difficult meaningfully to discuss the concept of constitutional democracy without acknowledging the normative components of both terms. This book is based on the premise that both democracy and constitutionalism are "good" and compatible. While the figures on the spread of democracy shown in Table 1.1 are promising in this sense, the questions raised by more qualitative assessments are not as encouraging. The spread of democracy is less good if, like a cheap paint job, it only faintly covers the deeper blemishes. Constitutions are essentially about limits, but they are also about governance and it is important that the limits not be so cumbersome as to prevent it. A government need not be activist to be effective, but it needs to be capable of acting: "The difference between effective and impotent government is that the former may decide against doing something, whereas the latter cannot do what it would like to do."[31] The badness of bad government may be lessened by ineffective government, but effective government is a risk we must take, if for no better reason than that the alternatives are worse.[32] Even Adam Smith, the apostle of free enterprise, was emphatic in his defense of state protection against foreign invasion; the "duty of protecting, as far as possible, every member of the society from the injustice or oppression of every other member of it, or the duty of establishing an exact administration of justice; and . . . the duty of erecting and maintaining certain public works and certain public institutions which it can never be for the interest of any individual, or small number of individuals, to erect and maintain."[33]

There has to be effective government before one can talk realistically about limited government. "The legal codification of rights," as Stephen Holmes puts it, "has little meaning when political authorities lack enforcement powers. As a consequence, a constitution that does not organize effective government will wholly fail to protect rights."[34] "Good" government is an elusive concept since even the most corrupt is good for someone (such as the corruptees), and the varieties that can be encompassed under the rubric of "constitutional democracy" are many. But a case can be made not just that democracy is normatively good, but that it is a system uniquely appropriate to the contemporary world. Gellner argues that democracy is neither "inherent in human nature" nor "valid for humanity as such," but that it is highly appropriate to modern times: "A society committed to growth and hence to occupational instability is thereby also committed to a basic egalitarianism. . . . This society needs economic pluralism for productive efficiency, and it needs social and political pluralism to counteract excessive tendencies to centralism."[35] It needs constitutional democracy. Whether it can sustain it is another question.

Notes

1. Heinz Klug, *Constituting Democracy: Globalism and South Africa's Political Reconstruction* (New York: Cambridge University Press, 2000), 12.

2. The Constitution left the issue of who could vote to the states, most of which required property ownership, a requirement that was gradually abolished in the nineteenth century. Former slaves were legally enfranchised by the Fifteenth Amendment, though some states continued to discriminate into the 1960s. Women were given the vote in Wyoming in 1890, but nationally not until the Twenty-second Amendment in 1920.

3. Walter F. Murphy, "Constitutions, Constitutionalism, and Democracy," in *Constitutionalism and Democracy: Transitions in the Contemporary World,* ed. Douglas Greenberg et al. (New York: Oxford University Press, 1993), 6.

4. *West Virginia State Board of Education v. Barnette,* 319 U.S. 624 (1943), 638.

5. Reinhard Bendix, *Kings or People: Power and the Mandate to Rule* (Berkeley: University of California Press, 1978), 248-49.

6. Bendix, *Kings or People,* 249.

7. Bendix, *Kings or People,* 601.

8. Ernest Gellner, *Conditions of Liberty: Civil Society and Its Rivals* (New York: Penguin Press, 1994), 188.

9. Daniel S. Lev, "Social Movements, Constitutionalism, and Human Rights: Comments from the Malaysian and Indonesian Experiences," in Greenberg et al., *Constitutionalism and Democracy,* 139.

10. Carlos Santiago Nino, *The Constitution of Deliberative Democracy* (New Haven: Yale University Press, 1996), 3.

11. Nino, *The Constitution of Deliberative Democracy,* 4.

12. Nino, *The Constitution of Deliberative Democracy,* 12.

13. Cass Sunstein, "Constitutionalism and Secession," *University of Chicago Law Review* 58 (1991), 635.

14. Robert A. Dahl, *Polyarchy: Participation and Opposition* (New Haven: Yale University Press, 1971).

15. Robert A. Dahl, *Democracy and Its Critics* (New Haven: Yale University Press, 1989), 167.

16. Dahl, *Democracy and Its Critics,* 167.

17. Sunstein, "Constitutionalism and Secession," 644.

18. Murphy, "Constitutions, Constitutionalism, and Democracy," 7.

19. Donald S. Lutz, "Toward a Theory of Constitutional Amendment," *American Political Science Review* 88 (June 1994), 369.

20. Giovanni Sartori, *Comparative Constitutional Engineering: An Inquiry into Structures, Incentives, and Outcomes* (New York: New York University Press, 2nd ed., 1997), 197.

21. Lutz, "Toward a Theory of Constitutional Amendment," 367.

22. Jefferson's letters on this subject, written between 1789 and 1824, can be found in most editions of Jefferson's works. Madison's replies, in the *Federalist,* Number 49 and in a February 4, 1790 letter to Jefferson, can be similarly found in his. The correspondence is nicely summarized and elaborated in Stephen Holmes, "Precommitment and the Paradox of Democracy," in *Constitutionalism and Democracy,* ed. Jon Elster and Rune Slagstad (New York: Cambridge University Press, 1993). This quote appears in Holmes, 205.

23. Jefferson in Holmes, "Precommitment," 206.

24. Madison in Holmes, "Precommitment," 217, 216.

25. Madison in Holmes, "Precommitment," 217.

26. Michael Crozier, Samuel P. Huntington, and Joji Watanuki, *The Crisis of Democracy* (New York: New York University Press, 1975).

27. Samuel P. Huntington, *The Third Wave: Democratization in the Late Twentieth Century* (Norman: University of Oklahoma Press, 1991).

28. Larry Diamond, *Developing Democracy: Toward Consolidation* (Baltimore: The Johns Hopkins University Press, 1999), 34.

29. Susan J. Pharr, Robert D. Putnam, and Russell J. Dalton, "A Quarter Century of Declining Confidence," in *The Global Divergence of Democracies,* ed. Larry Diamond and Marc C. Plattner (Baltimore: The Johns Hopkins University Press, 2001), 295.

30. Robert Luckham, Anne Marie Goetz, and Mary Kaldor, "Democratic Institutions and Democratic Politics," in *Can Democracy Be Designed? The Politics of Institutional Choice in Conflict-Torn Societies,* ed. Sunil Bastian and Robin Luckman (New York: Zed Books, 2003), 19.

31. Sartori, *Comparative Constitutional Engineering,* 112.

32. Sartori, *Comparative Constitutional Engineering,* 113.

33. Adam Smith, *The Wealth of Nations* (London: Everyman's Library, 1910, originally published in 1776), vol. 2, 180.

34. Stephen Holmes, "Constitutionalism, Democracy, and State Decay," in *Deliberative Democracy and Human Rights,* ed. Harold Hongju Koh and Ronald C. Slye (New Haven: Yale University Press, 1999), 120.

35. Gellner, *Conditions of Liberty,* 187, 188.

Chapter 2

The Origins of Constitutions

Because most contemporary constitutions derive from widely-recognized written documents, the idea of constitutional democracy is sometimes wrongly conflated with a text. As Murphy reminds us, "We need to distinguish between the authority a text asserts and the authority it exerts."[1] A text-oriented system, such as that of the United States, is at least superficially different from one rooted largely in tradition and statute law, such as Great Britain. But even in the presence of an identified legal document, "Constitutional texts fall along a spectrum of authority. At one extreme are shams, such as those of Stalin and Mao. At the other extreme should be those whose provisions are fully operative; but no constitutional text operates with complete authority."[2] Constitutions, as we have described them in chapter 1, both constitute and limit government, but they have other functions as well.

To some degree or another, all constitutions are shams, or, to put it less bluntly, have mythic or cosmetic functions that, if nothing else, "allow a nation to hide its failures behind idealistic rhetoric."[3] The act of constitutional creation, in fact, often takes place *before* the bonding of disparate parts into an actual nation. Although Indonesia celebrates the year 1945 as its year of constitutional birth, the reality of national sovereignty was not achieved until 1948, and there are some who still see it more as "a nation in waiting" than a fully-constituted nation-state.[4] The Indonesian constitution is not a sham, and more than a myth; but it is hardly a binding statement either of rights or of governing prerogatives. At this point in time, and indeed through most of the Sukarno and New Order years, the Indonesian constitution, and the five basic rights—collectively known as Pancasila—that are its foundation, has been more a symbol and set of aspirations than a charter for government or guardian of rights. This is in no way to underestimate its significance. "Pancasila democracy," as Schwarz noted at the height of Soeharto's rule, "includes many of the features of democratization— secret balloting, universal adult suffrage, regular elections—but relatively few of the individual and group freedoms on the liberalization agenda."[5] This may be "formalistic democracy that is not easy to distinguish from authoritarian rule;" as Schwarz concludes, but as the post-Soeharto years show, forms have meaning; the empty shell of New Order democracy is filled with free expression, sensitivity to public opinion, and a governing elite that is sensitive to the substance as well as the symbolism of democratic procedures. In this sense at least, Indonesia provides an interesting case of what Sklar has labeled "democracy in parts," where such institutions as semi-autonomous courts and a partially-free press allow democratic procedures to gestate prior to the full, formal establishment of democratic institutions.[6]

Formative Forces

Indonesia's written constitution, in common with many, was drafted as both a declaration of independence and a constitution. Combining fervor with substance it has few of the limits on authority characteristic of most constitutional regimes. This is one reason for a growing consensus on the need for substantial constitutional reform that has produced a series of major changes in the basic text. As these amendments take shape they are serving both to construct a new edifice of institutions and give substance to the Pancasila ideals of independence, tolerance, and national unity outlined in 1945, much as the 1789 Constitution of the United States limited and substantiated the ideals of the Declaration of Independence of 1776.

It is difficult through two centuries of hindsight to realize how "revolutionary" the American constitution was. Coming out of a British tradition in which constitutional limitations evolved out of incremental negotiations, there was widespread skepticism that any group of mortals could describe a government on paper in much the same way as a chef might write a recipe. "It seems to have been reserved to the people of this country," Alexander Hamilton wrote in defense of the American constitution, "to decide . . . whether societies of men are really capable or not of establishing good government from reflection and choice, or whether they are forever destined to depend for their political constitutions on accident and force."[7] Hamilton was perhaps exaggerating the abstract nature of the process: "How the framers at the Federal Convention thought about such major theoretical issues as representation and the separation of powers," as Rakove points out, "was largely a response to their assessment of the relevant provisions and practices of the state constitutions," which, for a decade or more "had served, in effect, as the great political laboratory upon whose experiments the framers of 1787 drew."[8] And it would be naive to argue that there wasn't a lot of political wheeling and dealing at the convention.

What was nonetheless extraordinary about the process in 1787 was its deliberative, even theoretical character. Rummaging through history, philosophy and their state experiences, Hamilton and his colleagues set out to *plan* a government.

The American experience notwithstanding, the question of whether such planning is possible remains very much alive. Political scientists debate which was the greater failure: the widespread adoption of British parliamentary models in post-colonial Africa, or American presidential models in Latin America. The result was essentially the same. "Whatever the explanations for these Third World failures, they gave credit during trying times for democracies to a line of theoretical pessimism: if democracy was chancy in its origins, then it must be even more so in its replicas."[9] On the other hand, the constitutions not just imported but imposed on Germany and Japan after World War II have held up well for more than half a century. Many other recent transitions to democracy have been at least as successful. Particularly as constitution makers have become more sophisticated in borrowing bits and pieces from different systems and adapting them to local circumstances, there is a growing sense of confidence that constitutions can be built.

"There is," as the editors of one recent volume of case studies conclude, "a kind of hubris in the idea that constitutional experts, political scientists, donor agencies or even national decision makers can assure democracy or solve conflicts by designing institutions. Indeed institutional design is a kind of oxymoron."[10] As experience with different institutional forms in diverse settings multiply, however, so does our ability to evaluate the ways in which particular configurations of the rules are likely to structure the ways in which they are likely to work. Successful constitution-building processes, moreover, encourage others through what Di Palma calls "demonstration effects."[11] It thus seems increasingly possible, as Hamilton and the American Federalists argued, to craft democracies, and even to export significant parts of them to other cultures. What are the rules of such craftsmanship?

To begin, the organic or cultural perspective is impossible to ignore. In some cases, constitutions evolve almost entirely out of historic experience. In what was almost a real-life replication of social contract theory, the Icelandic Althingi—the world's oldest parliament—emerged in just this manner. Iceland's early settlers, arriving in the 10th century, had no native people to subdue, and needed only to find a way to live among one another. Disputes were resolved face-to-face, often by violence. The accounts of the early sagas reveal a world much like the philosopher Thomas Hobbes's state of nature in which life was "nasty, mean, brutish, and short." To bring order to a growing society, the early settlers soon began a series of periodic town meetings, called *things,* which met peacefully to resolve conflicts. Thus if Olaf found a whale beached on Magnus's land, and both claimed the rights to carve it up for meat and oil, the dispute would be taken to the local *thing* for resolution.

By the time a third or fourth whale had washed up in similar circumstances, these decisions had become fairly routine: each Icelandic *thing* began to develop what the English and Americans call a common law tradition. The next step was to make these traditions uniform across the island, hence the development of the *Althingi* (an annual meeting of all the *things*) and the codification of the various rulings into something very much like statutory or parliamentary law. As in many contemporary societies, the reality of justice in Iceland was considerably more complex. By one count of cases recorded in the Icelandic sagas, 297 of the 520 cases described led to bloody violence.[12] As Ziolkowski concludes, "The law is known to everyone, and the cases are meticulously presented in the courts; but if matters do not turn out satisfactorily, even the greatest lawyers resort to violence."[13] What is most interesting historically, however, is the movement in Iceland— absent a feudal heritage to overcome—toward something very much like the social contract myths constructed by later political theorists to justify constitutional government.

The glory days of Icelandic democracy (if they were indeed that glorious) were cut short by colonization, and few societies have been sufficiently isolated to evolve so rich a heritage; but the traditions of the *thing* have survived in Iceland and continue to inform the country's politics. While it need not take hundreds of years for democratic traditions to evolve, there must be considerable congruence between a nation's "civic culture" and its formal system of rights and rules. Although the postwar constitutions of both Germany and Japan were written largely by Americans, and imposed essentially by occupying troops, their longevity can be attributed in no small part to the sensitivity shown by the drafters of those constitutions to local conditions. Countries whose constitutions derive from hegemonic relations have not usually been so fortunate. Despite the original optimism of many policymakers in the United States, few students of constitutional democracy shared their enthusiasm for the prospects of postwar democratization in Iraq.

Achieving Legitimacy

In early Iceland, the "legitimacy" of the government was never at issue. Systems whose constitutions evolve and whose principles need not be proclaimed—Great Britain serving as a contemporary model—have little need to justify themselves. Most governments, however, are born in cataclysm: to the extent that they want to base their authority in consent, to that extent must they cultivate both the myth and the genuine imprint of popular support. Whatever Sukarno and Hatta may have lost by not proclaiming independence on the day following Japan's surrender in 1945, they gained in the perception that they were not tools of the Japanese, that the struggle for independence from the Dutch was not a by-product of World War II but an assertion of genuine *Indonesian* nationalism.

Let us look at this issue more abstractly. Suppose, as Bruce Ackerman hypothetically suggests, that you and your friends believe yourselves to be badly governed. "Despite its undisputed mastery of established legal forms, you say that you—and your comrades—are the true representatives of the people."[14] How do you convince your compatriots of this position? A true believer might argue that the opinions of others are of no concern, that Jesus, Marx, Allah, or the International Monetary Fund has shown you the way. If your beliefs are strong, you may go ahead to begin the revolution regardless of what others think. But if you want to win, and especially if you believe in democracy, you will want to show not just that your cause is just but that it is for the greater good. Since your takeover is, from the perspective of the old regime, illegal, you would want to persuade your countrymen that it is nonetheless legitimate. Ideally, as Ackerman puts it, "the leadership's claims to legitimacy must be validated by the *concrete assent* given by faithful followers, who recognize them as the true representatives of the people despite the fact that their meetings lack the formal sanction of law."[15]

But once new leadership is in place, the battle for legitimacy has only begun. "Revolution," after all, "is a game any number can play. Just as you challenged established authority, so can the next fellow."[16] Unless you are willing to accept a state of permanent revolution, the task of affirming your right to rule remains. Force provides one easy answer, adopting what Ackerman calls "revolutionary amnesia," you may ask people to forget how you got there and to shut up and obey. It might work, but you are unlikely to go down in history as a hero. A new regime must mark a clean break with the past in such a way that it (a) does not do so much violence to the nation's traditions or the interests of powerful elites that they will turn on it for revenge; (b) convinces a large sector of the public that the new government has the right to rule and is able to control enough of the state apparatus to allow it to do so; and (c), while reassuring people that it will not become more of a threat to their core interests than was its predecessor, create a government powerful enough to act. None of these are easy tasks, particularly in divided societies.

These problems are further compounded when the old regime engaged in widespread abuses of power. In contrast with defeated colonial liars, sadists, and cheats, the evil elites of many displaced third wave regimes are still around. Where there was what Stephen Holmes calls "a socially diffuse sense of complicity," that is where a system of corruption or brutality permeated the system, it may even be impossible to contemplate a working government that does not include substantial remnants of the old order.[17] The problem of "transitional justice"—confronted by South Africa with regard to apartheid, in Eastern Europe with a variety of crimes against humanity, and in the Philippines and Indonesia with manifest and pervasive corruption—yields no simple solutions. The process of "lustration," used in both Germany and the Czech Republic to identify and eliminate from government but not criminally prosecute the worst elements of the old order, was in a sense similar to the South African Truth and Reconciliation Commission's refusal to make revenge its primary goal. However much such "soft" treatment of manifest "villains" may violate the spirit of the new order one is hoping to introduce, the fact is that many of these same "villains" may be among the few in emergent order who know how to keep the trains running, the water flowing, and the police enforcing the law. And there are ethical problems as well. Even in the relatively mild process of lustration, prosecutors begin, as a rule, with the inherently suspect records of the old order, and the high probability that some of the worst offenders may have been better able to cover their tracks and shift blame to others. The very serious question of applying today's standards to conduct in the past becomes a particularly serious issue when applied to lower level bureaucrats, but can also serve more to distract from current problems than to solve them. Laws punishing the old regime, moreover, skate very close to the thin ice of the *ex post facto* laws that are anathema to democracy. Clearly, the higher the degree of continuity between regimes, the more serious these problems become.[18]

A Constitution for What Country?

More than half of the "countries" represented in the United Nations today were created by colonial office bureaucrats drawing lines over the maps of lands they had never seen. Boundaries that have no relationship to natural features, nor to such demographics as religion, ethnicity and race are the norm in many parts of the world. Yet despite the artificiality of these constructs, it is plausible to argue that "nationness is the most universally legitimate value in the political life of our time."[19] The importance of these "imagined communities," as Anderson calls them, is relatively recent yet remarkably potent. Few forces are more subversive of the implementation of democratic constitutions than the continuing pull of subnational loyalties, or the longing of some citizens to be part of another state. To construct a democracy it is important to know who the *demos* in question are.

The idea of imagining a nation coincides, in a rough sense, with the rise of constitutionalism. Its roots, moreover, are found in many of the same forces we discussed in our chapter 1 discussion of the transition from tradition-based monarchial systems to more modern states. Ironically too, the foundation of "nationness" in many postcolonial regimes is built almost entirely on colonial ground, within the boundaries enforced by occupying powers. It was the Dutch, not the Javanese, who created Indonesia; the British who carved out Kenya and Belize; Stalin who defined modern Azerbaijan and Kazakstan. Even the long-established countries of Europe have, through war and diplomacy, shifted the boundaries of what we call "France" or "Poland" so many times that old maps are obsolete.

It is remarkable how well some of these artificial constructs we call nations survive. Belgium—two countries in ethnicity, language, and religion—remains viable and whole as does India (plus or minus Kashmir). Yet the record of failure is high with the dizzyingly fast and brutal dissolution of what once was Yugoslavia a vivid contemporary example. In dramatic form, the Yugoslavia case underscores the very significant differences between the problem of nation-building and coherence in authoritarian and democratic regimes. The general argument is that,

Agreements about the territorial domain of the state are not necessarily prior for a nondemocratic regime. A nondemocratic regime may be able to impose acquiescence over a large group of people for a long period of time without threatening the coherence of the state.

In sharp contrast, the very definition of a democracy involves agreement by the citizens of a territory, however specified, on the procedures used to generate a government that can make legitimate claims on their obedience.[20]

While it seems almost axiomatic that, "The most basic presupposition of democracy is *the existence of a community within which it may be operative,"*[21] it is also true that, "democratic theorists almost invariably take the territorial limit as given, discussing neither how it ought to be established in the first place nor under what conditions, if any, democratic principles would justify part of a democracy in seceding from the whole."[22] The contemporary situation in Iraq raises still another set of questions about the burdens placed upon a regime whose autonomy is in question. Elected or not, the ability of a new Iraqi regime to establish its legitimacy is almost necessarily in question for as long as it appears to be founded in a foreign military occupation. The success of the allies in installing what have proven to be remarkably enduring constitutional democracies in Austria, Germany, Italy, and Japan continues to serve as the exceptions that test the rule. There are few other analogies.

As important as the boundary problem is, there are numerous cases in which tenuous communities have survived: there is at least one thriving democracy like Belgium for every one that has split like the Czech Republic and Slovakia; one multicultural Switzerland for every Yugoslavia. A case might even be made that a democratic regime may, in some ways, be capable of binding a nation together more enduringly than can an authoritarian one. Linz and Stepan use the term "state-nations" (as opposed to nation-states) to describe those countries which "are multicultural, or even multinational states, which nonetheless manage to engender strong identification and loyalty from their citizens, an identification and loyalty that proponents of homogeneous nation-states perceive that only nation-states can engender."[23] If Walker Connor's 1972 calculation that only 12 of the 132 nation-states then in existence were "essentially homogeneous from an ethnic view-point,"[24] it would seem as if quite a number of stable democracies have been able to overcome such rivalries to produce such loyalties.

Perhaps the best case for reversing the traditional order and seeing democracy as a source rather than a derivative of national unity is found in the *Federalist Papers,* the first nine of which are devoted, as Jay wrote, to "whether it would conduce more to the interest of the people of America that they should, to all general purposes, be one nation, under one federal government, or that they should divide themselves into separate confederacies, and give to the head of each the same kind of powers which they are advised to place in one national government."[25]

It took nearly seventy-five years to answer this question. That secession was frequently advocated even by some who had participated in establishing the union;

and that the question of national union was only resolved by a bloody civil war is an historical fact that Americans are inclined to forget in looking at the contemporary problems of a nation-in-waiting like Indonesia. The question of nation-ness that weighed heavily on the American founding fathers has, moreover, received little attention from students of American political history. Of the thirty or so texts and books of readings on my bookshelves, for example, virtually all include one or more selections from the *Federalist Papers,* but not one refers to the issue of nation-building that Publius himself considered problem number one.

The U.S. founders were deeply concerned with questions of identity. The *Federalist Papers* begin, as noted, with a discussion of the problem and end with Hamilton's observation that "A nation, without a national government is, in my view, an awful spectacle."[26] Noah Pickus makes a very convincing case that,

> The entire argument of *The Federalist* itself constituted an attempt to overcome the colonist's deeply rooted habit of thinking in regional, ethnic and religious parts by elaborating a history of "the people." We begin to see Publius's artifice as a constitution maker, his artfulness and his skill, when he utilizes a great jumble of principles, culture, and experience to portray subnational identities as less real than what the colonists share. "Harken not the unnatural voice," he warns, "which tells you that the people of America, knit together as they are by so many cords of affection, can no longer live together as members of the same family."[27]

In retrospect the founders may have been wrong in their ultimately unsuccessful attempt to sweep the issue of slavery under the rug of federalism; but their recognition that nation-building is a process that both informs and derives from constitutional democracy remains very much on the mark. Rather than finding community in small, homogeneous enclaves where citizens are so similarly situated as to have few significant conflicts, Publius saw the process of finding agreement beneath sharp differences as essential to the development of a civic culture. The very act of acting democratically, in other words, is part of what makes democracy work.

> The ideal citizen should not retreat into an Anti-Federalist defense of small, homogeneous communities or into a thin, minimalist position that champions tolerance as the preeminent good. Doing so undermines the constant effort to bind citizens together that being a free people requires. . . .
>
> The process of finding agreement beneath differences sustains attachment to a common citizenship.[28]

Democracies are built less on the foundations of cohesive communities and human virtue than on institutional configurations that take people as they are. "The inference to which we are brought," in Madison's words, "is that the *causes* of faction cannot be removed, and that relief is only to be sought in controlling its *effects.*"[29]

To put this in the terms of more contemporary social science, civil societies can be made as well as born. The imagined communities that form the basis of nationness can be constructs of human contrivance. "Publius (and especially Madison)," as Pickus suggests, "conceived citizenship to be neither a matter of cultural belonging nor of assenting to a settled set of political principles. For Publius, American citizenship meant attachment to a common identity that is itself subject to change. He tried to forge a shared identity without foreclosing deliberation over the nature of that identity."[30]

A system thus built on conflict as much as consensus, and virtue is the product rather than the generator of social conflict must be carefully constructed. Democracies that are not organic, that are born in conflict or founded in diversity, the American experience suggests, can be viable. In his provocative history of the American effort to achieve political and social integration, Rogan Kersh distinguishes between membership in a cultural community or ethnic group and belonging to a polity. "The sustainable-union idea of belonging to the polity," he argues, "suggests a promising basis for integration today, in that a variety of immigrant groups joined the American national whole in the eighteenth and nineteenth centuries without having prized aspects of their traditional cultures automatically stripped away."[31] How to do this is tricky, described by Kersh as "one of the most compelling dilemmas for would-be modern unionists;"[32] but it remains one aspect of the American experience most worthy of emulating.

State Institutions and Political Power

John Harbeson has argued that the prevailing manner in which political scientists have tended to conceptualize the state has seriously hindered our ability to understand the process of democratic transition. In the emerging democracies of southern Africa that have been the focus of Harbeson's attention, few governments—whether ostensibly democratic or not—have been able to extend their rule throughout the jurisdictions they supposedly govern.[33] Whether they have the cultural identity or sense of union we have just discussed, they lack the material resources and what Evans calls the "embedded autonomy" to extend their rule throughout what the maps define as their jurisdictions.[34] Because the institutions and trappings of government are in place, including elected officials, appointed bureaucrats and diplomats occupying real offices, it is easy (falsely, Harbeson argues) to assume that they constitute a state.

The term "banana republic" was once used derisively to describe a group of countries in Central America which—despite the putative existence of formal governments—were so deeply in the thrall of foreign fruit companies that their actual powers were trivial. At the other end of the spectrum, many fully sovereign states, through their constitutions, place more or less strict limits on the scope of government power. We will analyze these kinds of chosen limits in chapter 4. Our point here is simply that many societies lack the luxury of such choice: "states," to put it mildly, "are not likely to be equally capable of intervening in different areas of socioeconomic life."[35] Dominant industries, such as the fruit companies that effectively ruled much of Central America in the early twentieth century; and hegemonic neighbors like the Soviet Union and the United States at the height of the Cold War, sharply constrain the ability of a nation to craft its own effective constitution. In Indonesia, the military has its own sources of revenue, and a structural apparatus reaching from every village to the top of the cabinet. Even with its role in the parliament curtailed, the independent authority of the military is a basic fact of Indonesian political life, no matter what the constitution says. "Institutional choices," as Bastian and Luckham say, "are never made in a political and economic vacuum; they are often tailored to suit the narrower political and economic agendas of those making them."[36]

To some degree or another, of course, all governments are in thrall to the "hidden" powers of some military, economic, or social cabal: the discipline of political science never would have differentiated itself from the study of law if what is written in statutes and constitutions provided a true guide to power. We will return repeatedly to the question of the degree to which the real "state" coincides, or fails to coincide with the formal institutions of the government. The point here is more limited: the range of options available to those crafting constitutions is far more limited in some societies than it is in others. *All* societies, moreover, are sharply constrained by a rich variety of cultural, economic, ethnic, international, and other forces that to a very large degree predetermine the outcome of their constitutive deliberations. The Constitution of the United States was, to a remarkable extent, the product of "reflection and choice;" but it is quite remarkable, in retrospect at least, how little of this reflection and choice involved the question of slavery.

Constitutional Transitions

Constitution-making in countries in which the constitution evolved out of longstanding practices is essentially a process of solidifying existing unions. For newer or less homogeneous societies, the problem of legitimacy is both more complicated and more important. How can constitutional democracy in a country like the United States in 1789 acquire sufficient legitimacy to constrain and channel methods of resolving conflict? Even if the founders were right in seeing the process itself as a force for cohesion, by what means can such processes be put in place? Political legitimacy—the psychological bond between a people and its government—tends to be associated with stability, effectiveness, accountability, and so on. While anarchy and lawlessness may suit the interests of some people in the short run, few people benefit from it as a daily diet. Other things being equal, constitution makers should seek processes of creation or change that maximize the prospects of sustainable and accountable government.

If constitutional moments have generally occurred in the wake of revolution, the end of colonial rule, or the fall of empire, many recent transitional regimes, as with the United States, have been blessed with time to plan. They are, in this respect, able to benefit from the experience of others. The American founding fathers did three things that are frequently held up for emulation. The first was to construct a constitutional convention that transcended the established process. The flaw in the existing system that most needed change was the requirement that all acts of the Continental Congress—including changes in the Constitution—be by unanimous vote of all thirteen states. The Constitutional Convention that convened in Philadelphia in 1787 simply by-passed this procedure. Despite its dubious legal origins, however, the Convention included many of the new nation's most learned experts in law and history, as well as seven present or former state governors, twenty-eight members or former members of Congress; and, as its presiding officer, the commander-in-chief of the Armies of the Revolution, George Washington. They were a landed aristocracy well aware of their own prerogatives, but they were also representatives of the new nation's diverse regional interests, and uncommonly able as a group to transcend factional disputes and command public respect.

The second defining characteristic of the Constitutional Convention was its determination to negotiate whatever compromises were necessary to produce a consensus document. Some of these compromises were neither moral nor enduring. Failure to confront the issue of slavery led ultimately to civil war, and the initial absence of a Bill of Rights was an oversight that even the founders felt a need quickly to remedy. But the work of the convention in crafting a nation out of thirteen diverse states, of drafting a document that (the Civil War notwithstanding) has worked for more than two centuries, was really quite remarkable.

The third and perhaps most important characteristic of the American process was its self-imposition of downstream constraints. By subjecting its work to a subsequent ratification process, the convention was energized both by the need to achieve a consensus among the delegates and later to sell the product to a skeptical electorate. Sold as a package, the new Constitution had to balance the interests of small states and large, South and North, without offending a diversity of minorities. All of these elements, and more, were stunningly well-incorporated into the transitional process in South Africa where a relatively stable, democratic regime was crafted out of what was, arguably, the most intractable of world conflicts. Perhaps the most important aspect of the process in South Africa was its final result, "that no single party could claim that the Constitution was theirs and theirs alone. All parties (it was hoped) would be able to say 'We influenced and helped shape this Constitution.' The Constitution could not reflect everything that every party wanted. Every party was required to compromise on some features of its text, but also to see its influence on other features."[37]

Few nations celebrate their constitution days with anything like the patriotic fervor that generally accompanies celebrations of independence; but constitutions do have symbolic, even mythic functions that play important roles in defining the legitimacy of regimes. What the United States and South African cases suggest is that, "Constitutionalism . . . stands for the rare moments in a nation's history when deep, principled discussion transcends the log-rolling and horse-trading of everyday majority politics, the object of these debates being the principles which are to constrain future majority decisions."[38] Whether most modern states can afford the luxury of a drawn-out process of deliberation is another question. The two years that it took the U.S. founders, from their first meeting in 1787 to the inauguration of President Washington in 1789, were smoothed by the continued functioning of state governments, the absence of economic or international crises, and the far slower pace of economic and political life. In a case like that of Indonesia, by way of contrast, it was necessary both to develop a new post-Soeharto constitution and to fill the void in governance that his swift departure had left. A new government arising from the ashes of a discredited old regime is doubly damned. It can build a foundation of legitimacy neither on the ruins of the old order's discredited legal system, nor on a claim that their current position of power is more than transitional. The first problem in such transitions inheres in the process itself. Absent the decisive break in leadership provided by revolution or expulsion of a colonial power, the moment of change is difficult to define. Instead of a decisive break with the past, many of the same faces inhabit many of the same offices; those who were part of the problem are suddenly expected to be part of the solution.

Following the break up of the Soviet Union, one of the first steps in most Eastern European countries was to amend the old constitution. Generally, "the amendments were the result of an elite agreement with the former Communist leadership. They were not intended to be expressions of the 'will,' values, or demands of the masses who in varying degrees participated in the process resulting in the collapse of Communist rule."[39] Whatever the need for change, those overseeing the process were also aware that beyond ideology and politics, their jobs were on the line.

What tended to happen in many of these regimes was that the process became drawn out, "not because democracy needs time but because democratization has met some hefty stumbling blocks."[40] The "halfway house" regimes that resulted were either what Di Palma calls "dictablandas" or "democraduras."

> *Dictablandas* are still noncompetitive dictatorships in which a degree of bland liberalization has been used to justify the status quo. They reflect the fact that institutional forces that define the dictatorship, usually the military or the single party. . . do not know how to relinquish power. . . .
>
> *Democraduras* go a step further and, in contrast to *dictablandas,* allow after a fashion a competitive system. But competition is limited in three ways by fairly explicit or formal pacts. Participation is restricted to usually conservative forces that exclude others; these forces share government offices according to consociational arrangements fairly independent of electoral verdicts; they also leave touchy issues out of the policy agenda.[41]

Instead of reworking the institutions of the state by crafting new constitutions, instead of involving a wider public in the process of change, these "halfway house" regimes tended toward reform at the margins of the old order, revising the existing constitution just enough to give the appearance of change, but keeping its human infrastructure basically small and intact.

At the same time, these more incremental processes of change need not lead to failure. What Lindblom classically defined as "the science of muddling through," is not without advantages. Instead of "starting from fundamentals anew," the process of "successive limited comparisons" gradually builds "out from the current situation, step by step and by small degrees."[42] No constitution is ever made once, and the process of "muddling through," for all its lack of drama and closure, has certain pragmatic advantages, and may even serve to reassure a skeptical public. Dramatic constitutional "moments" can reveal and exacerbate deep divisions as commonly as they can heal them, while incremental changes may—through the process of change itself—show the way to future methods of problem-solving. Di Palma argues that legitimacy, defined as a widespread allegiance to democratic values, is not a necessary precondition to stability.[43] What is necessary is the achievement of democratic agreement, a reasonably widespread consensus that the institutions of the democratic state are the best places in which conflicts can be resolved. There is no better way to achieve this kind of connectedness than through popular involvement in the process of change; whether this can be achieved incrementally as well as through a dramatic "constitutional moment" is not as clear. The failure of many third wave democracies to mark a clean break with the past is indeed looking better through the lens of time; and even the "dictablandas" and "democraduras" of eastern Europe are, in many cases, slouching their way toward democracy. Certainly, they are no worse off, at comparable stages in development, than many of the carefully planned designer democracies constructed by former colonial powers in democracy's second wave.

Is Indonesia "Ready for Democracy?"

The question of whether Indonesia (or any other country) is "ready for democracy" is mildly patronizing. But it is raised so often both in Indonesian and in the literature of comparative politics that it needs to be addressed both as regards Indonesia and the "third" world more generally. The question of whether Indonesia is an appropriate setting for "western" concepts of democracy, constitutionalism, and human rights comes in different guises. The oldest of these arguments, that democracy is a product of western European values and cannot be successfully grafted onto hostile roots, has been empirically demonstrated to be false in virtually every corner of the world. Whether it has worked better or worse (or just differently) in Japan than in Canada, in Costa Rica than in Italy is not the point. It has worked.

The more serious arguments, based on various notions of affinities between a nation's political culture and its constitutional system, is not as easily refuted if only because there are too many failures and too few long-standing successes to make a conclusive case. For many years, the prevailing wisdom among political scientists was that the underlying political order, in particular the existence of a strong civic culture, best differentiated successful democracies from failures. Yale University political scientist Robert Dahl's brilliant studies of democratic regimes have been particularly convincing on this point. Dahl concedes that constitutional forms can play a role in structuring the ways in which democratic systems function,[44] but the overall thrust of his argument is that the chances of sustaining democratic regimes in societies which are not "polyarchies," or do not have democratic political cultures, are low.

The foundation of a democratic civil culture, in Dahl's view, is a widespread willingness to lose. As a citizen I accept a contrary majority's decision because in the long run "I cannot satisfactorily gain my own ends unless I allow others an opportunity to pursue their ends on an equal basis."[45] In divided societies this means, at a minimum, a willingness to trust in the basic fairness of those who are not like you. Only a relatively small number of countries in the world meet this test. How then, can we account for the large number of seemingly successful transitions to democracy that the world has witnessed in recent years? One answer, suggested by Dahl in *After the Revolution?* is that the alternatives are even worse, as in the old saw, usually attributed to Winston Churchill, that democracy is the worst form of government except for everything else. Accepting the democratic bargain, as Di Palma puts it,

> may make sense not only to the convinced democrat, who needs no demonstration, but also to those who benefitted from the certainty of the old despotism and to those among its enemies who may otherwise long to replace it with their own brand of certainty. In the latter two cases, the bargain's open-endedness seems less costly, more promising, or downright inescapable when compared with preserving that certainty or replacing it with a new one.[46]

Note the parallel here with Publius. What the argument suggests is that whether "pre-conditions" for democracy exist or not, if the appropriate bargains can be made to put democratic institutions in place, there may be learning effects that help produce a culture of democracy. Rustow's classic argument, that democracy needs a phase of habituation lasting for at least a generation, before which any "conspicuous failure to resolve some urgent political question . . . may prove fatal" may still be valid.[47] Absent such failure, those who learn to play by the rules of democracy may learn to accept them as well. Halfway houses like New Order Indonesia, moreover may play important roles. Whether the underlying political culture meets Dahl's test, habituation in the rules and procedures of democracy—acting constitutionally—is itself an important force in sustaining successful transitions.

As much as some students of comparative politics might accept this argument, they might still contend that countries like Indonesia are "not ready for democracy" because they lack not only democratic political cultures but the underlying economic and social conditions necessary for them to develop.[48] But while the record of poor countries in sustaining democratic institutions is not sufficiently strong to question the general association between democracy and economic development, there are good reasons to be skeptical as to cause and effect. In much the same way in which constitutions can nurture democracy as well as reflect it, the correlation between affluence and democracy may not have been cast in the proper causal framework. In the Indonesian case,

> there is enough evidence to suspect the validity of democracy-as-effect and propose in its stead democracy-as-cause. Democracy provides a conducive climate for a healthy growth of the middle class, for the creation of economic wealth, and for the progressive equalization of income. We are thus reversing the-cart-before-the-horse argument in the contemporary literature of democratization.[49]

Giovanni Sartori has wryly noted that the idea of economic preconditions to democracy went unnoted for more than a century before suddenly becoming relevant for the "third wave," suggesting, as Pabottingi puts it that, "The bulk of factors Huntington calls preconditions to democracy pass better as its characteristics."[50]

In comparative perspective, Indonesia is probably neither worse off than some countries that have made successful transitions, nor better than some that have not. Its most troubling problem of transition lies in its ability to cohere as a nation; or, to put it more accurately, to develop a constitutional and democratic polity able to control and coexist with a national security apparatus that thrives on ethnic and regional conflict. Recent history offers a decisively negative answer to the question of whether constitutional democracy is essentially a western construct. It also makes it clear that a variety of "dictablandas," "democraduras," and democracies with adjectives, "Call for more nuanced definitions and descriptions of regime types which would transcend the simple dichotomy of authoritarianism versus democracy."[51] Truth be told, of course, such nuances have always existed even among the supposedly "developed" democracies of the west.

Democratization is a process, not an event. It requires effort to keep the process open yet stable. "Constitutional democracy," as Murphy puts it,

> needs a political culture that simultaneously encourages citizens to respect the rights of fellow citizens even as they push their own interests and hold their representatives accountable for advancing those interests—a culture whose force cannot diminish when private citizens become public officials. That such a political culture will pre-exist constitutional democracy is unlikely, making it necessary for the polity to pull itself up by its own boot straps by helping to create the very milieu in which it can flourish. Turning that paradox into a fait accompli is likely to require a generation.[52]

"Democracy," as Di Palma points out, "does not happen in an international vacuum,"[53] a proposition tellingly tested in the case of South Africa. Constitutional changes are promoted from such direct sources as military occupation and economic sanctions to the subtle influences of Di Palma's "demonstration effects." The demise of the world communist movement, while its manifest effects on transitions to democracy in Eastern Europe have been widely noted, has had an equally notable, if more subtle impact on those regimes where the Communist threat (and U.S. depictions of it) no longer serve as rationales for the maintenance of authoritarian governments. This does not mean that the United States (and other outside actors) will act as disinterested promoters of transitional regimes. The U.S. Agency for International Development has been aggressive in its promotion of transitions to democracy and sensitive in recent years to cross cultural exigencies; but national interests generally come first, and may not always encourage democracy building. Because constitutional legitimacy rests so heavily on a congruence between acts of creation and facts of culture, even the best intended efforts of outsiders, moreover, may prove counter-productive, without even considering the stigma such intervention may impart. But if one should be wary of outside intervention in crafting constitutions, it would be folly to ignore the experiences and examples of regimes that have both succeeded and failed, and there have been few other times in world history, it would seem, when the international environment has been so positive.

Notes

1. Walter F. Murphy, "Constitutions, Constitutionalism, and Democracy," in *Constitutionalism and Democracy: Transitions in the Contemporary World,* ed. Douglas Greenberg et al. (New York: Oxford University Press, 1993), 8.

2. Murphy, "Constitutions," 8.

3. Murphy, "Constitutions," 8.

4. Adam Schwarz, *A Nation in Waiting: Indonesia's Search for Stability* (Boulder, CO: Westview Press, 2nd ed., 2000).

5. Schwarz, *Nation in Waiting,* 294.

6. Richard L. Sklar, "Democracy in Africa," *African Studies Review* (1983), 26: 3-4.

7. Alexander Hamilton, James Madison, and John Jay (writing under the collective pen name of "Publius"), *The Federalist Papers.* These essays, available from many publishers, were originally published as a series of newspaper articles defending the new constitution during the fight for ratification in New York State. This quotation is from paper number one written by Hamilton. Because they are available in literally dozens of editions, I shall follow the practice of referring citations by the number of the paper, in the order in which they were printed, rather than to the page number in any particular reprint.

8. Jack N. Rakove, *Original Meanings: Politics and Ideas in the Making of the Constitution* (New York: Vintage Books, 1997), 31.

9. Giuseppe Di Palma, *To Craft Democracies: An Essay on Democratic Transitions* (Berkeley: University of California Press, 1990), 19.

10. Sunil Bastian and Robin Luckham, "Conclusion: The Politics of Institutional Choice," in *Can Democracy Be Designed? The Politics of Institutional Choice in Conflict-Torn Societies,* ed. Bastian and Luckham (New York: Zed Books, 2003), 304.

11. Di Palma, *To Craft Democracies,* 19.

12. These figures, compiled by Andreas Heusler in 1911 are taken from William Ian Miller, *Bloodtaking and Peacemaking: Feud, Law, and Society in Saga Iceland* (Chicago: University of Chicago Press, 1990), 236.

13. Theodore Ziolkowski, *The Mirror of Justice: Literary Reflections of Legal Crises* (Princeton, NJ: Princeton University Press, 1997), 56.

14. Bruce A. Ackerman, "Neo-Federalism?" in *Constitutionalism and Democracy,* ed. Jon Elster and Rune Slagstad (New York: Ca mbridge University Press, 1993), 159.

15. Ackerman, "Neo-Federalism," 159.

16. Ackerman, "Neo-Federalism," 159.

17. Stephen Holmes, "The End of Decommunization," in *Transitional Justice: How Emerging Democracies Reckon with Former Regimes,* ed. Neil J. Kritz (Washington, DC: United States Institute of Peace, 1995), 118.

18. Herman Schwarz, "Lustration in Eastern Europe," in Kritz, *Transitional Justice,* 461.

19. Benedict Anderson, *Imagined Communities* (New York: Verso, rev. ed., 1991), 3.

20. Juan J. Linz and Alfred Stepan, *Problems of Democratic Transition and Consolidation: Southern Europe, South America, and Post-Communist Europe* (Baltimore: The Johns Hopkins University Press, 1996), 27.

21. Carl Cohen, *Democracy* (New York: The Free Press, 1973), 41.

22. J. R. Pennock, "Introduction," in *Nomos XXV: Liberal Democracy,* ed. J. R. Pennock and R. W. Chapman (New York: New York University Press, 1983), 5.

23. Linz and Stepan, *Problems of Democratic Transition,* 34.

24. Walker Connor, "Nation-Building or Nation Destroying," *World Politics* 24 (1972), 320.

25. *Federalist,* Number 2.

26. *Federalist,* Number 85.

27. Noah M. J. Pickus, "'Hearken Not to the Unnatural Voice': Publius and the Artifice of Attachment," in *Diversity and Citizenship: Rediscovering American Nationhood,* ed. Gary J. Jacobsohn and Susan Dunn (Lanham, MD: Rowman and Littlefield, 1996), 72. The quote is from *Federalist* Number 14 (Madison).

28. Pickus, "Hearken Not," 78.

29. *Federalist,* Number 10.

30. Pickus, "Hearken Not," 64.

31. Rogan Kersh, *Dreams of a More Perfect Union* (Ithaca, NY: Cornell University Press, 2001), 293.

32. Kersh, *Dreams,* 292.

33. John W. Harbeson, "Toward Restoration of the Democratic State: The State of Democracy in Sub-Saharan Africa," (paper presented at the Annual Meeting of the American Political Science Association, Boston, MA, August 29-September 1, 2002).

34. Peter B. Evans, *Embedded Autonomy: States and Industrial Transformation* (Princeton, NJ: Princeton University Press, 1995).

35. Peter B. Evans, Dietrich Rueschmeyer, and Theda Skocpol, "On the Road toward a More Adequate Understanding of the State," in *Bringing the State Back In*, eds. Evans, Rueschmeyer, and Skocpol (New York: Cambridge University Press, 1985), 351.

36. Bastian and Luckham, "Conclusion," in Bastian and Luckham, *Can Democracy Be Designed?* 307

37. Nicholas Haysom, *Negotiating a Political Settlement in South Africa: Are There Lessons for Burma?* Report of workshops held in Chiang Mai, Thailand and New Delhi, India, April 2000 (Stockholm: International Institute for Democracy and Electoral Assistance, 2001), 31.

38. Jon Elster, "Introduction," in *Constitutionalism and Democracy*, ed. Jon Elster and Rune Slagstad (New York: Cambridge University Press, 1993), 6.

39. Andras Sajo and Vera Losonci, "Rule by Law in East Central Europe: Is the Emperor's New Suit a Straightjacket?" in Greenberg et al., *Constitutionalism and Democracy*, 328.

40. Di Palma, *To Craft Democracies*, 53.

41. Di Palma, *To Craft Democracies*, 154.

42. Charles E. Lindblom, "The Science of Muddling Through," *Public Administration Review* 14 (Spring 1959), 81.

43. Di Palma, *To Craft Democracies*, Chapter 7.

44. Robert A. Dahl, *Dilemmas of Pluralist Democracy: Autonomy versus Control* (New Haven: Yale University Press, 1982), 189-192. See also his *A Preface to Democratic Theory* (Chicago: University of Chicago Press, 1956); *Polyarchy: Participation and Opposition* (Yale, 1971); *Democracy and Its Critics* (Yale, 1989); and *After the Revolution* (Yale, 1970).

45. Dahl, *After the Revolution*, 12.

46. Di Palma, *To Craft Democracies*, 43.

47. Dankwart Rustow, "Transitions to Democracy," *Comparative Politics* 2 (1970), 359. Rustow's essay and a number of comments upon and extensions of his arguments can be found in *Transitions to Democracy*, ed. Lisa Anderson (New York: Columbia University Press, 1999).

48. See, for example, Howard Crouch, "Democratic Prospects in Indonesia," in *Democracy in Indonesia, 1950s and 1990s, ed.* David Bourchier and John Legge (Victoria, Australia: Monash University Papers on Southeast Asia, Number 31, 1994), 115-27; and R. William Liddle, "The Middle Class and the New Order Legitimacy," in *The Politics of Middle Class Indonesia*, ed. Richard Tanter and Kenneth Young (Victoria, Australia: Monash University Papers on Southeast Asia, Number 19, 1990); and Theodore Friend, *Indonesian Destinies* (Cambridge, MA: Belknap-Harvard University Press, 2003).

49. Mochtar Pabottingi, "In the Absence of Autocentricity: The Case of Historical Preclusion of Democracy in Indonesia," in *Crafting Indonesian Democracy*, ed. R. William Liddle (Bandung: Penerbit Mizan, 2001), 37.

50. Pabotting, "In the Absence of Autocentricity," 37.

51. Elke Zuern, "Bibliographical Essay: The Genealogy of Democratization," in Anderson, *Transitions to Democracy*, 287.

52. Walter F. Murphy, "Civil Law, Common Law, and Constitutional Democracy," *Louisiana Law Review* 91 (1991), 113.

53. Di Palma, *To Craft Democracies*, 183.

Chapter 3

Comparing Constitutions

The differences between the unwritten constitution of a country like Great Britain or New Zealand, and the carefully crafted, legalistic work of the American founding fathers, are not always significant. Citizens living in countries with some of the most lavish declarations of fundamental rights can hardly to be said to have more freedom than most Australians and Britons who have gone along quite nicely for all these years without a formal bill of rights. Juan Bautista Alberdi, the father of constitutionalism in Argentina, has argued that, "All constitutions change or succumb when they are but children of imitation; the only one which does not change, the only one which moves and lives in the country, is the constitution which that country has received from the events of its history, that is to say, from those deeds which form the chain of its existence."[1]

Even Alberdi, however, is aware of the important role that written words can play in politics: indeed he himself has devoted considerable attention to the nuances of a document that he hoped would be a shaping force in Argentina. Constitution makers understand that words on paper can be twisted or ignored, and few deny the importance of cultural and historic limits; but it is their acute awareness of these forces that pushes them to structure institutions and limit their formal powers in the hope of controlling excesses. "They are constantly concerned," says Murphy, "with the human penchant to act selfishly and abuse power. They want institutional restraints on substantive matters to prevent lapses into an authoritarian or even totalitarian system cloaked with populist trappings."[2] Cass Sunstein has used the

felicitous phrase "pre-commitment strategies" to describe the enabling and constraining mechanisms embodied in most written documents. "Like the rules of grammar, such provisions set out the rules by which political discussion will occur, and
in that sense free up the participants to conduct their discussions more easily."[3]

As with the rules of grammar, constitutional meanings evolve. Hamilton wrote
in the *Federalist* that, "Particular provisions, though not altogether useless, have
far less virtue and efficacy than are commonly ascribed to them."[4] But Hamilton
and the rest of the delegates to the American constitutional convention sometimes
went for days at a time attending to the linguistic nuances of a single phrase. To a
remarkable degree, moreover, subsequent debates in American political history have
been structured in accord with those nuances, debated in terms of the grammar of
meanings established in 1789.

Length, Detail, Flexibility, and Authority

The Constitution of the United States is remarkable for its brevity. At about 7,500
words it can be read in a short sitting. Most countries and all but one of the 50 U.S.
states are more verbose, with some written constitutions running to more than ten
times that length. Many countries and states have gone through more than one round
of constitution-making. Since 1789, for example, each of the American states has
averaged three constitutions. My own state of New York replaced its original
constitution in 1822, again in 1846, and yet again in 1894. It has, moreover, held
five constitutional conventions, in 1801, 1867, 1915, 1938, and 1967, which, though
they did not produce a new text, frequently resulted in significant amendments. In
contrast with the national constitution, which has been amended twenty-seven times
since 1789, New York's 1894 constitution has been amended more than 200 times.

James Madison argued, and most scholars have tended to agree, that constitutions should be short, sparing in structural detail, and largely free of substantive
content. Most of the American states, and some newer nations fail these tests very
badly. In the United States,

> On average, current state constitutions contain 828 provisions, and 324 are devoted
> to particularistic or statutory-type issues. This means that 39% of the typical state
> constitution is devoted to matters that most scholars consider extraneous at best.
> Compared to the U.S. Constitution, which devotes only 14 (about 6%) of its 240
> provisions to particularistic issues, the degree to which the state documents violates
> the Madisonian model becomes much clearer. On average, they contain 23 times
> more particularistic provisions than the U.S. Constitution.[5]

Some of these provisions are very particularistic indeed, such as the clause in the
New York state constitution that specifies the width of hiking trails in the Adiron-
dack State Park, or Alabama's provision of help to peanut farmers whose crops are

damaged by frost. Some of these provisions, a growing number unfortunately, are lobbied into constitutions by interest groups hoping to wall special privileges off from the normal democratic process. In contradiction to Madison and the accepted wisdom of political science, however, it seems that the more particularistic provisions a state constitution includes the longer it is likely to last. Although this rather clear and consistent finding "implies that constitutionalization of statutory policies maintains political stability rather than destroys,"[6] this could be a uniquely American phenomenon, or one that applies best at the subnational level.

The tendency to legislate in constitutions, rather than simply define the powers, processes, and limitations on government, is far less common in national constitutions than it is in the American states. As in the United States, however, world constitutions are growing longer, particularly in countries with federal systems. The Austrian constitution, for example, includes more than seventy separate articles spelling out the relative powers of national, provincial, and local governments. If we take Professor Sunstein's view of constitutions as pre-commitments, it would follow that constitutional wordiness is part of a strategy more tightly to bind future generations. The Indonesian Constitution—among the world's briefest—was kept short because it was seen as more as a declaration of independence and aspiration than a constitution. Whether it was intended to serve only as a transitional document is not clear, but it does seem that its lack of precision has made it unusually susceptible to multiple interpretations. As a general proposition, the more detailed the language, the more it would seem to serve as a barrier to subsequent reinterpretation, though this has not always been the case. In the American experience such vague phrases as "due process of law" and "unreasonable" searches and seizures have been debated, defined, redefined, and litigated thousands of times without satisfying anyone. But even when the language of the founding fathers seems clear and unambiguous, as when the First Amendment says that "Congress shall make no law. . . abridging the freedom of speech," few politicians or judges have taken this language to ban libel laws, laws punishing hate speech, or laws banning various forms of supposedly subversive activities.

However much the constitution restricts or seems to restrict the scope of government, questions of structure are, in the long run, probably more important than abstract strictures. In the *Federalist Papers* Madison wrote "that mere declarations in the written constitution are not sufficient to restrain the several departments within their legal rights."[7] Instead, he suggested, "the great security against a gradual concentration of the several powers in the same department, consists in giving to those who administer each department the necessary constitutional means and personal motives to resist the encroachments of others."[8] While this argument is usually associated with Madison's subsequent defense of separated powers, the more general point is interesting as well, for what Madison is arguing is that governments should not be made more efficient than they need to be. "If men were angels, no government would be necessary;" but since they are not, "auxiliary precautions" are called for, even in a democracy. If we cannot turn mere mortals into angels, we can, "through the whole system of human affairs, private as well as public" prevent any single set of individuals from dominating others. In all important distributions of power, "the constant aim is to divide and arrange the several offices in such a manner that each may be a check on the other—that the private interests of every individual may be a sentinel over the public rights."[9]

If this sounds like a political version of Adam Smith's defense of capitalism, it should come as no surprise. And that it leads logically in the *Federalist* to the separation of powers makes sense as well. But what is easy to overlook here is the more general defense of what political scientists now call pluralism and the idea that a more diverse and complicated society is often a society with more real freedom than one that is better unified. Highly unified, neatly structured societies— like their economic counterparts—may be more efficient in the short run than those that are fragmented and diffuse, but they are also far more capable of destroying individual freedom. And if constitutional government is limited government, it would stand to reason that most constitutions concern themselves more with mechanisms promoting freedom than efficiency. We will return in a later chapter to Madison's argument on pluralism and to more recent updates of the debate; but let us turn first to the questions of mechanics embedded in the United States and other constitutions.

Questions of Structure: Presidential, Parliamentary, or Mixed

The idea of the separation of powers is an idea, an artifact, a tool of written constitutions designed to frustrate and prevent hasty governance. None of the countries that I can think of as being organic in evolution—not Great Britain or most of its former colonies nor the long evolving democracies of the Nordic countries—has a formal separation of legislative, executive, and judicial institutions, though the judiciary in some of these systems has carved out a modest degree of independence. In these and other parliamentary regimes, the executive branch, known collectively as the cabinet, is chosen by the legislature typically from among its own members. Members of the cabinet remain members of parliament and also serve in executive capacities as ministers in charge of various government departments. If there is a president (or monarch), his or her role is largely ceremonial with real executive power in the hands of the prime minister. Typically, too, the cabinet appoints the judiciary.

In theory, the central, defining characteristic of a parliamentary system is that of *cabinet responsibility,* the ability of the parliament to force the government to resign and either form a new cabinet or call for new elections. The "executive branch," including the prime minister and the various ministers in charge of agriculture, finance, and so on, are both drawn from the parliament and collectively responsible to it. A cabinet that can no longer reach a consensus on its own, or that can no longer get its way in parliament, must give up its right to control the government.

In presidential systems, chief executives are elected on their own, usually by direct popular election; and they serve for fixed terms rather than at the pleasure of the parliament. Neither the president nor any of his department heads is a member of parliament, and the president's cabinet is essentially responsible to him or her. It is characteristic of presidential systems to blend legislative and executive power as, to use a familiar example, in the United States where the president may veto an act of Congress and the Congress may, in turn, override the veto by a two-thirds vote. It is important in these systems to include clear methods of resolving power struggles between the branches, a job partly given in most presidential systems to a more-or-less independent judiciary. Finally, "parliamentary systems have collective or collegial executives whereas presidential systems have one-person, non-collegial executives."[10] Whether, as Lijphart argues, this is a defining distinction between presidential and parliamentary systems is not clear. Although Switzerland has a plural executive, it is not strictly a presidential system since its executive council is chosen by parliament rather than direct election.[11] Uruguay and Lebanon have also experienced periods of governance under a dual executive structure designed to give permanent status to both of the divided nations' polarized factions, and a similar arrangement in Cyprus was even more short-lived. Failures such as these have led most observers to question the viability of plural executives under systems of separated powers. Shugart and Carey argue that "a collegial presidency might be applicable to societies divided by deep partisan or ideological divisions as well as societies . . . with ethnic or other subcultural divisions;"[12] but in practice there are no strictly presidential systems functioning today with plural executives.

A growing tendency in constitution-making is toward creation of hybrid, or mixed presidential-parliamentary systems in which there is both a prime minister selected by the legislature and a president elected by popular vote. The aspect of the system that makes this form of government unique is that while the prime minister is politically responsible to parliament, the president has some real powers. In Finland, one of the more stable and successful premier-presidential regimes, the president has generally had virtually a free hand to deal with issues of foreign policy and to appoint the Chancellor of Justice, but has rarely intruded on domestic policy issues. In countries like Ireland and Austria, on the other hand, the strength of parties in controlling the legislature has prevented a supposedly autonomous executive from carving out an independent role. Shugart and Carey conclude that although "the specific combinations of responsibilities can vary. . . the performance of premier-presidential regimes. . . will depend on the clarity of the division of executive responsibilities between president and cabinet."[13] Even where those divisions seem clear, moreover, the dynamics of the system can vary markedly from year to year. France's ostensibly mixed system, usually described as "semi-presidential," has swung between periods of executive domination under Presidents de Gaulle and Pompidou to periods of very real balance between the powers of the president on the one hand and the parliament and cabinet on the other. As can be seen in the

Appendix, parliamentary systems are the most common today, accounting for more than half of all democratic systems, followed by presidential and only a scattering of mixed systems.

Checks and Balances

The differences between presidential systems on the one hand, and those lacking a separation of powers on the other, are important largely because of the different ways in which they respectively channel the flow of political power. The fundamental rationale for a system of separate powers, and for the checks and balances it includes, is an extension of the idea that the primary function of a written constitution is to limit government. Even in a democracy, the argument holds, "a majority might well take actions that would destroy the system; hence some method of minority veto may be necessary to prevent this."[14] While these vetoes are not absolute, a system of checks and balances provides points at which minorities can slow government action or require some form of extraordinary majority. In the United States, to give one example, the president's ability to veto an act of Congress is not absolute; but it takes a two-thirds vote of both houses of Congress to override a presidential veto. In the American system, such checks and balances are sustained by the separation of powers. Here, "the preservation of liberty," is dependent, in James Madison's words, on giving each department "a will of its own" and being "so constituted that the members of each should have as little agency as possible in the appointment of the members of the other."[15] But while it is often the case that unitary systems more clearly focus political power in their legislatures and the cabinets they select, parliamentary regimes are seldom without similar checks on government power. Madison's argument, as Dahl has pointed out, "exaggerates the importance. . . of specified checks to governmental officials by other specified governmental officials" at the same time that "it underestimates the importance of the inherent checks and balances existing in every pluralistic society."[16]

Absent such social pluralism, presidential systems are often found wanting in their ability to govern, particularly in periods of transition from authoritarian rule. Drawing on the Latin American experience, Nino argues that,

> the main challenge faced by processes of transition in consolidating democratic institutions is the containment of the network of de facto power relationships that corporations weave, as they take advantage of the vacuum left by representatives of popular sovereignty. Under authoritarian rule, social groups representing particular interests carve a place for themselves after some bargaining, which includes their offer of support for the regime. Such groups are the military themselves, the religious organizations, coalitions of entrepreneurs, trade unions, and even the press. Of course these groups resist relinquishing their power to the representatives of the people once democratic rule is established.[17]

The ability of these groups to exercise veto powers under a system of checks and balances can produce regimes that effectively lack the ability to govern in any meaningful sense. Unable to challenge the old order, they either lose their ability to mobilize mass publics, or look for the kinds of strong leaders that can transcend the institutional barriers imposed by the constitution. The result in many cases is either *"conditioned democracies* that achieve stability as a result of a sort of enduring truce with corporative power,"[18] or a reversion, often through popular election, to some form of authoritarian rule. This experience is not confined to Latin America. Whether it is more likely to happen in presidential as opposed to parliamentary regimes is a more complicated issue.

In a widely-cited 1988 study of the connections between presidentialism and instability in Third World countries, Fred Riggs traced the collapse of more than thirty such regimes.[19] While there are a number of reasons for the failures of democracies, Riggs and many subsequent researchers concluded that the rate was substantially higher for presidential than parliamentary regimes. Mainwaring, in 1992, for example, listed thirty-two democracies that had been continuously democratic for at least twenty-five years, twenty-three (or 72 percent) of which were parliamentary.[20] It seemed clear from most of these early studies of the issue that a system of separated powers, by making it more difficult to put together the coalitions needed to provide effective governance, makes a presidential regime almost inherently less stable than one which requires the building of parliamentary coalitions.

The idea that presidential systems are less stable has become less certain as newer governments and other factors are taken into account. One problem with many of the studies that highlighted the supposed fragility of presidential regimes is that most were conducted before a number of third wave transitions had time to demonstrate their stability. Updating the numbers, and using a shorter time span, Shugart and Carey calculated a failure rate of 50 percent for presidential regimes compared with 43.8 for parliamentary.[21] In most cases, moreover, it can be argued that it is the failure of linking political institutions, parties in particular, more than any inherent flaws in presidential systems that account for the problem. Where parties are cohesive and strongly organized, they can provide the links between the separate institutions of the government that make it possible to transcend constitutional boundaries and provide the kind of government that can govern effectively.

The price of such efficacy can be high. Because it has a separate institutional and political base, the strong executive in a presidential system is sometimes positioned to turn the legislature and judiciary into rubber stamps. In Argentina it was known as Peronism, in Indonesia as Guided Democracy. Where parties are too weak to pull the separate institutions together, the resulting failures to govern tend, all too often, to invite military intervention and the displacement of elected regimes. Di Palma goes so far as to suggest that the United States is virtually alone among presidential systems that have endured, and that "the notion that presidentialism introduces a beneficial system of checks and balances" is simply wrong.

A president can rarely perform the moderating role that a head of state performs in a parliamentary system. In the last analysis, he is an elected partisan. As to the presence, separate from the president, of an equally elected parliament, chances are that . . . it will produce an often unreconcilable duality of powers, each appealing to its own source of legitimacy. Only in the United States, for reasons that go beyond the constitutional intent of presidentialism and have to do with the American party system and other American constitutional features, has presidentialism operated as a system of countervailing power.[22]

One problem with Di Palma's argument is that the United States, as Shugart and Carey's tables reveal, is the only developed nation with a presidential regime. Indeed if we control for economic development, "parliamentarism has not fared any better in the Third World than presidentialism; arguably, it has fared worse."[23] What this suggests, of course, is "that the first and crucial variables to which political scientists must direct their attention are social and not political."[24] Separate governmental institutions can remain separate and function effectively enough to sustain the system only in a political atmosphere that is sufficiently diverse (polyarchal, to use Dahl's term) to keep them afloat: "in so far as there is any general protection in human society against the deprivation by one group of the freedom desired by another, it is probably not to be found in constitutional forms. It is to be discovered, if at all, in extra-constitutional factors."[25]

There is also some question whether the reality of power in many cabinets is as collegial as traditional typologies suggest. The prime minister is as firmly in charge of the government in many parliaments as are many a supposedly-independent presidents. While almost everyone in Great Britain, for example, would agree "that cabinet ministers *should* collectively participate, and . . . both should and *could* collectively deliberate upon policy," as David Judge puts it, "The changing relationship between the prime minister, cabinet, cabinet committees and departments of state has generated heated academic debate."[26] In Belgium, where coalition governments are the norm, party leaders frequently bypass the parliament entirely.

This has made the principle of collegial and collective cabinet decision-making more difficult to realize. The most important issues, in terms of political delicacy or complexity, are increasingly settled in formal . . . or informal meetings between the prime minister and vice-prime ministers, who are the heavyweights of each coalition party in the cabinet. Once an agreement is reached the matter is transferred for final approval to the council of ministers, where it is usually rubber-stamped with little discussion and even fewer amendments.[27]

Sartori has effectively debunked the myth that parliamentary regimes are inherently more efficient than presidential. Where *parliaments,* as opposed to strong party cabinets, rule, the situation can be very much analogous to that in divided governments in presidential systems. Coalitions may persist, but they do not necessarily govern without very significant checks and balances. "Government stability," as Sartori puts it, "stands for a mere *duration;* and governments can be at once long-lived and impotent. . . . Indeed, in most parliamentary systems which require government by coalition, governments prolong their survival by doing next to nothing."[28]

Somewhat more subtly it can also be argued that presidential systems have the greater capacity to focus public attention. For better or worse—and it certainly can work both ways—presidents tend to crystalize public opinion and capture media attention. They help to simplify (some would say, oversimplify) politics and thus tend to be popular with mass publics. Brazil in 1993 put the question of parliamentarism vs. presidentialism to a referendum with the latter winning over-whelmingly.[29]

But this is only the beginning of this debate. More generally, the issue is probably better framed in terms of checks and balances. Even with divided government, presidential systems have shown a capacity to govern effectively that flies in the face of conventional wisdom, and parliamentary systems, it appears, are susceptible to the same problems of deadlock and deference to corporatist and military influence as presidential. The simple existence of a parliamentary form, moreover, is not a guarantee of consensual politics. Sri Lanka's parliaments, instead of building inter-ethnic coalitions have tended to exacerbate conflicts, limit democracy, and oppress the Tamil minority. "The extremely adversarial nature of political contestation inhibited the growth of consensual political decision making. The unitary Westminster model adopted from the British appeared to foist a polarized polity on Sri Lankan reality."[30] Whether Sri Lanka would have been able to overcome these problems by choosing a different electoral system, or by giving the Tamil area partial autonomy we will never know. In the luxury of hindsight it is easy, though not necessarily accurate, to attribute both failures and successes to questions of design. But it does seem clear that majoritarian democracy, untempered by institutional checks on majority power, and/or unrestrained by effective bills of rights is unlikely to provide lasting justice or stability in divided nations.

Federalism

Many of the same arguments that have been made with regard to the separation of powers between government branches can be made about the division of powers between the national government and local entities. A federal system can remain viable only where its institutional forms are reinforced and supported by complementary social and political forces. A former Speaker of the United States House of Representatives is often remembered for his frequently-voiced argument that "all politics is local." "Tip" O'Neill's quip neatly encapsulates the territorial nature of American politics, and it serves also to explain why its federal system has endured. In strictly legal terms, federalism has all but ceased to exist in the United States: congressional and Supreme Court interpretations of the Constitution's "commerce," "due process," and "equal protection" clauses have erased virtually all areas of policy once regarded as strictly local; and the Congress has used its taxing and spending powers to fill in whatever additional areas of policy it chooses to usurp. In strictly legal terms, states rights are largely what the national government says they are; the states remain important in the United States essentially because, as I have argued elsewhere, "all local is politics."[31] Whatever the legal reach of federalism in the United States, its political role is potent and enduring.

Switzerland provides a rare example of a federal system which has evolved more or less organically out of a gradually tightening confederation of states whose political autonomy has declined in roughly inverse proportion to their growing economic integration and social homogenization. Most other federal systems have, in the long run, proven either cosmetic or unsustainable. When regional differences are sufficiently strong to require a division of powers, they are often too strong to sustain a national government. When, conversely, there are national issues that override local concerns, the tendency is for the society's political institutions to organize along these lines and to leave sectoral politics largely behind. Former Canadian prime minister Pierre Trudeau once said that "federalism is ultimately bound to fail if the nationalism it cultivates is unable to generate a national image which has immensely more appeal than the regional ones."[32]

Canada is an exception that tests the rule because it remains almost unique in combining federalism and parliamentary democracy. Because the logic of parliamentary politics pushes party cohesion, the tendency is either to sublimate regional differences or make them part of a national agenda. In the former case, the exigencies of the need to win some piece of the national cabinet require local units to cohere to national party platforms. In the latter case, regions whose parties lose national elections often see autonomy as the better choice. True federalism survives best, it would seem, in presidential systems or, at a minimum, in political systems whose parties are as loosely disciplined as those of most presidential systems.

As with the separation of powers, federalism is in part a matter of degree. Just as there are hybrids of the parliamentary-presidential model (parliamentary systems such as that of India with autonomous courts, for example; or France where executive power is divided between a president and a prime minister), some federal systems are more centralized than others. The German system, in which the administrative process is largely decentralized, provides an interesting model for developed democracies. By centralizing major policy decisions but allowing regions to decide such details as the citing of public works projects, it combines many of the virtues of uniformity with local control.

The German system does not, however, address problems of ethnic and religious conflict that often underlie demands for decentralization. Here, the Indian model combining parliamentary government with a high level of state autonomy, has been generally successful in giving minority groups some sense of self-determination and keeping high conflict issues out of national politics. While it has been unable to deal with Kashmir, and is often in a state of flux, India's combination of parliamentary democracy, division of powers, and decentralization,

> lays the ground for a high degree of political inclusiveness. At the same time it strengthens the capacity of political parties. The parliamentary form of executive selection stimulates such tendencies as well. The very fact, moreover, that India has managed to uphold a plural practice for such a long time has had favorable consequences. Over a period of a hundred years, a process of trial and error has been operating, leading to an unusually far-reaching—for third-world conditions—conciliatory capacity in political life.[33]

"But decentralization alone does not address the political weakness of the socially excluded. Away from the scrutiny of central authorities, local class, ethnic, racial or patriarchal tyrannies can sometimes be more extreme."[34] The effectiveness of decentralization, as I will argue in subsequent chapters, depends in large part on the degree to which it is democratic rather than bureaucratic and—to no small degree—how meaningfully it fits in with and is integrated into other state institutions.

Effective federalism is defined less by structures than by processes. An important component of this dynamic is the "training" for democracy that citizens in the federal systems of countries like India derive from experience at the local level. De Tocqueville, early in the history of the American system, stressed the importance of decentralization in developing what contemporary social scientists call a "civic culture," or the habits of participation that nurture a respect for the process of getting along with others, a force we will return to in chapter 5.[35] If we think of federalism more as a system of devolving power than of localizing institutions, it can work in this way. But the cautionary notes of the skeptics need also be heard: the smaller, the more homogeneous the community, the greater the danger of intolerance and the greater the consequent need for constitutional restraints.

Bills of Rights

In many histories of the United States, the failure of the founders to include a Bill of Rights was a simple oversight quickly corrected when the new government convened. While this is substantially what happened, a good argument was made for *not* including one at all. Bills of rights, as Hamilton argued in the *Federalist,*

> are not only unnecessary in the proposed Constitution, but would even be dangerous. They would contain various exceptions to powers not granted; and on this very account, would afford a colorable pretext to claim more than were granted. For why declare that things shall not be done which there is no power to do? Why, for instance, should it be said that the liberty of the press shall not be restrained, when no power is given by which restrictions may be imposed?[36]

Hamilton lost, and most contemporary observers are glad he did. The Bill of Rights may be no more than a parchment barrier, and it may in some cases invite rather than deter evasion; but in broad outline it probably does make a difference.

The contrast with Great Britain is instructive. In terms of popular support for basic freedoms, the British record is probably superior, comparatively unmarked by some of the nastier manifestations of racism and anti-immigrant hysteria that have sometimes overwhelmed the United States. The absence of a written guarantee of free speech in Great Britain, moreover, does not mean that parliament is totally unfettered in its legal ability to override free speech claims and other rights. Yet,

> The absence of a textual provision undoubtedly circumscribes the British judiciary's ability to vindicate speech interests. . . . Any analysis of the strength of free speech interests in English law must begin with the frank recognition that if Parliament acts clearly and unambiguously, a claim of privilege under some notion of free speech will fail in British domestic courts. This illustrates the most obvious effect of a textual speech clause: such provisions legitimate—and often necessitate—judicial review of legislative enactments for consistency with the asserted speech right.[37]

This brings us back to the question of institutional forms. It is an open question whether the power of the courts in the United States to override acts of elected officials is "democratic." Whatever the answer to this question, however, there is no denying the importance of the courts in American politics both as actors in their own right and as deterrents to others. Their role, as well with regard to the national courts in India, has been particularly important in applying the Bill of Rights to the states. Whether this role is compatible with what we think of as democratic government returns us to the question of the role played by constitutional words and forms the process of governance.

Constitutional Forms and Political Realities

There is probably no student of politics who has given more sustained attention to the question of what makes democracy work than Yale professor Robert Dahl.[38] It is noteworthy that almost nowhere in his many works does Dahl give serious attention to constitutional forms. "To assume that [the United States] has remained democratic because of its Constitution," he wrote in 1956, "seems to me to be an obvious reversal of the relationship; it is much more plausible to suppose that the Constitution has remained because our society is essentially democratic."[39] In later books, Dahl concedes that constitutional forms can channel the ways in which democratic forces flow, listing, for example, four significant consequences of the ways in which the U.S. Constitution organizes power;[40] but the fundamental lesson he draws from the case of the United States is that a democratic culture can sustain itself despite a structure that "is neither consensual nor majoritarian but . . . possesses the vices of both and the virtues of neither."[41] The overall thrust of Dahl's argument—that the chances are poor of sustaining democratic regimes in societies that do not have strong democratic cultures—makes a good deal of intuitive sense and has, in the long run, been validated. The exceptions, however, are sufficiently numerous and interesting seriously to question the rule. The United States itself, as more than one Briton noted in the 1790s, was not then ready for democracy either.

However much we hope that constitutional democracies can sustain themselves, there is no doubt that the prospects for success are higher in some societies than others. Civil society is part of the equation, closely linked to economic development, and a historical tradition of democratic procedures. Democracies "are extremely fragile when facing poverty,"[42] yet not all poor democracies fail. The prospects for sustainable democracy are similarly bleak in nations divided by ethnic or religious conflict. But even here, as the examples of such diverse countries as Belgium, Canada, India, and Switzerland show, constitutions have ways, in the long run, of increasing their own chances of survival. As people become habituated to working through certain defined procedures, as they accustom themselves to a common rhetoric of rights, the constitution itself becomes part of a shared political culture that takes on a life of its own.

The prospects for successful constitutional "engineering," for using institutional forms as tools for overcoming deficiencies in civil society, should not be overestimated. Most of all, there are no "one-size-fits-all" solutions to the problem of building sustainable democracies. The attempts during what is sometimes called the "second wave" of democratization following World War II were most successful when—as in Germany and Japan—constitutions were tailored to social realities. By retaining the ceremonial importance of the Japanese emperor, by reconstructing Germany as a federal state, the foundations were laid for viable systems. The attempts, at the other extreme, to impose virtual carbon copies of the American constitution in the Philippines and many Latin American countries, or of British institutions in Africa, can be seen, in retrospect, as doomed to failure.

Institutions matter. But citizens matter too. As Larry Diamond puts it:

> The mass public matters for democratization in two senses: in its often pivotal role (too little appreciated by the scholarly literature) in helping to effect a transition to democracy, and in the never-ending quest to deepen democracy beyond its formal structure. If we think of democracy in developmental terms, as a political system that emerges gradually in fragments or parts, and is always capable of becoming more liberal, inclusive, responsive, accountable, effective, and just, then we must see democratization not simply as a limited period of transition from set of formal regime rules to another, but rather as an ongoing process, a perpetual challenge, a recurrent struggle.[43]

Most important, constitutions succeed or fail in their entirety: while it is useful for analytic purposes to compare the workings of federal and non-federal, or parliamentary and presidential systems, in the actual functioning of a political system it is the meshing of its various parts—both structural and cultural—that most impacts its ability to cohere. Governments failed to resolve ethnic conflicts in Sri Lanka not because they were parliamentary in form, but because an electoral system that over-rewarded the majority ethnic group negated the need to form coalition cabinets.

Notes

1. As quoted in Dick Howard, "The Indeterminacy of Constitutions," 31 *Wake Forest Law Review* (1996), 402.

2. Walter F. Murphy, "Constitutions, Constitutionalism, and Democracy," in *Constitutionalism and Democracy: Transitions in the Contemporary World*, ed. Douglas Greenberg et al. (New York: Oxford University Press, 1993), 6.

3. Cass Sunstein, "Constitutionalism and Secession," *University of Chicago Law Review* 58 (1991), 637.

4. *Federalist,* Number 83.

5. Christopher W. Hammons, "Was James Madison Wrong? Rethinking the American Preference for Short, Framework-Oriented Constitutions," *American Political Science Review* 93 (December 1999), 840.

6. Hammons, "Was James Madison Wrong?" 846.

7. This quotation is from *The Federalist Papers,* number 49, the authorship of which was long in dispute but which is now generally attributed to Madison.

8. *Federalist*, Number 51.

9. *Federalist,* Number 51.

10. Arend Lijphart, *Patterns of Democracy: Government Forms and Performance in Thirty-Six Countries* (New Haven, CT: Yale University Press, 1999), 118.

11. Switzerland's seven-member executive council is selected by the parliament but may not be replaced. Its president (also appointed by parliament) has little independence of the executive council and must step aside after one year in favor of the appointed vice president.

12. Matthew Soberg Shugart and John M. Carey, *Presidents and Assemblies: Constitutional Design and Electoral Dynamics* (New York: Cambridge University Press, 1992), 104-5.

13. Shugart and Carey, 75.

14. Robert A. Dahl, *A Preface to Democratic Theory* (Chicago: University of Chicago Press, 1956), 55.

15. *Federalist,* Number 51.

16. *Federalist*, Number 22.

17. Carlos Santiago Nino, "Transition to Democracy, Corporatism, and Presidentialism with Special Reference to Latin America," in Greenberg et al., 47.

18. Nino, "Transitions to Democracy," 51.

19. Fred W. Riggs, "The Survival of Presidentialism in America: Para-constitutional Practices," *International Political Science Review* 9 (1988), 247-63.

20. Scott Mainwaring, "Presidentialism, Multi-Party Systems, and Democracy: The Difficult Equation," *Comparative Politics* 25 (October 1992), 21-43.

21. Shugart and Carey, 41.

22. Giuseppe Di Palma, *To Craft Democracies: An Essay on Democratic Transitions* (Berkeley: University of California Press, 1990), 217.

23. Shugart and Carey, p. 42.

24. Dahl, *A Preface,* 83.

25. Dahl, *A Preface,* 134.

26. David Judge, *The Parliamentary State* (London: Sage Publications, 1993), 141.

27. Lieven de Winter, "Parliament and Government in Belgium: Prisoners or Partiocracy," in *Parliaments and Governments in Western Europe* ed. Philip Norton (Portland, OR: Frank Cass Publishers, 1998), 100-101.

28. Giovanni Sartori, *Comparative Constitutional Engineering: An Inquiry into Structures, Incentives, and Outcomes* (New York: New York University Press, 2nd ed., 1997), 113.

29. John Peeler, *Building Democracy in Latin America* (Boulder, CO: Lynne Reiner, 1998), 82.

30. Radhika Coomaraswamy, "The Politics of Institutional Design: An Overview of the Case of Sri Lanka," in *Can Democracy Be Designed? The Politics of Institutional Choice in Conflict-Torn Societies,* ed. Sunil Bastian and Robin Luckham (New York: Zed Books, 2003), 145.

31. Edward Schneier and John Brian Murtaugh, *New York Politics: A Tale of Two States* (Armonk, NY: M. E. Sharpe, 2001), 63.

32. As quoted in Peter H. Russell, *Constitutional Odyssey: Can Canadians Become a Sovereign People?* (Toronto: University of Toronto Press, 2nd ed., 1993), 80.

33. Axel Hadenius, *Institutions and Democratic Citizenship* (New York: Oxford University Press, 2001), 126.

34. Robin Luckham, Anne Marie Goetz, and Mary Kaldor, "Democratic Institutions and Democratic Politics," in Bastian and Luckham, *Can Democracy Be Designed?* 32.

35. Alexis de Tocqueville, *Democracy in America* (New York: Alfred A. Knopf, 1945), vol. I, 68. Originally published in Paris in 1835.

36. *Federalist,* Number 84.

37. Ronald J. Krotosyzynski, Jr., "Brind and Rust v. Sullivan: Free Speech and the Limits of a Written Constitution," 22 *Florida State Law Review* (1994) reprinted in Vicki C. Jackson and Mark Tushnet, *Comparative Constitutional Law* (New York: Foundation Press, 1999), 1377.

38. The books by Robert A. Dahl that are most cogent to the topics of this book are, in chronological order: *A Preface to Democratic Theory* (Chicago: University of Chicago Press, 1956); *After the Revolution* (New Haven: Yale University Press, 1970); *Polyarchy: Participation and Opposition* (Yale, 1971); *Dilemmas of Pluralist Democracy: Autonomy vs. Control* (Yale, 1982); *Democracy and Its Critics* (Yale, 1989); and *How Democratic Is the American Constitution?* (Yale, 2001).

39. Dahl, *A Preface,* 143.

40. Dahl, *Dilemmas,* 189-192.

41. Dahl, *How Democratic,* 188-89.

42. Adam Przeworski et al., *Democracy and Development: Political Institutions and Well-Being in the World, 1950-1990* (New York: Cambridge University Press, 2000), 269.

43. Larry Diamond, *Developing Democracy: Toward Consolidation* (Baltimore: The Johns Hopkins University Press, 1999), 219.

Chapter 4

The Scope of Constitutional Regimes

Constitutions limit the scope of government power, some considerably more than others. The traditional means of distinguishing forms of government on the basis of the locus of sovereignty—democracy, oligarchy, monarchy—derive with surprisingly little change from Aristotle. A second continuum, ranking governments along a dimension of their capacity and willingness to control individual and social behavior, is a more recent product of the forces of technological change that have made possible whole new dimensions of control. While there is no such thing, even in fiction, as a truly *totalitarian* government in which the Big Brother of state power is able to control every moment of every citizens' life, the examples of Nazi Germany and Stalinist Russia offer chilling reminders of how powerful a force the modern state can be.

At the other end of the scale are states in which resources are so scarce as to make the government virtually irrelevant to many citizens. There are jungle villages in Papua so unreachable by land, sea, or air that they have never had meaningful contact with any agency of the Indonesian government. And there are governments in other less developed nations that are almost as irrelevant to their citizens throughout the country as successive Dutch and Indonesian governments have always been in these remote villages. A "marginal state" such as this is one that "exhibits certain outward attributes of statehood, but which can penetrate its territory only to a very low degree. Society here is highly autonomous. The state has but a minimal governance capacity. Its task may be primarily symbolic and ritualistic in nature."[1]

While this kind of marginal state most commonly appears in the wake of the collapse of a central state—as in pre-Taliban Afghanistan when the warlords moved in to displace the fallen Soviet-backed state—it is also characteristic of regimes that simply lack the assets to develop the infrastructure of the modern state. With a per capita gross domestic product of less than $500, the 12.7 percent of its resources that a country like Cameroon spends on government is enough to sustain only the most basic public services. Of more interest here are those states that have the resources but simply choose not to invest them in public sector activities. In welfare states as diverse as Sweden, Kuwait, Israel, and the Netherlands, nearly half of every dollar spent is spent by the government to provide a mix of services such as medical care, housing, national defense, and social security. Similarly affluent countries, including the United States (22.7 percent), Singapore (15.9 percent), and South Korea (17.7 percent) *choose* to leave far higher proportions of the nation's resources in private hands, or for the use of state and local governments.[2] Limited governments such as these are kept relatively small both by politics and, in many cases, by constitutions that sharply circumscribe the role of the state.

The Scope of the Political

Ignoring philosophical questions about the nature of free will, some things are, in all societies, matters of individual choice: whether you put sugar in your coffee, whether you place your left leg in your pants before the right, whether you sleep on your stomach or your back. A smaller domain of behavior is regulated, often unevenly, by social forces through norms of conduct as well as economic and social sanctions. It is not illegal in most societies for adults to sing in elevators or to play with their food. It just isn't done. For their practitioners, the rules of behavior described by various religions are comparable to or stronger than secular laws, as are rules dictated by those with economic power. An employer's strictures against smoking in the office, observing dress codes, or requiring union membership as a condition of employment are the functional equivalents of laws for employees. Few countries ban the wearing of blue jeans: in most countries, most questions of attire are outside the scope of the political. But if your employer requires you to wear a tie or observe other dress codes, the effect on you is pretty much the same as a law on attire. You won't go to jail or be fined for wearing jeans, but you will pay a price in terms of demotion or being fired.

The lines dividing the spheres of the personal, the social, and the political are not always clearly defined. Many social norms are so deeply ingrained in a culture that they have become part of most person's world maps (Freud labeled these internalized norms the "super ego"). And some social norms are given added sanction by law. It is not only uncouth to spit on the Metro, it is illegal as well. A private employer can fire you for violating certain rules only if the state allows it.

Despite these ambiguities and areas of overlap, the distinction between the spheres of the personal, the social, and the political is important. Many of the most bitter and enduring arguments in politics concern the definition of these boundaries, and the ways in which political systems differently define the scope of the political is as important in describing them as is the question of who has power. Students of comparative politics need ask not only "who governs?" but "how much?"

The rights most appropriately designated off-limits to government usurpation, it is widely agreed, are those that support the functioning of the system itself, those we labeled "functional rights" in chapter 1. Most democracies, for example, protect the franchise and free speech in ways that make it difficult, if not legally impossible, to change the rules regarding elections or debating public issues. How far the state should or will go positively to protect and extend these rights is more controversial. Citizens in Great Britain can and do speak on any topics they want in Hyde Park; but the London police will not protect that same citizen's "right" to give the same speech in the entryway to Harrod's Department Store.

Beyond functional rights, variations abound. As we have argued, some constitutional prohibitions on state action have philosophical or ideological origins that often trace back into theories of natural law. Some rights, it is argued, are inherently individual such as the right to life itself, to property, or to privacy. Because democracies tend logically toward values of legal equality, it often follows that their constitutions require equality in the enforcement as well as the making of the law. And it is possible to go beyond simple restrictions on state power into the area of positive political acts designed to restrict social actors. Here we get into another important way in which constitutions deal with questions of power and autonomy. To prohibit the state from taking a life or invading privacy is one thing; but to protect the individual from social invasions of his or her privacy or right to life is quite another. The Constitution of the United States is virtually devoid of positive protections of rights: it proscribes government action in a variety of spheres but tacitly at least permits private action that might accomplish the same ends.

Many other constitutions, including those of the American states, attempt in some way to define positive rights. Most state governments in the United States, for example, guarantee a right to free public education. Here the constitution acts, not to constrict the scope of the public but rather to expand it into areas that previously had been considered social (mostly in the form of church-sponsored schools) or personal (in the form of home schooling). A comparison of similar clauses in the constitutions of the United States on the one hand, and that of the state of New York on the other is nicely illustrative.

The U.S. Constitution protects rights mostly through clauses that *prohibit* government action. The First Amendment, for example, says that "Congress shall make no law respecting an establishment of religion, or prohibiting the free exercise thereof. " Contrast this language with a similar provision in the constitution of New York: "The free exercise and enjoyment of religious profession and worship, without discrimination or preference, shall forever be allowed in this state to all mankind." While the national constitution prohibits Congress from passing laws abridging certain specified freedoms, it is silent on other acts of discrimination, such as those committed by private individuals. Because its language is directed at Congress, the protection it provides is only from government action, except insofar as the Congress decides to go beyond those boundaries. In some cases, it has done exactly that. It is, for example, illegal to wiretap your neighbor's phone not because the First Amendment protects your neighbor, but because Congress has chosen to provide such protection. The more positive wording of the New York State constitution requires no such legislative action. The State Court of Appeals, ruling in a 1986 free speech case, described the results of these differences in the following terms:

> Freedom of expression in books, movies and the arts, generally, is one of those areas in which there is a great diversity among the states Thus it is an area in which the Supreme Court has displayed great reluctance to expand Federal constitutional protections, holding instead that this is a matter essentially governed by community standards. . . . However, New York has a long history and tradition of fostering freedom of expression, often tolerating and supporting works which in other States would be found offensive to the community. . . . Thus the minimal national standard established by the Supreme Court for First Amendment rights cannot be considered dispositive in determining the scope of this state's constitutional guarantee of freedom of expression.[3]

Although New York's protections of privacy extend to private attacks as well as governmental, many of the positive rights guaranteed by constitutions must be implemented and enforced by courts and elective bodies. Many of them, particularly those guaranteeing economic justice, sound better than they actually prove in practice. Guarantees against poverty and exploitation are considerably more common in constitutions than they are in real life, particularly when they require the commitment of economic resources for their implementation or seriously challenge entrenched interests. In practice, such "rights" often turn out to be largely rhetorical, interpreted in most societies as symbols of aspiration rather than as mandates for action. Typically, New York's Section 1 of Article 17, which seemingly mandates a state obligation to provide for "the aid, care, and support of the needy" has been rendered essentially meaningless by court rulings that it is up to the legislature to decide who is "needy." Constitutions do not provide the courts with very effective means of implementing such decisions, even where they might be inclined to make them. Nowhere are they empowered actually to appropriate government funds; but a court decision that generally mandates such expenditures has more than just moral and political force, as the failure to implement court-ordered changes can result in private lawsuits that add extra weight to the original court order. In one set of cases in New York City, the reluctance of the government to respond to a court order on prison overcrowding was overcome by a threat to order the release of individual prisoners citing the original decision.

Because they are so seldom substantiated, positive rights—such as those "guaranteeing" employment, housing, education, or health care—are sometimes called "aspirational" rights, telling us more about what a government should do rather than what it may or may not. A telling exception to this rule is the extraordinary 2000 decision of the Supreme Court of South Africa pushing enforcement of the "right" to adequate housing that seems quite unique in its forthright intrusion into an area of "rights" enforcement that traditional theory has assigned to the legislature. "In the end," as Sunstein suggests, "the argument for socioeconomic rights was irresistible, in large part because such guarantees seemed an indispensable way of expressing a commitment to overcome the legacy of apartheid—the overriding goal of the new constitution."[4] Despite this appropriate cautionary note, I suspect that decisions such as these are not as uncommon as they seem, especially in countries with strong judiciaries. A number of American state courts have, for example, forced the legislative and executive branches significantly to modify their methods of funding public education, caring for the mentally ill, or treating prisoners.

The Government and Private Property

For most of the twentieth century the cutting edge issues distinguishing the roles and rights of governments, social institutions, and individuals have been economic. The expansion of corporate powers across local, provincial, and national boundaries called forth a reassessment of the roles of governments. Where once government had been the only institution capable of repression on a national scale, the rise of the modern corporation necessitated a re-examination of the boundaries between public and private. "A modern society," as one Scandinavian scholar says,

> needed more government. A strong state could also serve as an instrument in the emancipation of underprivileged groups. However, whereas the latter looked upon the growing state power as a good in itself, others looked upon it as a threat to liberty. Both sides could agree, however, that the development pointed out a new way of governing society. . . . which ultimately led to the constitutional conflict in the years following the Second World War [over] discretionary power beyond the limit of the old rule-of-law state. The change implied a new role for the administration, which could no longer limit itself to the nondiscriminatory establishment of a general framework within which private interests could take initiatives.[5]

In the first wave of this conflict, the issue was largely regulatory: whether the state should have the power to regulate social and economic institutions such as corporations. For many conservatives "property was, and should be, not only the symbol, but the source and guarantee of individual liberty,"[6] but what became increasingly clear as the nineteenth century unfolded was that, in the concentrated hands of the very few, it could become a threat to freedom as well.

Property rights and liberal democracy are perhaps most clearly linked in the U.S. Constitution, and it is in the United States that the fight to expand the role of government has been most persistent. The argument in general terms is accepted by most supporters of democracy. If the government controls your economic destiny, your ability to act as an autonomous citizen is limited. It is difficult to oppose the re-election of your employer, hard to editorialize about the flaws of a government that owns the media you work for. Even such rights as those of privacy and freedom to worship can be indirectly limited absent private property, as when the government as landlord is free to make inspections of your home that the government as policeman could not, or when the government "allows" freedom of religion but refuses a particular sect a building to house its church. While some early twentieth century reformers conceded these basic points, they also noted that these same arguments could be reversed. As Sunstein puts it,

> If the central concerns are citizenship and democracy, the line between negative rights and positive rights is hard to maintain. The right to constitutional protection of private property has a strong democratic justification: If people's holdings are subject to ongoing governmental adjustment, people cannot have the security and independence that the status of citizenship requires. . . . But the same things can be said for minimal protections against starvation, homelessness, and other extreme deprivation. For people to be able to act as citizens . . . they must have the kind of independence that such minimal protections ensure.[7]

The first wave of the assault on property rights in the United States focused on regulation. Government action was seen less as an assault on the right to property itself than on its use to encroach upon the rights of others. Many early state regulations, such as those controlling bank or insurance fraud, could be seen less as restrictions on business than as acts to protect the market system, or to defend the property rights of legitimate enterprises from the dishonest. The role of government was one of controlling rather than displacing market forces. Despite the vehement protests of many capitalists and economic conservatives, this relatively limited expansion of state power gained gradual acceptance as compatible with the continued existence of a right to property. While it seems difficult to believe that people defended the right to sell contaminated meat, defraud investors, or operate factories without fire exits, there are—even in the contemporary world—a number of people who, theoretically, at least, defend virtually all rights based on economic ownership as particularly worthy of protection. "In most societies," as Charles Lindblom puts it,

> the law broadly prohibits one person from inflicting injury on another: prohibits, for example, physical assault, theft, libel, and conspiracy to injure. Even threats are illegal. But it leaves one great exception: injury through termination of an exchange relationship. It is easy to see why it must allow that exception if a market system is to persist. But it is an exception to which classical liberal theory on liberty seems blind.[8]

Classical liberals have been joined by many so-called public choice theorists in continuing to accord property rights a preferred position, as an essentially inherent part of individual liberty. The extreme position using the argument to oppose all government regulations is seldom heard; but there is a surprisingly tenacious movement in the United States that continues to "urge a return to the good old days when the courts protected property rights and economic liberties, in keeping with the intent of the framers' and the basic values of American constitutional system."[9]

More threatening than the rise of the regulatory state is the notion, dramatically expressed in socialist thought, that private property itself might be incompatible with constitutional democracy. An independent system of private property, as Macpherson puts it, "leads necessarily . . . to an inequality of wealth and power that denies a lot of people the possibility of a reasonably human life."[10] When government sets out positively to redress these inequalities through public ownership of key institutions, the questions raised are different in kind from those raised by government regulation of institutions in private hands. Not surprisingly, fights over this changing role of the state were at the root of constitutional crises in many societies, and of revolutions in some. While the idea of democratic socialism has many overt and covert supporters, the notion that democracy and socialism are fundamentally incompatible has regained much of its old force in recent years.

Indeed one could argue that the twentieth century saw an almost total reversal in the direction of the conflict over public ownership. Early in the century, the struggle, particularly in Western Europe, was one of overcoming legal and philosophical barriers to the nationalization of private property. By the middle of the century, virtually every mode of transportation, communication, and energy production had been nationalized. Most countries had socialized medicine as well, and many governments had taken over basic industries such as mining, steel, aircraft manufacturing, and tourism. By the end of the century, privatization swept through both Western and Eastern Europe and became a world force. In Eastern Europe and in the new countries once part of the old Soviet Union, the transition has been difficult, and may, in the opinion of some observers, be unobtainable in the short run. The essence of the problem, to abstract from Jon Elster's longer argument, is found in the tensions between capitalism's need for stability and the mass public's predictable reaction to painful change. The prerequisites to free enterprise—stable currencies and banking systems, protections of property rights, freedom from wage and price controls—must be firmly enough locked in place for investors to believe that their businesses can endure. Such reforms, however,

are also incompatible with political democracy, if they lead to the best-off being very well off. Private ownership leads to income inequalities that are unacceptable to large segments of the population. . . . By a twist of history, the workers of China and the Soviet Union now brandish the egalitarian ideology against the regime itself. . . . In doing so, they find natural allies among the conservative bureaucratic forces who want nothing more than the failure of the reforms.[11]

Most third wave constitutions have taken a cautious, middle road toward the protection of property. With a few short-lived exceptions, the extreme libertarian position of public choice theorists and American conservatives has not been embraced, nor, however, has any significant support for socialism appeared. Most references to public ownership in existing constitutions, at the same time, have been either quietly ignored (as in Indonesia) or actually rescinded (as in Madagascar) to allow for the privatization of state enterprises and generally to move toward more mixed economies. If modern constitutions seldom proclaim socialism and government control over major industries as an objective of the state, there are equally few that leave the poor to the mercy of market forces for basic sustenance, education, and other aspirational rights.

The Scope of the Political in Transitional Regimes

The problem of redefining the scope of the political is particularly acute in systems attempting simultaneously to democratize and move toward market economies. Writing from the perspective of Eastern Europe, Lena Kolarska-Bobinska argues that "during the transition period the role of the state is particularly essential and undoubtedly different from that played by the state in a stabilized market system." The "old bureaucratic structures," particularly at the lower levels, are difficult to replace, yet if change is to be meaningful they "must redefine their role and that of their of their apparatus."[12] The past few years in Indonesia have shown in less sweeping ways the essence of this dilemma: you can bring in people who are fully committed to the need for change, but don't quite now how to achieve it; or you can rely on those who know very well how changes could be effected, but have little interest in achieving it. In Eastern Europe and the former Soviet Union, "privatization" often meant having the same bureaucrats keep their jobs and run their companies for profit instead of for the state. Wearing their free enterprise hats, the same party functionaries who once ran things for the state now command disproportionate influence through their control of private economic resources.[13]

A similar kind of problem has emerged in other countries that were not formally socialist, but in which the line between the public and private sectors was blurred at best. Such "corporatist arrangements pose a serious threat to democracy in countries with a history of authoritarian state corporatism, such as Mexico, Egypt, and Indonesia, where the state has created, organized, licensed, funded, subordinated, and controlled 'interest groups' with a view to cooptation, repression, and domination rather than to ordered bargaining."[14] A quasi-market system in which foreign and domestic capitalists have established privileged positions in their relationships with state institutions cannot be replaced overnight. Those who have profited from the old order will be in very strong positions to resist change. To pull the plug on a major industry or financial institution and open the market to competition is to risk major economic disruptions. But because these industries have such strong economic powers, they tend also to have disproportionate weight politically.

> Limited economic development, or the absence of a fully functioning market economy, further increases the danger that corporatism will stifle civil society, even under a formally democratic framework, because there are fewer autonomous resources and less interest pluralism in society. Even in countries that have vigorous market economies and now rate as liberal democracies, like South Korea and Taiwan, the state corporatist legacy casts a neoauthoritarian shadow over the structure of interest representation.[15]

In Indonesia, these problems are compounded by pervasive patterns of corruption that tightly link corporate interests, political parties, and state institutions, the military in particular. The Indonesian military has long been a major player in the economy, controlling both legitimate businesses and supporting some less savory enterprises. It also has strong political roots at the local level where it was often the only organized group allowed to operate throughout the Soeharto years. Abuses of human rights by the military should not go unpunished, and the government is under strong international pressure to convict some of the worst offenders. But the military also has a vital role to play in holding the country together; and it is also, not coincidentally, a powerful political force in its own right, quite possibly capable of toppling the civilian government.[16] Both in terms of wealth and military power the people most likely to be elected to the legislature and elevated to other positions of power, moreover, are often the same people who have profited most from the system as it was. They are not easily displaced.

A second, and often related, problem in transitional regimes is that one of the key institutions in dealing with corruption—the judiciary—is likely itself to be deeply enmeshed in the intrigues and abuses of power of the old order. Yet it too is difficult to replace or reform. Constitutions are probably not good places for addressing these problems. As the experience in Eastern Europe and the former states of the Soviet Union show, there is no one path to change. Economic reform comes in fits and starts. To define the boundaries between the state and private enterprise in constitutional terms is to guarantee that the constitution will either be frequently amended or frequently ignored. To those impatient for change, there is a strong temptation simply to bypass the courts and other regular channels of constituted authority by granting special, supposedly temporary or emergency powers to a strong central authority. But as Professor Kolarska-Bobinska asks, "Is the recourse to such undemocratic means justified by considerations of efficiency and speed? Will not the use of means whose logic is contradictory to the nature of the system that is the goal deform the shape of its solutions? Should that be sanctioned by the constitution?"[17] The very steps that might be needed, in the short run, to facilitate changes to a market system, to displace the worst features of the old order and generate confidence in the capacity of the new regime to govern, may be the steps that—in the long run—contain the seeds of the destruction of democracy.

Different, but equally daunting, problems confront transitional regimes in countries with abiding ethnic conflicts. Established democracies as diverse as Canada, Costa Rica, Switzerland, and—for that matter the United States—have been able to function democratically and at least contain episodes of major violence. But enduring conflicts in Nigeria, Sri Lanka, Ethiopia, Cyprus, and other second and third wave transitions have frustrated otherwise promising processes of democratic consolidation. The dramatic contrast between the success of authoritarian regimes in Yugoslavia and the failure of what followed have tended to confirm the hypothesis that democratization is likely to fail in the face of such divisions. The logic here is simple. "A nondemocratic regime," as Linz and Stepan put it,

> may be able to impose acquiescence over large groups of people for a long period of time without threatening the coherence of the state. In a nondemocratic regime, the fact that central authority is not derived and maintained by free electoral competition means that separatist or irredentist aspirations, if they exist, are not routinely appealed to in the course of normal politics and can possibly be simply repressed.[18]

The problem this poses for transitional regimes is intense. Not only are the ethnic and religious conflicts previously suppressed likely to explode out of the bottle when the cork is removed, but in many cases the conflicts have been exacerbated by the very regimes that seemingly had kept them under control. Ethnicity and religion have often been politicized by those seeking a return to authoritarian rule. In "country after country in Africa," ethnic and religious conflict has been less "the result of 'primordial' bonds among fellow members of ethnic or religious groups" than the "often strategic, self-serving actions of politicians. . . who, in striving to create or retain support for their bids for power, help to perpetuate the notion that ethnically or religiously divided African states cannot develop recognizably democratic political systems."[19]

One possible solution to this problem is to take the most troubling issues of conflict off the table, to create a constitution that in one way or another places questions of ethnic or religious controversy beyond the scope of national politics. Through federalism, issues such as these can be kicked downstairs with the hope of regionalizing the problem. Linguistically, Switzerland is four countries, and it works. Canada has been somewhat less successful in satisfying its largely Quebecois, French-speaking minority, but so far the system coheres. But even though the federal solution more-or-less worked for seventy years in the United States, Lincoln was almost certainly right when he said that it was impossible to sustain a nation half slave and half free. Systems that provide local autonomy can, to be sure, take the pressure off the national government, but when devolution goes too far it becomes secession—as with the Czech Republic and Slovakia—when it does not go far enough it festers or erupts.

The stresses on multicultural regimes are compounded in the modern world by outside forces. The Cold War proved particularly cruel with both sides frequently intervening on behalf of dissident ethnic groups as a means of embarrassing regimes friendly to the other side, as when the United States armed and encouraged the Taliban in Afghanistan simply because it was fighting a pro-Soviet regime. Further compounding ethnic conflicts are the active diasporas of nationalist emigres whose enthusiasms for ethnic causes know few bounds. There is both irony and tragedy in the fact that the most enthusiastic and effective supporter of the more violent aspects of the Irish Republican Army is likely to be "the determinedly 'Irish' Bostonian who knows no Irish literature, plays no Irish sports, pays no Irish taxes, serves in no Irish army, does not vote in Irish elections, and has only holiday conceptions of the Old Sow as she is today."[20]

In an earlier chapter we suggested that one prerequisite to democratic consolidation is a willingness to lose. But if nobody likes a sore loser, sore winners can be even more dangerous. While the tendency of economic and ethnic elites stubbornly to insist on the retention of old privileges, the threats from those who want immediate transfers of both power and wealth can be disruptive as well. Those who were formally excluded from participation, or forced into compromises they were not consulted in approving, may be particulary (and understandbly) aggressive in trying to overthrow the old order. Studies of the process of democratization, however, have generally shown "that deradicalization and even demobilization of popular forces are intrinsic to late-twentieth century democratization. Political participation is also exchanged for substantive inequities prompted or deepened by market-based strategies."[21] The willingness of the African National Congress to strike socialism from its platform and allow whites essentially to dominate the post-apartheid economy served enormously to aid South Africa's transition to democracy.

State Institutions and Political Power

We began this chapter by suggesting that governments differ from one another not only in the ways the answer the question "who governs," but also in delimiting the scope of the political, in deciding how much the government shall and shall not control. To what extent, if any, are these two questions interrelated?

In one of the most provocative books ever published in political science, E. E. Schattschneider argued that the questions of scope and power were closely linked. To view politics as a simple "tug of war of measurable forces," Schattschneider argued in *The Semisovereign People*, was to ignore the equally important

> struggle between the conflicting tendencies toward the privatization and socialization of conflict. . . . A long list of ideas concerning individualism, free private enterprise, localism, privacy and economy in government seems to be designed to privatize conflict or to restrict its scope or to limit the use of public authority to enlarge the scope of conflict. A tremendous amount of conflict is controlled by keeping it so private that it is almost completely invisible.[22]

Sometimes these methods of restricting the scope of conflict are sewn into the fabric of the constitution through provisions that either put some issues off-limits or restrict the ability of certain kinds of majorities to coalesce. If certain issues are walled out of politics, some citizens will be less likely to participate. If some citizens, conversely, are not allowed to participate, the issues that might interest them are not likely to be articulated.

What Stephen Holmes calls "gag rules" are more prevalent in world politics than is commonly acknowledged. "Although seldom studied in a systematic manner, strategic self-censorship seems to be an almost universally employed technique of self-management and self-rule."[23] By putting certain issues off-limits to politics, or by devolving them to local governments, constitutions can sidestep or at least defer conflicts that might threaten system stability. This is precisely what the American founding fathers did with the question of slavery and—more successfully in the long run—with religion.

Restricting the scope of conflict directly carries with it the risk of future eruptions, if not civil war. By keeping some issues out of politics, moreover, one risks making politics irrelevant, and thus threatening the very purpose of democracy. A strong argument can be made, however, that democracies can be structured in ways that mitigate conflict without gag rules. Although they disagree strongly at times on the particulars of the best approach, Arend Lijphart and Donald Horowitz have been most prominently associated with the argument that institutional choices—particularly those revolving around the electoral system—can have a profound impact on the ways in which political conflicts work themselves out.[24] Just as Madison argued in the tenth *Federalist*, that it was both possible and desirable to control the *effects* of factions without destroying the liberties that allowed them to exist, so do contemporary scholars like Lijphart and Horowitz believe that function can be made to follow form.

Whether the system created is federal or unitary, parliamentary or presidential, it is argued, makes a difference in the ways in which conflicts are resolved. Electoral systems especially can be structured to promote bargaining across ethnic group lines. The art of constitutional engineering is not to develop one ideal set of institutions, but rather to fit a system to its underlying civic culture.

Notes

1. Axel Hadenius, *Institutions and Democratic Citizenship* (New York: Oxford University Press, 2001), 251.

2. The figures cited here are taken from the World Bank's compilation for 1995 as reported on its very useful website. Because they include only the expenditures of the national government, they underestimate the public sector's share of GDP in a federal system such as that of the United States where state and local governments account for an additional 14 or 15 percent.

3. *People ex. rel. Arcara v. Cloud Books* 68 New York 2nd 553 (1986), 558.

4. The case of *South Africa v. Grootboom* is nicely summarized and analyzed in Cass R. Sunstein, *Designing Democracy: What Constitutions Do* (New York: Oxford University Press, 2001), 225.

5. Francis Sejersted, "From Liberal Constitutionalism to Corporate Pluralism: The Conflict Over the Enabling Acts in Norway After the Second World War and the Subsequent Constitutional Development," in *Constitutionalism and Democracy*, ed. Jon Elster and Rune Slagstad (New York: Cambridge University Press, 1993), 276

6. Jennifer Nedelsky, "American Constitutionalism and the Paradox of Private Property," in Elster and Slagstad, *Constitutionalism and Democracy*, 242.

7. Sunstein, *Designing Democracy,*223.

8. Charles E. Lindblom, *Politics and Markets: The World's Political-Economic Systems* (New York: Basic Books, 1977), 48.

9. Nedelsky, "American Constitutionalism," 242.

10. C. B. Macpherson, "Human Rights as Property Rights," *Dissent* (Winter 1977), 73.

11. Jon Elster, "The Necessity and Impossibility of Simultaneous Economic and Political Reform," in *Constitutionalism and Democracy: Transitions in the Contemporary World*, ed. Douglas Greenberg et al. (New York: Oxford University Press, 1993), 270.

12. Lena Kolarska-Bobinska, "The Role of the State: Contradictions in the Transition to Democracy," in Greenberg et al. *Constitutionalism and Democracy*, 309.

13. Kolarska-Bobinska, "The Role of the State."

14. Larry Diamond, *Developing Democracy: Toward Consolidation* (Baltimore: The Johns Hopkins University Press, 1999), 250.

15. Diamond, *Developing Democracy*, 250.

16. R. William Liddle, "Indonesia's Unexpected Failure of Leadership," in *The Politics of Post-Suharto Indonesia*, ed. Adam Schwarz and Jonathan Paris (New York: Council on Foreign Relations Press, 1999), 16-39.

17. Kolarska-Bobinska, "The Role of the State," 310.

18. Juan J. Linz and Alfred Stepan, *Problems of Democratic Transition and Consolidation: Southern Europe, South America, and Post-Communist Europe* (Baltimore: The Johns Hopkins University Press, 1999), 27

19. Jeff Haynes, *Democracy in the Developing World: Africa, Asia, Latin America, and the Middle East* (Malden, MA: Blackwell Publishers, 2001), 143.

20. Benedict Anderson, *The Spectre of Comparisons: Nationalism, Southeast Asia, and the World* (New York: Verso, 2000), 72.

21. Richard Joseph, "Democratization in Africa after 1989: Comparative and Theoretical Perspectives," in *Transitions to Democracy*, ed. Lisa Anderson (New York: Columbia University Press, 1999), 249.

22. E. E. Schattschneider, *The Semisovereign People: A Realist's View of Democracy in America* (New York: Holt, Rinehart, and Winston, 1960), 6, 7.

23. Stephen Holmes, "Gag Rules and the Politics of Omission," in Elster and Slagstad, *Constitutionalism and Democracy*, 57.

24. Arend Lijphart, *Democracy in Plural Societies: A Comparative Exploration* (New Haven: Yale University Press, 1977) and David L. Horowitz, *Ethnic Groups in Conflict* (Berkeley: University of California Press, 1985).

Chapter 5

Conflict and Consensus: The Civic Culture of Democracies

The argument that constitutions are of secondary importance to social and economic variables has a long history. In extreme form, it is argued that a true understanding of how people are governed is to be found only in the underlying dynamics of specific cultures in defined stages of development. A classic formulation of this notion is in Karl Marx's depiction of the polity as a "superstructure," dependent almost entirely upon the underlying control of the means of production. Few other students of politics have put the issue as starkly as Marx and his disciples; but there is, and long has been, a rather strong consensus that "political-institutional changes in the direction of democracy are the consequence of transformations in economic and social life."[1] The core argument of this book is that institutional, socioeconomic, and cultural variables are interrelated: democracies often thrive in places where the underlying culture seems hostile at best, it fails in places where it should not; but that there are generally predictable patterns to this dynamic. What this chapter tries to do is to sort out the variables scholars have found most consistently associated with stable democracy; to examine the logic of predicted associations; and to examine the various dynamics of actual institutional response to these elements of civic culture.

Three related sets of variables have traditionally been identified as being most closely related to the emergence and persistence of democracy. For many years it was argued that size was important; that democracy fared best in small places, or at least in communities that were uniform and cohesive, undivided by significant ethnic or social cleavages. A second school, while not necessarily disagreeing on the importance of national unity, places the emphasis on economic development. "Any casual glance at the world," as one study puts it, "will show that poor countries tend to have authoritarian regimes, and wealthy countries democratic ones."[2] Finally, there are a number of studies indicating that neither social unity nor economic development explains sustainable democracy but rather the patterns of conflict that underlie them. "The study of the conditions encouraging democracy must therefore focus on the sources of both cleavage and consensus."[3] There is, in this view, a particular kind of civil society, a deeply-ingrained set of social relations that facilitates democratization and helps sustain it.

To the extent that any of these approaches downplay institutional variables and elite agreements, they probably overstate their case. Some societies, at the same time, are far more likely to sustain constitutional democracy than others. And the ways in which institutions work and constitutions evolve are strongly related to the ways in which societies are structured in terms of cultural cohesion and division, size, and economic development.

Size and Democracy

In classical political theory it was generally assumed that democracies could survive only in small communities. Aristotle, for example, suggested a walled city state in which one could see one rim from the other, and Plato flatly declared 5,040 the optimal number of citizens.[4] The central issue, in this classic conception, was one of civic unity and trust. "In a large republic," as Montesquieu put it, "the common good is sacrificed to a thousand considerations; it is subordinated to various exceptions; it depends on accidents. In a small republic, the public good is more strongly felt, better known, and closer to each citizen; abuses are less extensive, and consequently less protected."[5] James Madison's most enduring contribution to political theory was to turn this argument on its head to suggest that larger democracies were more secure than small. Madison and the Federalists ultimately prevailed in this argument, but not without a fight. Many of those who opposed ratification of the Constitution put the issue of size at the center of their case. In the debate over ratification, indeed, it is plausible to argue that "size *was* the issue."[6] The core of the anti-Federalists case against the Constitution was a shared conviction that a nation-state as large and diverse as that proposed by the Federalists would invariably become tyrannical.

There is a strong logic to the anti-Federalist argument. Pure mathematics suggest that the smaller the country the greater the chance that any individual's voice will be heard. There are devices, such as decentralization, representative bodies, public opinion polls, and so on, that can amplify individual voices in larger societies. But there is no getting around the essential problem of how larger and larger numbers of citizens can participate in any direct sense in the policy process. In the Athenian Assembly, as Dahl and Tufte point out, "it was easier for Pericles to speak to all of the citizens than for all of the citizens to speak to Pericles."[7] In the much larger democracies of today, the mass media make it possible for political leaders to communicate with the citizens almost as easily as could Pericles. But although the absolute number of people who can communicate directly with their leaders is about the same as it was in Pericles' Athens, the lines are much, much longer. The gap between the politician's ability to talk to his constituents and their ability to talk to him grows with size. Where once members of the U.S. Congress had "connections of blood, of friendship, and of acquaintance"[8] with their constituents, one member today represents more than 600,000 people. At twenty seconds each, working eight hours a day, it would take the modern congressman six months just to meet *half* of his or her constituents.

More important, the citizens of a large democracy have fewer chances to talk with *each other*. The face-to-face communications of the old New England town meeting were important in helping to create and sustain what modern theorists call "the civic culture" of democracy, and we will return to this dynamic later in this chapter. The essential point, as Dahl and Tufte put it, is that,

> If individuals in the smaller system foresee that whenever group conflict emerges they will have to pay dearly for it in their personal relationships, conflict is likely to be less frequent than in the larger system. Organized group conflict entails extra costs in the form of individual antagonisms among people who must frequently confront one another . . . in the small system, the further group conflict is pressed, the higher the stakes become.[9]

The sense of community that can, and often does, develop in such societies can be highly conducive to democratic governance. Where people negotiate their problems in an atmosphere of personal proximity, the habit of compromise is likely to grow. But even here, a case can be made on the other side. Small communities are not known for their tolerance. "Participation in face-to-face democracies," moreover, "is not automatically therapeutic: it can," as Mansbridge found in her study of New England town meetings, "make participants feel humiliated, frightened, and even more powerless than before."[10]

Modern political scientists seldom directly address the issue of size. The proposition that republican government can survive only in small states, it is generally argued, "was surely given the coup de grace by the American" case.[11] Very small states, like Barbados, Liechtenstein, and Tonga, are often more like semi-autonomous provinces or colonies than sovereign nations. In a global economy, moreover, they suffer from an inability to provide a full range of public services and opportunities. A relatively large small country the size of Iceland (300,000), Cape Verde (400,000), or Guyana (800,000) can have a university, but is unlikely to support a full medical school or advanced training in physics or political science. It may take great pride in its cultural heritage, but unless its citizens are fluent in a more universal language, they will be dependent in many respects on others, and more subject to the erosion of their traditions. Iceland's popular musician Björk has a worldwide following, but more than 95 percent of Iceland's popular culture is imported. She herself sings more songs in English than Icelandic. In a more disastrous sense, small states are unusually susceptible to external pressures and threats. The history of Cyprus provides a depressing example of a situation in which relatively minor local frictions have been ratchetted up by Britain, Greece, and Turkey to the extent that "the principal determining factors for ethnic conflict have not been cultural or religious differences, but the policies pursued by interested powers, external to Cyprus."[12]

Despite these difficulties, as can be seen in Table 5-1, very small countries are considerably more likely to be democratic than large ones. Interestingly, most of the world's micro-democracies are island communities. But whether islands in the sea or islands between more powerful mainland neighbors, most are only recently independent and remain strongly tied to their former colonial masters. Whether democracy in Cayman flowed up from the essential cultural unity of the islands or down through a long tradition of increasing autonomy under the British system is not clear. What is clear is that very small countries, internally democratic though they may be, are frequently derivative of their sovereignty and—by implication if not in fact—of their democratic institutions as well.

Size and Diversity

The argument that small societies are more likely to be democratic is, on closer examination, not always an argument about size. In stressing the importance of personal trust, the argument for small democracy has less to do with the direct interpersonal nature of communications than with their content. The essential idea is that democracy is best planted in "a shared affective identity in terms of a common sentiment/belief that 'we' belong together."[13] It is helpful if not essential that there be a sense of "nationness" underlying any constitutional system; but the argument here goes further to suggest that democracy in particular requires interpersonal trust. Only where there is such national solidarity can you be confident of survival if you lose an election. At the very least, citizens must share a sense of loyalty to the same set of institutions. Even if they are not quite comfortable with each other in cultural terms, "a shared sense of identity based on belonging to the same polity may be sufficient to buttress liberal democratic practices."[14]

Harry Eckstein's classic study of Norway makes this point in concrete terms. Although Norway is certainly less diverse in most ways than, say, Great Britain or the United States, it is hardly a uniform society.

Table 5-1

Size and Democracy: Types of Government in the World's Largest and Smallest Countries (1950-2002)

	25 Smallest Countries	25 Largest Countries
Mostly Democratic	Antigua and Barbuda, Barbados, Belize, Cape Verde, Dominica, Grenada, Iceland, Malta, Marshall Islands, St. Lucia, St. Kitts and Nevis, St. Vincent, San Marino Sao Tome and Principe, Tuvalu, Vanuatu	France, Germany, India, Italy, Japan, Korea, Mexico, Turkey, United Kingdom, United States
Mixed	Andorra, Comoros, Liechtenstein, Monaco, Seychelles, Solomon Islands	Bangladesh, Brazil, Indonesia, Nigeria, Philippines, Thailand
Mostly Authoritarian	Brunei, Maldives, Tonga	China, Congo, Egypt, Ethiopia, Iran, Pakistan, Russia, Ukraine, Vietnam

Source: Population figures are those reported for the year 2000 on the web site of the United States Census. Judgments as to whether countries like Andorra should be classified as nations are based on membership in the United Nations or recognition by various regional associations such as the European Union. Countries are classified as democratic, mixed, or authoritarian largely in accord with the general ratings of Freedom House (see appendix A). "Mixed" systems are those that either combine (as in Monaco) a strong hereditary monarch with an elected government, or those that have mixed at least ten years of democratic rule into the past forty years.

If the model "small society". . . is something as intimate, neighborly, and internally accessible as . . . an Aristotelian city-state, then clearly international power and numbers of people signify less than geographic area, communications, contiguity, and constant intercourse among citizens. From all these standpoints, Norway comes closer to being immense than small. . . . Her territory is 30 per cent larger than the United Kingdom's; communications among many places even today are difficult and earlier in the century were virtually impossible much of the year; the population is the most scattered in Europe, except for Iceland's; and there is in consequence much regional diversity. . . . She has about as complex a social structure (diverse regions, dialects, occupations, economic interests, cultural stances, voluntary organizations, and political organizations) as much less stable societies.[15]

Despite this apparent diversity, Norway, in Eckstein's argument, is a cohesive society in terms of its attitude toward the institutions of the state. "The idea of democracy is imbibed through the earliest socialization process . . . and is central to the Norwegians conception of their national essence. . . . Fidelity to democracy is a principle that simply is not subject to dispute."[16] This suggests that there are two ways of talking about consensus: in the social and cultural sense that people "have a common history or distinctive culture," and in the narrower sense that they "share a sense of belonging to a polity" with which they identify. Citizens, as Andrew Mason puts it, and as Eckstein basically argued with regard to Norway, might "have a sense of belonging to their polity without thinking that there is any real sense in which they belong *together*."[17]

The evidence on the importance of the first of these connections is not strong. Democracies as diverse as Belgium, Canada, India, and Switzerland have long survived despite sharp ethnic, religious, and linguistic splits. The more recent successes of democratic transitions in Spain and South Africa underscore the point. And as sensible as it sounds to say that there needs to be some basic political consensus and regime loyalty, the evidence here isn't very strong either, though the longer people become acclimated to democracy, the more they tend to support it. In order to establish a constitutional democracy there must be, to be sure, a national entity; and there probably needs to be fairly strong agreement that the existing way of doing things—whether through violence, autocracy, or colonial rule—can be improved upon. But this doesn't mean that there has to be consensus on values.

> Diverse groups hold together, firstly, because they have a common interest in sheer survival, and, secondly, because they practice politics—not because they agree about "fundamentals," or some such concept too vague, too personal, or too divine ever to do the job of politics for it. The moral consensus of a free state is not something mysteriously prior to or above politics: it is the activity (the civilizing activity) of politics itself.[18]

Similarly, Rustow has suggested that, "The basis of democracy is not maximum consensus. It is the tenuous middle ground between imposed uniformity (such as would lead to some form of tyranny) and implacable hostility (of a kind that would disrupt the community in civil war or secession)."[19] Within the broad confines of this middle ground, moreover, it matters a lot what kind of a democracy is put in place, how it operates, who it includes. The argument from political culture runs the danger of confusing and effect. It seems at least tacitly to assume "that social and economic conditions are somehow more basic, and that we must look for the significant relations in this deeper layer rather than in the "superstructure" of political epiphenomena."[20] While constitutions do not make democracies, they can go a long way toward shaping the processes of bargaining needed to bridge social and cultural conflicts.

Economic Underpinnings

It is bit of a stretch to describe Tanzania as "mostly democratic," or Haiti as having a "mixed" history of democracy and authoritarianism as I do in Table 5-2. Yet even by these generous standards it is striking that only one of the world's poorest countries has been mostly democratic over the past half century, while ten have yet to experience more than a fleeting taste of nonauthoritarian rule. With the exceptions of Singapore and Hong Kong, two oil-rich Arab monarchies, and the unusual case of Taiwan, conversely, every country in the world whose citizens average over $8,000 a year is a democracy. The correlation between affluence and sustainable democracy is clear and remains one of the most enduring facts of comparative political analysis. The question has not been whether this is true but why.

"From Aristotle down to the present," Lipset says, "men have argued that only in a wealthy society in which relatively few citizens lived at the level of real poverty could there be a situation in which the mass of the population intelligently participate in politics and develop the self-restraint necessary to avoid succumbing to the appeals of irresponsible demagogues."[21] This view, that the relationship between income and politics is related to education and a low rate of poverty, continues to have widespread support. In somewhat more nuanced form, Huntington suggests that economic development creates a "much more diverse, complex, and interrelated economy, which becomes increasingly difficult for authoritarian regimes to control." It does so, first, by creating,

> new sources of wealth outside the state and a functional need to devolve decision making. Second, economic development increases the levels of education in society. . . . More highly educated people tend to develop the characteristics of trust, satisfaction, and competence that go with democracy. Third, economic development makes greater resources available for distribution among social groups and hence facilitates accommodation and compromise.[22]

Finally, Huntington connects political democracy with the expansion of the middle class, or, at least, the absence of huge gaps between rich and poor. "Democracy is difficult," he argues, "in a situation of concentrated inequalities in which a large, impoverished majority confronts a small, wealthy oligarchy."[23]

Adam Przeworski and his colleagues examined almost every country that had its own government between 1950 and 1990 and compared their politics with a variety of economic and social indicators. Their data indicate that while "per capita income generally [is] by far the best predictor of political regimes," affluence in it-

Table 5-2

Per Capita Income and Democratization in the World's Richest and Poorest Countries

	25 Richest Countries	*25 Poorest Countries*
Mostly Democratic	Australia, Austria, Belgium, Canada, Denmark, Finland, France, Germany, Iceland, Ireland, Israel, Italy, Japan, Netherlands, New Zealand, Norway, Sweden, Switzerland, United Kingdom, United States	Tanzania
Mixed	Hong Kong, Taiwan	Benin, Burkina Faso, Burundi, Central African Republic, Haiti, Kenya, Madagascar, Mali, Malawi, Mozambique, Niger, Nigeria, Rwanda, Zambia
Mostly Authoritarian	Kuwait, Singapore, United Arab Emirates	Azerbaijan, Bangladesh, Burma, Chad, Ethiopia, Guinea, Nepal, Tajikistan, Togo, Zaire

Source: World Gross Domestic Product figures can be found in accessible form on the web at www.geocities.com. On the classification of political systems see the note to Table 3-1 on page 69.

self is not automatically associated with democracy: while few very poor countries are democratically governed "there are countries in which dictatorships persist when all the observable conditions indicate they should not; there are others in which democracies flourish in spite of all the odds."[24] The Przeworsiki study begins by examining countries that underwent a transition from dictatorship to democracy and vice versa. Seeking confirmation of an old notion that there might be some sort of "take-off" point, a level of affluence at which the demands for participation become irrepressible, they found few consistent patterns. Economic development may create "prerequisites," preconditions, or even a demand for democracy, but the idea it leads in some inevitable sense to the end of autocracy is not confirmed. Indeed "the causal power of economic development in bringing down dictatorships appears paltry. The level of development, at least as measured by per capita income, gives little information about the chances of transition to democracy."[25]

Where overall economic development matters most is in established regimes. Once a country adopts a democratic constitution, the chances that it will revert to dictatorship (without outside intervention) are problematic in poor countries, virtually nonexistent in the rest. Affluence is important in part because it tends to be associated with education. And education is connected to democracy both because it increases the possibility of informed consent and policy dialogue, and because it tends to increase citizen involvement. Formal schooling imparts skills and "increases one's capacity for understanding and working with complex, abstract, and intangible subjects, that is, subjects like politics. . . . Learning about politics doubtless heightens interests; the more sense one can make of the political world, the more likely that one is to pay attention to it."[26] More crudely, rich governments "buy" support with better roads and schools than poor countries. Even where there are disagreements as to how resources should be allocated, money is divisible. It can be bargained in amounts in ways that cultural and linguistic favors cannot. And if wealth is good, growing wealth is better. As Dahl says, "economic growth . . . fosters the belief that joint gains may be shared from an increase in outputs; in political life, the game of politics need not be zero-sum; if politics is not zero-sum, political opponents are not necessarily implacable enemies; and negotiation and compromise can lead to mutually beneficial compromises"[27] Beyond gross income, patterns of distribution are also linked with democratization in most studies, though there is less consensus as to how. In his classic study of historic transitions, Barrington Moore disparaged the roles of peasants and urban workers, emphasized the role of the middle class, and attributed the primary blocking role to an entrenched landowning class.[28] While a number of subsequent scholars have echoed Moore's emphasis on the middle class,[29] the tendency in more recent studies has been to focus less on class than on the dynamics of interaction between and among sectors of the economy, and the willingness of the economic elite to risk certain forms of power sharing. If shifts in the balance of class power are basic to the process of democratization, they are less "ahistorical givens" than "constructed by movements, organizations and leaderships that act in some particular environment."[30]

Division, Cohesion, and Political Stability

At the time of the drafting of the U.S. Constitution, conventional wisdom held that democracy could survive only in a relatively small, homogeneous society. Madison's answer was that diversity and distance might actually prove to be moderating forces. His argument, as brilliantly outlined in *Federalist* Number 10, was that although individual and group conflict was inevitable in human society, its causes could be controlled either "by destroying the liberty which is essential to its existence," or "by giving to every citizen the same opinions, the same passions and the same interests. . . . The second expedient," he continued, "is as impracticable as the first would be unwise."[31] Thus unable or unwilling to control the sources of faction, we should concentrate on controlling its effects. This could be accomplished less through constitutional limits on power, than by so expanding the citizen base to the point at which no single group would so dominate as to be able to impose a "tyranny of the majority." Although Dahl has shown that Madison's logic on the issue of majority tyranny is flawed, Dahl and others have tended strongly to the basic argument that diversity—instead of tearing a country apart—can be a source of unity or at least tolerance. While the stability of the system may require some consensus on the system itself, a highly diverse population is not necessarily destined to fly apart or succumb to dictatorship. Dahl calls this *polyarchy*.

> As compared with the political processes of a dictatorship, the characteristics of polyarchy greatly extend the number, size, and diversity of the minorities whose preferences will influence the outcome of governmental decisions. Furthermore, these characteristics evidently have a reciprocal influence on a number of key aspects of politics: the kinds of leaders recruited, the legitimate and illegitimate types of political activity, the range and kinds of policies open to leaders, social processes for information and communication—indeed upon the whole ethos of the society. It is in these and other effects more than in the sovereignty of the majority that we find the values of a democratic process.[32]

From Dahl's perspective (and perhaps, by implication, Madison's), the link between affluence and democracy is largely associational. The more complex the economy, the less likely it is that a single sector will predominate. The most salient feature of what he calls a modern dynamic pluralist society is the dispersion of "power among a number of relatively independent actors" that have sufficient resources to bargain with each other. Characteristic of pluralist .society "is a dispersion of *political resources,* such as money, knowledge, status, and access to organizations; of *strategic locations,* particularly in economic, scientific, educational, and cultural affairs; and of *bargaining positions,* both overt and latent, in economic affairs, science, communications, education, and elsewhere."[33] Or, as Madison put it, "Extend the sphere, and you take in a greater variety of parties and interests; you will make it less possible that a majority of the whole will have a common motive to invade the rights of other citizens; or if such common motive exists, it will be more difficult... to act in unison."[34] In a dynamic pluralism, individuals have multiple identities: conflicts between rich and poor, men and women, workers and retirees, Blacks and Whites do not overlap. Your ally on one issue may be your opponent on the next. To return, then, to a point raised earlier, the argument here is less about size *per se* than diversity. The more diverse the society, the less likely that political divisions will overlap. Dynamic pluralism arises from "cross-cutting cleavages," where "politically inconsistent affiliations, loyalties, and stimuli reduce the aggressiveness involved in political choice."[35] Modern societies,

> with their complex social differentiations and networks of interest, their wide political participation and highly organized political groups, are on the face of it . . . likely to be what one could call mechanically integrated systems: systems in which cohesion results largely from political divisions themselves, either directly through their countervailing effects on one another or indirectly through the moderating effects—the tendency to scale down political demands—that [some scholars] attribute to overlapping memberships.[36]

The Civic Culture of Democracy

A good argument can be made that a strong associational life is important in itself. This was a key facet of Alexis de Tocqueville's perspective on the vigor of democracy in the United States, made viable through a dense network of voluntary associations. When people "happen to have a common interest in some concern . . . they meet, they combine, and thus, by degrees, they become familiar with the principle of association. The greater the multiplicity of small affairs, the more do men, even without knowing it, acquire facility in prosecuting great undertakings in common."[37] Associational activities teach democracy. They instill habits of cooperation and compromise, and a sense of community strong enough to transcend differences on particular issues. He was particularly drawn to the New England town meeting, a form of governing in which the citizen "practices the art of government in the small sphere within his reach; he accustoms himself to those forms without which liberty can only advance by revolutions; he imbibes their spirit; he acquires a taste for order, comprehends the balance of powers, and collects clear practical notions on the nature of his duties and the extent of his rights."[38]

In a modern variant of this argument, pluralism and active citizen participation at all levels are held to strengthen civil society and undergird the democratic state. In Putnam's study of Italy, both the quality and quantity of civic engagement in different regions explained the rather markedly different political cultures of the north and south. The northern tradition of well-elaborated social networks, in which people wielded civic power, helped to reinforce the bonds of trust that formed the foundations for economic and social progress not found in the more authoritarian south.[39] "Tocqueville," he concludes, "was right: Democratic government is strengthened, not weakened, when it faces a vigorous civic society."[40]

Putnam followed his study of Italy with a widely praised analysis of the contemporary United States in which he traces a growing alienation of modern citizens from both their government and each other. Using the vivid metaphor of "bowling alone" to contrast the social experience of a league, he suggests that even such seemingly uncivic associations as bowling leagues contribute to pluralistic democracy through their effects on personality and character.[41] There are limits to this kind of analysis. Distinguishing between bowling leagues on the one hand, and more explicitly political organizations like Greenpeace, the Ku Klux Klan, and the National Organization of Women, John Ehrenberg argues that, "People bowled, played soccer, and sang in choral groups in Jim Crow Mississippi and in New York City, but that does not mean that their civil societies were remotely similar . . . and if South Africans played rugby in conditions of apartheid it makes a world of difference that they do now in conditions of freedom."[42]

Experience in working with others, in other words, may or may not contribute to the development of a democratic civic culture. Too often in the literature,

> nary a word is said about how civic associations may be cross-cut by deep ethnic, religious, or ideological divides. Unfortunately for those who place all of their democratic eggs in the civil society basket, history shows us time and again that civic associations can be organized in a manner consistent with existing ethno-religious divisions in society. History also shows us that, rather than serving as social capital for democracy, at times these divisions can engender debilitating social rivalries that diminish rather than enhance the prospects for civic decency. To put the matter bluntly, then, civil society is not always "democracy-good." As with right-wing militias or the Ku Klux Klan in the United States, there is nothing at all unusual about certain "civil" organizations becoming, as far as citizenship and democracy are concerned, deeply "uncivil" in their behavior.[43]

Despite these reservations, vigorous civil societies mediate between individuals and their governments. Their effectiveness is measured not simply by quantitative estimates of how many people are connected to each other in how many organizations, but by qualitative estimates as well that "make the right kinds of distinctions—distinctions that capture the diversity of associational goods, powers, and structural locations, and then compare these with the many different kinds of democratic functions associations might serve."[44] If association life is to contribute to a culture of democracy, it helps if they are self-governing and enmeshed in what Putnam calls "networks of civic engagement."[45] "Civil society," in this sense,

> delineates a sphere that is formally distinct from the body politic and state authority on the one hand, and from the immediate pursuit of self-interest and the imperatives of the market on the other. Political activities, even when they are driven by narrowest motives of individual gain, occur in an area that addresses society's broadest questions. Economic activities, even when they take shape in the most cosmopolitan international arenas, are more narrow because they are frankly organized around the pursuit of advantage. Civil society can be found in the grey areas between these two spheres.[46]

It is in these "grey areas" that collective action fosters coalition building and tends to be most productive of the kind of civic culture that sustains democracy. This kind of "associational life," as Hadenius puts it, "cannot be permeated, directed, and 'used' by the agents of the political sphere."[47] Nor, in its most developed form, is it supportive of a democratic polity where it is rooted in traditional patterns of authority. Patronage systems, in which traditional village or tribal leaders, land or factory owners effectively dominate associational life, may be a first step toward the development of civil society; but because the client-patron system is essentially one of dominance and subordination, associations in such cultures provide neither effective counterweights to authority nor training for citizenship.

While there are a number of other qualifications that have been applied to the civic culture hypothesis, the core argument boils down to three main points: first, that associational life itself, democratic associational life at least, serves as a training ground for citizenship. Second, that associational life has a tendency to blunt or moderate political conflicts by channeling them through intermediary institutions and by exposing citizens to conflicting points of view in non-authoritative situations. Before they instruct their lobbyists, for example, political interest groups must first define their own negotiating positions, as their opponents must define theirs. In pluralistic organizations, the process of negotiating each group's bargaining position has already begun the process of blunting conflict. It accustoms people to settling for half a loaf, to understanding that their individual preferences can be accommodated to those of others with different points of view.

Finally, a society with a rich associational life—or a strong civic culture, to use contemporary terminology—is more likely to have the virtues of Dahl's pluralist society. In both the civic culture approach and the case for pluralism there is a stress on those intermediary institutions that operate in the realm between the individual and the state, between a country's economic system and its other socio-cultural institutions. Particularly important in pluralist democracies are the patterns of associational life: the civic culture that works is comprised of associations that cross rather than reinforce other lines of conflict and encourage "cross-cutting clea-vages." The "chances for stable democracy," as Lipset wrote, "are enhanced to the extent that groups and individuals have a number of crosscutting, politically relevant affiliations. To the degree that a significant proportion of the population is pulled among conflicting forces, its members have an interest in reducing the intensity of political conflict [and] . . . in protecting the rights of political minor-ities."[48]

The chances that such conflicting forces will emerge are, in turn, greater in more complex societies. Associational life and pluralism are, in other words, by-products of economic development. Thus if the parallels between the arguments regarding civic culture and pluralism are strong, so in many ways, are virtually all of the connections that relate socioeconomic variables and stable democracy. What each of them has in common can perhaps best be expressed in negative terms: dem-ocracy is difficult, if not impossible, to sustain in a country that is severely underdeveloped or sharply divided. Small societies, or, one might better say, highly cohesive societies, are clearly advantaged. But absent a strong consensus on basic values, or even in the presence of economic, ethnic, and religious diversity, democracies appear to thrive with equal likelihood of success in societies that are highly fractured, highly organized, and both economically and socially diverse.

Political Cultures, Elites, and Democracy

Whatever their individual loading, the collective social, economic, and cultural variables discussed in this chapter are clearly predictive of stable democracy. In a 1980-1988 study of 147 countries, Tatu Vanhanen constructed a rather elegant set of measures of these variables, and compared them with a measure of "democratization." The fit was good: small and homogeneous societies at one end; and highly pluralistic, economically-complex countries at the other, tended to be far more democratic than those that were torn by ethnic rivalries, deep poverty, class divisions, or organizational simplicity. In all but the smallest countries, the more diverse the population, the greater the likelihood of sustainable democracy. Interestingly, Vanhanen's "Index of Power Resources," which combines indicators of the breadth and complexity of economic and organizational power resources, predicts democratization better than a comparable study of public opinion and democracy conducted a decade later. In this study, Ronald Inglehart compared surveys in more than seventy societies measuring overt public support for the ideal of democracy. His findings were "unambiguous. Although overt lip service to democracy is almost universal today, it is *not* necessarily an indicator of how deeply democracy has taken root in a given country."[49] The two countries in which 99 percent of those polled described a democratic system as a "very good" or "fairly good" way of governing a country, for example, were Albania and Egypt, putting them more than 10 percent higher on a support for democracy scale than many manifestly more democratic countries. More important than such overt expressions of democratic values, Inglehart found, were people's feelings of economic well-being, their tolerance of diversity, and—most important—"self-expression. . . ." In general outline, "economic development leads to a growing emphasis on self-expression values, a syndrome of tolerance, trust, a participatory outlook, and emphasis on freedom of expression . . ." which in turn "is conducive to democratic institutions."[50] These are, we should note, precisely the kinds of values that the proponents of both pluralism and civil society attribute to the associational life they correlate with democratization.

Some of the more interesting findings in the Vanhanen and Inglehart studies concern countries that deviate most sharply from the general patterns. In 1980, for example, fourteen countries on Vanhanen's scale of democratization had considerably lower scores than their indices of power resources would have predicted.

Eleven of the fourteen were nondemocracies. "It is remarkable that seven (South Korea, Uruguay, Argentina, Chile, Poland, Panama, and Turkey) of the Non-democracies were ruled by military or semimilitary governments in 1980 and that in the other four (Yugoslavia, the Philippines, Mexico and Jordan) cases governments rested on the support of the military."[51] Equally interesting, from the perspective of hindsight, is that twenty years later *all* of these countries except Jordan are generally counted as democracies.

"China, Vietnam, and Iran," in Inglehart's study, "have lower levels of democracy than their publics' values would predict: a determined elite, in control of the military, can repress mass aspirations."[52] A number of "under-democratic" countries in both studies—Bosnia, Croatia, Nigeria, Serbia, and Uganda—have faced sharp ethnic tensions. And Vanhanen found that some countries (including the United States), whose levels of effective democracy were lower than expected, were countries in which there are electoral systems (such as the electoral college) that significantly distort popular preferences. What emerges from virtually all of these studies is a general rule that democracy is considerably more likely to emerge and continue in some kinds of societies than others. Small, highly cohesive societies at one end, and economically developed, highly pluralistic societies at the other, dominate the landscape of democratic governance. A rich associational life and the self-expression values it tends to engender appear to be the bridge that links economic development to the democratic state. But these correlations are by no means absolute or linear. Democracies and societies are created and sustained by people in governments: who they are and how they are organized is important.

> We have absolutely no a priori reason to believe that only one set of circumstances produces and sustains democracy, even if during the last few hundred years' experience particular circumstances have often nurtured democracy. The most we can reasonably hope to get from scrutinizing historical cases of democratization is a map of alternative paths by which the process has occurred, an indication of sufficient—not necessary—conditions for that transformation, and a specification of general mechanisms that play a part in producing or sustaining democratic institutions.[53]

The role of key elites and even particular individuals cannot be ignored either in crafting democracies or in destroying them. It is almost impossible to imagine the emergence of a democratic South Africa absent Nelson Mandela and F. W. de Klerk, who won the Nobel Prize for their efforts. No matter how "ripe" the social conditions in South Africa were for change, it simply would not have happened absent their work. With negotiation having displaced revolution as the most common road to democracy, the roles of nondemocratic elites—former autocrats and their supporters, the military, and the larger economic enterprises—are often crucial in deciding when and how the transition will take place. And even when they have taken place, the old order—or at least some part of it—frequently lurks behind the curtains of the new parliaments setting the parameters of permissible democracy. Rustow argues that "consensus on fundamentals is an implausible precondition of democracy."[54] Born in compromise, it is almost impossible to think of a new democracy that is built exclusively on the foundations of its civic culture, however defined. "To survive and prosper," as Murphy says,

> constitutional democracy needs, perhaps more than any other kind of political system, leaders who have both patience and wisdom, virtues that have never been in great supply. Constitutional democracy also needs a political culture that simultaneously encourages citizens to respect the rights of fellow citizens even as they push their own interests. . . . That such a political culture will pre-exist constitutional democracy is unlikely, making it necessary for the polity to pull itself up by its own bootstraps by helping to create the very milieu in which it can flourish.[55]

Thus it matters just what kind of democratic transition the old order negotiates. Those who emphasize the importance of social forces in developing democracy provide what Rustow described as "a necessary corrective to the sterile legalism of an earlier generation." But to the extent that this underestimates the importance of constitutional forms, "We have been in danger of throwing away the political baby with the institutional bathwater. . . . Any genetic theory of democracy would do well to assume a two-way flow of causality, or some form of circular interaction, between politics on the one hand and economic and social conditions on the other."[56] Democratic transitions rise and fall, in most cases, according to the fit between the institutions of the newly crafted system to the changing realities of its civic culture.

Notes

1. Alex Hadenius, *Institutions and Democratic Citizenship* (New York: Oxford University Press, 2001), 72.

2. Adam Przeworski et al., *Democracy and Development: Political Institutions and Well-Being in the World, 1950-1990* (New York: Cambridge University Press, 2000), 8.

3. Seymour Martin Lipset, *Political Man: The Social Bases of Politics* (New York: Doubleday, 1960), 1.

4. Almost nowhere in the modern world could these standards of size be met. Plato's 5,040 citizens did not include women, children, or slaves which means, presumably, that democracy might survive his test in the modern world with a population of, say, thirty thousand. Even if we stretch it to 100,000, there are only thirty-three more-or-less self-governing territories that small. Almost all of these "countries" such as Liechtenstein, Greenland, and Bermuda, actually share their sovereignty with some larger country. The two fully independent countries that come closest to the Platonic ideal are Nauru, with a population of 11,845, and Tuvalu with 10,838.

5. Baron de Montesquieu, *The Spirit of the Laws*, translated and edited by Anne M. Cohler, Basia Carolyn Miller, and Harold Samuel Stone (New York: Cambridge University Press, 1989), vol. I, bk. 8, 123.

6. Rosemarie Zagarri, *The Politics of Size: Representation in the United States, 1776-1850* (Ithaca, NY: Cornell University Press, 1987), 83.

7. Robert A. Dahl and Edward R. Tufte, *Size and Democracy* (Stanford, CA: Stanford University Press, 1977), 74-75.

8. *Federalist*, Number 49.

9. Dahl and Tufte, *Size and Democracy,* 93.

10. Jane Mansbridge, *Beyond Adversary Democracy* (Chicago: University of Chicago Press, 1983), 71.

11. Scott Gordon, *Controlling the State: Constitutionalism from Ancient Athens to Today* (Cambridge, MA: Harvard University Press, 1999), 303.

12. Adamantia Pollis, "Colonialism and Neo-Colonialism: Determinants of Ethnic Conflict in Cyprus," in *Small States in the Modern World: The Conditions of Survival*, ed. Peter Worsley and Paschalis Kitromilides (Nicosia: The New Cyprus Association, 1977), 73.

13. Arash Abizadeh, "Does Liberal Democracy Presuppose a Cultural Nation? Four Arguments," *American Political Science Review* 96 (September 2002), 507.

14. Abizadeh, "Does Liberal Democracy?" 507.

15. Harry Eckstein, *Division and Cohesion in Democracy: A Study of Norway* (Princeton, NJ: Princeton University Press, 1966), 23-24.

16. Eckstein, *Division and Cohesion*, 17.

17. Andrew Mason, *Community, Solidarity, and Belonging* (Cambridge: Cambridge University Press, 2000), as quoted in Abizadeh, "Does Liberal Democracy?" 507.

18. Bernard Crick, *In Defense of Politics* (New York: Penguin Books, rev. ed., 1964), 24.

19. Dankwart A. Rustow, "Transitions to Democracy: Toward a Dynamic Model," in *Transitions to Democracy,* ed. Lisa Anderson (New York: Columbia University Press, 1999), 36. Rustow's article was originally a paper presented at the 1969 Annual Meeting of the American Political Science Association in New York.

20. Rustow, "Transitions to Democracy," 19.

21. Lipset, *Political Man,* 31.

22. Samuel P. Huntington, *The Third Wave: Democratization in the Late Twentieth Centruy,* (Norman: University of Oklahoma Press, 1993), 30.

23. Huntington, *The Third Wave*, 32.

24. Przeworski et al., *Democracy and Development*, 88.

25. Przeworski et al., *Democracy and Development*, 98.

26. Raymond E. Wolfinger and Steven J. Rosenstone, *Who Votes?* (New Haven: Yale University Press, 1980), 18.

27. Robert A. Dahl, *Democracy and Its Critics* (New Haven: Yale University Press, 1989), 252.

28. Barrington Moore, *The Social Origins of Dictatorship and Democracy* (Boston: Beacon Press, 1966).

29. See especially Lipset, *Political Man.*

30. Evelyne Huber, Dietrich Rueschemeyer, and John D. Stephens, "Economic Development and Democracy," in *Classes and Elites in Democracy and Democratization,* ed. Eva Etzioni-Halevy (New York: Garland, 1997), 144.

31. *Federalist,* Number 10.

32. Robert A. Dahl, *A Preface to Democratic Theory* (Chicago: University of Chicago Press, 1956), 133-34.

33. Dahl, *Preface.*

34. *Federalist,* Number 10.

35. Lipset, *Political Man,* 77.

36. Eckstein, *Division and Cohesion,* 193.

37. Alexis de Tocqueville, *Democracy in America,* revised and edited by Phillips Bradley (New York: Alfred A. Knopf, 1945), vol. 2, 115.

38. Tocqueville, *Democracy in America,* vol. 1, 68.

39. Robert Putnam, *Making Democracy Work: Civic Traditions in Modern Italy* (Princeton, NJ: Princeton University Press, 1993), 173-75.

40. Putnam, *Making Democracy Work,* 182.

41. Robert Putnam, *Bowling Alone: The Collapse and Revival of American Community* (New York: Simon and Schuster, 2000).

42. John Ehrenberg, *Civil Society and Democratic Politics* (New York: New York University Press, 1999), 235-36, 239.

43. Robert W. Hefner, "Introduction," in *The Politics of Multiculturalism: Pluralism and Citizenship in Malaysia, Singapore, and Indonesia,* ed. Robert Hefner (Honolulu: University of Hawaii Press, 2001), 9.

44. Mark E. Warren, *Democracy and Association* (Princeton, NJ: Princeton University Press, 2001), 11.

45. Putnam, *Making Democracy Work,* 167.

46. Ehrenberg, *Civil Society,* 235.

47. Hadenius, *Institutions,* 34.

48. Lipset, *Political Man,* 77-78.

49. Ronald Inglehart, "How Solid Is Mass Support for Democracy—And How Can We Measure It?" *PS: Political Science and Politics* 36 (January 2003), 51.

50. Inglehart, "How Solid Is Mass Support?" 56-57.

51. Tatu Vanhanen, *The Process of Democratization: A Comparative Study of 147 States, 1980-88* (New York: Crane Russak, 1990), 79.

52. Inglehart, "How Solid Is Mass Support?" 55.

53. Charles Tilly, "The Top-down and Bottom-up Construction of Democracy," in Etzioni-Halevy, 281-82.

54. Rustow, 18.

55. Walter Murphy, "Civil Law, Common Law, and Constitutional Democracy," *Louisiana Law Review* 91 (1991), 114.

56. Rustow, 19.

Chapter 6

Matching Cultures and Regimes:
Elites, Pluralism, and Electoral Systems

In all but the most dramatic situations of conquest and revolution, the old order casts more than a passing shadow on the new. "Competence is always in short supply and the new political leaders have to confront the urgent task of reforming political institutions while keeping economic institutions running."[1] Where the break is abrupt—as in the French Revolution, the decolonization of India, or the overthrow of Saddam Hussein—a segment of the old order is exiled or destroyed. In most transitions, however, the old order tends to be very much a part of the process of creating the new. Whether they represent segments of the existing government, the military, trade unions, or farmers, the men and women who actually sit down and draft constitutions are the leaders—sometimes self-appointed—of significant groups in society.

Classes and Elites in the Process of Democratization

Societies with vibrant civil cultures are likely to be democratic. Where associational life is weak, it is also likely to be skewed: certain groups are less likely to be organized than others, or to have widely recognized leaders. In such societies, when a new constitution is negotiated and community leaders summoned to plan the new order, the unorganized are not at the table. Neither slaves, women, nor tenant farmers were among the founders of the United States. Charles Beard's argument that the founders were not a representative sample of the American people, and that they created a constitution supportive of their own class interests[2] has been challenged as oversimple. "The Framers," as John Diggins suggests, "would have been both amused and appalled by Beard's inability to comprehend what they were up to."[3] In fact, he says, they "were a rarity in the history of political thought, perhaps the first class-conscious elites who used their talents to check the power of their own class."[4] Diggins' argument that instead of creating a constitution to protect their economic privileges, the founders actually used their privileges to preserve their country, is a useful corrective to Beard's economic theory. But the notion that they acted in disregard of their own interests is equally simplistic; if they were the first to construct a document that both protected and put some of their privileges at risk, they were not the last. Repeatedly, in the history of constitution-making, elites have tended—even as they protect their core interests—to create documents that have the potential to erode their dominance of political power. This implicit exchange, or "trade-off between participation and moderation," is what Huntington calls, "the democratic bargain."[5] What the U.S. founders may have given up was compensated by checks and balances that limited the government's ability to act; assurances of the protection of slavery; and the creation of a central government able to establish a stable currency, control popular uprisings, and protect against foreign intrigues that might jeopardize their wealth.

Unless democracy results from the complete breakdown of the established system, as in some parts of Eastern Europe and the former Soviet Union, the process of establishing new regimes almost inevitably includes bargaining of this kind. Democracy, as Przeworski says, "Can be established only if there exist institutions that would make it unlikely that the competitive political process would result in outcomes highly adverse to anyone's interests given the distribution of economic, ideological, organizational and other relevant resources."[6] These bargains are usually imbedded in institutional formulas that insure a continuing ability to maintain an enclave of power. "Democracy cannot be a result of substantive compromise, but it can be a result of an institutional compromise."[7] That is, powerful elites understand that the only deals that can assure continuing security are those that guarantee institutional influence. A deal, for example, that stipulates that tax rates cannot exceed a certain level is worthless as soon as a new election empowers a government determined to do exactly that. But a deal that writes into the constitution a clause that requires a two-thirds vote to raise taxes, or that skews the electoral system in ways that favor the rich, may secure the same end more surely. While there is no guarantee that these devices will work forever, "a particular institutional arrangement may render some outcomes quite unlikely."[8]

Why would the poor and middle classes accept such a deal? Generally, their acceptance starts with a recognition that those who control major resources—economic and military most obviously, but including bureaucratic skills—cannot be displaced without major upheavals. If brought under a democratic tent, however, the old elite will have to fight its battles on terrain that in the long run favors those who are more numerous. In the words of a member of the executive committee of Spain's Socialist Party, "Democracy and its consolidation come first, before our political programs . . . because the Spanish right has shown that it can live very well under both authoritarian and democratic regimes, while the left can only survive within a democratic framework."[9] Much the same argument applies in the case of ethnic divisions where it involves crafting rules that simultaneously allow majority rule and wall some issues off-limits or subject them to minority veto.

The most ineluctable problems of democratic transition tend to stem from the reserve powers of a hierarchical military. Poorly disciplined armies that are themselves fractured by ethnic and economic divisions, tend to be roughly reflective of the society as a whole and pose few serious challenges. But those that have organized themselves effectively, particularly in internal military operations (as in fighting a regional insurgency), are difficult to bring into the democratic tent.

> More than any of the . . . other kinds of organizational bases found in nondemocratic regimes, a hierarchical military possesses the greatest ability to impose "reserve domains" on the newly elected government, and this by definition precludes democratic consolidation. This is a particularly acute problem if the hierarchical military have been involved in widespread human rights violations and conditions their loyalty, as part of the state apparatus, upon not being punished by the new democratic government. Such a legacy of human rights violations presented severe problems for democratic consolidation in Argentina and Chile.[10]

In cases where long simmering ethnic, religious, and regional conflicts have served as justification for military privileges within the larger system, the challenge, "is to gradually roll back these prerogatives and refocus the military's mission, training, and expenditures around issues of external security,"[11] an outcome almost impossible to achieve in the face of internal security problems.

Whether military and economic elites achieve their privileged roles through direct negotiations or through tacit recognition of their special abilities to threaten emerging regimes, this way of looking at the ways in which constitutional democracies evolve forces a reconsideration of the balances between popular sovereignty and elite powers that constitutions provide. In earlier chapters—and in most of the literature on constitutional democracy—limits on majority rule have been treated as devices for the protection of minority rights. When the protected "minority" consists of wealthy landowners, generals, or corrupt commissars, the principle is the same, but the moral loading of the issue changes. The bargains that must be made to establish a "democratic" system might, on the one hand, be so protective of the old order as to make the new system a sham at best. Nino use the example of Argentina to argue that, the attempt to have a better form of democracy may ultimately result in a more degraded form of democracy or even to authoritarian regimes, since many people are threatened by the political participation of the least-favored sectors of society. This is one reason why democratic systems have not produced the just social states one would expect from the epistemic value they offer. In improving the value of the process through a more extended participation, we must be careful not to produce social reactions that may undermine the whole democratic process.[12]

Despite the obvious perils, this danger has led many advocates of democratization to accept systems of checks and balances that deliberately protect the core interests of the privileged. Since the old elites would almost certainly have retained their privileges *without democratization* (which is what happened in most parts of the former Soviet Union) to protect those privileges as part of a transition to democracy is to preserve what probably would have been protected anyway.

Just as James Madison and the U.S. founders sought to devise a constitution that would both enhance democracy and protect all citizens (including themselves) from the "tyranny of the majority," there are many contemporary analysts who enthusiastically support devices designed to limit majority power, even if it protects the prerogatives of an old order. Madison's vision of democracy, with its emphasis on limited government at the expense of popular sovereignty "fell far short of the requirements that later generations would find necessary and desirable in a democratic republic,"[13] but it was still remarkably progressive for its day. In a similar manner, a contemporary constitution, no matter how protective it might seem of the old elites, is a step forward insofar as it allows for an expansion of the wider public's role. Compared with "either civil war or authoritarian regimes and the complete absence of all democratic process, a model that requires the circulation of elites through competitive elections is not so quickly to be dismissed."[14]

> Actors will support the new democratic regime if it is in their interest to comply with the democratic rules. In other words, the new democracy is accepted when it is the best deal the actors can obtain given the current balance of power. . . .
>
> It is not typically the result of republican idealists negotiating with the nation's interest foremost in mind. Rather, democracy is arrived at through realistic, self-interested calculation and protracted bargaining among hostile actors representing diverse social groups.[15]

Most constitutions are thus shaped by two key factors: the participants, on the one hand, and each of their respective calculations, on the other hand, of how various procedures and rules will effect their long-term abilities to achieve their goals.

The first of these forces—the question of which groups and interests are participants in the process of crafting the new regime—is the point at which arguments on the nature of civil society meet the issue of constitutional design. "During constitutional reform negotiations, the problems of the country tend to take a back seat to the problems of the people at the negotiating table."[16] Since it is almost a given that some representatives of the old order will be there, the crucial question revolves around the opposition. Because authoritarian regimes generally seek to destroy or manage all significant organizations, they tend to leave what Johnson, in the case of Eastern Europe, calls an "associational wasteland" in which all significant organizations were essentially those of the suddenly discredited and collapsing state.[17] Here, as in South Africa, what opposition leaders there were came to the negotiating table, quite literally, from jail or exile. They, and others at the table, could only guess at the actual extent of their popular support. In those unusual moments when new constitutions are negotiated (or old ones revised), it would be overly cynical to argue that motives of self-interest are completely dominant and that constitutions are nothing more than partisan attempts to secure current advantages from future majorities. Whether looking at the deliberations in Philadelphia in the late 1700s or Jakarta in the early 2000s, it is impressive how seriously constitution-makers approach their job. Increasingly, moreover, "the world community is embracing a shared normative expectation that all states seeking international legitimacy should manifestly govern with the consent of the governed."[18] Along with a shift toward democratization, however, there is a growing awareness of the ways in which agreements negotiated in the crafting of constitutions can have long-term consequences both normatively and in shaping future power relationships.

The possibilities of engineering the system to produce desired outcomes are now widely recognized, openly debated, and frequently a force in shaping periods of transition. "Constitutions are pathways. They do not establish that the citizens of [what-ever country] must all march in unison to the heavenly city."[19] Nor is the heavenly city their only goal. As much as international pressures have diffused the ideal of democratization, the spread of knowledge about how systems work gives an edge to those who do their homework, who best understand how to tilt the system to their advantage, and who understand that the rules defined by constitutions affect the allocation of power.

Electoral Systems and Their Consequences

Subsequent chapters will look at the ways in which the designs of bureaucracies, legislatures, courts, and local governments affect the allocation of power. Our concern here is with representation. Most scholars agree that the design of the electoral system is "probably the most powerful instrument for shaping the political system."[20] *Who* is represented in the system and *how?* Electoral systems in most nations can be changed by simple majority; but it is not at all uncommon to find the basic outlines embedded in the constitution or insulated from politics in some other way.[21] Until the 1980s electoral systems were seldom changed; but some of the newer democracies have fiddled with their systems two or three times, and a number of older systems—Italy, Japan, New Zealand, Peru, and Turkey among them—have significantly altered the ways in which they vote.

Who Votes?

In strictly legal terms, most modern democracies are founded on systems of universal suffrage. There are exceptions, particularly with regard to non-natives. Some countries have literacy requirements, and others (including most of the U.S. states) deny the vote to ex-felons and people with mental disabilities. Five countries deny the vote to active members of the military, and government employees in general are disenfranchised in Ethiopia. Qatar, in 2003, became one of the last countries to extend the franchise to women. Iran recently raised the minimum voting age from 15 to 17, but five countries continue to put the age of voting at 16. Most put it at either 18 or 21, with El Salvador and Mongolia highest at 25.

Where suffrage requirements differ is not so much in terms of what they are as to how they are administered. Some countries make it easier to vote than others. In many countries, as in most of the U.S. states, a citizen must decide weeks or even months before the actual election that he or she wants to register to vote. In others, registration is automatic and permanent. Some very poor countries that require voters to pre-register disenfranchise literally thousands of voters every election through lost or mangled records. Instances of overt intimidation in which citizens are forcibly kept from the ballot box recur regularly.

The table in Appendix A lists the countries that have held more than one recent election, ranked according to the percentage of the adult population actually voting in all elections between 1945 and 2002. The variations are enormous, from the more than 90 percent of the voting age population that typically votes in each parliamentary election in Italy, to fewer than 45 percent in Colombia, Mali, and Monaco (which has the world's lowest turnout). Because they are calculated in terms of the total population, countries with large proportions of non-citizens, such as Luxembourg and Switzerland, have higher rates of citizen participation than indicated here. Elections in some countries, moreover, are more meaningful than in others. And there are countries in which non-voting is sometimes encouraged as an act of protest. (Turnout in Fiji, for example, dropped from 90 percent in 1999 to 78.6 percent in 2001 as more than 100,000 people risked substantial fines by refusing to vote. Another 12 percent cast blank or invalid ballots.) Some Latin American countries have long traditions of voting with an obscene word to protest the available choices, though this is, in a sense, an act of participation.[22]

On average, in countries with relatively free elections, about two-thirds of those eligible actually vote. Socioeconomic factors account for some of the variation. Better educated people are more likely to vote: hence the higher rates, generally, for countries in the developed world. Of the countries listed in Appendix A, the twenty with the highest per capita GDP have averaged voter turnout rates of 76.8 percent, the twenty lowest, 58.6 percent; but the numbers are muddier in the middle, and overall correlation between economic development and voting participation is weak. It is likely that low turnout in the very poorest countries may be more the product of imperfect election procedures than citizen choice. Political variables are more important, with elections that people think will be closely contested more attractive than those that are not. But electorates are also artifacts, tools that can be used to make some people more likely to vote than others.

In some cases, the relationship between election rules and voter participation is clear and direct. An enforced system of compulsory voting, such as that used in Australia, where there is a fine for not voting, inflates turnout. Even those countries with unenforced compulsory voting laws, or with trivial penalties (as in Argentina where the fine is about ten cents) tend to have higher rates of participation.[23] Lower rates of participation are found in countries that require voluntary personal registration, which, one study concluded, accounted for declines in participation rates of as much as 30 to 40 percent.[24]

The history of voting participation in the United States, a country that makes it relatively difficult to vote, provides telling indicators of the ways in which election laws can be used to manipulate not only how many people are likely to vote, but what kinds. Without actually mentioning race, a variety of laws adopted at the end of Reconstruction successfully disenfranchised most African-Americans in the South. Many states, for example, adopted so-called grandfather clauses in which only those whose grandfathers had voted—meaning those whose ancestors had not been slaves—were eligible to vote. When these laws were ruled unconstitutional, the states adopted "literacy" laws which were administered in such a way as to accomplish the same objective.[25] A more subtle form of discrimination was practiced by the Republican Secretary of State in Florida in 2000 where a private firm was hired to provide a list of convicted felons who, under state law, were forbidden to vote. A list provided by Republican consultants, was used to purge the voter roles of some 57,000 people, more than half of them African-American, but 90 percent of whom—as it turned out—were innocent of any crime. Given the close outcome of the presidential election in Florida (where the African-American vote was overwhelmingly for Gore), a case can be made that this manipulation of the voting lists won the election for George W. Bush.[26]

U.S. politicians have long been adept at manipulating voter rolls for partisan advantage; but what is most striking is the low and steadily declining rate of participation that place the U.S. average—even if we include presidential elections—in the bottom decile of world electorates. Restrictive registration requirements explain at best a small part of this sorry story, as these years of decline have been years in which voting rules have generally been made less severe. Contrary to expectations, moreover, declines in participation in the United States have taken place despite substantial increases in literacy and formal education. "In every political system," as Burnham says, "there is an irreducible minimum of adult citizens who are apolitical or disaffected or for other reasons abstain." Even in Australia, there are people who would rather pay a ten dollar fine than drag themselves to the polls.

> But in most other democratic-capitalist polities, this minimum is relatively small. The body of nonvoters in these polities seems on the whole not to reflect systematic biases along sociological lines of obvious political importance, and tends to be highly stable. . . .
> In the United States, by contrast, there is overwhelming evidence of systematic participation biases along sociological lines of political significance.[27]

The poor in the United States, quite simply, do not vote to the degree that their more affluent fellow citizens do, nor that they do in most other countries. Burnham attributes this largely to "the comparatively defective mobilizing and educating capacities of today's American major parties."[28] Unlike the Social Democratic parties of Western Europe, for example, the Democrats in the United States make little effort to register and mobilize their potential supporters in the working class.

From a broader comparative perspective, this failure can also be traced in some part to constitutive factors. So-called first-past-the-post electoral systems, such as that used in the United States, are about 6 percent lower on the list than those with proportional representation, largely, one suspects, because they tend to be less competitive. Where elections become more meaningful, participation rates can shoot up dramatically. Voter participation in countries as diverse as Botswana, Chile, Cyprus, and Mexico jumped by anywhere from 15 to 25 per cent when it became apparent that voting might make a difference. Voter "fatigue" may also be a factor for Americans who are called upon to go to the polls at least every two years for national elections, and sometimes in between for state and local contests. Only the citizens of Micronesia (also among the lowest in participation rates) are called upon to vote so frequently. Finally, voters in parliamentary systems have voted at an average rate of 70.4 percent as compared with 55.9 percent in contests for the legislature in presidential systems. Turnout is generally higher in voting for presidents than for their legislative counterparts, which is the most important reason for this difference; but it may also be attributable to the tendency of legislatures in presidential systems to use first-past-post election systems and to be less politically competitive.

Electoral System Design

Electoral systems provide the means by which votes cast by the people are translated into the offices won by politicians. Regardless of how many popular votes are cast for particular candidates, different electoral systems can translate them into dramatically different political outcomes, as former U.S. Vice President Al Gore can testify. Gore, though winning the popular vote in 2000, lost the presidency to George W. Bush who won a majority of votes in the Electoral College. It was the fourth time in U.S. history that a person winning fewer votes than his opponent had gone to the White House through the device of this singular institution.

The U.S. Electoral College is unique, but systems that in some sense or another skew the ways votes are added up are quite common. Twice in modern elections for Great Britain's House of Commons (in 1951 and 1974) the party winning the most votes nationally failed to win a majority of seats. As with the American Electoral College, there was relatively little public outcry. "Considered more a quirk of a basically sound system . . . than an outright unfairness which should be reversed," most people intuitively understand that there are trade-offs embedded in electoral systems that may produce minor skews of this kind. Conversely, in Mongolia in 1992 a system of "block voting" that allowed the ruling party to win 92 percent of the seats with 57 percent of the votes "was considered by many to be not merely unfair but dangerous to democracy, and the electoral system was consequently changed for the election of 1996."[29]

"There are," as Benjamin Reilly says, "countless electoral system variations, and countless ways to classify them." Reilly groups them according to "ten main formulas which fall into three broad families: plurality-majority systems, semi-proportional systems, and proportional representation (PR) systems."[30] These basic varieties are summarized in Figure 6-1.

Plurality-Majority Systems

Perhaps the most easily understood systems are those like that of the British House of Commons where each member represents a single geographic district. The British, Canadian, and U.S. variants of this system are called either "first-past-the-post" (FPTP) or "plurality" systems, meaning simply that the person with the most votes wins.[31] Almost a third of the world's democracies use an FPTP system in which the country is divided into legislative districts that each elect one member of the lower house. While most FPTP systems use single-member districts, there are a few—mostly in small countries—that elect three or more representatives from each district and allow the voter to cast as many votes as there are seats to be filled. In most of these so-called Block Voting (BV) systems, voters are free to vote for individual candidates. In six *"Party* Block Vote" systems, voters choose between lists of party candidates in each district and are not allowed to split their votes. A problem with both of these Block Voting systems is that they tend to greatly exaggerate the strength of the majority party, as in the case of Mongolia mentioned earlier. In 1995 in Mauritius, as well, one party's 65 percent of the popular vote captured every seat in parliament. The Block Voting system was replaced.

Figure 6-1

World Electoral Systems

Plurality-Majority Systems

First-Past-the-Post	Block Vote	Alternative Vote	Two Rounds
Canada, India	Fiji, Kuwait	Australia	France, Mali
U.K., U.S.	Philippines		Iran, Ukraine

Semi-Proportional Systems

Parallel Voting	Single Non-Transferable Vote
Ecuador, Ireland,	Jordan, Taiwan,
Japan, Russia	Indonesian Regional Assembly

Proportional Representation

Party List	Mixed Member	Single Transferable Vote
Chile, Finland, Israel	Germany, Hungary,	Ireland, Malta
South Africa, Turkey	Mexico	

Source: Adapted from Andrew Reynolds and Benjamin Reilly, *The International IDEA Handbook of Electoral System Design* (Stockholm: International Institute for Democracy and Electoral Assistance, 1997).

One problem with single-member district systems is that they can elect people who are opposed by a majority of their constituents. If there are more than two candidates, it is possible to win with less than a majority. In 1988, to offer a graphic example, Ngiratkel Etpison won the presidency of Palau with just 26 percent of the vote. In Canada in the 2000 elections, nearly 40 percent of the elected parliamentarians failed to win a majority, some won with fewer than 40 percent. "Spoiler" candidates, common in these systems, can confuse results in unexpected ways. To prevent such distortions, "majority" variants of the system, such as France's two-round vote, require the plurality leader to participate in a second round of voting against the second highest vote getter. The two-round system, widely used in presidential elections, is unusual for legislators outside of France, its former colonies and some U.S. party primaries.[32] Largely because it is expensive to run two elections, some countries (and the U.S. city of San Francisco) have adopted a system that accomplishes the same objectives in one election. Under "alternative vote" (AV) systems, voters rank candidates in order of choice. A first round of counting looks only at those ranked first and, if there is no majority winner, distributes the second choices of the candidate with the lowest number of first preference votes, until a majority winner is found.[33] These refinements of the basic single-member FPTP system improve the process in some ways, complicate it in others; but do not address what has traditionally been the primary objection to the system, that it tends to underrepresent or exclude minority candidates. Various methods of *proportional representation* (PR) address this problem by allocating the seats won by parties or groups according to the number of votes they win.

Proportional Representation

Almost half of the world's legislatures are chosen through some variant of PR.[34] The two most widely used systems either allocate seats solely according to a proportional formula, or use PR to supplement an FPTP system. In a "pure" PR system, parties produce lists of candidates, voters choose among the lists, and seats in the legislature are allocated according to each party's share. A party getting 40 percent of the popular vote gets 40 percent of the seats, a party getting 12 percent gets 12. In "mixed" PR systems, candidates run both in districts—as in FPTP systems—and on regional or national party lists which are used to adjust overall totals. In Germany, for example, if three parties split their district votes, one party could win, say, half of the single-member districts with only 40 percent of the total popular vote. Under a mixed PR system, they keep these seats; but minor parties are compensated with a bonus reflecting their national percentages. The German system is very confusing, even to Germans. Its essence is to give voters a sense of having their own district representatives while simultaneously giving all parties representation proportionate to their share of the vote. In one recent election, for example, the Christian Democrats won 68 percent of the district seats and the Social Democrats all the rest. But to make the results proportional, two parties (the Free Democrats and the Greens) that failed to win a single district seat were rewarded nearly 20 percent of the seats in the Bundestag. And the Social Democrats, though finishing second in district races were compensated with 107 list candidates to the Christian Democrats' fifty-four, thus making the parties' numbers in the legislature essentially proportional to the national vote.[35]

The critical questions in PR systems are those relating to "thresholds," and the ways party lists are compiled. In Israel, each party runs a single list of up to 120 candidates, and voters cast a single ballot for the list of their choice. With this large a list, the threshold, or minimum vote required to win a seat, is very low: a party with less than 2 percent of the vote can win a seat in the Knesset. South Africa's national threshold is even lower, with candidates able to win with less than 1 percent of the national vote, but the threshold is actually high in the parallel system of multi-member districts. Few PR systems are quite so sensitive to the nuances of minority politics as those of Israel and South Africa. The systems used in Finland since 1906 are more typical. Instead of a single national list, candidates for parliament run from fifteen districts of relatively equal size. With only fifteen candidates in each race it takes 7 to 10 percent of the vote for a minority candidate to win. In the 2000 elections, eight parties won one seat or more, but the three largest parties won nearly three-quarters of all seats. The contrast between the 7 to 10 percent it takes to elect a legislator in Finland, and the fraction of 1 percent it takes in South Africa is only part of the story. The second set of issues in PR systems revolve around the ways voters' choices are structured. In Finland until the 1954 elections, the lists were compiled and ranked by the executive committees of the parties, the method used in most PR systems. The power this gives to party leaders is enormous: if they know, for example, that they are likely to win, say, two or three of eight seats in a district, their power to rank the candidates lets them decide which two or three of their eight candidates will win.

In order to give the voters more say in what individuals are elected, the Finnish system was changed in 1954 to combine inter-party competition with competition on the party list. Individual voters, rather than the parties, rank the candidates. Recent changes in the election laws in Israel are even more dramatic where the power to produce party lists has given party voters a system similar to U.S. party primaries. The result has been a dramatic fragmentation of the parties, because dissidents know they have a better chance of being elected as the top candidate on a small party's list than as a lower-ranked candidate on a major party's.[36] In the 1980s, Israel's two major parties, Likud and Labor, held more than 95 percent of the seats in Knesset, a percentage which has declined to 48 percent and falling.

Mixed Systems

"Parallel" systems use both winner-take-all districts and proportional representation. Unlike the German mixed PR system, however, they do not compensate for disproportionate results in the district elections. Japan was for many years the primary exemplar of parallel voting, but has recently been joined by Russia and a number of the newer democracies. Mixed systems offer the advantage of a chance to choose both a local representative and a national party, though depending upon the numerical balance between local and national candidates, they may not be very proportional and may have districts that are too large to have local meaning.

"Parallel systems," as Reynolds and Reilly put it, "are also relatively complex, and can leave voters confused as to the nature and operation of the electoral system."[37]

Mixed systems are often selected as means of compromising diverse interests. Russia's adoption of parallel voting for its Duma, for example, was the product less of ideology than of "compromises among parliamentarians, the Russian president, and the legacy of past practice," combined with very hard-nosed calculations of who would most benefit and lose through the adoption of each kind of voting system.[38] Another way of achieving balances of this kind is by creating a bicameral legislature with one house elected on the basis of PR and the other designed to reflect regional interests. This was the path chosen by Indonesia in 2003 in converting what had been a partly-appointed, partly-elected upper house into a body specifically structured to represent the nation's provinces and regions.

Electoral Systems and Their Consequences

The compromise that created the system for electing the Russian Duma is hardly unique. As with the so-called Great Compromise that created a population-based U.S. House of Representatives and state-based Senate, the founders of both nations recognized, as Madison dryly observed, "that the result will be somewhat influenced by the mode."[39] The fundamental and most far-reaching choice is between systems that are essentially territorial, on the one hand, and proportional on the other. Probably the most widely noted result of using PR is to increase the number of parties in the legislature. In his classic study of *Political Parties,* first published in 1951, Maurice Duverger formulated what has become known as "Duverger's Law" which suggests that the plurality system in single member districts tends to produce two-party competition. The cause of this tendency—Duverger himself never called it a law—is a process that takes place over a series of elections in which voters gradually become aware of the futility of voting for fringe parties. As voters realize that candidates who win with less than a majority could have been defeated, opposition parties will increasingly coalesce.[40] Over time, in theory, the number of parties diminishes to two which, in turn, are basically moderate. There are voters who do not accept such calculations and will vote for candidates they know will lose. Thus Duverger's law does not always work. The forty-one FPTP countries listed in Appendix A elected representatives from an average of 3.6 parties in their most recent elections. Only twelve had just two parties, and nine had five or more. But the tendency for winner-take-all elections to reduce the number of competing parties is comparatively strong. The median number of parties holding at least 2 percent of the seats in all 124 countries is three in countries with FPTP systems, four in mixed systems, and five in those using LPR.

More sophisticated studies of elections system have increasingly refined these observations. Giovanni Sartori, for example, has shown that it is possible to engineer a reduction in the number of parties competing in LPR systems. Sartori put all systems on a single continuum from FPTP—called "strong" party systems—to the most "feeble," or LPR systems with large districts.[41] A large district system, such as that of Israel, particularly one that sets a very low threshold for election, encourages the proliferation of parties, while one that has proportionality but small districts or high thresholds is much like a system of single-member districts. The Irish transferable-vote system, for example, is similar to LPR, but because elections are conducted in districts of only three to five seats, a party that does not receive at least 20 to 25 percent of the vote is deprived of representation. The logic of voter choice is not much different than in FPTP systems: votes for minor party candidates are wasted on those who cannot win. Whether voters actually make these calculations is matter of some dispute. Gary Cox has suggested that voters tend to follow a rule in which they will ultimately reduce the effective number of competing parties to one more than the voting system allows: if a district can elect four representatives, a maximum of five parties are likely to have a chance.[42]

What Sartori and Cox have done is to shift attention away from a simple distinction between PR and FPTP to a focus on the magnitude of the district. The size of the district also appears to have effects on the ways in which individual legislators think about their roles. It has long been noted that U.S. senators—with entire states as their "districts"—are less parochial and more moderate than representatives in the House. With larger constituencies, they represent a greater diversity of interests: unlike House districts, which can be almost entirely African-American, rural or urban, the states as districts are more complex. "Senators, facing a daunting array of state interests, are often compelled to take stands that involve politically painful choices. They are prevented from adopting the strategy of merely conforming precisely to the interests of their constituencies because their constituencies are states, where it is unavoidable that there will be interests that will clash."[43] Smaller districts, conversely, allow a more personal form of representation. Even within FPTP countries, there is substantial difference in the interactions between legislators and their constituents in a country like the Baha-mas, with one representative for every 8,000 people and India, with one per 1,846,000.

Electoral Engineering

There is no exact science as to the description of how electoral systems work. Cultural factors and formal rules interact with each other to produce patterns that are often as confounding as they are predictable. FPTP systems are associated with two dominant parties, as clearly illustrated in the Bahamas, Paraguay, and the United States, but can accommodate as many ten in India. PR systems that predictably allow nine or ten parties to win seats in the parliaments of the Netherlands and Belgium empowered only two in the most recent elections in Chile and Turkey.

Despite these anomalies, those who study election rules are increasingly convinced that they can be fit to cultural and political conditions in ways that substantially affect system performance. Politicians, who have long been aware of these effects, are becoming increasingly sophisticated in how to deploy them.

> In many nations the rules of the electoral system, for many decades accepted as stable and immutable, indeed often bureaucratic and technical, have become increasingly politicized and contentious. The wave of constitution building following the surge of newer democracies in the early 1990s generated a series of negotiations about electoral laws that needed to be resolved before other constitutional issues could be agreed. After the first elections, far from being settled, the consolidation process in these nations has frequently seen continued adjustments in electoral regulations, such as threshold levels, the use of electoral formula, and the size of legislative bodies. . . . Disentangling the effects of formal rules and cultural modernization is important, not only for the understanding it provides into the behavior of politicians, parties, and citizens, but also because this gives insights into the possibilities and limits of electoral engineering.[44]

Some relationships, if not consistent, are clear. Despite exceptions, the more proportional the system, the larger its districts and the lower the thresholds, the greater the number of parties. And the greater the number of parties, the more difficult it is to maintain governing coalitions.[45] This facet of system design plays a central role in the power sharing mechanisms favored by advocates of "consociational" democracy. By allowing more minorities representation in parliament, list PR, particularly in large, low-threshold districts, fragments the parliament and favors development of the broad coalitions favored by the consociational approach. This perspective, tellingly argued in the works of Arend Lijphart, has been questioned on both theoretical and empirical grounds. Both sides agree strongly with the proposition, long associated with Sir Arthur Lewis, that, "The surest way to way to kill the idea of democracy in a plural society is adopt the Anglo-American system of first-past-the-post."[46] They disagree largely over questions of whether ethnic and other cleavages are best be negotiated between narrowly-based parties in fragmented parliaments, or within broader coalition parties, both in the government and in creating electoral lists. Those who Reilly describes as "centripetalists,"

> argue that the best way to mitigate the destructive effects of ethnicity in divided societies is not simply to replicate existing ethnic divisions in the legislature, but rather to utilise electoral systems which encourage cooperation and accommodation between rival groups, and therefore work to break down the salience of ethnicity rather than foster its representation in parliament.[47]

Low thresholds and large districts, from this perspective, may serve as much to intensify as to mitigate regional and ethnic divisions and produce governments that are too weak to work effectively.

Research on the actual effects of different systems have found that the connections between electoral systems and outcomes are more complex than a purely mechanical model might suggest. Formal rules, such as those that use high thresholds to discourage minor parties, do inhibit fragmentation; but there are cultural and psychological factors that can also "affect the readiness of voters to vote for small parties," and which both reinforce and counter formal rules.[48] Studies in Latin America indicate that these relationships are more complex, and may even work in reverse, in presidential systems.[49]

Some attempts at electoral engineering have manifestly failed. The enormous diversity and size of the Indian electorate, for example, has increasingly defied the "normal" tendency of FPTP systems to reduce the number of effective parties. The more profound objection to electoral engineering is that it can have self-defeating biases. On the one hand, as argued with regard to South Africa, a system that is successfully "consociational" may in the long run so moderate conflict as to render elections trivial. Even worse, on the other hand, are electoral laws so transparently rigged that they not only do not work but also "raise the likelihood that extremist parties will seek redress outside the democratic process." In Fiji, the system of Alternative Voting proved at best a diversion from the real problems of land use and ethnic balance in the civil service: "'Electoral engineering' provides no solution to these inflammatory ethnic issues, but it does imply a willingness to intentionally politicize election laws."[50] The Fiji case is extreme, and perhaps intractable under any system; but Fraenkel's caveat on electoral engineering is well-taken. Electorates are artifacts only to a degree. More important, we should not lose sight of the fact that the primary purpose of elections has nothing to do with mathematical models, and everything to do with choosing real governments that make decisions that affect peoples' lives. There are many ways in which elections can be rigged that range from the kinds of rules changes discussed here to outright fraud. The work of organizations like the Carter Center and the United Nations Development Program have been very helpful in monitoring and controlling the worst kinds of abuse; and a growing number of nations have set up their own domestic, non-partisan election commissions. Even in mature, advanced democracies, however, free and fair elections do not occur automatically. You cannot have democracy without elections, but you can—and too often do—have elections without democracy.

Notes

1. Ezra Suleiman, "Bureaucracy and Democratic Consolidation: Lessons from Eastern Europe, " in Lisa Anderson, *Transitions to Democracy* (New York: Columbia University Press, 1999), 160.

2. Charles A. Beard, *An Economic Interpretation of the Constitution of the United States* (New York: Macmillan, 1913).

3. John P. Diggins, *The Lost Soul of American Politics: Virtue, Self-Interest, and the Foundations of Liberalism* (Chicago: University of Chicago Press, 1984), 27.

4. Diggins, *The Lost Soul of American Politics*, 97.

5. Samuel P. Huntington, *The Third Wave: Democratization in the Late Twentieth Century* (Norman: University of Oklahoma Press, 1991), 169.

6. Adam Przeworski, "Democracy as a Contingent Outcome of Conflicts," in *Constitutionalism and Democracy,* ed. Jon Elster and Rune Slagstad (New York: Cambridge University Press, 1988), 66.

7. Przeworski, "Democracy as a Contingent Outcome of Conflicts," 64.

8. Przeworski, "Democracy as a Contingent Outcome of Conflicts," 68.

9. As quoted in Giuseppe Di Palma, *To Craft Democracies: An Essay on Democratic Transitions* (Berkeley: University of California Press, 1990), 60.

10. Juan Linz and Alfred Stepan, *Problems of Democratic Transition and Consolidation: Southern Europe, South America, and Post Communist Europe* (Baltimore: The Johns Hopkins University Press, 1996), 67-68.

11. Larry Diamond, *Developing Democracy: Toward Consolidation* (Baltimore: The Johns Hopkins University Press, 1999), 113.

12. Carlos Santiago Nino, *The Constitution of Deliberative Democracy* (New Haven: Yale University Press, 1996), 159-60

13. Robert A. Dahl, *How Democratic Is the American Constitution?* (New Haven: Yale University Press, 2001), 15

14. Ian Shapiro, *Democracy's Place* (Ithaca, NY: Cornell University Press, 1996), 82.

15. Gretchen Casper and Michelle M. Taylor, *Negotiating Democracy: Transitions From Authoritarian Rule* (Pittsburgh, PA: University of Pittsburgh Press, 1996), 244.

16. R. Kent Weaver and Bert A. Rockman, "Institutional Reform and Constitutional Design," in *Do Institutions Matter? Government Capabilities in the United States and Abroad*, ed. Weaver and Rockman (Washington, DC: The Brookings Institution, 1993), 465.

17. James Johnson, "Inventing Constitutional Traditions: The Poverty of Fatalism," in John Ferejohn, Jack N. Rakove, and Jonathan Riley, *Constitutional Culture and Democratic Rule* (New York: Cambridge University Press, 2001), 87.

18. Diamond, *Developing Democracy,* 57, 58.

19. Giovanni Sartori, *Comparative Constitutional Engineering: An Inquiry into Structures, Incentives, and Outcomes* (New York: New York University Press, 2nd ed., 1997), 199.

20. Arend Lijphart, "The Alternative Vote: A Realistic Alternative for South Africa?" *Politikon* 18 (June 1991), 91.

21. Andrew Reynolds, "Designing Electoral Systems," in *International Encyclopedia of Elections*, ed. Richard Rose (Washington, DC: Congressional Quarterly Press, 2000), 58-66.

22. Spoilt ballots, which became familiar to Americans in the controversy over Florida in the 2000 presidential election, average fewer than 2 percent in most world elections, 4 percent in countries with compulsory voting. Poorly designed ballots—such as those used in parts of Florida—can produce high rates of error; but in general, "The evidence seems to show that invalid ballots . . . are not ballots with mistakes, but ballots of protest." Reynolds, "Designing Election Systems," 254.

23. In Belgium, curiously, the penalty for repeated failure to vote is the loss of one's right to vote.

24. Paul Kleppner, *Who Voted?: The Dynamics of Electoral Turnout, 1870-1980* (New York: Praeger, 1982), 113-46.

25. For documentation and analysis of these subterfuges, see United States Commission on Civil Rights, *Voting* (Washington, DC: Government Printing Office, 1961).

26. Greg Palast, Will Hutton, and Joe Conason, *The Best Democracy Money Can Buy* (New York: Pluto Press, 2002).

27. Walter Dean Burnham, "The Turnout Problem," in *Elections American Style*, ed. A. James Reichley (Washington, DC: The Brookings Institution, 1987), 132.

28. Burnham, "The Turnout Problem," 104.

29. Andrew Reynolds and Benjamin Reilly, *The Internaional IDEA Handbook of Electoral System Design* (Stockholm: International Institute for Democracy and Electoral Assistance, 1997), 11-12.

30. Benjamin Reilly, *Democracy in Divided Societies: Electoral Engineering for Conflict Management* (Cambridge: Cambridge University Press, 2001), 14.

31. The basic classification of election systems presented here, and most of the descriptions, are derived from Reynolds and Reilly, *IDEA Handbook*.

32. Most U.S. states have *primary* elections in which, typically, voters registered with a party vote for the candidate they want to see face the other party's nominee in the general election. In many states, these primary elections require a candidate to win a majority vote in a runoff election if necessary.

33. Reynolds and Reilly, *IDEA Handbook*, 16.

34. Reynolds and Reilly, *IDEA Handbook*, 60. If we count the electoral systems in all 212 countries and related territories that directly elect legislators, the numbers break down as follows: plurality-majority, 109; proportional, 74; semi-proportional, 29. Reynolds, "Designing Electoral Systems," 63.

35. For a more detailed explanation of how this complicated system works, see Harmon Zeigler, *Political Parties in Industrial Democracies* (Itasca, IL: Peacock, 1993), 175-79.

36. The importance of nominating systems cannot be underestimated. On this too-often neglected topic see Gideon Rahat and Reuven Hazan, "Candidate Selection Methods: An Analytical Framework," *Party Politics* 7 (May 2001), 297-322.

37. Reynolds and Reilly, *IDEA Handbook*, 56.

38. Wilma Rule and Nadezhda Shvedova, "Russia: An Evolving Parallel System," in Reynolds and Riley, *IDEA Handbook*, 59.

39 Quoted in Justice Harlan's dissent in *Wesberry v. Sanders*, 366 U.S. 1 (1963), 32.

40. Maurice Duverger, *Political Parties: Their Organization and Activity in the Modern State* (New York: John Wiley and Sons, 1954). See also Duverger's delightful essay, "'Duverger's Law': Forty Years Later," in Bernard Grofman and Arend Lijphart, *Electoral Laws and Their Political Consequences* (New York: Agathon Press, 1986), 69-84.

41. Sartori introduced this continuum in a 1968 article and elaborated it in *Parties and Party Systems: A Framework for Analysis* (New York: Cambridge University Press, 1976).

42. I am oversimplifying the much more sophisticated argument in Gary W. Cox, *Making Votes Count: Strategic Coordination in the World's Electoral Systems* (New York: Cambridge University Press, 1997).

43. Ross K. Baker, *House and Senate* (New York: W. W. Norton, 3rd ed., 2001), 134.

44. Pippa Norris, *Electoral Engineering* (New York: Cambridge University Press, 2004), 178.

45. Carsten Anckar, "Effects of Electoral Systems: A Study of 80 Countries," paper presented at the Swedish Center for Business and Policy Studies Seminar in Stockholm, September 28-29, 2001. This useful research summary can be found at www.sns.se.

46. W. Arthur Lewis, *Politics in West Africa* (London: Allen and Unwin, 1965), 11.

47. Reilly, *Democracy in Divided Societies,* 21.

48. Anckar, "Effects of Electoral Systems," 15.

49. Mark P. Jones, "Electoral Laws in Latin America and the Caribbean," *Electoral Studies,* 12 (1993), 59-75.

50. Jon Fraenkel, "The Alternative Vote System in Fiji: Electoral Engineering or Ballot-Rigging," *Journal of Commonwealth and Comparative Politics* 39 (July 2001), 8.

Chapter 7

Bureaucracy and Democracy

General classifications of regime types only begin to describe the actual roles of institutions. Constitutions vary, moreover, in the degree to which they specify these structures. The very important appellate powers of the U.S. Supreme Court, for example, and some of the government's most important institutions— from the Air Force to the Central Intelligence Agency—are defined by statutes, not the constitution. If "constitutions are 'forms' that structure and discipline the decision-making processes,"[1] we must move considerably beyond the constitutional texts in order to describe real-world variations in institutional structures.

Bureaucracies

For most citizens, most of the time, the bureaucracy is the government. "The actual conduct of foreign negotiations," as Hamilton wrote in 1789, "the preparatory plans of finance, the application and disbursement of the public moneys in conformity to the general appropriations of the legislature, the arrangement of the army and the navy, the direction of the operations of war, these, and other matters of a like nature, constitute what seems to be most properly understood by the administration of government."[2] Despite their importance, the U.S. founders virtually ignored administrative issues in drafting the constitution. Article I, on the powers of Congress, is more than twice the length of Article II, on the executive (most of which relates to the process of electing the president). The constitution assumes the existence of an army, navy, ambassadors to foreign nations, and various unspecified "executive departments." It authorizes the president, with the advice and consent of the Senate, to appoint the heads of these agencies "and all other officers of the United States, whose appointments are not herein otherwise provided for." Essentially, however, the structure of the federal bureaucracy and its relationship to state and local bureaucracies are not found in the constitution.

This lack of attention to administrative issues was justified by the need for flexibility. Distinguishing legislation from administration, Hamilton argued that the process of *making* laws is inherently subject to abuse. The "jarrings of parties in that department," he said of Congress, must be carefully checked by explicit constitutional provisions. "In the legislature, promptitude of decision is oftener an evil than a benefit." Executive vigor, on the other hand, "is a leading character in the definition of good government. . . . A feeble Executive implies a feeble execution of the government. A feeble execution is but another phrase for bad execution; and a government ill executed, whatever it may be in theory, must be, in practice, a bad government."[3]

Despite the anti-government rhetoric of some politicians, it is widely agreed that Hamilton was right, and that the private sector, no less than the public, can function effectively only in the context of a professional administrative state. "Democratic government in modern industrial society," as Schumpeter argued, "must be able to command, for all intents and purposes . . . the service of a well-trained bureaucracy of good standing."[4]

> It is no accident that modern mass democracy and the development of what came to be recognized as the modern bureaucracy went hand-in-hand. The modern democratic state was built upon the bureaucratic structure that undergirds this state. Political leaders of the emerging democratic states from the early nineteenth century to the late twentieth century recognized that whatever the goals of the state—controlling a vast empire, creating an educational system, guaranteeing democratic procedures, conducting war, establishing the welfare state, collecting taxes—each necessitates a highly organized, basically non-political instrument at its control.[5]

The importance of a strong bureaucracy is perhaps best measured by its antithesis. Holmes' description of post-Communist Russia makes the point, similar to Hamilton's, that "liberal values are threatened just as thoroughly by state incapacity as by despotic power. Destatization is not the true solution, it is the problem. . . . The rights inscribed in the 1977 Brezhnev Constitution went unprotected because of a repressive state apparatus. The rights ascribed in the 1993 Yeltsin Constitution go unenforced because the government lacks resources and purpose."[6]

Most modern constitutions leave control over the bureaucracy largely to politics, but there are exceptions. The location of final executive authority is almost always specified, as is the existence of certain key departments. Embedded in many constitutions are particular agencies empowered to perform specific roles in isolation from direct legislative or executive control. In most cases, methods of hiring and firing administrators are spelled out in detail. Some constitutions—particularly in countries emerging from authoritarian rule—specifically constrain the army and police. Finally a number of constitutions, especially in federal systems, contain provisions that govern relations between national and local administrators, though few are as detailed as Austria's specific reference to ski instructors.[7] The key questions in these areas revolve around issues of control: by whom and through what mechanisms will issues of executing the laws by decided?

Staffing the Bureaucracy

A century ago, Max Weber correctly predicted that bureaucracy—because of its technical superiority—would become the dominant institution of the modern state.[8] Systems based on patronage or family ties are found less and less frequently. Where patrimonial structures endure, their inability to regularize relations between the government and business or guarantee the security of contracts, has inhibited the emergence of both capitalism and democracy. An entrenched oligarchy able to use the state apparatus to discourage competition is antithetical to development. The patronage-based system Riggs called "bureaucratic capitalism" has been highly resistant to forms of government and business that base such relations in laws and market forces.[9] With a substantial influx of foreign capital—in Indonesia with oil, in Thailand with spillover U.S. money from Vietnam—a more assertive business class can push through some of the reforms needed to level the playing field, making patron-client relations less implacable than Rigg's early Thailand might suggest. More advanced parts of the bureaucracy, such as the increasingly professional army in Indonesia, may also push for rationalization of the process.[10] Weberian reform of the Indonesian and Thai bureaucracies is, however, far from complete, has barely scratched the surface in the Philippines, and is virtually nonexistent in much of Africa. If economic expansion can "challenge the foundations of the patrimonial administrative state," the process is protracted and difficult.[11]

The ability of elected officials to define public policies, and rely upon neutral civil servants to implement them was what led Weber to associate the rise of bureaucracy with development of the modern state. If many countries are unable to develop such capacities, problems can also arise from overdevelopment of bureaucracies in established states. The gloomy side of Weber's scenario was that elected politicians would increasingly stand hopeless as dilettantes against the expert advice of the bureaucrats. Growing complexity raises the possibility that the civil service will become an almost autonomous ruling class. Civil servants in France, for example,

Especially at the highest levels, represent a closed and elite group of specially educated and usually well-born or well-connected men, and to a far lesser extent, women, who move easily from one management position to the next, regardless of whether it is in the public domain or in the private domain. The resulting interpenetration of elites (administrative, political, and economic) is the most extensive in Western Europe. . . .

Although this background has certainly produced a state administration characterized by efficiency, stability, and expertise, it is not a system designed to promote equal opportunity, transparency, or democratic accountability.[12]

If few public services are as elitist as the French, the tendency for a trained bureaucracy to become a force unto itself is strong. In economically underdeveloped societies the gap between the educated elite that forms the core of a bureaucracy and the rest of the population is a source of tension, particularly in postcolonial regimes where the experts most needed by the new regime were trained by the old. Even in established democracies with few such tensions, and absent the French aristocratic tradition, the increasing complexity of the administrative apparatus poses a growing threat to democratic institutions. Combined with what Paul Light calls the "thickening" of government, bureaucrats become isolated from both clients and superiors. In one form, that Light calls "vertical thickening," the layers of management grow at an exponential rate. My own look at one large, typical, department in New York State found a vast and growing array of "executive deputy commissioners," "first deputy commissioners," "deputy commissioners," "directors," "executive directors," "assistant directors," and so on, that dramatically increase the distance along the chain of command from the head of the department to the people who actually serve the public.[13] "Horizontal" thickening, at the same time, produces literally dozens of redundant agencies that blur both responsibility and control, and layer on top of that a growing array of auditing and control agencies that further blur the chain of command. One recent study estimated that a third of all U.S. federal civilian employees are engaged in managing, checking, and auditing the ones who actually do the work.[14] Carried to an extreme,

The laws themselves become mere authorizations for the administration which determines their interpretation. The parliamentary regime is dependent on the legislative control exercised by its executive bodies, but this control is no longer able to supervise all the technical details and ramifications of public administration. For in order to be effective, parliamentary control needs information, for which it depends in large measure on the administrative apparatus. The member of parliament is bewildered by the skilled way in which the administration advances its explanations; and parliament is also dependent on the administration for the legislation to be enacted, since the latter works it out.[15]

Top civil servants, as the once-popular BBC television series *Yes Minister* humorously showed, have policy agendas of their own and can become quite adept at misleading their less experienced, nominal superiors.[16] And lower level civil servants often respond as much to their political environments as they do to commands from ministers or presidents. "Corporatist politics," as they are called in Europe, or in the less formal "iron triangles" of the United States, bring civil servants into regular, often cooperative, contact with client groups in a "blurring of the lines between public and private" that derives less from conspiracy than from "the nature of industrial society itself."[17] To function effectively bureaucracies must become increasingly specialized. It takes a rocket scientist to design a rocket, a pharmacologist to test the safety of a new drug. That these experts will relate regularly and well with others in their fields, make it almost inevitable that they will form what Emmette Redford calls "functional oligarchies" that "concentrate influence in strategic locations," and hide it "within complex organizations. . . . To be democratic," Redford suggests, "the process of decision within functional complexes will have to be open to outside influence."[18] Runaway bureaucrats who cater inordinately to special interests are not likely to promote democratic values or inspire public trust. Insofar as constitutional democracy is about the rule of law, it is important for those who make the laws to have control over those who implement them. The methods of securing such control are of enduring concern.

The Structures of Command

The most direct way of establishing a command structure is by linking the making and execution of policy, as in the British Cabinet where members of the cabinet collectively advise the prime minister on legislative issues and individually administer government agencies. This linking of rule-making and enforcement roles attenuates what rational choice theorists call the principal-agent problem:

> An agency head, being a member of parliament, can both convey the intent of parliament to the agency and information from the agency to the parliament about the costs and constraints of pursuing different policies. As a member of parliament of the majority party, the agency head has a strong incentive to shield the agency from pressures from the minority party(-ies) or outside interest groups that would thwart the majority party's objectives. Parliament members also have an extra incentive to monitor and control the agencies they lead so as to ensure that they pursue the agenda legislated by the parliament.[19]

This assumes that there *is* a majority. In parliamentary systems in which coalition governments are the norm, issues of enforcement blend with issues of lawmaking in crafting coalitions. A rural party, for example, might forgo part of its legislative program in exchange for the Ministry of Agriculture. It thus achieves its objectives less through the transparent process of lawmaking than through biased enforcement. In rational choice terms, the agent becomes, in reality, a principal in disguise.

A second disadvantage with the cabinet system is its tendency to make ministers of people with little administrative expertise. "Individuals rise to the top of a party because of their parliamentary skills, loyalty to the party, ability to formulate policies, effectiveness as campaigners, etc. None of these assets may prove very useful when it comes to directing a bureaucracy."[20] To avoid some of these problems, most mixed parliamentary-presidential and some parliamentary systems allow various outsiders to serve. In France, for example, cabinets always include a mix of parliamentarians and celebrities or experts from other fields.

In presidential systems, agency heads are typically not members of the legislature. Indeed, under the U.S. Constitution, a member of Congress may not hold an administrative position. Many countries go still further in denying the legislature any role whatsoever in choosing agency heads. In their study of forty-five past and present systems with elected presidents, Shugart and Carey found twenty-nine in which the president alone has the power to appoint and dismiss members of the cabinet.[21] The president of the United States appoints his or her cabinet with the "advice and consent" of the Senate, but the constitution is silent on the question of the right to fire. Many modern constitutions grant presidents the right to appoint their cabinets, but subject the appointees—both individually and collectively—to parliamentary sanction. This sort of mixing of the personnel powers were found in nine of the Shugart-Carey regimes. At the other extreme were the elected presidents of Ireland and Bulgaria, who have no role at all in staffing the cabinet, and Slovenia, where the parliament appoints individual ministers and may actually "reject a proposal for the dismissal of a minister by the leader of the government."[22]

The U.S. Congress has largely abstained from using its formal power of "advice and consent" in the appointment process, and allowed the president to sink or swim with a cabinet and staff of his or her choice. Oversight is exercised not by a formal power of dismissal, but by fairly strong legal and political powers of formal investigation and through the dynamics of a political process that makes the president's power of appointment less formidable than it at first appears. Collectively, as Fenno wrote, "the Cabinet draws its life breath from the President, but as individuals the Cabinet members are by no means so dependent on him. In many instances, we are presented with the paradox that in order for the Cabinet member to be of real help to the President in one of his leadership roles, the member must have non-presidential 'public' prestige, party following, legislative support, or roots of influence in his department."[23] The general consensus among students of the presidency has been, that if significant direction of some agencies can be maintained in the short run, sustained control over literally thousands of agencies, bureaus, and field offices is essentially unattainable.[24] Congress too, though sometimes excessively involved in the details of policy, is generally acknowledged to have little capacity for sustained oversight. What controls it provides, moreover, tend to be exercised through committees and subcommittees that may not represent the views of the Congress as a whole.

Paradoxically, the overall U.S. system of executive and legislative control—through a combination of weak lines of command, interest group diversity, and legislative powers of both appropriations and exposure—combine with a civil service tradition to provide "a sometimes painful, inevitably self-interested process of consultation and second-guessing that reasonably well keeps administration sensitive to the concerns of persons and groups affected" by agency policies.[25] How consistently this system works is a matter of continuing dispute; but as long as the major actors are able to enforce a relatively high degree of transparency in the bureaucracy, it is unlikely to escape some form of control. Key to the success of this system—sometimes statutory, sometimes constitutional—is the institutionalization of administrative procedures that maximize visibility. *Command* is rare, but this does not mean that the bureaucracy functions without significant *controls*. The most effective of these derive less from sustained, institutional efforts or, what McCubbins and Schwartz call "police patrols," than from the "fire alarms" set by interest groups, insiders, and citizens who use the visibility of the bureaucracy to keep it under constant scrutiny.[26]

Important devices in facilitating such oversight in the United States are the Administrative Procedures Act and its state counterparts. Under these laws, government agencies must publish notices of proposed rules thirty days before they take effect, a period in which public comments are invited. It is generally true that the only audience for these notices are the legislative committees that drafted the original bills and the interest groups most affected by them. As fire alarms, they may not always be heard by those with the greatest need to be warned. But they do have a tendency to discourage administrative end runs around the legislature and are, if for this reason only, generally worth having on the books.

Independent Agencies

In theory it would seem that democracies would maximize the extent to which elective politicians control the policy process. There are, however, a growing number of agencies whose powers are deliberately sheltered from either executive or legislative interference, most commonly in the areas of banking, auditing, and election administration. In many countries, largely autonomous agencies controlling the money supply are embedded in the constitution. The directors of the German Federal Bank (*Bundesbank*), for example are appointed to fixed eight-year terms by the president on the advice of the chancellor, and cannot be removed. The Federal Reserve in the United States, as with similar institutions in other countries, was created by statute but enjoys what Elster calls "quasi-constitutional force" by virtue of similarly long terms of office and extensive powers.[27] Both the Bundesbank and "the Fed" have been criticized for being too isolated from the political needs of the administration, or of being what William Greider, with regard to the Federal Reserve calls "an anti-democratic enclave of corporate power in uncomfortable contradiction with the civic mythology of self-government."[28]

In 1991 the Argentine Congress prohibited the Central Bank from printing new money, and reasserted its own right to determine monetary policy. One close student of Argentine politics argued in 2000 that, "The law was an immediate, stunning, and lasting success. It has become the anchor of Argentina's impressive macroeconomic performance in the 1990s. Only through democratic procedures could Argentina's economy finally achieve a turnaround."[29] Unfortunately for Argentina, its economy went into a spectacular fall just as this article reached publication, a collapse from which it is only very painfully beginning to recover, and which, ironically, has been widely blamed on the very "politicization" of the Central Bank's functions that were once so lavishly praised. Independent central banks are generally likely to pursue more cautious, business- and banker-friendly policies than are elected public officials; or at least that is the way in which they are widely perceived. The spectacular success and later failures of the politicized process in Argentina can be matched, less dramatically perhaps, by similar miscalculations in countries whose banking systems are independent.

Goodhart makes the analogy to an independent judiciary in the sense that both courts and central banks deal with complex, technical subjects that largely apply general guidelines set by the legislature. As with the law, sound "money can be seen as having a function in preventing chaotic violence and allowing the development of a stable society."[30] It is not clear, however, that the majority of supposedly independent banks are as autonomous as they appear to be, and whether they actually contribute to system stability or perform more cosmetic functions. It does appear that bank autonomy is associated with federalism,[31] and with fragmented systems more generally.[32] The reality for most emerging democracies, however, is that they don't have a choice in these matters: to join the European Union new members *must* establish independent banks and surrender considerable control over monetary policy to the European Bank; and developing nations around the world will find it almost impossible to get foreign loans without such bodies in place. Between 1989 and 1994 alone, "at least twenty-five developing countries legislated increases in the statutory independence of their central banks."[33]

Much of the reasoning that led to the creation of independent banks has led some democracies to establish autonomous auditing agencies. Almost half of the American states have separately-elected public officials who prescribe and enforce accounting rules for state and local agencies and performs periodic audits of their activities. Chile has a Comptroller General appointed for life, but is unusual in this respect. At the national level in the United States, the General Accounting Office performs these functions under the general supervision of Congress, and some countries entrust special auditing functions to designated parliamentary committees. In all these cases, the point is to have audits conducted by people who are not politically indebted to the executive official who runs the agencies in question.

Rather than appoint or elect independent auditors, the most common practice is to make the process of audit and control a part of normal politics. Legislative committees often perform these functions, and members of the shadow cabinet—opposition party members who would be in the cabinet if their party were in the majority—serve as watchdogs over their government counterparts. Few documents are more soporific than financial audits which rank high on the list of most unread documents. Their occasionally spectacular revelations, and their probable deterrent effects, however, are so substantial that it is surprising how little attention they have received either from political scientists or constitution-makers.

A third type of independent agency, mandated with growing frequency in modern constitutions, is an independent election commission. The debacle of the vote count in the 2000 presidential election in the United States brought into sharp relief the problems that can arise through partisan administration of elections. These problems of bias are compounded in countries without the resources to ensure ballot access or security. An IDEA report on Southern Africa summarizes the major considerations that should probably underlie such bodies, including, "independence from the sitting government, to further their operational autonomy and perception as neutral administrative bodies;" the capacity to conduct politically neutral voter education drives; "the need to seriously consider the fiscal sustainability of existing electoral systems . . . the human resources necessary for an effective and transparent electoral system;" and "plans for enforcing their regulations and dealing with actors breaking these rules."[34]

Countries with bodies that meet these criteria have generally been given high marks by impartial observers, and most new constitutions have provided for them. Many of the world's older democracies continue to rely on party competition and a sense of fair play to regulate elections. In the United States, in particular, election boards tend to be bipartisan (as opposed to nonpartisan), and tinkering with the rules for partisan advantage is considered part of the game. Perhaps the most egregious instances of such manipulation occur in the apportionment of legislative seats. One form of electoral engineering is malapportionment in which certain groups are spread across larger districts than their favored rivals. Great Britain's so-called rotten boroughs evolved out of a gradual shift in population from rural to urban areas whereby the failure to redraw district lines meant that a district in London might have hundreds of thousands of constituents while a representative from a declining rural area might have only a few hundred. The Constitution of the United States attempted to prevent this development by requiring that districts in the House of Representatives be readjusted after every census to reflect shifts in population, a practice that has been widely emulated in more recent constitutions and, by statute, in Britain itself. The seemingly academic requirement that there be an impartial, national census is in this sense a prerequisite to democratic elections.[35]

Even with districts of equal size, the American practice allowing elected officials to draw district lines can, through a process known as "gerrymandering," allow the party in control to exert considerable influence over electoral outcomes. A handful of states, and most other countries, have attempted to depoliticize the drawing of district lines by creating "nonpolitical" bodies like the Indian Delimitation Commission, which deals with both state and national districts, or the seven-member constituency committee which suggests changes to the German Bundestag. Many new democracies have created constitutionally-sanctioned permanent election commissions that are responsible for drawing districts lines and for virtually all aspects of election management.

In the cases of central banks, auditing agencies, and electoral commissions, the point of establishing their independence is to isolate them from "ordinary" politics. Quite a different set of motives explains the creation of agencies like the South African Commissions of Human Rights and Gender Equality that are essentially constitutionally empowered advocacy groups. In many systems, a form of corporatist thinking has led to the embedding of key economic groups in earmarked agencies. An interesting variation on this theme is the practice in many U.S. states of directly electing the heads of government departments. North Dakota, for example, elects a Secretary of State, Attorney General, Treasurer, Auditor; and Commissioners of Agriculture, Education, Insurance, Labor, and Taxes; and a Public Service Commission. Because they diffuse responsibility the elimination of such separately elected officials has been advocated by almost everyone who has studied them, but the average number of such officials per state dropped only from 10.7 in 1955 to 10.2 in 1995.[36] They remain almost unique to the U.S. states.

Privatization, Devolution, and Decentralization

In many countries, there has been a strong movement in recent years to privatize state functions. This tendency has been particularly pronounced in formerly socialist regimes where a wholesale process of denationalizing state enterprises marked the transition to market economics. While the scale of these transitions is unprecedented, the process is not. For much of the 20th century, European democratic regimes fluctuated between governments that were more or less favorable to socialism. In Great Britain, for example, there was a fairly predictable cycle which a newly-elected Labour government would nationalize such basic industries as coal and steel, Conservatives would denationalize them, Labour renationalize, and so on. This cycle ended in the last quarter of the century when a paradigm of privatization swept Great Britain and most of the industrial world.

Adminstrative decentralization has also been characteristic of modern governments. Motives for decentralizing often stem from the same political forces as for privatization. "Autonomy, decentralization, delegation, and federation insulate the politics of one set of activities from the politics of another. They localize attention and conflicts and reduce pressure on processes of democratic consensus."[37] The linking of decentralization with privatization in a general mistrust of central governments is at the core of the so-called new public management, which seeks to increase political control and cost-effectiveness by breaking bureaucratic rigidities.[38] "In the last two decades," as Suleiman shows "countries as different in traditional attitudes to public employment as the U.S. and Sweden have, alongside New Zealand and Finland, been those states that have implemented the strongest reforms aimed at reducing government employment. In all four countries, the efforts have shown a considerable degree of success, since the number of civil servants has declined, is some cases rather sharply."[39]

Instead of emphasizing central control, the public management movement has sought to make bureaucratic procedures more flexible and accountable in terms of results rather than rules. Lower level managers have more operational flexibility with closer ties, often commercial in nature, with their clients. Advocates emphasize three d's—devolution, decentralization, and deregulation—in what its most ardent advocates claimed are universal rules for improving both public and private bureaucracies[40] While these reforms can often be achieved piece by piece by statute or simple executive order, the detailed nature of many modern constitutions makes it necessary to move in a more comprehensive manner. In Brazil, for example, the 1988 constitution included a set of job guarantees for civil servants that made it necessary to amend the constitution even to begin the process of reform.[41]

With careful monitoring, devolution, decentralization, and privatization can be an effective device for increasing bureaucratic responsiveness. In many cases, however, power is more devolved than decentralized: it is spun out to local units that lack the will or capacity to perform the functions once run by the central government. Public policy is fragmented into weaker units more susceptible to special interest control, eroding "any notion of the public interest." It tends "to regard administrative reform as merely another public policy arena where policies are determined by the interplay of market forces."[42] When this takes place in arenas where market competition is weak, or where the devolved power is still a state monopoly, concepts of equity and balance disappear. Catherine Rudder's study of the delegation of the power to regulate the American accounting industry to the industry itself reveals a pattern of an increasing erosion of standards that may be endemic to the process itself. While the kind of "functional representation" that such delegations of power provide can be said to be less heavy-handed than government regulation, it presents, as Rudder argues, at least four basic problems:

- Legitimacy: By what authority does a private group make public policy?
- Accountability: To whom is this person or group responsible? Is the work of the group sufficiently transparent? How is accountability to the public ensured?
- Representativeness: Is the group sufficiently representative of the broader public? Are the group's positions representative of its own constituents?
- Independence of judgment: Are the decisions made in a disinterested, fair-minded manner?[43]

Rudder's study provides troubling answers to these questions of the accounting interest in particular, and, it suggests, to the concept of self-regulation in general.

A parallel trend to contract government functions out to private companies and nonprofit organizations has meant that a large proportion of nonprofit organizations—from church groups to charities—receive a majority of their funds from government sources. This creates many of the same problems of responsibility and control that occur with administrative decentralization; but has the added drawback of threatening the autonomy of recipient organizations. A study of thirteen of the larger nonprofits in the United States concluded that, "Contracting regimes homogenize the nonprofit agencies they work through, make government agencies less responsible, and destroy the ability of charitable organizations to stand as mediating forces between citizens and the state."[44] The problems raised by such policies in developing countries are even more troubling. In highly stratified or patrimonial societies, in particular, devolved powers tend to accrue to those local elites who can effectively control those bureaucrats who can longer count on backing from the central administration. The politics of what Paul Hutchcroft calls "booty capitalism," a patrimonial state typified by the business capture of government agencies was facilitated in the Philippines by a highly decentralized system of public administration.[45] Even in the United States, "grass roots" administration has often had more to do with grass tops than roots. Philip Selznick's classic study of the Tennessee Valley Authority revealed a process by which administrative decentralization resulted in many of the basic goals of the organization being "co-opted" by the local oligarchies the TVA had been created to challenge.[46]

A somewhat different pattern emerged in many post-Communist societies where state control was maintained less through a formal command structure than an elaborate parallel hierarchy of Communist Party functionaries positioned in every office. The survival skills that enabled many civil servants to wall themselves off from performing public services produced patterns of mutually reinforcing expectations that have proven resistant to change. With "a legacy of little capacity or initiative at the local level," and "a society that accepts indifference and control as an historic reality of government," it has been difficult—despite a variety of organizational experiments—to effect significant change. Whatever the title on the door, the average citizen still sees "the same faces behind the counter—even if the picture of Lenin has gone."[47] Decentralization in this context serves largely to protect the face behind the counter from reform from above.

Irving Kristol once wrote that "decentralization, if it is to work, must create stronger local authorities, not weaker ones. Effective decentralization does not diffuse authority; it takes the power that is diffused throughout a large bureaucracy and concentrates it into new nuclei of authority."[48] To the extent that these power centers can be controlled by competitive grassroots movements, privatization and decentralization may well enhance the prospects of democratic governance. Absent such guarantees, decentralization efforts have generally been, at best, ambiguous in their effects. Regimes, as Boone concluded in her study of Africa, "manipulate local power relations to their own advantage; they try to avoid moves that foment local challenge." This means that they "are unlikely to devolve real power and resources to rural leaders they do not trust and/or cannot control."[49]

The devolution wave seems to have crested in a growing recognition that the key problem in constituting bureaucracies is still one of control. One step toward facilitating this is giving elected officials the resources to act. Both the legislature and the executive can arm themselves against the greater information resources of the bureaucracy by hiring staff assistants of their own, a tendency epitomized in the United States. The number of personal assistants available to each member of the House of Representatives has grown from an average of four per member in the 1950s to seventeen in recent years; and from six to forty in the Senate.[50] Where Grover Cleveland was criticized in the 1880s for hiring a second personal secretary, the contemporary White House has more than 1,500 professional employees. How much this growing bureaucracy actually increases presidential control is not certain, but the growth of parallel institutions, such as the prime minister's staff on Canada's Parliament Hill, has been remarkable.

Whatever problems attend overstaffing,[51] the United States and Canada are not unique in giving elected representatives such help. Legislators, ministers, and presidents need staff assistance to monitor bureaucrats and keep in contact with their constituents. National libraries, computer facilities, budgetary and other experts, are minimally essential, as are methods of publicly disseminating legislative and executive decisions. In most new democracies, and in quite a few others, however,

> these functions are all very weak, and national legislatures lack the organization, financial resources, equipment, experienced members and staff to serve as mature and autonomous points of deliberation in the policy process. This does not always mean they lack authority. However, a congress that is constitutionally powerful but institutionally weak, as in a presidential system, is tempted to exercise its authority in destabilizing ways, through confrontation, obstruction, extortion, and corruption. This raises a related dimension of professionalization . . . with respect to executive branch bureaucrats. States (and peoples) get what they pay for. If they want civil servants and legislative staff with professional skill and dedication, and legislators more interested in representing interests than collecting bribes, they need to pay these officials reasonably well—and then vigorously punish illicit income.[52]

In the final analysis, constitutional devices do not control bureaucracies. Hamilton and the American founders were wise to leave such control to politics. What they could not anticipate, in terms of the growing complexity of administrative problems, has been largely provided for by the development of merit-based civil service systems. The danger that such systems can be transformed into self-serving, technocratic elites is real, making it important constantly to refine the systems of checks and balances developed to control the administrative state. Access to agency records, transparency, strong procedural guarantees, general public awareness, low tolerance levels for corruption: these are the most basic forces for control. What constitutions can do, in a negative sense, is to make such devices unworkable by denying elected officials the resources they need to govern. What they can do to help is provide elected officials with the forms of "energy" that Hamilton espoused in his discussion of the U.S. presidency, and to provide a framework of pluralism and transparency that keeps the general public in the picture.

The Special Problems of the Police and Military

The military often plays a decisive role in transitions to democracy, and its support for fledgling constitutional governments—particularly in divided societies—is often crucial to their success. Along with the internal security apparatus, it is often the single best organized public or private institution in the country. During the Cold War, the major powers trained and funded tens of thousands of third world soldiers, spies, and policemen compared with but a handful of other bureaucrats, helping to give these security forces an enormous edge in technical skills. Even today, the superiority of police and military organization and training is likely to be overwhelming.

Not surprisingly, military coups are far and away the most significant threats to the survival of constitutional democracies. But the military can more subtly play a role in subverting democratic regimes by serving as tools of repression for nominally civilian regimes. National security laws can serve as convenient covers for the enfeeblement of opposing groups. In Africa, in particular, national security alerts, or emergency powers, are often so vaguely defined as to have no real limits. In Kenya and Malawi, through a simple declaration by the government that an emergency exists,

> a whole set of measures, ranging from indefinite detention without trial, restriction of movement including the imposition of curfews, press censorship, to suspension of any legislation (other than the Constitution and the enabling Act itself) may be taken. . . . As a result, security powers are permanently available *and* exercisable. An important consequence of this is that the boundaries between security powers, strictu sensu, and ordinary criminal law are often blurred.[53]

The regime may thus continue to function in terms of a nominal constitution, hold sham elections, convene parliaments, and even follow constitutional procedures in confining political opponents. In their hearts, however, the leaders of these quasi-democracies know all too well that regime survival is essentially in the hands of those who they empower to enforce these acts of repression.

The first step toward civilian control over the military is the displacement of its civilian roles. In many countries, the armed forces control both the traditional military and the internal security apparatus. Frequently, the military is also deeply imbedded in political and economic life. This penetration of civil society was enunciated with unusual clarity in the Indonesian concept of *dwifungsi* (dual function), which prevailed throughout the Soeharto years. This doctrine, clearly articulated in Indonesia, but no less real in similar regimes, "insists that apart from its normal defence function, the military has a socio-political mission to promote national development and to ensure political stability."[54] More than a euphemism for repression, *dwifungsi* was unusual in giving the armed forces everything from assigned seats in parliament to real estate holdings, emergency relief operations, a for-profit airline, and control over the people hawking watches to tourists in Bali. More than half of the military's *legal* revenue still comes from sources other than government appropriations. Its independence from full civilian control is thus virtually assured, and with it its role in governance.

If the separation of the military from its domestic functions is the first priority of democratizing regimes, the establishment of civilian control—particularly in terms of the budget—is second. The idea that the military must contend and make its case in the political arena against other priorities is both a realistic and essential goal. In the long run, however, the establishment of civilian control over the military is probably less a product of constitutional fiat than of evolving patterns of trust. The process of producing a constitution may very well (and hopefully should) produce the preconditions. "As democratic institutions sink roots and as popular commitment to the constitutional system deepens, the scope for the military to intervene in politics diminishes. As economic development proceeds. . . the society becomes more educated and complex, and the plausibility of it ever being governable again by a centralized military recedes."[55] It is this dynamic that probably explains the tendency for military coups and coup attempts to take place almost entirely in economically underdeveloped countries. And there is also a strong tendency for democratization itself to lead to an increase in civilian control of the military. Wendy Hunter's study of Brazil has shown quite dramatically how a newly assertive legislature weakened the influence of the military—not for ideological reasons—but for electoral ones. Military budgets were cut in favor of more constituency-oriented policies.[56]

The threat posed by an overblown security apparatus is not confined to the third world. In the United States, "the adversarial process between political parties, which is considered a hallmark of democracy on domestic questions, simply has not worked on military issues."[57] The military and Central Intelligence Agency have frequently acted either without informing the Congress or in direct defiance of legal authority. Major strategic questions have been decided by a small elite, as have fundamental questions of resource allocation. "For all practical purposes, on these matters no public opinion existed and the democratic process was inoperable."[58] In broad scope, a large state security system "erodes democracy. . . by legitimizing institutions which are hierarchical, which thrive on secrecy and which, in an age of weapons of mass destruction, give a tiny group of people power over the future of life itself."[59]

The danger that a national budget top-heavy in military spending can erode the economic and social foundations of the state is clearly illustrated in the case of the Soviet Union. Its effects may be similarly corrosive in established democracies as well. High taxes and relatively low levels of spending for domestic services can lead, in the long run, to a widespread feeling that citizens are not getting their money's worth. And a large military skews the economy in more subtle ways by drawing scientific and engineering talent into designing weapons systems instead of consumer products, and by putting the nation at a competitive disadvantage with countries that can focus their resources on the development of market goods and services. Gregory Hooks makes the provocative argument that through its domination of the United States' most important planning tools, the Pentagon has implemented a "de facto industrial policy" that is "hostile or indifferent to the planning of civilian industries."[60]

In a famous article on garrison states, Lasswell expressed the fear that a crisis atmosphere, brought on by a "continued expectation of violence" could lead to routine acceptance of repressive measures on a permanent basis, and to a politics in which military concerns played a dominant role. "To militarize is to governmentalize. It is also to centralize. To centralize is to enhance the effective control of the executive over decisions, and thereby to reduce the control exercised by courts and legislatures."[61] That such centralization has been a salient aspect of politics is clear. The extent to which it is a product of militarization or modernization less so. The growth of executive power has manifested itself differently in different systems; but the bottom line, as Richard Kohn has written, is that,

> While many of the military's professional values—courage, honesty, sacrifice, integrity, loyalty, service—are among the most respected in human experience, the norms and processes intrinsic to military institutions diverge so far from the premises of democratic society that the relationship is inherently adversarial and sometimes unstable. . . .
>
> The point of civilian control is to make security subordinate to the larger purposes of a nation, rather than the other way around. The purpose of the military is to defend society, not to define it. While a country may have civilian control of the military without democracy, it cannot have democracy without civilian control.[62]

Bureaucracy and Democracy

Max Weber's ideal type bureaucracy was built on *hierarchy*, a system in which orders flow down through a clearly-defined chain-of-command; *specialization*, where hiring, firing, and promotion are based on merit, and tasks are performed by experts; and *fixed rules* that define relations between superiors and subordinates as well as ways of dealing with clients. Weber's argument that this form of organization was technically superior to organizations based on aristocratic privilege, patronage, or even election has been largely borne out. Countries and corporations that have abandoned patrimonial forms in favor of bureaucracy have generally outpaced their rivals to a remarkable degree.

But model bureaucracies seldom exist; and just as the study of medicine proceeds from healthy bodies to the far more interesting and clinically-relevant study of pathologies, so has the literature on bureaucracy tended to emphasize the dangers of red tape and insensitivity that mature bureaucracies are likely to display. Weber himself was acutely conscious of the extent to which a developed bureaucracy could use its skills to arrogate powers better placed in the hands of elected officials. Various models of bureaucratic reform, especially under the banner of the new public management movement in the 1980s and 1990s, have sought to address these pathologies through decentralization, devolution, and privatization. While some of these reforms have been more successful than others, the key to the proper functioning of bureaucracies in democratic societies continues to reside in the political process. Transparency is essential, and the more extensive the groups in civil society are able to sound the fire alarms of warning the better the likelihood of controlling abuse. Civilian control over the bureaucracy in general is as important to democracy as control over the military. It derives not just from the kind of vigor in the executive that Alexander Hamilton championed, but from comparable vigor in the legislature, the judiciary, and in the local communities of complex societies.

Notes

1. Giovanni Sartori, *Comparative Constitutional Engineering: An Inquiry into Structures, Incentives, and Outcomes* (New York: New York University Press, 2nd ed., 1997), 200.

2. Alexander Hamilton, John Jay, and James Madison, *The Federalist Papers*, Number 72.

3. *Federalist,* Number 70.

4. Joseph Schumpeter, *Capitalism, Socialism, and Democracy* (New York: Harper and Row, 3rd ed., 1949), 293.

5. Ezra Suleiman, *Dismantling Democratic States* (Princeton, N.J.: Princeton University Press, 2003), 7.

6. Steven Holmes, as quoted in Ezra Suleiman, "Bureaucracy and Democratic Consolidation," in *Transitions to Democracy*, ed. Lisa Anderson (New York: Columbia University Press, 1999), 144.

7. John A. Rohr, *Civil Servants and Their Constitutions* (Lawrence: University Press of Kansas, 2002), 167.

8. Max Weber's 1910 "Essay on Bureaucracy," and other essays on the same theme became widely available in the United States in Max Weber, *The Theory of Social and Economic Organization,* trans., A. M. Henderson and Talcott Parson (New York: Oxford University Press, 1947).

9. Fred W. Riggs, *Thailand: The Modernization of a Bureaucratic Polity* (Honolulu: East-West Center Press, 1966).

10. Harold Crouch, "Partimonialism and Military Rule in Indonesia," *World Politics* 31 (1979), 571-87.

11. Paul D. Hutchcroft, *Booty Capitalism: The Politics of Banking in the Philippines* (Ithaca, NY: Cornell University Press, 1998), 50.

12. Arista Maria Cirtautas, "France," in Jeffrey Kopstein and Mark Lichbach, eds., *Comparative Politics: Interests, Identities, and Institutions in a Changing Global Order* (New York: Cambridge University Press, 2000), 94.

13. Edward Schneier and John Brian Murtaugh, *New York Politics: A Tale of Two States* (Armonk, NY: M. E. Sharpe, 2001), 346.

14. Paul C. Light, *Thickening Government: Federal Hierarchy and the Diffusion of Accountability* (Washington, DC: The Brookings Institution, 1995), 63.

15. Henry Jacoby, *The Bureaucratization of the World,* trans. Eveline Kanes (Berkeley: University of California Press, 1973), 162.

16. I first became a fan of *Yes Minister* in an interview with Iceland's then Minister of Finance, who confessed that he tried never to schedule meetings on the evenings it was televised. Iceland has an interesting way of combining patronage and merit in choosing permanent secretaries. When vacancies occur, elected ministers are allowed to appoint their personal choices; but once these political appointees are in place they have permanent tenure. While this helps provide experience and continuity, it can also result in sharp ideological differences between ministers and their permanent secretaries. One permanent secretary was so mistrusted by his political superior that he spent his day reading newspapers while his job was performed by a "press secretary" who had the confidence of the minister.

17. Gerald Garvey, *Facing the Bureaucracy: Living and Dying in a Public Agency* (San Francisco: Jossey-Bass, 1993), 34.

18. Emmette S. Redford, *Democracy in the Administrative State* (New York: Oxford University Press, 1969), 60.

19. Dennis C. Mueller, *Constitutional Democracy* (New York: Oxford University Press, 1996), 249.

20. Mueller, *Constitutional Democracy,* 249.

21. Matthew Soberg Shugart and John M. Carey, *Presidents and Assemblies: Constitutional Design and Electoral Dynamics* (New York: Cambridge University Press, 1992), 155.

22. Marjan Brezovšok, "Democratic Government in Slovenia," in *The New Democratic Parliaments: The First Years,* ed. Lawrence D. Longley and Drago Zajc (Lawrence, WI: Research Committee of Legislative Specialists, 1998), 84.

23. Richard F. Fenno, *The President's Cabinet* (Cambridge: Harvard University Press, 1959), 248.

24. B. Dan Wood and Richard W. Waterman, *Bureaucratic Dynamics: The Role of Bureaucracy in a Democracy* (Boulder, CO: Westview Press, 1994), 21.

25. Christopher H. Foreman, Jr., *Signals from the Hill: Congressional Oversight and the Challenge of Social Regulation* (New Haven: Yale University Press, 1988), 6.

26. Matthew McCubbins and Thomas Schwartz, "Congressional Oversight Overlooked: Police Patrol Versus Fire Alarm," *American Journal of Political Science* 41 (1984), 165-77.

27. Jon Elster, "Constitutional Courts and Central Banks: Suicide Prevention or Suicide Pact?" 3 *East European Constitutional Review* (Summer-Fall 1994), 68.

28. William Greider, *Secrets of the Temple: How the Federal Reserve Runs the Country* (New York: Simon and Schuster, 1987), 12.

29. Jorge I. Dominguez, "Free Politics and Free Markets in Latin America," in *The Global Divergence of Democracies*, ed. Larry Diamond and Marc F. Plattner (Baltimore: The Johns Hopkins University Press, 2001), 251.

30. C. A. E. Goodhart, *The Central Bank and the Financial System* (New York: Palgrave-Macmillan, 1995), 197.

31. Arend Lijphart, *Patterns of Democracy: Government Forms and Performance in Thirty-Six Countries* (New Haven: Yale University Press, 1999), 240-42.

32. The strength of central banks is related in this analysis to having higher checks and balances in the system and more polarized parties. These findings are nicely summarized in George Tsebelis, *Veto Players: How Political Institutions Work* (Princeton, NJ: Princeton University Press, 2002), 239-46.

33. Thomas Kelly, "Central Bank Independence and Democratic Decision Making," in *Development and Democracy: New Perspectives on an Old Debate,* ed. Sunder Ramaswamy and Jeffrey W. Cason (Lebanon, NH: Middlebury College Press, 2003), 195.

34. International Institute for Democracy and Electoral Assistance, *Conference Report: Towards Sustainable Democratic Institutions in Southern Africa* (Stockholm: International IDEA, 2000), 43.

35. Benedict Anderson explores the connections between census taking and the rise of nation-states in *Imagined Communities* (New York: Verso, rev. ed., 1993), chapter 10.

36. Thad Beyle, "Enhancing Executive Leadership in the States," *State and Local Government Review* 27 (1995), 22.

37. James G. March and Johan P. Olsen, *Democratic Governance* (New York: The Free Press, 1995), 79.

38. See, for example, Peter Aucoin, *The New Public Management: Canada in Comparative Perspective* (Montreal: Institute for Research on Public Policy, 1996), 3-4.

39. Suleiman, *Dismantling Democratic States*, 117-18.

40. H. George Frederickson, "Comparing the Reinventing Government Movement with the New Public Administration," *Public Administration Review* 56 (May/June 1996), 263-70.

41. For an insider account, by the minister in charge, see Luiz Carlos Bresser-Pereira, "The 1995 Public Management Reform in Brazil: Reflections of a Reformer," in *Reinventing Leviathan: The Politics of Administrative Reform in Developing Countries,* ed. Ben Ross Schneider and Blanca Heredia (Miami: North-South Center Press, 2003), 89-107.

42. Suleiman, *Dismantling Democratic States,* 314.

43. Catherine E. Rudder, "The Ethics of Public Policy Making by Private Bodies: The Case of Independence of the Accounting Industry in the U.S.," a paper delivered at the June 28-July 4, 2003 meeting of the International Political Science Association in Durban, South Africa, 9.

44. Steven Rathger Smith and Michael Lipsky, *Non-Profits for Hire: The Welfare State in the Age of Contracting* (Cambridge: Harvard University Press, 1993), 98.

45. Hutchcroft, *Booty Capitalism.*

46. Philip Selznick, *TVA and the Grass Roots* (Berkeley: University of California Press, 1949). In a later essay, Selznick conceded that TVA's concessions to local interests, while sacrificing agricultural and social goals, gained both local and national support that enabled it "to ward off threatened dismemberment and to gain time for the successful development of its key activity—the expansion of electric power." Selznick, *Leadership in Administration* (Evanston, Ill.: Row, Peterson and Company, 1957), 44.

47. Randall Baker, "Comparative Overview and Conclusion," in Baker, ed., *Transitions from Authoritarianism: The Role of the Bureaucracy* (Westport, CT: Praeger, 2002), 294. See also the case studies in this volume by Harry Roots and Natalia Karotom on Estonia, Ljudmil Georgieve on Bulgaria, and Mik Strmecki on Slovenia.

48. Irving Kristol, "Decentralization for What?" *The Public Interest* (Spring 1968), 22.

49. Catherine Boone, "Decentralization as a Political Strategy in West Africa," *Comparative Political Studies* 36 (May 2003), 375.

50. Norman J. Ornstein, Thomas E. Mann, and Michael J. Malbin, *Vital Statistics on Congress, 2001-2002* (Washington, DC: American Enterprise Institute, 2002), 21.

51. There is a point of diminishing returns at which politicians, instead of increasing their effectiveness with more staff, become captives of their own mini-bureaucracies and the time it takes to run them.

52. Larry Diamond, *Developing Democracy: Toward Consolidation* (Baltimore: The Johns Hopkins University Press, 1999), 98-99.

53. H. W. O. Okoth-Ogendo, "Constitutions without Constitutionalism: Reflections on an African Political Paradox," in *Constitutionalism and Democracy: Transitions in the Contemporary World,* ed. Douglas Greenberg et al., (New York: Oxford University Press, 1993), 77.

54. Jun Honna, *Military Politics and Democratization in Indonesia* (London: Routledge-Curzon, 2003), 3.

55. Diamond, *Developing Democracy*, 115-16.

56. Wendy Ann Hunter, *Eroding Military Influence in Brazil: Politicians Against Soldiers* (Chapel Hill: University of North Carolina Press, 1997).

57. Robert C. Johansen, "Military Policies and the State System," in *Prospects for Democracy: North, South, East, West*, ed. David Held (Stanford, CA: Stanford University Press, 1993), 217.

58. Robert A. Dahl, *Controlling Nuclear Weapons: Democracy versus Guardianship* (Syracuse, NY: Syracuse University Press, 1985), 34. I find it curious that in the rich variety of his writings on democracy Professor Dahl almost nowhere gives serious attention to the profoundly important issues he discusses so eloquently in this short book.

59. David Held, *Democracy and the Global Order: From the Modern State to Cosmopolitan Governance* (Stanford, Calif.: Stanford University Press, 1995), 119.

60. Gregory Hooks, *Forging the Military-Industrial Complex: World War II's Battle of the Potomac* (Urbana: University of Illinois Press, 1991), 275.

61. Harold Lasswell, "The Garrison State," *American Journal of Sociology* 46 (1941), 111.

62. Richard H. Kohn, "How Democracies Control the Military," in Diamond and Platner, *The Global Divergence of Democracies,* 276-77.

Chapter 8

Chief Executives

Although the disagreements between Hamilton and Madison are muted in *The Federalist Papers,* their divergent attitudes toward the powers of the presidency have played a continuing bass line to the melody of American politics. While some presidents have been "stronger" than others, and some sessions of Congress more assertive, the Hamiltonian preference for a strong executive has increasingly held sway. Nor is this tendency confined to the United States. "There is near universal agreement that decision-making in Great Britain is executive-centric."[1] "Many Asian legislatures have become mere extensions of the executive with little power of their own."[2] "In Latin America, many casual and academic observers alike assume that legislatures often forgo their constitutional powers, abdicating in favor of the executive."[3] In both parliamentary and presidential systems, Madison's depiction of democracy as a system in which "the legislature clearly predominates" has been superceded by an increasingly powerful executive authority.

In chapter 3, we outlined distinctions between "parliamentary" and "presidential" systems, along with various hybrids combining aspects of both. While these distinctions generally shape the locus of decisions, what we hope to trace here are questions of power and authority: What kinds of constitutional rules tend to enhance or restrict the nature of executive power? How compatible is the centralization of power in the executive with democratization? Are tendencies toward executive authority that seemed to have been manifest in recent years likely to continue, or have they peaked in favor of resurgent legislatures?

Constituting the Executive Office

In Switzerland, executive power is lodged in a seven-member Federal Council each of whose members serve as heads of the major government departments. The presidency of the Council rotates every year. Other countries have experimented with rotating or collegial executives, but Switzerland is unique in sustaining a system with no fixed chief executive. In some parliamentary systems, particularly those that require multi-party coalitions to form a government, executive power is quasi-collegial. The cabinet in Iceland, for example, meets twice every week to hammer out both basic policies and strategies for achieving them. Each minister has a portfolio, such as Fisheries or Education, and is essentially responsible for running his or her department. The prime ministers, in such cases, preside over cabinet meetings, represent its collective decisions, and may have some executive powers. In general terms, the phrase "cabinet government" accurately describes the basic dynamics of these systems; but unlike Switzerland, they all have a single person, a prime minister who is, without question, first among equals.

Many countries also have separate heads of state who have more symbolic leadership roles. Kings, queens, and many elected presidents serve largely as symbols of the nation and frequently do little more than greet visiting dignitaries, celebrate the openings of new highways, and hope their children avoid scandals. Some heads of state, either through tradition or law, possess important residual powers that go beyond the powers defined in the constitution. In time of war or national crisis, powers are sometimes ceded to chief executives in tacit if not overt defiance of constitutions. Specific constitutional descriptions of executive powers, moreover, are seldom found. The Canadian constitution, at one extreme, does not even mention the office of the prime minister. Executive power is thus highly contextual, dependent to a great degree on time, place, and the kinds of decision-making skills Richard Neustadt emphasized in his study of the American presidency.[4]

The constitutional powers of presidents range from largely ceremonial to nearly absolute. The elected president of Iceland has no effective control over the administration and rarely plays a legislative role. At the other end of the spectrum is a country like Russia in which presidential powers shade toward dictatorship. The institutionalization of the executive office has served in virtually every system to strengthen it to the point that even relatively weak presidents (in personal terms) can command strong presidencies (or prime ministerships). Presidential and parliamentary systems work differently in a number of important respects, but,

> The parliamentary-presidential distinction does not bear directly on the distribution of power in executive-legislative relationships. In parliamentary systems one can find a rough balance of power between cabinet and parliament, as in Belgium, but one can also find clear executive dominance, as in the United Kingdom, New Zealand, and Barbados. The same range of variation occurs in presidential systems.[5]

Some of this variance is a function of traditions, individual skills, and party systems. Among the once Communist countries of the Soviet Union and Eastern Europe, for example, Moldavia and Romania have what are, on paper, the most powerful legislatures in the region; but traditions of executive power and the existence of dominant parties have instead produced highly concentrated systems of executive power. Strong executives can be checked by formal structures and rules, on the one hand, and by resource constraints on the other. The growth of executive power in most established democracies has come less through explicit constitutional provisions than through massive delegations of legislative power.

At the inner circle of executive offices are personal staff advisors. It is impossible accurately to quantify the size of these executive offices because most chief executives prefer to hide their true extent; because they have informal as well as formal networks of advisors, and because there is often a shadow network of government agencies (typically including the intelligence agencies) that tend to work particularly closely with the chief executive. Members of what U.S. president Franklin Roosevelt referred to as his "kitchen" cabinet (as opposed to the formal cabinet which presumably met in the dining room) are usually drawn from among the chief executive's closest friends. Chosen for loyalty as much as competence, members of this inner circle may or may not have formal positions, and may or may not be on the government payroll, but they are found in almost every country. This inner core plays a crucial role in advising the chief executive and channeling access to his or her office. Its scope tends to tighten in times of crisis, sometimes to the extent that even cabinet members find it difficult to get appointments to see the chief. The role of spouses in these inner circles is often exaggerated; but there is little doubt that some, such as Argentina's Eva Peron, were key players.

Presidents and prime ministers generally have less control over the second circle of power which consists of the formal cabinet and the heads of key agencies. The politics of cabinet-making and running the government make such control problematic. But chief executives usually do have greater staff resources. Cabinets do not often have press secretaries, prime ministers almost always do; and in both presidential and cabinet systems it is generally the chief executive who runs the budget office and other policy formulating staff offices. The legislative presidency is most fully developed in the United States. Its elaborate structure, increasingly emulated, by no means guarantees legislative success; but the elaboration of the budget office, the offices of legislative liaison, the press office, and others continue to transform the nature of legislative-executive relations.

Choosing the Team

A key factor in evaluating the relative powers of chief executives revolves around their ability to choose their governing teams. In parliamentary systems the process of forming the cabinet is one of the most important tasks that prime ministers confront: a former Canadian prime minister was only half kidding when he listed his occupation as "cabinet-maker." The process is particularly delicate in multi-party systems, when the balancing of who gets what ministries (or portfolios) is the key to whether a coalition can be crafted. The one power left to the monarch or elected president in many otherwise purely parliamentary systems is that of decid-ing who shall get the first crack at forming a government. Some constitutions require that the party with the largest number of seats try first, but in most it is a free-for-all of frantic bargaining in which the key problem is to allocate portfolios in a way that will secure the participation of enough parties to form a majority.

Where one party has a clear majority, the essential problem is one of dividing the ministries among individual members and factions, a process that has often taken place long before parliament convenes. Single party cabinets have been the norm in modern Britain and many of its former colonies. In Western Europe, 30.9 percent of the 1945-1999 parliaments analyzed in one recent study functioned with single-party cabinets,[6] and some parts of the former Soviet Union, including Rus-sia, appear to be moving toward a similar pattern. The rest of the world is about evenly divided. As shown be seen in Table 8-1, just under a half (48 percent) of the world's parliaments had single-party cabinets in 2003.

A cabinet forged out of a coalition of two or more parties, no one of which can gain a majority vote on its own, requires a delicate process of bargaining both within and between party groups. A substantial literature has explored the logic of coalition development in such systems. The starting points in these models are the concepts of (a) minimal winning coalitions and (b) connected winning alliances.[7] The idea of the minimal winning coalition is that parties are unlikely to offer to share power with more representatives of other parties than it takes to win. The most obvious flaw in this theory is that it is blind to policy issues: two large centrist parties, for example, might form a grand coalition in which they give up seats in the cabinet rather than share power with a small party of extremists. Hence the idea of connected alliances, which suggests simply that the most likely alliances are between the parties most closely connected on a left-right ideological scale.

The combined predictive power of these two models is quite good, with the logic they embody underlying most recent research on the comparative politics of cabinet formation. Overall, as Laver and Schofield conclude, "the interaction of the deductive theory and the empirical analysis of government coalition formation has been relatively productive."[8] There are, at the same time, so many exceptions to the rules that these models have generated—and so many good reasons for those exceptions—that a good deal of skepticism is warranted. The most important of these relate to the multidimensional nature of issue differences, and the internal politics of parties engaged in coalition building. Our interests here are in the ways in which the rules of the game influence this process. The ways in which par-liaments are elected have a major impact. Of the thirty-three governments shown

Table 8-1

Number of Parties Represented in the Cabinets of
69 World Parliaments (2003)

Countries with One Party Cabinets (33):
Andorra,* Antigua and Barbuda,* Bahamas,* Barbados,* Belize,* Canada,* Greece, Grenada,* Guyana, Jamaica,* Kenya,* Liechtenstein, Malta, Moldova, Monaco, Mongolia,* Romania, St. Kitts and Nevis,* St. Lucia,* St. Vincent and the Grenadines,* Samoa,* Seychelles, Solomon Islands,* South Africa, Spain, Sri Lanka, Suriname, Sweden, Taiwan, Trinidad and Tobago, United Kingdom.*

Countries with Two Party Cabinets (18):
Australia, Austria, Denmark, Dominica,* Fiji, Germany, Hungary, Iceland, Ireland, Mauritius,* Netherlands, New Zealand, Poland, Portugal, San Marino, Sao Tome and Principe, South Korea,* Vanuatu.

Countries with Three Party Cabinets (8):
Bangladesh,* Italy, Japan,* Macedonia, Norway, Serbia and Montenegro, Thailand, Turkey.

Countries with Four Party Cabinets (6):
Albania, Czech Republic, Finland, Latvia, Slovakia, Slovenia.

Countries with Five or More Party Cabinets (4)
Guinea-Bissau, India,* Lithuania, Morocco.*

---

*Countries in which some or all parliamentarians are elected from first-past-the-post, single member districts.

Sources: www.electionworld.org; www.ipu.org

in Table 8-1 with single party cabinets, seventeen have first-past-the-post election systems. In a very broad sense, the more proportional the electoral system, the more complicated the cabinet. Only four of the cabinets with three parties or more have first-past-the-post systems. This association makes most devotees of consociational democracy advocates for PR, on the grounds that the broader the coalition cabinet the more likely it is to protect minority rights.

Beyond electoral factors, the process of cabinet formation can be shaped strongly by the rules. In the extreme cases of Belgium and Northern Ireland, the composition of the cabinet is virtually dictated by requirements that it include some proportion of various groups—Catholics and Protestants under the power-sharing agreement in Northern Ireland, Dutch and French-speaking members under Article 86B of the Belgian Constitution. Less formal norms have often operated to keep certain groups out of the government (and thus, by implication, kept certain others in). For many years, the Communist and neo-Fascist parties of France and Italy were in "permanent opposition," that is, not allowed to hold cabinet portfolios and narrowing the parties from which governing coalitions could be formed. In recent years, anti-immigrant groups have been given more or less the same kind of pariah status in some parts of Europe. The process of structuring a multi-party cabinet is generally facilitated when the chief of state has the power to invite a particular party or individual to go first in trying to put together a coalition. Systems such as that of Italy that automatically give the single largest party the right to try first, tend similarly to simplify and facilitate the bargaining process. Also important are rules on how cabinets are actually installed, whether, in particular, a formal rule of investiture requires a new government to be voted in by an affirmative majority of the legislature.

Forming a cabinet in presidential systems is also, less formally, an exercise in coalition building. True coalition government is founded in a binding agreement between factions or parties and seldom occurs in presidential systems. But less formal attempts to buy support in the legislature are common as Netto's study of Brazil shows. President Collor, in 1992, not only dismissed his entire cabinet, but openly consulted opposition party leaders to form what was, in essence, a coalition cabinet crafted to secure support in congress.[9] In countries like Brazil, where party discipline is loose and cabinet positions important sources of power and patronage, informal coalitions are quite commonly structured into both allocating ministries and reaching a consensus on policies. Stepan has shown that the average tenure of ministers in presidential democracies is considerably shorter than that of those in parliamentary systems. Presidents who do not enjoy party majorities in the legislature, he argues, are particularly likely to "resort to rapid ministerial rotation as a device in their perpetual search for support on key issues."[10]

Perhaps the most difficult executive office to define is that of the vice president. Former U.S. vice president John Nance Garner once described his role as that of a spare tire on the automobile of government: very important on the rare occasions when you need it, just taking up space most of the time. Some presidents have given far more power to their presidents than others: U.S. vice president Richard Cheney is frequently reported to be among President Bush's closest confidants; in South Africa, Nelson Mandela put his vice president (and ultimate successor) Thabo Mbecki in charge of much of the day-to-day management of the government. Regardless of how the office is filled, it is important that the succession be clearly defined. The superficially appealing idea of allowing the runner-up for the presidency to become vice president has not worked, as it puts the president's most bitter enemy a heartbeat from the office, and allows a certified loser to take over from the electorate's first choice. Extending beyond the question of who takes charge on the death of the president, a growing number of constitutions also make provisions for a longer chain of succession (in the event of a tragedy that took the lives of both the president and vice president), and for presidential disabilities. Amendment XXV to the U.S. Constitution, for example, specifies both the order of succession beyond the vice president, and a method by which a disabled president may relinquish his or her duties to the vice president on an acting basis. It also allows the cabinet, with the concurrence of two-thirds of the congress, to declare a president disabled even if he or she is unwilling or unable to do so. And it allows the president—with the consent of two-thirds of the Congress—to fill a vacancy in the office the vice president. One American political scientist has argued that "we would get better Vice Presidents" if all were nominated in this manner,[11] but the tendency in most presidential systems that have vice presidents is to elect them with and in the same manner as the president.

Staying in Power

The hallmark of parliamentary government is the need for the governing coalition to secure and retain the confidence of a parliamentary majority. Putting together a cabinet that the legislature will support is only a starting point, a point that is, moreover, intimately connected with that government's ability to stay in power. Here again, the rules play an important role. In the textbook model, drawn largely from Great Britain and the older parliaments of Europe, a government that loses an important vote must either resign or call a new election.

Europe's early parliaments were formed as checks on the powers of the monarch. The line of demarcation between the government (that is, the monarchy) and the legislature was clear, and as the office of the prime minister and his or her cabinet evolved, the government was seen as the instrument of parliamentary power: the stronger the cabinet, the stronger the parliament. But as these cabinets displaced monarchs as the effective executive powers, party discipline became a tool by which parliamentary government became, in effect, cabinet government. Particularly where a single party majority was able to form the government, a cabinet, once installed, was able through its control of the policy agenda and intra-party advancement, to stay in power throughout its constitutional term. Votes of no confidence became rarities. Even in coalition governments, the idea of collective ministerial responsibility combined with party discipline to separate governments from parliaments. The idea of collective responsibility is that however much the members of the cabinet might fight in chambers, they would show only a collective face to the outside world, speak with one voice to parliament, and stand or fall together. This mechanism works best where the parties are not so sharply divided that some of those inside the government will come to prefer the uncer-

tainties of change to a share of power in the existing government; but even in
highly conflicted systems, the tendency is increasingly to work things out within
the existing framework rather than face the uncertainties of a new election.

There are many variations on this theme. Germany, in its postwar constitution,
introduced a "constructive" vote of no confidence, a rule by which a cabinet cannot
be deposed without the simultaneous election of an alternative. Similar provisions
in the revised constitution of Belgium and Spain have probably increased government stability by forcing the opposition not just to vote the rascals out but to
agree on a substitute. In France, the requirement that a bill is adopted unless an
absolute majority votes affirmatively to censure the government, has had a similar
effect. Rules such as these serve largely to reinforce the tendency toward government stability. Even when votes of no confidence occur, few constitutions
actually *require* dissolution of the legislature, making it common for crises to be
resolved by rearranging the chairs while leaving the house intact. More than one
government may go down to defeat without the parliament being dissolved. "In
Italy, perhaps the most extreme case, six governments formed after each of the
1968, the 1972, and the 1979 elections. In Belgium, Israel, and The Netherlands,
it is not uncommon for up to three governments, often with quite different party
compositions, to form without an intervening election."[12] Even with a single, dominant party, a mid-term reshuffling of the seats often occurs, and may even go right
to the top, as in Margaret Thatcher's dramatic fall from power at the hands of her
British Conservative Party colleagues in 1990.

Döring describes the evolving pattern of relations between parliaments and
governments in Western Europe one of strengthening government control. Marked
by the decreasing likelihood of no-confidence votes, it is also reflected in domination of the parliamentary agenda, and growing restrictions on private member bills,
that is, bills introduced by ordinary backbench members.[13] While this was an evo-
lutionary process in most of the countries covered by Döring, a number of newer
constitutions include provisions that tend to produce comparable outcomes. The
dynamics of the relationship between the prime minister, the cabinet, and the
legislature in parliamentary systems make it difficult to trace the degree to which
parliaments actually control governments. One of the interesting aspects of Mrs.
Thatcher's forced resignation is that it took place in the context of a wave of both
journalistic and scholarly essays bemoaning the loss of parliamentary powers to the
prime minister. But if the Thatcher case shows that power relationships can shift
quite unpredictably, it is still generally possible to sketch a continuum that moves
from the center outward through four basic patterns. In the most centralized form
of prime ministerial government, called chancellor democracy in Germany, the
prime minister sits, to use Sartori's term, as "a first *above unequals . . .* for he or
she truly runs the government and has a free hand in picking and firing truly subordinate ministers."[14] In a less centralized variation of cabinet government— where
the prime minister in Sartori's terms is "a first *among unequals"*—the prime

minister picks his or her government and is clearly in charge, but governs collegially. It is the job of the prime minister in such systems not just to form a coalition that can command a parliamentary majority but to keep that coalition intact. In the third form of cabinet government, there are truly collegial cabinets, forged and maintained out of coalitions *among equals*. Finally, there are systems in which the cabinet remains essentially subservient to the parliament as a whole, or at least to the party caucuses of the governing parties.

The most important predictors of these patterns are found in electoral systems; but other constitutional devices play important roles. Surely, the German constructive vote of no confidence makes it far more simple to hold coalitions together. And the fact that the German parliament appoints only the chancellor, not the whole cabinet, reinforces the notion that the execucentric nature of German politics is sown into the rules of the game. Generally, however, the last third of the twentieth century was one in which, with few changes in the formal rules, both parliamentary and presidential systems turned toward executive power. What David Judge has written of Britain could apply to most parliamentary systems:

> At the time when collective responsibility became a cardinal feature of British politics, in the middle decades of the nineteenth century, it was feaslble that cabinet members both should and *could* collectively deliberate upon policy. . . . In the twentieth century, however, the sheer scope and activism of government reduced the capacity of cabinet to act as *the* collective point of decision and increased the centripetal tendencies for decisions to be made elsewhere, most particularly within departments or within 10 Downing Street.[15]

Anthony King has argued that because the leaders of the executive branch in a parliamentary system are themselves members of parliament, it makes little sense to use the term "legislative-executive relations."[16] I disagree, but King is right to highlight the importance of the relationships between cabinet members and those who sit on the backbenches of the parties in power. As Mezey argues,

> Although it may be rare for a legislator to defect from his or her party on a floor vote, research on the relationship between the government and its rank-and-file supporters in several European parliamentary systems suggests that the apparent support of legislators for the cabinet is often predicated on significant consultation between the two. The result of such consultation may well be that the government will not propose the legislation that it would if left to its own devices, but rather that the government will modify its preferences to produce a proposal that will minimize any incipient opposition among its supporters in parliament.[17]

In this sense, relationships between executives and legislators seem rather similar to those that obtain in systems that formally separate the branches. For while a president need not court members of her party in Congress to stay in power, the success of his legislative program generally depends on precisely that kind of effort. Indeed, a president's tenure in office may depend upon it as well. A defining characteristic of presidential regimes is that the chief executive is not removable in the same way as a prime minister. Many systems, nonetheless, provide mechanisms for the removal of the president that are modeled not on votes of confidence but on some variation of the impeachment clause of the U.S. Constitution. Procedurally, an president must first be formally indicted by a majority of the House of Representatives, tried on those charges by the Senate, and convicted by a two-thirds vote. Substantively, the sole grounds for impeachment are "high crimes and misdemeanors," which generally mean "large-scale abuses of distinctly public authority."[18] Something in the nature of what Sunstein calls a "common law constitution" has raised this standard to the level of an understanding "that impeachment is appropriate only in the most extraordinary cases of abuse of distinctly presidential authority."[19] The House of Representatives lowered this bar in voting along largely partisan lines to impeach President Clinton in 1997. Although it was never expected that the Senate would vote to remove Clinton, the partisan nature of the charge from the House creates a strong possibility that the "common law constitution" may be evolving more toward a system in which impeachment becomes more analogous to a vote of no confidence. This is already the case in some of the thirty other countries that have impeachment clauses in their constitutions.[20] Indonesia, to take an extreme case, deposed its first two presidents in the three years following the resignation of Soeharto. Presidents have also been impeached or forced to resign with charges pending in the Philippines (2002), Ecuador in both 1999 and 2001, Lithuania and South Korea (2004). The presidents of Paraguay and Nigeria have narrowly escaped similar charges.

This tendency toward the growing use of impeachment proceedings as a tool of legislative-executive politics represents a partial convergence of presidential and parliamentary forms. It may also reflect a resurgence of parliaments. Any such resurgence, however, comes in the context of a century-long trend in quite the opposite direction toward the consolidation of executive power in general and its concentration in the hands of a single chief executive.

The Office and Powers of the Chief Executive

Because formal constitutions are seldom specific on the extent of executive powers, they tend to be defined by a combination of traditional roles, statutes, and political dynamics. In many systems a whiff of monarchy surrounds the executive office in the form of such prerogatives as freedom from arrest, "executive privilege" (the ability to keep official secrets), and the power to grant clemency and pardons. Also operating in most systems is a sort of constitutional common law by which a power like that which makes the U.S. president "commander in chief of the armed forces," evolves into something quite new as weapons systems and the nature of warfare evolve. Executive power is also intensely political, dependent upon both the skills of incumbents, the contexts within which they operate, popular support, and the effectiveness of other actors in the system.

Once again, it is worth emphasizing the role played by the rules of the electoral system in structuring executive power. In parliamentary systems, the effective power of the chief executive increases markedly in systems that encourage single party majorities and cohesive parties. In presidential systems, it helps enormously if the president is elected at the same time as the legislature and can run again. Less tangible electoral factors—such as a consensus that a certain margin of victory has given the winners a "mandate" to pursue particular policies—also play a role. Regardless of the nature of such advantages, some chief executive come to the table with more chips and better cards to play.

Information and Agenda Setting

"Agenda setting is a selection process . . . by which people in and around the government implicitly attend to some subjects in the population of potential agenda items rather than others."[21] The ability to decide what gets decided is also the power to decide what does not. In formal terms, in the U.S. Congress, only a member can introduce a bill. At the other extreme are some parliamentary systems in which only government bills appear on the legislative agenda. Whatever the formal rules, the interesting questions revolve around questions of framing: "*The definition of alternatives is the supreme instrument of power;* the antagonists can rarely agree on what issues are because power is involved in the definition. He who determines what politics is about runs the country, because the definition of of the alternatives is the choice of conflicts, and the choice of conflicts allocates power."[22]

Increasingly in the modern world, governments are expected to have programs. Parties campaign on issues, or what Americans call "platforms," that are promises of what they will do in power. These promises most readily transfer into programs in parliamentary systems with single-party majority cabinets. In multi-party systems, major programs are usually negotiated as part of the process of forming a coalition cabinet. The situation is less precise in presidential systems where a separately elected legislature may not accept the president's agenda as its own. Nonetheless, the evidence is quite clear that presidents and prime ministers do try to put their campaign promises into effect. Even in the supposedly less programmatic parties of the Unites States, presidents "seek to redeem most of their specific promises about policy that they make in their campaigns."[23] The executive's ability to frame issues in this broad sense is of relatively short duration. As presidents and prime ministers succeed in getting their programs adapted, their agendas shift from those based on correcting errors of the past to defending the programs of today. New events, catastrophes, and the general category of what

Birkland calls "focusing events"[24] sometimes provide new opportunities for leadership; but once the honeymoon is over, agenda-setting advantages tend to derive from more mundane institutional advantages that vary from one system to another.

The ability to control the calendar of the legislature gives some executives a very important tool of agenda control. In the most extreme cases, the parliament gets to vote *only* on bills presented by the government, and these can be presented with no amendments allowed. In practice, this power is often not as formidable as it appears. The New York State legislature, for example, does not allow amendments, and the party leaders of the Assembly and Senate retain such tight control over what bills can considered on the floor that in most sessions no bill is ever defeated. Bills are, however, pulled back for modification or withdrawn completely when substantial opposition arises. Even with full agenda control and a no-amendments rule, in other words, it is possible for a legislative majority to bargain with the government by rejecting its initiatives until it gets a bill to its liking.

While only a few chief executives have formal agenda control, most have partial ability to define the alternatives considered by the legislature. The power is sometimes delegated to the minister of foreign affairs, and is uneasily divided in France between the president and the premier, but most executives have the authority to negotiate treaties which, when the assembled chiefs reach agreement, are presented to their respective legislature on a take-it or leave-it basis. While many presidents and prime ministers look homeward as they negotiate the details of international agreements, in most systems the legislature's role in such decisions is marginal. In fact the constitutions of France, Italy, and Portugal essentially adhere to the British tradition that "the executive is free to make treaties, parliament only being involved when legislation is necessary to fulfill treaty obligations."[25] In Germany, a distinction between "political treaties" that require legislative assent, and all others which do not has been narrowly interpreted by the Constitutional Court to give the legislature a role only in those unusual instances in which a treaty directly affects the existence of the country or its territorial integrity.[26]

A handful of presidential systems have followed the lead of the United States and made it constitutionally more difficult to ratify a treaty than to pass an ordinary bill (a treaty requires approval of a two-thirds majority in the Senate), but in most systems it is treated as an ordinary bill. Treaties, however, are not ordinary at all. Indeed many treaties not only reform national practices but commit their signers to the subsequent regulations promulgated by the international bodies the treaties create. Legislatures are seldom consulted in negotiating these downstream agreements. There is a widespread understanding among students of comparative politics that "the operation of states in an ever more complex international system both limits their autonomy (in some spheres radically) and impinges increasingly upon their sovereignty."[27] Virtually no attention has been given, however, to the impact of these same globalizing forces on the internal distribution of power. Yet clearly when a country's legislature ratifies a treaty that, for example, establishes a free trade zone, it has also signed itself out of any future participation in setting the parameters of trade relations which will be negotiated by representatives from the executive branches.

To a lesser but still significant extent, the executive branch generally has a strong agenda setting role in public finance. The U.S. Constitution grants Congress the power of the purse. Until passage of the Budget and Accounting Act of 1921, individual bureaus and agencies submitted their budget proposals to the Secretary of the Treasury who compiled them into estimates submitted directly to congress. Presidents from time to time commented on these estimates and suggested revisions, but such interventions were rare and no president ever presumed to prepare a budget of his or her own. As developed in subsequent years, the powers of the president's Office of Management and Budget have expanded to encompass the power to clear any legislative request from the bureaucracy and to prepare the president's budget. It is this budget that become the starting point for legislative action. Although Congress has delegated these framing powers to the White House and its O.M.B., it has retained a far greater share of its traditional powers of the purse than most other world legislatures. With the Budget and Impoundment Act of 1974, Congress set up its own mechanisms for checking the overall figures presented by the president, and the congressional budget office's independent analyses of projected revenues have frequently served to undermine presidential projections. A number of other countries have begun to develop such capacities. Their effectiveness appears to be more a question of politics than of constitutional provisions as shown in the contrast between Chile and Mexico.

In Mexico, where Article 74 of the constitution clearly sites budget authority in the legislature, congress "has *always* approved the budget, even when it was clear that the executive had ignored the approved budget" of the year before.[28] The Chilean constitution, by way of contrast, places most formal budgetary powers in the hands of the president, giving congress only sixty days to consider it, and automatically putting the president's numbers in force if congress fails to act. Congress is prohibited, moreover, from proposing additional spending or moving funds between categories. Yet the reality of Chilean politics is that, "Legislators have been successful in altering the initial proposals of the presidents." Although these changes have been relatively small, "final budgetary numbers are not the whole story in terms of legislative influence. . . active lobbying takes place by legislators in both the proposal and consideration stages. . . [and] the president maintains constant contact with the legislative leadership of both his own party and the opposition."[29]

There are similar variations in parliamentary systems which also appear more related to political contexts than constitutional provisions. In Belgium, for example, the budget was typically presented to the parliament at the last moment and pushed through by the governing coalition with little debate. A series of reforms enacted in 1989 set certain regular deadlines and created legislative committees to oversee the budget; but although the process is now more transparent, it is only marginally less concentrated in the hands of the cabinet than it was before the reforms.[30] The extent to which party leaders consult rank-and-file members in constructing the budget varies enormously, as does the relative influence of cabinet members. My own sense is that prime ministers (and their staffs) are increasingly usurping the roles of ministers of finance in coordinating budget preparations, and that the cabinet as a whole is increasingly marginalized. But its also true that no central agent could ever really construct anything as technically specialized as the budget of a large, modern state. Even when "the finance minister and the prime minster play an important role in setting the political agenda, that agenda must inevitably be constructed out of policy proposals that are generated departmentally."[31]

However centralized the cabinet, once it has reached agreement on a budget, parliamentary approval is usually routine, serving largely to confirm compromises already worked out. The exceptions to this rule occur largely in highly fragmented systems, those with loose party discipline, or those with minority governments. In some parliaments, budget committees have been established to give more careful scrutiny to the government's numbers. Slovenia has adopted procedures that leave budget initiatives with the cabinet; but gives the legislature the opportunity to send the preliminary draft back for revision, allows close questioning of individual ministers on each aspect of the package, allows the Finance and Monetary Policy Committee to develop an alternative set of numbers, and finally allows the parliament to amend or reject the overall budget. Although this system seems, as one close observer puts it, "quite sensible and rational,"[32] it is also quite unique.

Policy Making Powers

The power to set the legislative agenda is at once more and less formidable than it appears. Even in systems where the legislature has little visible role, it is almost impossible to know to what extent, if any, the executive branch took legislative preferences into account in drafting its proposals. There are, at the same time, many instances in most systems in which such calculations are largely unnecessary since the rules of the game don't involve the legislature at all. The enormous complexity of policy issues, particularly those of a technical nature, necessitates—as indicated in our chapter 7 discussion of the bureaucracy—the delegation of rule-making powers to the executive branch. It is important not to confuse such delegations of power with the powers of presidents and prime ministers, as the overwhelming majority of these bureaucratic rules fly in at levels far below the radar screens of chief executives. But there has been a tendency in the United States and in some of its states for the president or governor to use this rule-making authority in a more sweeping manner. Particularly in the areas of land preservation and environmental protection, the Clinton administration was unusually proactive in using executive orders to broaden and extend the meaning of statutes passed before Republicans took control of Congress. His successor, George W. Bush, has been equally aggressive in rolling back many of those same executive orders and reinterpreting the original statutes themselves.

Emergency Powers

Many constitutions go beyond administrative regulations to give their chief executives emergency and decree-making powers that allow them to bypass the legislature on key issues. Extending beyond the power simply to fill in the details of legislation, a number of constitutions grant the power to suspend certain liberties and rule by decree under emergency conditions. In many countries, such states of emergency must be approved by a majority vote of the legislature, or, as in Costa Rica and Namibia, by two-thirds. More commonly, they reverse the dynamic of the normal legislative process. In Argentina, for example, "necessity and urgency" decrees can only be reversed or "vetoed" by a two-thirds vote of the legislature. Some constitutions limit the duration of the emergency to three or sixth months. But some, especially it seems in Africa and Latin America, are quite vague, much like that of France which requires only that the president "consult" with various people when the "integrity" and "independence" of the country are threatened, or Brazil where, until recently, three month "emergencies" could be extended again and again. What are called "states of exception" in some countries were used to suspend basic rights in Paraguay for forty years and in Columbia for almost thirty.

> The seriousness of the continuous use of constitutional states of exception in Latin America lies in the extremely subjective interpretation of the criteria that make them admissible, a practice that rapidly erodes the legitimacy of the constitutional order. . . . The derogation of rights based on these states of exception winds up weakening the political and judicial control of the acts of the government, particularly with respect to individual rights . . . [and] often lead to the granting of new political functions to the armed forces, with consequences that may become extremely serious for the preservation of democracy.[33]

Emergency powers clauses are more often found in the constitutions of presidential than parliamentary regimes, in part because prime ministers are better able to use the levers of cabinet responsibility to push through the emergency measures a president might not be able to get through a separately-elected legislature. Italy, at the same time, has one of the world's most permissive emergency power clauses, while Brazil—which copied the Italian article almost word-for-word—has recently modified it to make it far more difficult to use. What Brazilian legislators learned from hard experience is that it is important to include strict time limits on emergency power and require specific and periodic re-authorizations from the legislature.

Referendums

Somewhat analogous to emergency powers, in the sense that they can be used to bypass the legislative process, are constitutional clauses that allow chief executives to legislate by referendum. Some constitutions, particularly in the U.S. states, require certain issues—such as capital borrowing plans—to be put to a public vote. Referendums allow governments to put issues to the public when consensus is difficult to achieve, or when it seems important to give greater symbolic weight to decisions (as the 1992 vote by South Africa's white minority to abolish apartheid). The seemingly democratic idea of going directly to the people loses some appeal when wealthy interests are able to mount expensive campaigns to hide their real intentions, and by some attempts to use the device to invade minority rights. Butler and Ranney argue that this danger may be endemic to the process: "Because they cannot measure intensities of beliefs or work things out through discussion and discovery, referendums are bound to be more dangerous than representative assemblies to minority rights."[34] But in the country that uses referendums the most, Switzerland, where the public may initiate ballot propositions, it seems not to have worked that way at all. "Here," Lijphart argues, "the referendum and initiative have given even very small minorities a chance to challenge any laws passed by the majority of the elected representatives." In this context, "it can be seen as a strong consensus-inducing mechanism" that in fact protects minority rights.[35]

Our main point here has less to do with referendums as tools of democracy than with their impact on the relative powers of legislatures and chief executives. Through direct and subtle means of manipulating the media, it is possible for quasi-authoritarian chief executives to use referendums as tools for consolidating power at the expense of the legislature. Even where such demagogic appeals are not a factor, the simple ways in which referendum questions are typically phrased (usually in a sentence or two as compared with the multiple pages that a legislative statute might require), take the nuances out of the policy process and hand their interpretation to the bureaucracy and the courts. California's vote to eliminate affirmative action, for example, has led to a flurry of executive orders, resolutions by the boards of various semi-public institutions, lawsuits, and court cases that will probably drag on for years, but that are unlikely to involve the members of the elected legislature at all.

In the final analysis, the need for sweeping executive decrees and emergency powers is not clear. Democracies have usually proven adept at pulling themselves together in the face of outside threats. Their record of meeting internal crises by giving emergency powers to a single leader is, conversely, rather poor. The primary danger that inheres in grants of emergency powers lies in their tendency to erode the system of checks and balances that keep systems democratic. The involvement of chief executives in the policy process should be structured more around persuasion than command. It is the essence of constitutional democracy that major legislation involves the kinds of interactions that require bargaining and compromise. In both presidential and parliamentary systems, the political skills of chief executives are key variables in this equation. Neustadt's famous dictum that presidential power is the power to persuade applies to prime ministers as well. In both cases, however, the reality of these powers emerge from an amalgam of personal skills, political dynamics, and formal powers.

Where one party controls the government and party discipline is strong, the executive powers to set the agenda and sell a program come to the fore; in divided government, particularly in presidential regimes, the focus shifts to blocking powers, the tools the Constitution gives the president to stop action or force legislative leaders to the bargaining table. Among the most formidable of these is the power to veto acts of the parliament. The nature of the veto power varies enormously. Some presidents, particularly those in semi-presidential systems, have little more than the ability to express disapproval of a bill and perhaps delay final passage. At the other extreme are constitutions that make it very difficult for the legislature to override a veto, and give the president the ability to be very precise in deciding which parts of a bill to block. Following Shugart and Carey, these can be broken into three categories: item vetoes, pocket vetoes, and requirements for overrides.[36]

Item Vetoes

Legislatures can sometimes force presidents to accept policies they do not want by embedding them in complex bills filled with items that they do. The president of the United States can veto an entire bill on the grounds that it contains items of which she disapproves; but he runs the risk of having the Congress refuse to pass the bill at all. The governors of forty-three U.S. states, and of the Philippines and some Latin American countries do not face this problem because they have line item veto powers that enable them to send particular lines of a bill back to the legislature while signing the other parts into law. In some of these systems, the line-item or "partial" veto power applies only to money bills; but it is, in any instance, a powerful executive tool.

Pocket Vetoes

Most presidential and mixed systems give their chief executives a week or two either to sign a legislative act into law or to veto it. A tradition has evolved in many of these systems that allows this period to expire if the legislature is not in session. This allows the president to kill a bill either through a formal veto, which the legislature is no longer present to override, or by simply not signing it. If the chief executive alone has the power to call a special session of the legislature, such inaction—known as a "pocket veto"—kills the bill at least until the legislature reconvenes. The constitutions of Guatemala and Honduras explicitly prohibit the pocketing of bills, and many state legislatures in the United States curtail their use by going into recess at the end of the session rather than a formal adjournment.

Overrides

In most mixed systems, the veto power is only "suspensive," serving the symbolic function of informing the public and parliament of the president's objections and suspending implementation until the parliament votes a second time. In most pure presidential systems, it takes an extraordinary majority to override a veto, usually two-thirds of those present and voting, three-fifths in some cases, sometimes an absolute majority of all members. Although "there is no logic inherent to presidential government requiring the two-thirds cutoff," it has become "the focal point for constitution builders" and serves as the magic number in a majority of presidential systems.[37] Since this precedent was set by the United States, it is interesting to note that the American founders were by no means wedded to this or any other number. The convention voted down proposals to give both the president and the judiciary "revisionary" power over legislation, rejected attempts to give the president an absolute veto, and actually at one point voted 6 to 4 in favor of requiring a three-quarters majority in both houses to override. "These persistent efforts," as one historian notes, "displayed clearly the strong fears of democracy felt by leading members. Their versatility in this was as remarkable as their tenacity. There was no precedent for an absolute veto in republican government. Its connection with monarchy deterred most but not all of them."[38] And so two-thirds became the standard number as the compromise figure leaning clearly toward those who most feared and mistrusted the elected legislature.

Vetoes are not common. Even with the government divided between the parties through most of the period, only an average of six vetoes a year were cast in the United States in the 1990s. Most vetoes, moreover have a ritualistic nature in which both sides know it is coming and, for one reason or another, want it. The institutionalization of the legislative presidency has made it unnecessary for presidents to use vetoes to send messages to Congress, the message being sent is to the public. The importance of the veto power in the United States lies in its ability to transform (a) the visibility of the issue and (b) the rules of the legislative game from one that requires simple majorities to one requiring two-thirds. Since everyone knows this math, formal vetoes occur largely when both the Congress and the presidency want them to occur, that is, when they are searching for campaign issues or hoping to arouse the public. The true *power* of the veto lies in its threat: like the shotgun in the corner, it works best when it isn't used.

Implementation

The president of the United States is constitutionally required to see that the laws be faithfully executed. The linguistic quirk that gives us a word that can mean either to carry out or to kill is expressive of an often overlooked aspect of executive power. Vetoes are dramatic manifestations of the power to kill legislation, but are increasingly preludes to election campaigns and part of the bargaining process between legislatures and executives. Inaction, if only because it is more difficult to detect, can be at least as effective. Under pressure from a variety of domestic and international forces, for example, Indonesia has adopted a number of very tough statutes protecting its lush forest resources. They are a travesty. Those charged with enforcing the laws have *as a rule* either lacked the resources to act, looked the other way as massive violations occurred, or profited themselves from illegal timber operations.[39] The lawmaking process means little in countries that lack the resources or the will to enforce their own laws.

But nonenforcement is not simply a matter of weakness and corruption. It is also an artifact of executive power. In some cases, the most decisive act of the executive is to not act at all. A president who is hostile to an agency's mission can effectively cripple it by appointing as directors people hostile to its mission, or by simply not filling key vacancies. Every system must allow some flexibility in spending appropriated funds: if money is budgeted for snow removal, for example, and it doesn't snow, it would be folly to call out the plows. Explicit in some, implicit in most constitutions is the power to impound, defer, or transfer the expenditure of appropriated funds. Richard Nixon's clear abuses of this authority led the U. S. Congress to enact the Impoundment Control Act of 1974 establishing procedures for legislative control over executive actions that delay or cancel expenditures approved by congress. Routine, relatively trivial acts (as in our case of snow removal) require more paperwork but have been largely unaffected by these procedures. What Allen Schick calls "policy impoundments . . . when the President decides that he does not want the program or project, or wants it on smaller scale than that authorized by Congress" have become relatively rare,[40] but by no means unknown. When successful, they amount to what one clerk to the U.S. Congress once called "de facto vetoes . . . more effective than any veto you could write into a statute."[41]

Problems that arise from moving funds from one account to another are more intractable and largely reliant upon the effectiveness of the legislative oversight activities we will discuss in chapter 9. In less mature systems, problems of both impoundment and switching are likely to plague both chief executives and legislatures as lower level bureaucrats play fast and loose with the accounts. In presidential systems, legislative control is strongly related to the strength of the legislature's committee system, and they can be a control factor in parliamentary systems as well. In most parliamentary systems, however, the processes of financial management take place within the government as the various ministers, bureaucrats, the prime minister, and minister of finance, jockey for control.

Just as cabinet systems diverge in the degree to which policy agendas are collectively forged, so, it seems safe to assume, are differences at the enforcement stage. Having a cabinet position does not necessarily mean that one controls his or her ministry; but even in systems of strong, collective responsibility there remains a tendency to leave each individual minister in charge of his or her portfolio. In cabinet government "office *is* important," in particular the degree to which coalition governments almost always allocate portfolios in rather strict proportion to the size of coalition partners.[42] While this tendency has been difficult to explain in terms of rational choice theory or policy agendas, it makes very good sense if we assume that having the formal position of being the minister of X means that one can have substantial influence over how the laws are enforced and funds allocated with regard to X. The Minister of Fisheries may not be able appreciably to increase his agency's overall budget, but she is often able to decide the politically more valuable question of which port gets a new pier. Both presidents and prime ministers are, to some degree, at war with their own cabinets in trying to control such administrative decisions. These battles are generally fought at the staff level and sometimes triangulate through the finance ministry or the legislature; but the tension between the forces of central control and administrative decentralization is a constant in both presidential and parliamentary democracies.

The Growth of Executive Power

The struggle for institutional power is not a zero-sum game in which the growing powers of one branch result in declines in another. Growing government, or a growth in the technical capacity of the government to control the policy-making process, can mean growing influence for both the legislature and the executive. A chief executive or legislature that delegates trivial chores may actually gain power by increasing his, her, or its capacity to focus on important issues. In both relative and general terms, however, most modern democracies are decidedly more executive-centered than standard theories would suggest. Nowhere has this issue been more thoroughly analyzed and debated than in the United States.

To some extent, the rise of what Arthur Schlesinger called "the Imperial Presidency" is an American phenomenon. As commander-in-chief of the most powerful armed forces in world history, the president—for so long as Congress appropriates the money—is enormously capacitated to act on the international stage. The sheer scope of its economy also sets the United States apart. But the growth of presidential power is ultimately rooted in the same forces that have produced similar shifts in other systems. A new wave of democratization and legislative empowerment may be rolling back the tide, but the rise of the Imperial Presidency has roots that extend around the world. Globalization provides a major force in this direction. Summit meetings, whether regional or global, are meetings of presidents and prime ministers, not legislators. And as global issues intrude increasingly on domestic, so does power become centralized. To allow the nation to speak with one voice, virtually every constitutional democracy gives nearly unfettered authority to its chief executive to speak on the country's behalf. Day-to-day contacts often take place at the staff level, and consultation with key cabinet or congressional leaders is often the norm; but it is chief executives who set the agendas and make the deals.

Much the same is true in the area of national security. In spite of their disagreements over the proper extent of executive authority, one of the things on which Alexander Hamilton and James Madison agreed was in opposition to "the existence of standing armies in time of peace." Hamilton's argument was that because "the whole power of raising armies was lodged in the *Legislature*, not in the *Executive*," there would "be a great and real security against the keeping up of troops without evident necessity."[43] Since the beginning of World War II, however, that necessity has been continuously evident to most Americans. The existence of a standing army has given the president, as commander in chief, a great deal of discretionary authority to act around the world. A War Powers Act, passed in the 1970s to require consultation with Congress, has been generally ineffectual. Through his control of the national security apparatus, moreover, more than one president has stretched the concept of national security to cover other objectives.

Elected executives have almost always been able to capture public attention and support in ways that representative assemblies seldom can. The rise of the mass media, television in particular, has enabled modern chief executives cultivate the kinds of personality cults once associated with emperors and kings.[44] The U.S. president, because he or she is both the ceremonial and political leader of the country, is unusually well-positioned to use the media: like the royal family member who cuts the ribbon at the opening of a new highway or pins the medals on national heroes. In many parliamentary systems, a separately elected president performs these duties. Together with the heads of about twenty other countries, U.S. presidents are both royal and political, leaders in the sense of both the sacred and the profane. Even where these powers are relatively distinct, however, governments tend increasingly to speak to the people through the media rather than through parliament. As the media become national in scope, and focused more on short sound bites than on detailed explanations, executive advantage grows. In both, the office of the press secretary is one of the largest and closest to that of the president or prime minister. The power to persuade has been institutionalized.

The growth of central staff, both absolutely and relatively in comparison to that of national parliaments, has been a prominent aspect of both parliamentary and presidential systems. The growing number and complexity of the issues with which governments now deal puts an ever-increasing premium on expert knowledge, access to which is frequently centralized. Elgie's study of political leadership in six major democracies shows that "there is no clear relationship between staff size and the ability to exercise leadership."[45] There seems, however, to be an inverted U-curve in which chief executives such as those in Italy who enjoy few staff resources are constrained by their lack of resources, while those with strong backing are so involved in control and coordination that they have little time for personal leadership. The highly institutionalized White House, it can be argued, produces a strong *presidency,* but an increasingly weak and manipulated chief executive who becomes more prisoner than ruler of his or her castle.

Many of the forces tending toward the growth of executive power are so deeply embedded in global socioeconomic tendencies as to make them virtually axiomatic. There are, however, any number of ways in which the growth of executive power can be checked, and the mechanisms for balancing power invigorated. They begin with parliaments.

Notes

1. David Judge, *The Parliamentary State* (Newbury Park, CA: Sage Publications, 1993), 133.

2. Gordon R. Hein, "Strengthening Legislatures in Asia: The Challenges of Institution Building, Political Power, and Popular Legitimacy," in *Working Papers I: The Role of Legislatures and Parliaments in Democratizing and Newly Democratic Regimes,* ed. Lawrence D. Longley (Appleton, WI: Research Committee of Legislative Specialists, 1994), 362.

3. Scott Morgenstern, "Towards a Model of Latin American Legislatures," in *Legislative Politics in Latin America,* ed. Scott Morgenstern and Benito Nacif (New York: Cambridge University Press, 2002), 6.

4. Richard E. Neustadt, *Presidential Power: The Politics of Leadership* (New York: John Wiley, 1960).

5. Arend Lijphart, *Patterns of Democracy: Government Forms and Performance in Thirty-Six Countries* (New Haven: Yale University Press, 1999), 127.

6. Wolfgang C. Müller and Kaare Strøm, "Conclusion: Coalition Governance in Western Europe," in *Coalition Governments in Western Europe,* ed. Wolfgang Müller and Kaare Strøm (New York: Oxford University Press, 2000), 561.

7. The seminal work in this field is William Riker, *The Theory of Political Coalitions* (New Haven: Yale University Press, 1962). A nice summary and critique of both the theoretical literature and some of the empirical work applying it to Europe is Michael Laver and Norman Schofield, *Multiparty Government: The Politics of Coalition in Europe* (Ann Arbor: University of Michigan Press, 1998).

8. Laver and Schofield, *Multiparty Government,* 143.

9. Octavio Amorim Neto, "Presidential Cabinets, Electoral Cycles, and Coalition Discipline in Brazil," in Morgenstern and Nacif, *Legislative Politics,* 77.

10. Alfred Stepan, *Arguing Comparative Politics* (New York: Oxford, 2001), 275.

11. George Anastaplo, *The Amendments to the Constitution: A Commentary* (Baltimore: The Johns Hopkins University Press, 1995), 214.

12. Laver and Schofield, *Multiparty Government,* 212.

13. Herbert Döring, *Parliaments and Majority Rule in Western Europe* (New York: St. Martin's Press, 1995).

14. Giovanni Sartori, *Comparative Constitutional Engineering: An Inquiry into Structures, Incentives and Outcomes* (New York: New York University Press, 2nd ed., 1997), 102-3.

15. Judge, *The Parliamentary State,* 141.

16. Anthony King, "Modes of Executive-legislative Relations: Great Britain, France, and West Germany," *Legislative Studies Quarterly,* 1 (February 1976), 37-65.

17. Michael L. Mezey, "Executive-Legislative Relations," *World Encyclopedia of Parliaments and Legislatures,* ed. George Thomas Kurian (Washington, DC: Congressional Quarterly, 1998), II, 784.

18. Cass R. Sunstein, *Designing Democracy: What Constitutions Do* (New York: Oxford, 2002), 122.

19. Sunstein, *Designing Democracy,* 124.

20. Argentina, Azerbaijan, Bangladesh, Belarus, Brazil, Chile, Colombia, Costa Rica, Croatia, Dominican Republic, Ecuador, Greece, Guatemala, Honduras, Hungary, India. Indonesia, Italy, Kyrgyzstan, Lithuania, Nepal, Nicaragua, Paraguay, Russia, Slovenia, Sri Lanka, Taiwan, Tanzania, Uruguay, and Venezuela.

21. John W. Kingdon, *Agendas, Alternatives, and Public Policies* (New York: Harper Collins, 2nd ed., 1995), 231-32.

22. E. E. Schattschneider, *The Semisovereign People: A Realist's View of Democracy in America* (New York: Holt, Rinehart and Winston, 1960), 68.

23. Jeff Fishel, *Presidents and Promises* (Washington, DC: Congressional Quarterly, 1985), 214.

24. Thomas A. Birkland, *After Disaster: Agenda Setting, Public Policy, and Focusing Events* (Washington, DC: Georgetown University Press, 1997).

25. Erik Jurgens, "Parliaments and Treaty-Making," *Journal of Legislative Studies,* 1 (Summer, 1995), 178.

26. Excerpts from the Federal Constitutional Court's opinion can be found in Vicki C. Jackson and Mark Tushnet, *Comparative Constitutional Law* (New York: Foundation Press, 1999), 717-18.

27. David Held, *Democracy and the Global Order: From the Modern State to Cosmopolitan Governance* (Stanford, CA: Stanford University Press, 1995), 135.

28. Ma. Amparo Casar, "Executive-Legislative Relations in Mexico," Morgenstern and Nacif, *Legislative Politics,* 119.

29. Peter M. Siavelis, "Exaggerated Presidentialism and Moderate Presidents: Executive-Legislative Relations in Chile," Morgenstern and Nacif, *Legislative Politics,* 97.

30. Lieven de Winter, "Parliament and Government in Belgium: Prisoners of Partiocracy," *Parliaments and Governments in Western Europe*, ed. Philip Norton (Portland, OR: Frank Cass, 1998), vol. I, 97-122.

31. Michael Laver and Kenneth A. Shepsle, *Making and Breaking Governments: Cabinets and Legislatures in Parliamentary Democracies* (New York: Cambridge University Press, 1996), 285.

32. Bogomil Ferfila, "The Budget of the Republic of Slovenia and Budgetary Procedure in the Slovenian Parliament," *Working Papers on Comparative Legislative Studies III: The New Democratic Parliaments: The First Years*, ed. Lawrence D. Longley and Drago Zajc (Appleton, WI: Research Committee of Legislative Specialists, 1998), 259.

33. Hugo E. Frühling, "Human Rights in the Constitutional Order and Political Practice in Latin America," in *Constitutionalism and Democracy: Transitions in the Contemporary World*, ed. Douglas Greenberg et al. (New York: Oxford University Press, 1993), 89.

34. David Butler and Austin Ranney, "Theory," *Referendums: A Comparative Study of Practice and Theory*, ed. David Butler and Austin Ranney (Washington, DC: American Enterprise Institute, 1978), 36.

35. Arend Lijphart, *Patterns of Democracy: Government Forms and Performance in Thirty-Six Countries* (New Haven: Yale University Press, 1999), 231.

36. Matthew Soberg Shugart and John M. Carey, *Presidents and Assemblies: Constitutional Design and Electoral Dynamics* (New York: Cambridge University Press, 1992), 134.

37. Shugart and Carey, *Presidents and Assemblies,* 136.

38. Thornton Anderson, *Creating the Constitution: The Convention of 1787 and the First Congress* (University Park: Pennsylvania State University Press, 1993), 143.

39. *Which Way Forward? People, Forests and Policymaking in Indonesia,* ed. Carol J. Pierce Colfer and Ida Aju Pradnja Resosudarmo (Washington, DC: Resources for the Future, 2002).

40. Allen Schick, *Congress and Money: Budgeting, Spending and Taxing* (Washington, DC: The Urban Institute, 1980), 403.

41. Stanley M. Brand, testimony before the House Committee on Rules, "The Deferral Process after Chadha," *Hearings,* 99th Congress, 2nd sess. (1986), 99-100.

42. Laver and Schofield call this "one of the most striking non-trivial empirical relationships in political science," *Multiparty Government,* 193.

43. *The Federalist,* Number 24.

44. For forceful elaborations of this argument see Theodore J. Lowi, *The Personal President* (Ithaca, NY: Cornell University Press, 1985), and Samuel Kernell, *Going Public* (Washington, DC: Congressional Quarterly Press, 1986).

45. Robert Elgie, *Political Leadership in Liberal Democracies* (New York: St. Martin's Press, 1995), 282.

Chapter 9

Legislatures

Legislatures are the defining institutions of representative democracy. Democracy is consolidated to the extent that sovereignty resides in the legislature, endangered to the extent that it is not. Legislatures, at the same time, are not known for efficiency. The more complicated the task of governing, the greater the tendency toward executive power. As Sartori says, "parliamentary government works when its name is something of a misnomer," when it is supplemented, checked, and balanced by more efficient institutions, "when it acquires—we could say—a semi-parliamentary form. Somewhat paradoxically, the less a government is truly parliamentary, the better it performs."[1]

This paradox of parliamentary power is illustrated in the concept of "institutionalization" that Nelson Polsby used to describe the maturation of the U.S. House of Representatives. Necessary if not sufficient steps toward a legislature's capacity for governing are found, he argues, in its ability to develop a stable membership; organizational complexity; and institutional autonomy.[2] Poorly organized, and lacking experienced members, many world legislatures simply lack the resources to make policy, or counter the executive. The paradox lies in the fact that the further the legislature goes in gaining such autonomy, particularly in parliamentary systems, the greater the danger of losing its capacity for representation. In "isolating itself from its environment . . . legislatures are simply unable to go very far down the road of institutionalization."[3] In particular, "where party leadership roles are conjoined with executive hierarchies, as in Westminster systems, then the constitutional design of those systems militates against . . . the autonomy of legislatures as defined by Polsby."[4]

Samuel Huntington's suggestion that this paradox can be resolved by sur-rendering policy powers, conversely, sacrifices democracy on the alter of effici-ency.[5] It *is* important that legislatures have strong shares in determining the ways in which courts and bureaucracies rule. At the same time, the role of parliament cannot simply be scored by chalking up points. "Muscularity is not a particularly useful way to think about parliament's role as an institutional arena in which representative democracy actually takes place."[6] During consensual periods of democracy in Scandinavia, for example, it would be silly to argue that parliament was weak because it was not blocking the actions of the executive.

Various schema for assessing the role and importance of legislative bodies measure important distinctions. One frequently used classification suggests a con-tinuum that ranges from legislatures that serve largely as arenas of debate—revert-ing to the traditional role of a *parliament,* a place where people "parl" or speak—to those that exercise significant policy-making roles. Others stress the relative powers of legislatures in comparison with other branches of government. Blondel's concept of "viscosity," for example, is used to measure the legislature's ability to resist executive initiatives, or, in Tsebelis's terms to exercise significant veto power.[7] These classifications, though important, have proven difficult to apply, as even the same legislature can vary significantly from one session to another; and because legislatures—as representative institutions—play essentially contingent roles. The manageable questions are not so much about whether parliaments *do* act independently to shape public policy, but whether they *can*.

Constituting Legislatures

Most constitutions go into considerable detail in describing the composition and powers of the legislature. Although most of them have evolved into different insti-tutions than their creators would have predicted, some very basic decisions embod-ied in these texts strongly prefigure how subsequently elected parliaments act.

Membership

The most fundamental distinctions between legislative bodies derive from differing modes of selection. Legislatures differ from pre-parliaments and advisory bodies to the extent that they have their own electoral base. The key stage in the evolution of early parliaments was the point at which they were no longer assembled only at the monarch's call. The difference between the pre- and post-Communist parliaments of Eastern Europe is similarly grounded in their members not being prese-lected by the Communist Party. Among true legislatures, the most important dis-tinction is between parliamentary, presidential, and mixed systems in which mem-bers are elected either in conjunction with or separately from the executive. There are also significant differences that arise from the method of election, in particular between single-member districts and various forms of proportional representation. Where parliament shares sovereignty with an elected or hereditary executive, questions about legislative autonomy come to the fore. This begins with what Blondel called issues of "symbolic authority," of which there are three indicators.[8]

About two-thirds of the parliaments Blondel surveyed in the 1970s accorded their members parliamentary immunity, the right to make statements in debate that cannot be prosecuted. Parliamentary immunity laws can be abused to protect cor-rupt legislators who can use them to extract bribes and threaten enemies. Where such protections are lacking, conversely, legitimate opposition becomes difficult. A 1998 no-confidence debate in Thailand was all too-typically clouded by threats to arrest key opposition figures on charges of corruption (some true) that sharpened animosities while contributing nothing to the public debate.[9] Despite such poten-tials for abuse, the freedom to debate is so fundamental to parliamentary autonomy that its occasional use for corrupt purposes is probably a price that has to be paid, with other means being found to curb its abuse.

A second of Blondel's indicators is procedural independence, the ability of the legislature to make its own rules. Most constitutions formally provide for such independence, though the issue is more complicated in cabinet systems where, typ-ically, the government can push through a change in the rules almost at will. One of the ways in which power has been tilted toward the executive branch in Russia and other former Soviet states is through close leadership control of legislative proceedings. Newly assertive legislatures in some of these systems (and in South and Central America) have increasingly taken control of the process, but can find their efforts hampered by the absence of constitutional limits on executive power.

Third on Blondel's list, the right to meet and adjourn, is the least frequently granted either internationally or in the U.S. states. In his survey of 109 world parliaments, "a large majority of constitutions restrict[ed] the periods of meetings of legislatures to sessions specified in the constitution (eighty-four countries), and only in half the polities with assemblies (fifty-four) [was] it possible for the legislature to decide on its own about extraordinary sessions."[10] Half of U.S. states can convene themselves; the others only on dates specified in the constitution or at the call of the governor. This inability to convene or to determine session length weakens legislative ability to check and balance executive power.

There is considerable appeal to the ideal of a citizen legislature, a body of amateurs who meet to make policy and go home to "real" jobs. Professionalization depends, conversely, on having a physical presence in the capitol, and on having legislators who know what they are doing. Legislatures work better when a substantial proportion of the members understand parliamentary procedures, know something about the issues being considered, and know each other. "Political tourism," the term Attila Ágh uses to describe the failure of East European parliamentarians to run for reelection, is common in newer democracies and subverts their legislatures' work capacities. These parliaments, "although they are already democratic enough as formally and legally representative bodies . . . are still too volatile or 'fluid' and, for this reason, are not yet performing well." They "have been 'filled' from cycle to cycle with 'first generation type' MPs who start their political learning process almost from the same departure point, always anew."[11]

At the other extreme are legislatures such as the U.S. House of Representatives where turnover rates average less than 15 percent, and the median representative is entering his or her ninth year of service. A strong "term limits" movement has been ruled unconstitutional as it applies to Congress, but it has been implemented with regard to a number of subnational offices. The results of these limitations have played to mixed reviews, but there seems little doubt that legislatures with high rates of incumbency return are less dependent upon either the executive branch or private association lobbyists than are low-turnover institutions. Constitutions, such as that of Costa Rica, which limit parliamentarians to one term, virtually guarantee weak legislatures. More subtle ways of discouraging legislative tenure include low salaries and poor working conditions. In U.S. state legislatures, "pay and advancement prospects have been found to be the best predictors of membership stability."[12] Such reward structures clearly distinguish "career" legislatures from "dead ends;" but it also appears as if there are what Squire calls "springboard legislatures," that retain members by promising "access to resources and positions of power needed to advance their political careers."[13] Unitary and parliamentary systems serve this function better than those in federal or separation of powers systems where parallel career ladders, through state, local, and national executive branch positions in effect "compete" with legislative careers.

> In most parliamentary systems . . . only one political career ladder exists. The jobs at the top of the ladder are all in the cabinet (that is, in the executive branch); but the only way to reach the top of the ladder is by starting to climb it at the bottom (that is, in the legislative branch). In most parliamentary systems in order to become prime minister or a leading member of the cabinet one has to become, and remain, a member of the legislature. In this way, all of a country's political talent is sucked into the country's parliamentary assembly, even though the assembly itself might not be very important.[14]

Constitutions provide some markers on the road to office: citizenship requirements are nearly universal; and while most constitutions use the same minimum age for office as for voting, a significant number require MPs to be at least twenty-five, thirty, or in a few cases, thirty-five. A number of parliaments exclude members of the military, civil servants, those with criminal records, and, in a few cases, members of certain ethnic or political groups. Despite efforts to encourage diversity, parliamentarians are almost invariably older, wealthier, more male, and more reflective of large ethnic and religious groups than the general population.

There is no compelling reason to believe that an elderly, rich, majority male cannot represent the interests of the young, the poor, or whatever. Nor do those with appropriate descriptive characteristics always represent the interests of their class, clan, or gender. But "descriptive representatives . . . who possess mutual relationships with their constituents . . . provide that group with a stake in politics."[15] And there is a growing consensus that "the extent to which a politics of presence can include those who have been systematically excluded from political life is also the extent to which a politics of presence can bolster democratic participation and the legitimacy of democratic institutions."[16] Ethnic set asides and electoral rules that favor groups concentrated in particular geographic areas are of variable effectiveness, dependent, as argued in chapter 2, on a matrix of historic and socioeconomic variables. The dimension of descriptive representation that resonates around the world is that of gender. Despite recent attempts to increase their parliamentary representation, only about 6,000, or 15 percent, of the world's 40,000 plus lower house parliamentarians are women. Not a single parliament has a female majority. The top three countries are Rwanda (49 percent), Sweden (45 percent), and Denmark (38 percent), but there are seven with zero and the median for 176 national legislatures in 2004 was 11.5 percent.[17]

Women, and presumably other political minorities, tend to be more successful in electoral systems using proportional representation,[18] which allows

> for multiple candidates to be elected from the same party in a given district. This facilitates parties nominating candidates of both genders. . . . Indeed, in a PR system a party can actually go so far as to institute quotas, as was first done on a broad basis in Norway. If a party fails to nominate many women this is much more visible to the average voter than in single-member systems. Finally, since the success of new, smaller parties is much greater in a PR system, if the traditional parties do not nominate many women, both the reality of, and the threat of, forming a new women's party are far greater.[19]

Some of the newer democracies, Indonesia for one, have attempted to impose such quotas on the parties; but if outcomes of the 2004 legislative elections are an indicator, the quotas can be technically met while producing few tangible results.[20] With the best of intentions, the temptation is strong to put better known names and those of incumbents at the top of the party list; and that means mostly men.

Countries in which the symbolic importance of having more women in the legislature is highest are precisely those in which cultural barriers are greatest. And the fact that even the egalitarian societies of the Nordic democracies still have a male to female ratio of nearly two to one suggests that the barriers remain formidable. Even in the absence of quotas, however, it seems likely that "the proportions of women in legislatures will increase steadily but incrementally . . . [and] that at certain times, the proportion of women in legislatures will increase in substantial spurts."[21] But it will almost certainly be a long time in most countries before women are proportionately represented, longer still before they are fully equal.

Organization

Legislatures are organizations. Designed less for efficiency than representation, the "ideal type" legislature contrasts with Weber's model bureaucracy in three ways. First, although some MPs are more powerful than others, there is no formal hierarchy. Second, legislators are not hired or fired according to merit. While party leaders sometimes attempt to purge useless or disruptive MPs, merit is seldom a factor in finding replacements. Partly because of limits on their ability to recruit, legislatures—even in the highly-structured committees of the U.S. Congress—are generally less able than bureaucracies to sustain specialized subunits. Finally, legislatures structure themselves. Constitutions define the general parameters, but the contours of executive power are specified by statute as well. The legislative "division of labor," as Hall puts it, "is not authoritatively imposed. It bubbles up, as it were, from individual members' day-to-day choices about which matters warrant their time, energy, and staff attention."[22]

If legislatures function more to represent constituents than to make policy, the difference between a representative assembly and a true legislature lies in the ability of the latter to participate in making laws. To do this it must organize, and to stand up to the more efficient structure of the bureaucracy, it must organize in ways that, ironically, borrow from the bureaucratic model. Some of the world's smallest legislatures may be able to work effectively simply on the basis of deliberation and consensus. Such "small group" legislatures can be found among the eleven countries with parliaments of fewer than twenty-five members, and even in the seventeen that have between twenty-six and fifty. But the "average" parliament, with a mean of 166 members in its lower house, is too large to be run collegially. Organizational complexity is a necessity in larger bodies, such as the British House of Commons (with 659 MPs), the German Bundestag (603), French Assemblée Nationale (577), or the Grand National Assembly of Turkey (550).[23]

Committees
Bureaucratic emulation begins with professionalization. While MPs cannot expect tenure, they can promote policies that keep themselves in office. Pay and perquisites are part of the package, as are less tangible "intrinsic rewards. . . encompassing the satisfaction that derives from the on-the-job consumption of such things as importance of the position, public admiration and respect for the office, national visibility, influence, power, and public service."[24] The more mature the democracy,

the more likely a career legislature, increasingly dominated by those whose personal ambitions are linked to the institution's effectiveness. Beyond incumbency, development of these capacities combines hierarchy and specialization that parallels the organizational efficiency of the executive branch. Committees provide MPs with a means simultaneously of strengthening the institution and their own place in it. Through specialization, the institution increases its ability to process information and communicate with experts in the bureaucracy and private sector. When a legislature divides its work among committees, moreover, it gains an ability to engage in numerous tasks simultaneously. Where individual members choose their own committees, they gain power in policy areas they care about. They may not fully match the specialized knowledge of full-time civil servants, but they are often, *more* knowledgeable than the ministers to whom civil servants report.

> Executives throughout the democratic world have added departments and personnel whenever the need has arisen. In the legislatures, on the other hand, the number of members rarely rises—and never due to the pressure of an increased workload. The only response the legislative branch can offer, in order to effectively influence, scrutinize, and control the executive, is to improve the efficiency with which its membership is utilized. This includes the use of staff and experts, but more significantly it means to rationalize and adapt committees.[25]

Although sometimes subordinate to party control, strong committees provide ancillary benefits. Their small-group atmosphere is better suited to deliberation and compromise than more visible, scripted, and formal plenary sessions. Junior members gain leadership training, and, as Shaw puts it, "are indoctrinated into political norms and prepared for roles in the political system, inside and outside the legislature. Values and constraints are learned and political skill, visibility and prestige are acquired."[26] Finally, committees contribute to the civic culture by enhancing access to the process "by citizens, interest groups, civil servants, and political executives. This occurs," Shaw suggests, "when written or oral evidence is contributed to committees and when informal interactions take place. . . . The utility of such a contribution to the governmental process can easily be underestimated. It provides a distinctive type of linkage between government and the people."[27]

If committees are playing an increasingly important role in world legislatures, what is perhaps most surprising is just how subordinate a role they tend to play. Nowhere have they attained the importance of those in the United States, where, "the committee system," as Lees and Shaw argued in 1976, "is not only the strongest system in the present study; it is *by far* the strongest. . . . in some ways a deviant case."[28] Despite considerable convergence in recent years as party leaders have become increasingly assertive in the United States, and committees more important in other systems, American exceptionalism is still the rule. The ability of committees to call upon expert witnesses, deliberate the details of legislation, and amend both government and individual bills has grown in most systems; but nowhere are committees as well-staffed or have the same stability of membership and as active a role in making public policy. Committees in only four of seventeen European parliaments studied by Döring could initiate bills or subpoena government documents; and only eight have the power to amend.[29] The committee system of the Japanese Diet, though modeled on that of the United States, has never emerged as a significant force. There, as in most parliamentary systems, particularly in those dominated by a single party, ministerial control tends, through party discipline, to trump committee power.

For many years, party- and committee-based systems were regarded as contradictory modes of internal organization. One had either "government by the standing committees of the Congress," in Woodrow Wilson's famous phrase, or a system like the British in which the cabinet was thought to be the only committee needed. While U.S. legislative committees are still considerably stronger than those of all other parliamentary bodies, and the British cabinet far more dominant than most, the mix of party and committee powers is far more complicated in most of the world. The balance between these forces, moreover, is seldom stable. With the U.S. Congress, three approaches, roughly paralleling changes in the nature of Congress itself, have successively dominated. In the late 1950s and early 1960s, a distinction was made between the so-called seniority leaders, committee chairs whose positions came from continuous service, and the elected leaders. Under the forceful guidance of Speaker Sam Rayburn and Senate Majority Leader Lyndon Johnson, the policy expertise of committee chairs was harnessed to develop a legislative agenda and balance executive power. Under weaker party leaders in the 1970s, power drifted to a wider array of independent policy entrepreneurs and mid- to high-seniority legislators in a period characterized in most texts as "subcommittee government." Rather than party leaders coordinating the specialized policy work of a few "whales" (as Majority Leader Johnson dubbed the key committee chairs), there was a dispersion of influence to subgovernments. Finally, in a period epitomized by Newt Gingrich's first term as Speaker of a newly Republican House of Representatives in 1994, there was a rather dramatic centralization of power where the party caucuses accorded hierarchical powers to their elected leaders in choosing committee chairs, and bypassing the standing committees in processing legislation. None of these systems was particularly pure: legislative institutions resist dramatic change, and it is clear that however much we emphasize particular aspects of the balance between them, elements of both hierarchy and specialization have continuously competed for control.

Much the same can be said of Great Britain. Not until the 1970s were there any committees of fixed jurisdiction in the House of Commons, or, for that matter, in most parliaments. In 1973, Blondel attributed the "disfavor in which legislative committees have tended to be held in Western European countries" both to the control over procedures exercised by the executive and to the role played by party committees or legislative-executive commissions in the framing of legislative issues.[30] Only in France and Italy were committee deliberations a significant aspect of the legislative process; but their ability to complicate the passage of legislation was specifically limited by the constitution of the Fifth Republic adopted in 1958, and by recent reforms in Italy. By the time of Döring's 1996 survey of European parliaments, however, all eighteen had standing committees, sixteen of them with significant legislative roles.[31]

A number of parliaments, including Britain's, continue to rely largely on temporary, "select" committees to work out the details of particular bills. While these committees usually have marginal powers to modify government proposals, the growing number of parliamentary committees with fixed, long-term jurisdictions often do considerably more. In many newer Eastern European parliaments, budgetary and other key committees were established by formal constitutional clauses. In general, bills introduced by individual members or developed by the cabinet are referred to a committee for consideration. Following U.S. practice, many committees conduct hearings to which they may summon ministers and top civil servants, and, in some cases, issue subpoenas to compel testimony. Committees then proceed to what are called "mark-up" sessions, in which they rewrite draft bills. In separation of powers systems, these marked bills either go directly to the floor or through a screening process (the Committee on Rules in the United States, the Special Committee on Legislation in Bulgaria, or the Portfolio Committee in South Africa) that gives party leaders some ability to screen and schedule committee products before they come to a plenary vote.

In parliamentary systems where bills go to committees first, the cabinet controls committee deliberations through party caucuses. In most of Scandinavia, for example, each party group discusses the positions its members will take in committee. In the German Bundestag there are actual parallel structures of party and parliamentary committees, both structured along policy lines. Although there is "genuine give-and take on substantive points" in the official committees, party groups almost always meet first to determine both policy and tactics. These party groups, moreover, "form subcommittees, receive written testimony, meet with civil servants, ministers, and spokesmen for interest groups, and are aided by small staffs."[32]

It would be misleading to describe the German or Scandinavian systems as "committee dominated" in anything like the sense in which it was once common to speak of subcommittee government in the U.S. House. But the once-firm notion that strong committees were found only in separation-of-powers settings is no longer viable. In a number of presidential systems, conversely, party discipline is firmly enough exercised to make committees basically marginal to the overall process. This seems to be particularly true in newer legislatures where turnover rates are high, committees understaffed, and the kinds of policy specializations that are at the root of committee power are consequently underdeveloped. Where committees are strong, the "challenge of legislative organization," as Krehbiel puts it, "is to capture gains from specialization while minimizing the degree to which enacted policies deviate from majority-preferred outcomes."[33] For while strong committees clearly enhance the legislature's ability to act, they can also distort the policy process through "collective action dilemmas," in which the rational behavior of individual politicians seeking to get more for their constituents can result in group decisions that leave everybody unhappy. Committees intensify these tensions by institutionalizing policy fragmentation. "Biased" committees, stacked with disproportionate numbers from, say, agricultural or maritime districts are protected by norms of comity and reciprocity that "make it difficult for non-committee members to monitor committee behavior."[34] Committee members may also bargain among themselves to give particular benefits to their own local districts.[35]

Even without committees, the half dozen or so "micro" legislatures in which the cabinet seldom meets as a separate group have often been unable to establish clear policy priorities. The absence of "firm party loyalties" or strong executive powers in the small legislatures of many Pacific democracies, for example, "has driven successive prime ministers to the distribution of political patronage in their effort to win and retain their parliamentary majorities,"[36] and contributed to high levels of government instability. Where there is no separate executive to set priorities and exercise veto powers, most legislatures discipline themselves through strong parties. Even some of the world's smallest parliaments, such as that of St. Kitts and Nevis with fifteen MPs, have elaborated structures of party leadership.

Legislative Parties

The struggle for legislative power reflects a tension similar to that which pervades bureaucracy: whether the locus of power should flow largely down from policy generalists to experts in implementation, or up from policy experts to those whose job is to coordinate the technical decisions of specialized units. In the debate over the 1979 decision by the British House of Commons strengthen its committees, two normally divergent MPs, Labourite Michael Foot and Conservative Enoch Powell, both cautioned against allowing too much specialization to destroy what Foot called "the distinctive qualities of the British House of Commons."[37] To transfer the scrutiny of legislation to specialized bodies, they argued, would come at the expense of debate in plenary. In a similar vein, though a different context, then House Speaker Newt Gingrich in 1994 put through a series of rules changes giving him more ways of overseeing and circumventing the work of the standing committees in the U.S. House. He also expressed the hope that the committee system as a whole could be replaced by party task forces.[38] Committees have become a more important part of the process in Great Britain and, since Gingrich's departure, have been gradually reasserting their influence in the United States; but in both parliamentary and presidential systems, the interplay between parties as centralizing forces and committee-based forces of decentralization define the locus of institutional power.

The case for cohesive parties rests on the premise that public policy should essentially be founded in the will of the majority which "can best be established by popular choice between and control over alternative responsible political parties; for only such parties can provide the coherent, unified sets of rulers who will assume collective responsibility to the people for the manner in which government is carried on."[39] This is not the place for an extensive discussion of the conceptual problems hidden in this seemingly simple statement. From an organizational perspective, however, party-dominated legislatures and committee-dominant legislators differ in large part in the ways in which they "solve" the problem of representation. From one perspective representation can be viewed "almost exclusively in terms of a particular legislator and the constituency that elected that legislator; conversely, representation can be though of in terms of institutions collectively representing a society or people."[40] A system of independent committees, by making the legislature more responsive to specialized constituencies, may thus undermine the institution's ability to represent broader majorities. Party government restores the power of national majorities at the expense of strong minorities, and the connections between individual representatives.

Most legislatures balance these systems. In party-dominant legislatures, party cohesion depends in part upon the abilities of party leaders to satisfy the policy demands of rank-and-file party members. A parliamentarian from a district needing a new highway, who might work through the members of the public works committee in the U.S. Congress, shifts his or her focus to the appropriate minister in a parliamentary system. It is more difficult to trace the locus of influence in these kinds of exchanges, but there is little doubt that logrolling and favor trading are not the exclusive provenance of separation-of-powers legislatures. "Party discipline may be partially the product of anticipated reaction—that is, leaders deciding not to propose policies that they know their followers will oppose,"[41] and—it need hardly be added—of proposing policies their followers would like them to propose.

In theory it should be possible to rank legislatures along a continuum of the leadership's abilities to enforce discipline. In practice it is difficult to know the extent to which party cohesion is achieved by agreement or force. The ultimate tool, known in Britain as withholding the whip, or denying a candidate a place on the party's ballot, is not always available to party leaders; cumbersome in the sense that it can only be used once; and may backfire by allowing the martyred MP to beat the party's new candidate anyway. Of far greater importance is the ability continually and in the short run to reward cooperation. From cabinet positions to committee chairmanships, and appointments to attend international conferences and fund local projects, the reward structure in parliamentary regimes winds through party leaders, particularly those in the governing coalition. In presidential systems, the executive has a similar variety of favors to exchange for votes on its legislative program. What Brazilians call *emperguismo*, "creating public sector jobs for political purposes," has become so common in much of Latin America as to weaken "the legislature's ability as a collegial body to develop coherent public policy alternatives."[42] Constitutions and legislatures can restrict the administration's ability to negotiate these kinds of deals by, for example, limiting executive control over resource allocations, limiting patronage, or giving the executive few resources for negotiating. But executive influence in both parliamentary and presidential systems almost invariably becomes a favor-trading game.

The ability of presidents and prime ministers to play these games has strong institutional foundations. In presidential systems, most chief executives and many department heads have offices dedicated to legislative liaison. The U.S. president's Office of Management and Budget also serves as an office of central clearance for policy and routinely articulates the president's position. When the president's party controls the House or Senate, it is rare for a committee to schedule action on a bill until it has been cleared by OMB. Presidents, however, seldom have the kinds of controls over legislative institutions that prime ministers enjoy. In the most centralized systems, the government can also call upon lesser party officers, usually including a party "whip" system whose functions is to assure member attendance and encourage them to vote the party line. Some countries rely almost entirely upon the whip systems to maintain party cohesion. In others, informal communications or regular meetings of party members serve the same function.

Legislative party institutions tend to be similar though less elaborate in presidential systems; the crucial difference being that they are to some degree independent of the executive. Thus even when the president and a legislative majority are of the same party, presidents often find themselves having to negotiate with their fellow partisans in the legislature, negotiations that can be difficult in systems that do not elect the president and the legislature in concurrent elections. The president's party almost always loses legislative seats in midterm. While such elections can serve as useful correctives, they are more likely to produce deadlock and instability. Shugart and Carey argue that nonconcurrent elections are undesirable in presidential systems absent the "institutional means of reconstituting the government" that one finds in mixed premier-president regimes.[43]

Rules

"It is much more material that there should be a rule to go by than what that rule is," Thomas Jefferson wrote in his manual of rules for the U.S. House of Representatives.[44] Rules, at the same time, bias outcomes for the legislature in general, and, within the legislature, that optimize the influence of individual members. Committees have a tendency to do both, giving a larger number of individual MPs access to power and providing organizational vehicles for its exercise. But if "strong committees . . . are at least a necessary condition for effective parliamentary influence in the policy-making process,"[45] their ultimate roles depend as much upon the rules of the legislative game as on their organizational capacities. They are strongest when the rules require committee consideration of all bills; when they have the power to summon witnesses and mark-up bills; and when they have some control over plenary consideration of bills under each committee's jurisdiction.

The ability of party leaders to control the policy outputs of legislatures is also shaped in part by the flexibility allowed them in setting the legislative agenda. Using the U.S. House as an example, Cox and McCubbins make a convincing case that party leaders shape policies less by influencing the ways in which members vote than determining what they vote on.[46] Such control tends to be far more extensive in parliamentary systems in which the cabinet decides essentially what bills come to the floor and when, what will be debated and put to a decision on any given day, and what kinds of amendments can be proposed. In the most restrictive systems, only the cabinet can introduce a bill. This does not mean that back-benchers are totally impotent when it comes to putting their ideas on the table, only that they must sell them to party leaders if they hope to put them in play.

Many constitutions give the executive branch more power to shape certain aspects of the legislative agenda, such as treaties and budget bills, than others. Döring has identified six more general agenda setting prerogatives in seventeen European parliaments.[47] Control is most centralized in Greece, where the governing coalition has access to all six. To begin, the government has nearly complete control over the plenary agenda. An elected committee, dominated by the majority, "examines the legislative business for the coming week, determines the duration of debates, and decides which issues are to be debated."[48] The majority can also juggle committee memberships and end debate. Individual MPs are restricted in their ability to initiate legislation, and cannot increase appropriations. At the other European extreme, "Executive-parliamentary relations in Sweden are a mixture of cooperation and conflict, with a strong tradition of bargaining between parties. MPs are engaged in preparing government proposals for decision, proposing motions on an individual basis, and presenting questions to ministers."[49]

Döring notes that "the rich nuances of different countries' peculiarities cannot be measured" by formal powers. The Greek cabinet's control of the agenda is only as strong as its ability to hold the allegiance of backbenchers; and cohesive majorities in Sweden can push through almost any legislative package they bring to the floor, and indeed often do. In separation of powers and semi-presidential systems there is a similar range of central agenda control. Where a cohesive party controls the presidency and a legislative majority, the system can resemble, as it long did in Mexico, a cabinet-dominated parliament in which all legislation originated in the executive branch and was enacted without amendment. But the Mexican president's power, unlike the Greek premier's, was more political than constitutional. There are presidential systems in which the formal powers of the chief executive approach those of the Greek cabinet, but they are increasingly rare. In Latin America in particular, presidents retain the power to initiate the budget and most major legislation, but they have lost control over the legislature's ability to debate, amend, and sometimes significantly modify these initiatives.

The minute-to-minute management of legislative business—strongly shaped by the cabinet in parliamentary systems—is usually conducted by an elected, non-ministerial MP. In the Westminster model, the speaker is essentially nonpartisan, "elected to the chair because he has taken no prominent part in controversy."[50] The Speaker of the U.S. House, conversely, while expected to be fair, is also emphatically leader of the majority party. The ironic reversal here is that the British system, in which the substantive agenda is most tightly controlled, is among the most open to backbenchers in daily debate. By formal rule or tradition in most legislatures the speaker never speaks but decides who does. Debate is controlled both to maintain order and to set time limits on talking so that decisions can be made.

The need for a method of ending debate was famously manifest in the U.S. Senate when President Woodrow Wilson's opponents, though lacking the votes to block the Treaty of Versailles, talked it to death. Shortly thereafter, the Senate adopted a "cloture" rule allowing a two-thirds majority (later changed to 60 percent) to end debate; but even at 60 percent the Senate's tradition of unlimited debate (know as a "filibuster") is, to my knowledge, unique among world legislatures. In effect it raises the number of votes needed for the Senate to act;[51] but it also makes the Senate what is, with respect to presidential power, the most powerful legislature in the world. Only four of the European legislatures examined by Döring allow a parliamentary majority to extend debate.[52] Gag rules, not filibusters, are the norm.

Many legislatures routinely use voting methods that hide member records from the public. While the U.S. founders specified that "each house shall keep a journal of its proceedings," and include "the yeas and nays of the members" at the request of one fifth of them, a surprising number of legislatures vote by methods such as voice votes that are nearly impossible to trace, or by such methods as a show of hands that are not of public record. Sometimes the order of voting can influence their relative likelihood of passing an amendment or bill, and practices differ widely.[53] A determined majority can, in most legislatures, reset the government's agenda; but party discipline generally tightens on procedural votes and the number of members who know how to mount such challenges is usually small. The importance of legislative rules such as these have made it increasingly likely that they will receive some attention in constitutions, particularly those that aspire to transparency. Few of the basic perquisites of democratic government can be guaranteed absent public access to the full records of the legislature.

Bicameralism

Of the 171 legislatures listed in a 2003 guide, more than a third (36 percent) were bicameral.[54] Most of the "upper" houses in these two-chamber legislatures, like Britain's House of Lords, are largely symbolic. Often sites of lively debate, they have little formal authority. Only a handful of constitutions, mostly in the Americas, give basically equal powers to two chambers. In the asymmetric bicameralism of most systems, the "lower" house, usually popularly elected, has a stronger role. "Upper" house powers range from the dilatory and advisory powers of the Mexican Senate to the formal (if seldom used) veto power of the Dutch Eerste Kamer.

Early "upper" houses had their origins, like the House of Lords, in a tradition of according special status to the "upper" classes from which they were drawn. The U.S. Senate derived from a different model, based on the so-called great compromise which balanced the arguments of large states for representation by population with the smaller states case for representation for each state. The U.S. model has become, with few exceptions, the paradigm for bicameral systems in which "upper" house represents local entities as opposed to "lower" houses based on population. A third model, in which two chambers are drawn from essentially identical constituencies, is difficult to justify. Particularly where parties are strong, and both houses have similar constituencies, "upper" houses are either marginal or redundant. As one classic text argues, "The persistence of bicameralism in nonfederal systems is a remarkable example of the tenacity of organizational forms well after their original purpose has disappeared."[55] Thus although South Africa and a number of Eastern Europe democracies have installed bicameral legislatures, most have not. Where Blondel found "almost half the countries in the world" having two houses, or 52 of 108 in 1971, the current ratio has dropped to 62 of 171.[56] Nine countries that were originally bicameral by tradition or colonial heritage, beginning with New Zealand in 1950, and including Denmark (1954), Kenya (1966), Sweden (1971), Portugal (1976), Zimbabwe (1990), Iceland (1991), Peru (1992), and Venezuela (1999), have abolished their upper houses.

The continuing exceptions are the U. S. states where the Supreme Court ruled in 1964 that seats in *both* houses of the state legislatures must be apportioned solely on the basis of equal population.[57] The forty-nine states that have retained two-house legislatures (Nebraska has not) stand virtually alone among world legislatures in having two generally equal legislative bodies with neither diverse constituencies nor disciplined parties. This persistence of bicameralism seems to be based on tradition, the reluctance of upper houses members to vote themselves out of jobs, and a belief that it serves to improve the quality of legislation by adding impediments to precipitous action. "It doubles the security of the people," Madison wrote in the *Federalist,* "by requiring the concurrence of two distinct bodies in schemes of usurpation or perfidy."[58] Despite frequent repetition of this argument, it is not by any means an open and shut case. Two houses are going to disagree, but it is also likely that a more diverse group of legislators will have more ideas. "Thus, any conclusion regarding the *net* effect of second chambers on legislative production must take into account not only the effect of the second chambers' *veto* power, but also the effect of the second chambers' *origination* power."[59] It must also consider the norms of reciprocity that often develop in legislatures and make cooperation rather than conflict characteristic of inter-chamber relations. Roger's data on the U.S. states show no tendency for bicameralism to reduce the volume of legislation, and throws considerable "doubt on the widespread belief that bicameralism is necessarily a 'conservative' institution, in the sense of reducing overall legislative production."[60]

In Latin America, it has been argued that bicameralism tends to produce deadlocks that increase the risk of the government failure. While this argument apparently won the day in both Venezuela and Peru when they abolished their senates, defenders of the upper house raised important questions. In an interesting twist on the notion that bicameralism serves as a restraint on executive power, Victor Combellas, a member of the Venezuelan constituent assembly, suggested that the opposite might be true when a swing of control to the opposition in a unicameral system, "in midterm elections, for example— spells a head-on clash between the branches, whereas bicameralism holds out the possibility that the president can triangulate, building alliances with legislators in the less hostile chamber. By providing a lifeline for an embattled president, then, bicameralism might encourage negotiation and moderation."[61] Governors in the U.S. states have long understood this process.

Legislative outcomes in bicameral systems often depend on the rules that regulate relations between the two houses. Not surprisingly, cabinet systems that generally vest the power cabinet dissolution in the lower house, have closer linkages. Some systems minimize inter-house friction by sharply distinguishing the legislative responsibilities of each chamber. One of the more interesting two-house legislatures is that of Germany where bicameralism is an integral part of the federal system. The upper house, or Bundesrat, is comprised of local government officials, and its jurisdiction is limited to issues that involve provincial concerns. The framers of Germany's basic law apparently anticipated that only about 10 percent of all national statutes would invoke local issues important enough to require approval by the Bundesrat; but in practice bargaining between the legal committees of both houses and various court decisions have enabled the upper house to wield power over closer to 60 percent.[62] Because of stronger party controls, the upper house in Austria—similar in composition and formal role to the German Bundesrat—has had much less influence.

Absent the kind of veto power exercised in Great Britain where the lower house can simply override the upper, there must be a method for reconciling differences between the houses. The most common and cumbersome procedure is a process of reciprocal amendment in which modified bills ping-pong back and forth until both houses adopt the same language. Sixteen percent of the laws enacted in one session of the U.S. Congress went back and forth in this manner three times; almost 4 percent, four times; and in one case, involving an oil and gas bill in 1982, it took seven tries before the House and Senate could agree.[63] In the majority of bicameral systems this process, supplemented by informal negotiations, is the only sanctioned method for coming to an inter-house agreement. Known as the *navette* (or shuttle) in France, the process can be ended by cabinet intervention to create a conference committee comprised of members from both houses, chosen by party leaders, and drawn as a rule from members of the committees that considered the original bills. The U.S. Congress and most American state legislatures also make extensive use of conference committees whose agreements are then reported back to the each house for final approval.

All but one of the fifty-three bicameral legislatures examined by Tsebelis and Money made use of navettes in cases of inter-house disagreements; but only twenty-eight made use of conference committees. Seven used joint sessions of the two houses, and about half gave the deciding vote in the case of continuing disagreement to the lower house. The rules in many systems were even more favorable to lower houses on budget bills.[64] Still, what is perhaps most surprising is the extent to which—even in cabinet systems—the two houses come to the bargaining table with substantially equal authority. Cohesive parties, as we have noted, can overwhelm the process and allow the majority coalition's position to prevail. In Germany, for example, when strong party coalitions replaced less-disciplined cabinets, it "not only decreased the length of interchamber conflict. . . but they also made the bicameral checks and balances disappear."[65] Even in cases such as these, however, and in many cases where the rules allow the lower house ultimately to prevail, the very existence of a second house can change the strategic balance. We do not know in the German case, for example, the extent to which cabinets may have considered the preferences of members of the Bundesrat in preparing their legislative programs.

In sum, the effects of bicameralism are greatest when the two houses differ in composition; to the extent that they are equal in power; and to the extent that strong parties cannot override differences. Even absent these qualities, second chambers matter. The relatively toothless House of Lords can embarrass the government, or even force it to reconsider legislation: its amendments, indeed, "are usually accepted by the Commons."[66] More important, the second house's *potential* for later action enters into the calculations of what the first house will propose. Bicameralism, in this sense, is associated with the consensus model of democracy, forcing a broader coalition and thus, presumably, offering greater protection to minorities. But two houses also provide two arenas in which to inject new ideas. In presidential systems, it may increase distributive policies as three players (both houses and the chief executive) vie for approval by topping rather than blocking initiatives.

The danger of deadlock is severe when a parliamentary government confronts an independent upper house. In 1975, the Australian senate refused to pass the cabinet's appropriation bills. Crisis was averted by intervention of the governor-general on what Sartori calls "dubious legal grounds,"[67] not available in most systems. Whether the Australian experience was unique, Lijphart's suggestion that differences between "two mutually hostile majorities" can be avoided by the consociational formation an oversized coalition cabinet[68] is oversimple at best. In parliamentary systems, Sartori's argument that symmetric bicameralism is "a macroscopic instance of ill-conceived constitutionalism"[69] is more widely accepted. But whatever the arguments with regard to parliamentary systems, many of which have disempowered their upper houses, bicameralism is and will continue to be norm in large, presidential democracies, particularly those with federal systems.

The Functions of the Legislature

Conventional wisdom during the Cold War, when emphases on stability dominated both the study and practice of comparative politics, was that legislatures should be peripheral to policy making. Except perhaps in linking citizens with government, debating domestic priorities, and holding bureaucrats accountable, legislatures were to take a back seat to the more efficient and better-informed governing core of the executive branch. There has, however, been a revival of appreciation for the roles played by parliamentarians in presidential and cabinet systems. Because these "powers" derive from elections and other exogenous forces, it is virtually impossible to measure the power of a legislature. Capabilities differ widely. This makes it difficult to develop a taxonomy of legislatures,[70] but all the more important to recognize the ways in which they differ in their ability to perform basic functions.

Personal Representation

Broadly speaking, legislators "represent" their constituents in virtually everything they do. They personally represent by who they are, what they do for individuals, and how they express constituency views. Constituent service—from tours of the capitol to patronage and help with the bureaucracy—is a function familiar to many legislators; especially in systems with single-member districts. Relatively small, single-member districts encourage a politics of service in which legislators enhance their reelection chances and fulfill their representative roles less through ideology and party than through parochial and individualistic activities.

At its best, "casework," where legislators intervene with the bureaucracy on behalf of aggrieved constituents provides "a kind of appeals process for bureaucratic decisions." From the perspective of legislators, it is both "an important political asset" and "inherently satisfying to help people in these ways, where the results are frequently more immediate and tangible than in legislative work."[71] Even in Britain, where parties discourage particularism, recent interviews "found that over two thirds of the members listed 'constituency work' as their major job."[72] No legislature has refined the art more thoroughly than the U.S. House of Representatives, where some offices handle as many as 500 "casework" items a week.[73] As much as such service personalizes government, it can also distort the representative relationship by making public policies less equitable, and protecting incumbents through activities that have little to do with issues.[74]

Following the lead of Sweden, a number of countries have established a separate office of "ombudsman" to depoliticize interventions with the bureaucracy. By 1981 there were nineteen national ombudsman, and at least fifty regional and local offices responding to constituent complaints,[75] and the number has grown substantially. There are now thousands of such offices for governments, international agencies, and even private corporations. In parliamentary systems in particular, the advantage of such independent offices is that they are not constrained by party loyalty; neither, however, do they have the power to back complaints with action. The result, in the apt analogy of one study of developing nations is that the office of ombudsmen, while not very effective at hunting lions "can certainly swat a lot of flies."[76] Lion killing, in this sense, probably depends upon the ability—which ombudsmen do not have—to use their cumulative findings of bureaucratic error to pursue legislative remedies. Members of the U.S. Congress and its state legislatures frequently cite the importance of constituency complaints in guiding their oversight of how the laws are being implemented. The underlying question of whether a legislator best "represents" his or her constituency when acting narrowly on its behalf or broadly as an aspect of the nation as a whole is of perennial interest. In rational choice terms, personal favors are poor foundations for law. But to constrain legislators from dealing directly with constituency concerns is both to disconnect citizens from their government and to weaken the role of the legislature. As Mustapic argues with regard to Argentina, the legislature's "concentration on microinitiatives," rightly "tarred in text-books . . . is still an indicator of the representative function that legislators carry out as part of the relations that they maintain with the social fabric."[77] But excessive parochialism can also distort legislative priorities and the nature of the represent-ative relationship. If individual legislators cultivate followings based on personal services rather than policy, how democratic is the system? The issue is particularly pointed in cabinet systems that depend on party discipline. If the rise of party voting in Britain signaled the decreasing importance of the individual MP, it is possible that the opposite might happen if MPs are given the resources to develop individual ties with their constituents. "Increase the level of the personal vote, and the shape of parliamentary institutions will change to accommodate it, party cohesion will decline, and policy making will decentralize."[78]

The Informing Function

In Woodrow Wilson's view, "even more important than legislation is the instruction and guidance in political affairs which the people might receive from a body which kept all national concerns suffused in a broad daylight of discussion."[79] Wilson thought the U.S. Congress deficient in this regard because most of its real deliberations took place in the relatively closed chambers of its committees. No matter how well-informed members of committees might become, the point of information, in Wilson's view, was less to improve the technical quality of legislation than to inform the public on national issues through plenary deliberation.

To have a truly deliberative body, legislators need parliamentary immunity and access to a free press. It is important that there be records of debate, and a growing number of legislatures also provide full television coverage. Rules of parliamentary procedure designed to give a veneer of civility to controversy are designed to blunt the edge of controversy and encourage tolerance. But while it is almost axiomatic that the better and more thoroughly issues are debated, the better it is for democracy, debate can be polarizing as well as uniting. No matter how civil the rules, it seldom changes minds. Experienced legislators can count on the fingers of one hand the occasions in which parliamentary debate has changed votes. In fact the role of debate in politics is usually more that of reinforcing and explaining differences than of seeking consensus. Nor, in an age of mass media, is there any assurance that legislative debate will reach the public in any meaningful form. But if one takes the simple proposition that an informed decision is better than one founded in ignorance, and that in some long-range sense, wisdom will prevail, the case for open debate is a slam dunk. The question is, how can it best be conducted?

In a vague echo of Wilson, some students of constitutional democracy argue that parliamentary systems are superior to presidential, which focus "on individual persons who are candidates for the unipersonal center of power, instead of focusing on public ideals or substantive proposals."[80] But if deliberation in the U.S. Congress seldom provides the focus of the British House of Commons, the technical, less visible exchanges between senior committee members and bureaucrats in a congressional hearing are generally more informed and informative. Debate in a fragmented system seldom educates the general public in the ways that it can in a parliamentary system; but it probably has a greater overall impact on public policy.
.

Lawmaking

The word legislature comes from the Latin *legis latio,* lawmaking. In a general sense those assemblies named for their lawmaking powers tend to be more powerful than those known as parliaments. But the distinction between talking and doing is not easily sustained, particularly since legislative power is generally derivative and frequently depends upon others—bureaucrats, chief executives, private interests—to craft the laws it promulgates. The lawmaking function of the legislature is measured by the nature and extent of its processing activities and the extent to which it is the forum in which the balances between competing claims are weighed.

Constraints on this power come both at the initiation stage where constitutional structures or strictures prohibit legislative action and at the enforcement stage where they can be rendered nugatory. Many legislatures, as we have seen, are constitutionally barred from reviewing certain kinds of executive actions; and in many parliaments the government has control over the agenda. This is particularly likely to be the case in cabinet systems, but many South American presidents also have the sole power to initiate legislation in certain areas. More subtle constraints on lawmaking powers occur where constitutional rules, traditions, or political realities require the legislature to defer. Besides such obvious cases as those involving deference to state governments in federal systems, a number of constitutions vest quasi-legislative powers in institutions such as central banks. At the same time, all legislatures are more powerful today than a century ago simply because governments are more involved in the lives of citizens. The extension of the welfare state marked a quantum leap in the scope of the political in most democracies. Less noticed, but perhaps the greatest leap in the scope of legislative rule-making came about in a turn of the century shift toward statute law, most clearly manifest in the subnational governments of the United States. The change was not as dramatic in what are referred to as "code" rather than common law countries. But the shift toward statute law in Anglo-American democracies left in its wake a sea change in the ways in which the roles of legislatures are generally perceived. Law began increasingly to be seen not just as a means of establishing specific rules or dealing with particular controversies, but as a systematic attempt to furnish general rules for any new issues that might arise. This shift both broadened the scope of legislation and established what one legal scholar calls the "open-door" principle of legislative jurisdiction. Unlike the courts, which can only decide cases brought by litigants, "the legislature is free to make its own judgments as to what matters are suitable for legislative consideration. And the novelty of a proposal for legislation, or the fact that it will change prior common or statute law, raises no legal barrier to its adoption."[81] There is simply no way the modern welfare state could have emerged absent this shift from the common law paradigm.

Paradoxically, the growth of statute law has also produced a reversion of power back to the courts, to some extent, and to executive agencies even more. The power to fill in the details of legislation is increasingly delegated either by specific authorization, or by statutes that so vague as to leave it to others to provide finished rules. Legal challenges to such delegations are occasionally mounted, and still flame academic ire, but they are an almost universally-accepted part of the legislative process in democracies throughout the world. The growing challenge for legislators is to maintain a sufficient degree of supervision and control over these delegated powers to sustain the principle of legislative supremacy.

Oversight

Hierarchy works best when information flows up through the chain of command not out; when executives know what is happening from within their organizations rather than from outside. Bureaucracies are secretive. When legislatures delegate powers to bureaucracies, therefore, it is not always easy for them to find out how they are being implemented. Yet the increasingly broad scope of modern legislation makes even more trenchant Woodrow Wilson's argument that "vigilant oversight of administration" is "quite as important as law-making."[82] "Reviewing and investigating the conduct of lower-level administrative agencies is the type of legislative activity," as David Olson has noted, that even "dictatorships are likely to permit."[83] The question is, how best can such inquiries be conducted, by whom, and reaching how high into the administration?

There are a number of methods by which legislatures, their committees, or individual members can conduct oversight activities. One recent survey of eighty-two countries found two methods in use in 95 percent: committee hearings and oral or written formal questions.[84] The ways in which these tools are used vary. Committee hearings are the most regularly-used forums in the U.S. Congress, with hardly a legislative day going by without some ten to fifteen House and Senate committees engaged in formal inquiries. Whether there is an "innate disposition of the Congress to concentrate on administrative details rather than on basic issues of public policy,"[85] there is probably more committee oversight in the U.S. than in any other world legislature. Congress, on the other hand, has almost no mechanisms—as a plenary body—for questioning the administration. Unlike the British prime minister, who must face the Commons weekly for a formal question hour, the president of the United States never opens his or her office to direct questions from Congress or its committees. Committees in the House of Commons are becoming more assertive: for example, its Public Administration Committee in 2003 not only investigated the civil service system, but drafted its own bill for parliamentary action. Despite such newer uses of committees in the United Kingdom, oversight is far less specialized there, and in most parliamentary systems, than it is in the United States. The ultimate power of investigation, the ability to subpoena testimony, gives Congress a power which few other legislatures enjoy, but it is a power that seldom extends to the cabinet level. It is both the greatest weakness and the greatest strength of the U.S. Congress that it participates so actively in the day-to-day workings of the government. It is almost certainly the only world legislature "in which members of Congress and senior civil servants report more frequent contacts with one another than with department heads."[86] Through its well-staffed subcommittees, oversight is highly routinized in contrast with most other legislatures where, as Blondel puts it, "it seems to be used mainly when grave incidents have occurred and only rarely in relation to matters of intermediate importance concerning the day-to-day activities of the administration."[87]

Many world parliaments enjoy the power of what is called "interpellation," which empowers individual members to question ministers. The possibility that interpellation might serve as a sort of written equivalent of the British Question Hour has, however, seldom been realized. More typically, as in South Korea,

"Cabinet ministers often do not seem to provide sincere answers to the questions raised. Interpellation remains tedious and unmoving, no more than a blunt warning against executive mismanagement."[88] In some systems, casework provides a low-level equivalent of interpellation. Even in Britain, MPs are increasingly likely to go directly to lower level civil servants to solve individual problems rather than work through formal questions to the appropriate ministers. In well-staffed legislatures, oversight can also be achieved through laws requiring periodic reports. In 1989, one committee in the U.S. House received 278 mandated reports on how various agencies were administering their programs. The importance of these reports may be more in their crafting than in their contents, as they are not widely read; but the possibility "that some staffperson or lobbyist somewhere will sniff out the significant information and spread it" may make such reports effective.[89]

Pelizzo and Stapenhurst conclude that legislatures in parliamentary systems generally have more oversight tools than those in presidential, though they caution that a few tools used well provide more actual control than many that are unused.[90] There is also a distinction in the kinds of oversight provided by highly fragmented systems epitomized by the U.S. Congress, on the one hand, and the plenary pattern of the U.K. House of Commons and its progeny. Many of the differences between systems are also reflective of the general legislative powers of the legislatures in question, and, most important, in their control of government finances.

The Power of the Purse

"The power of the purse," as Richard Fenno wrote in his watershed study of the House Appropriations Committee, "is the historic bulwark of legislative authority. The exercise of that power constitutes the core legislative process—underpinning all other legislative decisions and regulating the balance of influence between the legislative and executive branches of government."[91] Although the U.S. Congress has delegated large chunks of control over the budget to the executive branch, the Constitution clearly vests the power of raising and spending money in the legislature. Congress, through its committees, frequently uses its appropriation power very specifically to direct just how each dollar will be spent; and, even when funds are not specifically earmarked, it is not uncommon for members of the House and Senate to lean on certain agencies in the hope of influencing decisions on where to site highways, military bases, and new post offices; and where not to site waste facilities. Just as important as its exercise of the power of the purse is Congress's ability to threaten an agency with budget cuts or reorganization.

The National Democratic Institute uses a typology developed by Warren Krafckik and Joachim Weaver to categorize the comparative roles of legislatures.[92] At the high end was the U.S. Congress which has the capacity not just to review and modify the executive budget but to bypass it entirely and formulate a budget of its own. Intermediate, or "budget influencing" power, found in Germany, India, the Philippines, and Poland, precludes adoption of a legislative budget, but grants the power to amend or reject. At the lowest level, are those parliaments, including those of Israel and most Commonwealth countries, that have only the power to debate and accept or reject the package. This power need not be trivial, as parliament can theoretically keep rejecting government budgets until it gets one it likes, especially in presidential systems where less disciplined parties combine with checks and balances generally to "encourage members of the legislature to play an active, sometimes adversarial, role vis-à-vis the executive."[93] Budget powers are also more likely to reside in legislatures with committee systems strong enough to provide institutional experts in the details of specific agency programs. And finally, parliaments with coalition cabinets are significantly more likely to play an active role in budgetary politics. One recent study of forty-four mostly-developed democracies found ten with strong constitutional restrictions on legislative amendments to the budget, and another six that allowed no amendments at all; yet nearly two-thirds of the countries studied reported at least minor changes having been made by the legislature in 2003.[94]

In most systems, the budgetary process begins and ends in the office of the chief executive. As governments grow, and budgets become more complex, central control structures become increasingly important. The U.S. Congress in 1921 delegated much of its power to negotiate agency budgets to a White House Office of Management and Budget, some form of which now exists in almost all large democracies (in parliamentary systems it is usually in the office of the Minister of Finance). The document produced by the budget office is generally the starting point for presidential and cabinet consideration, and in modified form goes to the legislature as the government's (or president's) budget. In the early stages of the process, when agencies submit their needs and wish lists to the executive budget office, ministers—particularly in coalition cabinets—and committee members can often exert considerable influence on the bargaining process. More than half of the forty-four national legislatures covered in a recent survey conducted formal pre-budget debates of some kind or another.[95] Many U.S. states precede consideration of the details of the budget with a debate and vote on its fiscal assumptions. In New York, the state senate and assembly both pay independent consultants to provide alternative fiscal assumptions to those of the governor. In Canada the legislature cannot amend the government's budget bill. "This 'all-or-nothing' system entails considerable risk for the government, and it actively seeks to consult with parliament prior to introducing the budget. The government withdraws elements of its budget for which majority support is not assured. Beginning in 1994, the Pre-Budget Consultation process was institutionalized in order to enhance transparency and allow the public to participate."[96]

Whether institutionalized or not, such consultations are increasingly common even in countries which grant their parliaments no formal powers of amendment.

Whatever their formal powers, however, many legislatures are simply not equipped effectively to evaluate the executive's budget, though this is beginning to change. The Norwegian parliament created a budget secretariat in 1997, the Czech parliament hired its first budget staff in 1998, Hungary and Italy in 1999; and there is a growing tendency for international donors to support parliamentary budget analysts, as the Ford Foundation has in Indonesia. None of these efforts provide close to the nearly 250 employees of the U.S. Congressional Budget Office; but there is a new willingness both to involve legislatures directly in the process and to require executive transparency in its preparation and presentation of the budget.

Functional Legislatures

Blondel described four archetypes of world legislatures in the1970s. The first and lowest type, the inchoate or nascent legislatures of largely authoritarian systems were not wholly rubber stamps, but their functions, even in debate or constituent service, were sharply constrained. At a second level *truncated* legislatures are those "where a number of bills, and occasionally general policies are discussed, and discussed with reasonable effectiveness, but where they constitute only a segment of the matters which 'should' come to the legislature."[97] The third type is a fully functional legislature that is poorly equipped or politically unable to stand up to the executive on major issues. We see this in both presidential systems in Latin America and Africa and in some the parliamentary democracies of the Commonwealth. Finally, there are those that to some degree or another successfully perform the "true" functions of lawmaking, oversight, and so on that we have just described.

What is perhaps most striking in looking now at Blondel's 1973 ranking is the remarkable degree to which scores have moved up. The truncated legislatures, not just of Eastern Europe and the former Soviet Union, but also in countries as diverse as Indonesia and Argentina, South Korea and South Africa are functional at least, and in many cases, true legislatures. If it was true, as David Truman wrote in 1965, that the twentieth century was "hard on legislatures,"[98] the twenty-first has witnessed a revival. There has also been an interesting reversal in concerns about the health of democratic legislatures from a focus on presidential as opposed to parliamentary systems, on the one hand, and from developing to developed democracies on the other. This debate returns us to a thorny set of questions about the nature of representative democracy that arises here in the form of the tension between the competing principals of representation reflected in parties, on the one hand, and committees on the other. Missing in much of this debate is the individual MP. Studies of party and executive leadership have tended to overemphasize the tools of control and discipline available to them without a corresponding recognition of how "backbenchers discipline leaders and get them to promote policies and positions that are to the backbenchers liking."[99]

Differences between legislatures with a single dominant party and those which depend upon coalitions to form cabinets or enact bills are substantial. In presidential systems, legislative-executive relations are likely to be smoothest when the president's party commands a legislative majority, though experience with divided government in the United States suggests that it may not always be a prescription for deadlock.[100] More generally, the idea that presidential systems—largely because of divided government—are inherently less stable than parliamentary is no longer unquestioned. What counts, it seems, is less the structure of the system than the political support, resources, and capacities of the legislatures themselves.

Notes

1. Giovanni Sartori, *Comparative Constitutional Engineering: An Inquiry into Structures, Incentives, and Outcomes* (New York: New York University Press, 2nd ed. 1997), 109.

2 Nelson W. Polsby, "The Institutionalization of the U.S. House of Representatives," *American Political Science Review* 62 (March 1968), 145.

3. John R. Hibbing, "Legislative Careers: Why and How We Should Study Them," *Journal of Legislative Studies* 24 (Summer 1999), 161.

4. David Judge, "Legislative Institutionalization: A Bent Analytic Arrow?" *Government and Opposition* 38 (Autumn 2003), 515.

5. Samuel P. Huntington, "Congressional Responses to the Twentieth Century," in *The Congress and America's Future*, ed. David B. Truman (Englewood Cliffs, NJ: Prentice-Hall, 1965), 6.

6. William R. Shaffer, *Politics, Parties, and Parliaments: Political Change in Norway* (Columbus: Ohio State University Press, 1998), 215.

7. J. Blondel et al., "Legislative Behaviour: Some Steps Toward a Cross-National Measurement," in *Legislatures*, ed. Phillip Norton (New York: Oxford University Press, 1970), and George Tsebelis, *Veto Players: How Political Institutions Work* (New York: Russell Sage Foundation, 2002).

8. J. Blondel, *Comparative Legislatures* (Englewood Cliffs, N.J.: Prentice-Hall, 1977), 31.

9. William Case, *Politics in Southeast Asia: Democracy or Less* (Richmond, UK: Curzon, 2002), 161-63.

10. Blondel, *Comparative Legislatures,* 31-32.

11. Attila Ágh, "Change and Continuity among the Members of Parliament: Low Incumbent Retention Rates in the New East Central European Parliaments," in *Parliamentary Members and Leaders: The Delicate Balance,* ed. Lawrence D. Longley, Attila Ágh, and Drago Zajc (Appleton, WI: Research Committee of Legislative Specialists, 2000), 27.

12. Peverill Squire, "Career Opportunities and Membership Stability in Legislatures," *Legislative Studies Quarterly* 13 (February 1988), 76.

13. Squire, "Career Opportunities," 77.

14. Anthony King, "How to Strengthen Legislatures—Assuming That We Want To," in *The Role of Legsilatures in Western Democracies*, ed. Norman J. Ornstein (Washington, DC: American Enterprise Institute, 1981), 80.

15. Suzanne Dovi, "Preferable Descriptive Representatives: Will Just Any Woman, Black, or Latino Do?" *American Political Science Review* 96 (December 2002), 738.

16. Dovi, "Preferable Descriptive Representation," 742.

17. The Inter-Parliamentary Union regularly updates its figures on "Women in National Parliaments" at its website, www.ipu.org/wmn.

18. Pippa Norris, "Choosing Electoral Systems: Proportional, Majoritarian, and Mixed Systems," *International Political Science Review* 18 (July 1997), 310.

19. Alan Sharoff, "Women's Representation in Legislatures and Cabinets in Industrial Democracies," *International Political Science Review* 21 (April 2000), 203.

20. Indonesian law requires each party to field slates that are at least 30 percent female; but because of lax enforcement and the structure of the party lists, fewer than 12 percent were actually elected in 2004, a substantial increase from 8 percent in 1999.

21. Sue Thomas, *How Women Legislate* (New York: Oxford University Press, 1994), 153.

22. Richard L. Hall, *Participation in Congress* (New Haven: Yale University Press, 1996), 10.

23. Inter-Parliamentary Union, *World Directory of Parliaments* (Geneva: Inter-Parliamentary Union, 2003).

24. Glenn R. Parker, *Congress and the Rent-Seeking Society* (Ann Arbor: University of Michigan Press, 1996), 39.

25. Reuven Y. Hazan, *Reforming Parliamentary Committees: Israel in Comparative Perspective* (Columbus: Ohio State University Press, 2001), 85.

26. Malcolm Shaw, "Legislative Committees," in *World Encyclopedia of Parliaments and Legislatures*, ed. George Thomas Kurian (Washington, DC: Congressional Quarterly Press, 1998), II, 793.

27. Shaw, "Legislative Committees," 792-93.

28. John D. Lees and Malcolm Shaw, eds. *Committees in Legislatures: A Comparative Analysis* (Durham, NC: Duke University Press, 1979), 387.

29. Herbert Döring, "Parliamentary Agenda Control and Legislative Outcomes in Western Europe," *Legislative Studies Quarterly* 26 (February 2001), 151.

30. Blondel, *Comparative Legislatures,* 69.

31. Herbert Döring, ed. *Parliaments and Majority Rule in Western Europe* (New York: St. Martin's Press, 1996).

32. Malcolm Shaw, "Committees in Legislatures," in Norton, *Legislatures,* 249.

33. Keith Krehbiel, *Information and Legislative Organization* (Ann Arbor: University of Michigan Press, 1991), 5.

34. Forrest Maltzman, *Competing Principles: Committees, Parties, and the Organization of Congress* (Ann Arbor: University of Michigan Press, 1998), 27.

35. On this process in Brazil, see David Samuels, "Progressive Ambition, Federalism, and Pork-Barreling in Brazil," in *Legislative Politics in Latin America*, ed. Scott Morgenstern and Benito Nacif (New York: Cambridge University Press, 2002), 315-40.

36. Graham Hassall and Cheryl Saunders, *Asia-Pacific Constitutional Systems* (New York: Cambridge University Press, 2002), 87.

37. Philip Norton, ed., *Parliaments and Governments in Western Europe* (Portland, OR: Frank Cass, 1998), 201.

38. Maltzman, *Competing Principals,* 160.

39. Austin Ranney, *The Doctrine of Responsible Party Government* (Urbana: University of Illinois Press, 1962), 12.

40. Glenn R. Parker, *Institutional Change, Discretion, and the Making of the Modern Congress* (Ann Arbor: University of Michigan Press, 1992), 106.

41. Michael L. Mezey, "Legislatures: Individual Purpose and Institutional Performance," in *Political Science: The State of the Discipline II,* ed. Ada W. Finifter (Washington, DC: American Political Science Association, 1993), 346.

42. Scott P. Mainwaring, *Rethinking Party Systems in the Third Wave of Democratization: The Case of Brazil* (Stanford, CA: Stanford University Press, 1999), 194, 203-6.

43. Matthew Soberg Shugart and John M. Carey, *Presidents and Assemblies: Constitutional Design and Electoral Dynamics* (New York: Cambridge University Press, 1992), 266.

44. William Holmes Brown, *Constitution, Jefferson's Manual, and Rules of the House of Representatives* (Washington, DC: Government Printing Office, 1979), 111.

45. Kaare Strøm, "Parliamentary Committees in European Democracies," in *The Changing Role of Parliamentary Committees*, ed. Lawrence D. Longley and Attila Ágh (Appleton, WI: Research Committee of Legislative Specialists, 1997), 64.

46. Gary W. Cox and Matthew D. McCubbins, *Legislative Leviathan: Party Government in the House* (Berkeley: University of California Press, 1993).

47. Döring, "Parliamentary Agenda Control," 149.

48. George Thomas Kurian, "Greece," in *World Encyclopedia of Parliaments,* I, 286.

49. Knut Heidar et al., "Five Most Similar Systems?" in *Beyond Westminster and Congress: The Nordic Experience,* ed. Peter Esaiasson and Knut Heidar (Columbus: Ohio State University Press, 2000), 37.

50. W. Ivor Jennings, *Parliament* (Cambridge: Cambridge University Press, 2nd ed., 1957), 15

51. The abundant literature on filibusters is well-summarized and placed in the larger context of Senate traditions in Burdett A. Loomis, ed., *Esteemed Colleagues: Civility and Deliberation in the U.S. Senate* (Washington, DC: The Brookings Institution, 2000).

52. Döring, "Parliamentary Agenda Control," 150.

53. The literature on this issue, and the complicated differences between the two major systems, are summarized in Bjørn Erik Rasch, "Parliamentary Floor Voting Procedures and Agenda Setting in Europe," *Legislative Studies Quarterly* 25 (February 2000), 3-23.

54. Inter-Parliamentary Union, *World Directory of Parliaments*.

55. Gerhard Loewenberg and Samuel C. Patterson, *Comparing Legislatures* (Boston: Little, Brown and Co., 1979), 121.

56. Blondel, *Comparative Legislatures,* 32.

57. *Reynolds v. Sims,* 377 U.S. 533 (1964).

58. *Federalist,* Number 62.

59. James R. Rogers, "The Impact of Bicameralism on Legislative Production," *Legislative Studies Quarterly* 28 (November 2003), 514.

60. Rogers, "The Impact of Bicameralism," 525.

61. John M. Carey, "Presidentialism and Representative Institutions," in *Constructing Democratic Governance in Latin America*, ed. Jorge I. Dominguez and Michael Shifter (Baltimore: The Johns Hopkins University Press, 2nd ed., 2003), 28.

62. This is the estimate of David Conradt as cited in Vicki C. Jackson and Mark Tushnet, eds., *Comparative Constitutional Law* (New York: Foundation Press, 1999), 842.

63. Edward V. Schneier and Bertram Gross, *Legislative Strategy: Shaping Public Policy* (New York: St. Martin's Press, 1993), 202.

64. George Tsebelis and Jeanette Money, *Bicameralism,* (New York: Cambridge University Press, 1997), 48-62.

65. Thomas König, "Bicameralism and Party Politics in Germany: An Empirical Social Choice Analysis," *Political Studies* 49 (2001), 433.

66. Philip Norton, "United Kingdom," in *Encyclopedia of World Parliaments,* II, 705.

67. Sartori, *Comparative Constitutional Engineering,* 186.

68. Arend Lijphart, *Democracies: Patterns of Majoritarian and Consensus Government in Twenty-One Countries* (New Haven: Yale University Press, 1984), 104.

69. Sartori, *Comparative Constitutional Engineering,* 187.

70. For provocative attempts, see especially Döring's earlier cited works on Europe; Michael Mezey, *Comparative Legislatures* (Durham, NC: Duke University Press, 1979); Nelson W. Polsby, "Legislatures," in *Handbook of Political Science,* ed. Nelson W. Polsby and Fred I. Geenstein (Reading, MA: Addison-Wesley, 1975);

71. David E. Price, *The Congressional Experience* (Boulder, CO: Westview Press, 2nd ed., 2000), 198-99.

72. David M. Olson, *Democratic Legislative Institutions: A Comparative View* (Armonk, NY: M. E. Sharpe, 1994), 17.

73. John R. Johannes, *To Serve the People: Congress and Constituency Service* (Lincoln: University of Nebraska Press, 1984), 34.

74. Morris P. Fiorina, *Congress: Keystone of the Washington Establishment* (New Haven: Yale University Press, 1977), 48.

75. Gerald E. Caiden, ed., *International Handbook of the Ombudsman* (Westport, CT: Greenwood Press, 1983).

76. Donald C. Rowat, *The Ombudsman Plan: The Worldwide Spread of an Idea* (Lanham, MD: University Press of America, 2nd ed., 1985), 170.

77. Ana Maria Mustapic, "President and Congress in Argentina," in *Legislative Politics in Latin America,* 43.

78. Bruce Cain, John Ferejohn, and Morris Fiorina, *The Personal Vote: Constituency Service and Electoral Independence* (Cambridge, MA: Harvard University Press, 1987), 219. The Gary Cox argument they cite is from his book *The Cabinet and the Development of Political Parties in Victorian England* (New York: Cambridge University Press, 1988).

79. Woodrow Wilson, *Congressional Government* (New York: Meridian Books, 1956, originally published in 1884), 195.

80. Carlos Santiago Nino, *The Constitution of Deliberative Democracy* (New Haven: Yale University Press, 1996), 160.

81. James Willard Hurst, *Dealing with Statutes* (New York: Columbia University Press, 1992), 3.

82. Wilson, *Congressional Government,* 195.

83. Olson, *Democratic Legislative Institutions,* 91.

84. Much of this data was drwan from a survey conducted by the Inter-Parliamentary Union in collaboration with the World Bank Institute in 2002, *Relations between the Legislature and the Executive in the Context of Parliamentary Oversight* (Geneva: IPU, 2002) as reported in Riccardo Pelizzo and Frederick Stapenhurst, "Legislatures and Oversight: A Note," paper delivered at the Annual Meeting of the Southern Political Science Association, New Orleans, Louisiana, January 7-10, 2004 and published in 2004 as an

occasional paper of the World Bank.

85. Harold Seidman, *Politics, Position, and Power: The Dynamics of Federal Organization* (New York: Oxford University Press, 2nd ed., 1975), 40.

86. Joel D. Aberach, *Keeping a Watchful Eye* (Washington, DC: The Brookings Institution, 1990), 7.

87. Blondel, *Comparative Legislatures,* 108.

88. Chan Wook Park, "Change Is Short but Continuity Is Long: Policy Influence of the National Assembly in Newly Democratized Korea, in Loewenberg, Squire, and Kiewiet, *Legislatures,* 347.

89. Eward V. Schneier and Bertram Gross, *Congress Today* (New York: St. Martin's Press, 1993), 307.

90. "Legislatures and Oversight," 14.

91. Richard F. Fenno, Jr., *The Power of the Purse: Appropriations Politics in Congress* (Boston: Little, Brown and Company, 1966), xiii.

92. National Democratic Institute for International Affairs, *Legislatures and the Budget Process: An International Survey* (Washington, DC: National Democratic Institute, 2003), 6.

93. National Democratic Institute, *Legislatures and the Budget Process,* 7.

94. Organization for Economic Co-operation and Development, *Results of the Survey on Budget Practices and Procedures* (Paris: OECD, 2004), Table 2.7.

95. OECD, *Survey of Budget Practices,* Table 2.7.

96. National Democratic Institute, *Legislatures and the Budget Process,* 25.

97. Blondel, *Comparative Legislatures,* 137.

98. David B. Truman, "Introduction: The Problem in Its Setting," in *The Congress and America's Future,* 1.

99. Shaun Bowler, David M. Farrell, and Richard S. Katz, "Party Cohesion, Party Discipline, and Parliaments," in *Party Discipline and Parliamentary Government*, ed. Bowler, Farrell, and Katz (Columbus: Ohio State University Press, 1999), 14-15.

100. Roger H. Davidson, "The Presidency and Three Eras of the Modern Congress," in *Divided Democracy: Cooperation and Conflict between the President and Congress*, ed. James A. Thurber (Washington, DC: Congressional Quarterly, 1991), 76.

Chapter 10

Federalism and Decentralization

As the institutions of the European Union gradually intrude upon such traditional functions of the state as coining money and regulating commerce, "classic accounts of state sovereignty as 'absolute,' 'indivisible,' and 'inalienable, in the sixteenth-century terms of Jean Bodin, have given way to a new discourse."[1] State sovereignty is increasingly challenged from above by the institutions and forces of globalization, and from below by variations on the themes of decentralization and devolution. The big three of federalism scholars—William Riker, K. C. Wheare, and Daniel Elazar—define federalism as a system in which legal authority is shared between a national government and its constituent provinces, but they offer significantly diverse standards for distinguishing just what it is that makes a system truly federal.[2] Riker, casting the broadest net, includes confederations; leagues of city states; and more modern states, such as the Soviet Union, which were federal more in form than in fact. Wheare, while excluding dictatorships, is less stringent than Elazar who requires a written constitution defining the jurisdictions of each level of power. Using this high standard, Elazar counted only twenty federations in 1996, but they contained nearly two-thirds of the world's population outside of China.[3] The Derbyshires described twenty-four of 192 world governments as having federal structures, with another thirty-five "highly decentralized."[4]

Retaining the core of the concept—the notion of dual sovereignty—helps to distinguish federal from unitary systems; but the growing variety of devices used to decentralize governance and devolve powers makes it almost impossible to draw absolute boundaries between regimes that are federal and those that are not. What matters in the crafting of constitutions are the ways in which different methods of allocating powers between levels of government affect the political process.

The Scope and Methods of Federalization

The classic model of federalism, epitomized by Switzerland, is one in which a group of small countries gradually drew together to enjoy the benefits of size and strength while retaining basic autonomy. Far more common, in modern times, are countries whose boundaries were already defined by precedent colonial or authoritarian regimes, which have adopted federal structures to diffuse internal conflicts. Brazil in 1891 and India in 1947 are relatively successful examples of this process. Finally, there are countries which have moved to federalism or some alternative form of devolution to accommodate the emergence or intensification of regional conflicts as in Belgium, Canada, and Spain.

Federal systems are forged through formal covenants that define the boundaries and powers of national and state governments. Unlike unitary systems, which frequently decentralize specific functions, a federal system has a division of power in which some matters are exclusively the concerns of its states or provinces and beyond the reach of the national government; and where certain other matters are guaranteed to the center. More important, a federal system requires a fairly well-fixed definition of its constituent units. Provinces or states may be divided, as has occurred quite frequently in India and Nigeria, and new ones created; but it is rare for regional governments to have their jurisdictions changed without consent.

Constituent Units

Sometimes the units of a federal system define themselves. Virtually unpassable Alpine ridges in Switzerland and Austria, or distinct islands—as in the ill-fated Federation of the West Indies—rather clearly demarcate boundaries. Belgium uses language groups for some political divisions, and India encourages some religious self-governance, in what is sometimes known as "sociological" federalism. In most cases, however, federalism implies geographic units; and the question of boundaries looms as a major issue invoking questions of size and diversity, and of matching territorial lines with less tangible but often more important questions of language, ethnicity, and religion. In the most minimal case—Trinidad and Tobago, for example—the "federal" system has but two units, the point being to assure the smaller island of Tobago aspects of its autonomy against its larger partner. At the other end of the scale are very large countries divided into many units, such as the United States with fifty states and India whose twenty-eight states include ten with populations of more than forty million persons each. The Russian constitution lists more than eighty-six republics, territories, regions, autonomous areas, and federal cities with supposedly distinctive powers.

Trinidad and Tobago aside, the record of small federations is poor. From the breakup of Pakistan and what is now Bangladesh, the secession of Eritrea from Ethiopia and the split between the Czech Republic and Slovakia, to current frictions between St. Kitts and Nevis, few of these two-unit federations have survived. The reality or fear that one of the two units must inevitably dominate makes separation likely, and suggests the general hypothesis that "A high number of differentiated regional units provides a more solid ground for a federal state than a low number."[5]

The units of federal systems are always of unequal size, sometimes strikingly so. To the extent that federalism is defended as a means of combining national government with the virtues of smaller units, some of these units can be quite large: India's Uttar Pradash, for example, would be the world's sixth largest country. Problems are most likely to arise, however, in smaller units. Recalling Madison's argument on pluralism and compound republics, the problem is that they may be too ethnically, linguistically, or religiously pure to fit in with the rest of the country, more susceptible to a situation in which "the ruling passion," runs roughshod over "both the public good and the rights of other citizens."[6] Because federalism creates a wall around its units against central intervention, care must be given to deciding just what powers are walled in. Federalism,

> gives regional governments exclusive authority over a given set of issue areas. Regional leaders can use this discretion to rule undemocratically over local governments or oppress citizens within their jurisdictions. In fact the same potential dangers of decentralization in general—authoritarian enclaves, discrimination against minorities, heightened geographical inequalities, inefficiency—are even more acute in a federal system, precisely because federalism entrenches the prerogatives of subnational governments.[7]

These problems are particularly acute where jurisdictions are established along ethnic, linguistic, or religious lines. The more that provincial governments are able to satisfy demands for purity, the more difficult they make life for those who are not part of the dominant group. Instead of providing a pluralistic, national solution to the problem, federalism flips the majority-minority relationship so that the once dominant English speakers in Quebec, for example, find themselves living in communities where all the signs are in French. Decentralization in Spain may similarly have "more or less satisfactorily met the demands of Basque and Catalán nationalists (thereby playing a crucial role in the consolidation of the constitutional monarchy), but it does not necessarily preclude majoritarian behavior on the part of the regional governments vis-à-vis minority linguistic groups falling in their own jurisdictions."[8] As necessary as such arrangements are, they often arouse resentment, especially where federalism is "asymmetric," that is, where minority provinces are allowed linguistic or other powers that other provinces are denied.

In theory, people can opt out of this dilemma by moving: "Each citizen chooses that polity which allows him to consume exactly the bundle of public goods and services he desires."[9] And if that still proves difficult, it is possible to cut the pie into smaller pieces: both India and Nigeria have increased the number of states from those established originally, and face persistent demands for further fragmentation. It is not by coincidence that this process is called "Balkanization," for an area in which "ethnic and political boundaries do *not* coincide in most cases, a fact that aggravates tensions and conflicts."[10] Whatever might have been done to prevent the ultimately violent breakup of the former Yugoslavia, and mitigate ethnic tensions in parts of the former Soviet Union, "the systematic narrowing of all relations in the community to relations among ethnic groups" is a recipe for trouble,[11] particularly when compounded by resource and income disparities. While such inequalities pose problems in all systems, the geographic labels that federalism sews into them can be troublesome both horizontally, between regions; and vertically, in forcing the central government to consider whether and how to deal with them. Even when ethnic tensions are not a factor, when one region has the sense that becoming part of a larger federation is likely to drag it down to the level of its poorer partner, the system is under stress. Jamaica's sense that it was being asked to carry too large a share of the economic burden played a major role in the breakup of the West Indies; and questions of relative economic power were similarly divisive in the unconsummated federation of Central Africa where, although the "actual break-up of the Federation started with Nyasaland's protests at discrimination and neglect, it is only too likely that Northern Rhodesia would have rebelled against being the perpetual milch cow of the Federation."[12]

In many instances, the boundaries of subnational units are drawn specifically to preserve and protect the political influence of rural areas. In Argentina, for example, federalism is as much a political device for checking the economic and numeric dominance of Buenos Ares as it is an instrument of regional autonomy. Its relatively poor, peripheral provinces have only 30 percent of the population, yet they hold 45 percent of the seats in the Chamber of Deputies, and 83 percent of those in the Senate, proportions that significantly distort the balance of political power. Many, if not most, federal systems give institutional advantages to rural interests and poorer provinces.

Roles

In their original designs, the differences between federal systems are striking in the diverse ways in which they allocate powers. Traditionally, federal nations have been symmetrical in the sense that the national/provincial division of powers is uniform with no local entity having independent powers not accorded to all; but formal asymmetries, such as those that give Quebec sovereign powers not granted other provinces, or the special autonomies of Catalonia, the Basque country, Galacia, and Navarre in Spain, are increasingly common. These asymmetrical patterns are the products of a shift in the origins of federal systems away from a process of gradual integration of diverse regions toward a tendency to give special status to particular subcultures in pre-existing regimes.[13] If "the federalist idea was not originally created for multinational or multilingual countries," most of the newer federal democracies were. "Federalism," as Illés argues with regard to Central Europe, "was not viewed as a guarantor of democracy for the whole country, but rather as a concession to minorities. This is one of the reasons why originally almost all Eastern European federations were asymmetrical constructions designed precisely for minorities, and why most of them remained so."[14]

The jurisdictional boundaries that define the roles of governments also vary.

> If anyone ever entertained the notion that there was a "normal" way for federalism to be structured, a comparison of the distribution of legislative power in the United States and Canada would dispel that notion. On one level, there are noticeable differences in where particular powers are lodged. Marriage and divorce and criminal law, for example, are governed by the central government in Canada but state governments in the United States, while labor law, nationalized in the United States, is an area jealously guarded by Canada's provincial government. Moreover, Canadian provinces have much more exclusive power over local commerce than U.S. states do.[15]

Legal analyses sometimes classify powers as exclusively national, exclusively provincial, or shared. Modern economies have made these distinctions increasingly opaque. Even the most clearly "national" power, that of conducting foreign policy, is blurred by the need for provinces to coordinate transportation systems, power grids, and so on with those of bordering countries, and to develop trade relations overseas: more U.S. state governments now have offices in Japan than in Washington.[16] And government functions that were once almost purely "local" bump into each so frequently as to call for coordinating mechanisms. In virtually all federal systems, the concept of exclusively provincial powers has given way to demands for national standards of economic and civil rights, of national laws protecting resources, and for more universal standards for education. Local control does not disappear under these pressures, but it is increasingly channeled and combined with other forces. Morton Grodzins rather famously described the idea of exclusive realms of national, provincial, and local powers as a "layer-cake" theory that failed adequately to describe the "marble cake" reality of powers that are more mixed than separated, and so thoroughly marbled that, "Wherever you slice through it you reveal an inseparable mixture of differently colored ingredients."[17]

Public choice theory supports the common sense notion that the roles assigned to the different levels of government in the political system should correspond with the scope of the issues involved. It makes little sense for the national government to run a town park or for each town to have its own army and navy: "the jurisdiction of government should extend as far, and no further, than the effects of the public goods it supplies."[18] The problem increasingly is that the growing mobility of goods and people blurs these lines and turns the focus of party leaders away from regionalism. Whatever the written constitution says about the division of powers, the actual distribution of relative influence depends on politics. The ability of Germany and Austria's strong parties to override, to some degree, the boundaries between the provinces and the central government confirms Riker's observation that, "the proximate cause of the degree of variations in the degree of centralization (or peripheralization) is the degree of party centralization."[19] What appears in formal terms to be a strict, logical division of powers between national and provincial governments works in reality as a negotiated process of interlocking problem solving.

Institutions

Switzerland is unique in having a three-tiered federal system in which sovereignty is divided between the national government and the cantons, and within the cantons with local governments. The Nigerian constitution officially recognizes some 770 local councils, but their actual autonomy has never been defined. Many provinces and states accord home rule powers to municipalities; but where cities and towns in the United States and in most other countries are creatures of the state and can theoretically be abolished by simple legislative act, Switzerland's municipalities enjoy the same essential constitutional status as the cantons. The European Union is moving toward a similar three-tiered system with a European government at the top, national governments in the middle, and the provinces of federal states such as Austria and Germany on the bottom. The proposed European constitution will seemingly be similar to Switzerland's in affording constitutional protections to these nested powers..

   In most federal systems, the two levels of government display parallel structures. Provincial parliamentary or presidential systems echo the configurations of their national counterparts, though—outside of the United States—relatively few subnational parliaments are bicameral. Bureaucracies tend also to be reiterative, so that national ministries share jurisdictions with their state counterparts. Some federal systems also follow the U.S. model of dual courts, with state and local courts chosen separately from their national counterparts and having overlapping but essentially distinct jurisdictions. True federalism walks the fine line between fragmentation and nationalization. Table 10-1 depicts the formal ways in which twenty-three federated democracies are structured. Most federal constitutions, it shows, empower a constitutional court, and most have bicameral legislatures, with the upper house generally designed to overrepresent the territorial dimensions of the polity. Few are parliamentary. The United States and six other countries allocate judicial powers to both state and national courts and thus allow differences in such areas as sentencing, family law, and even some aspects of the civil code. Many countries, federated or not, tolerate and even encourage regional variations in law enforcement and may allow some accommodation to ethnic traditions in deciding some kinds of cases; but the overwhelming majority of legal systems are hierarchically organized under a single tent. There are, in most cases, good cultural and historic reasons for the varying patterns of institutional arrangements depicted in Table 10-1; but what it most clearly shows is that a typology of federal systems would produce almost as many types as there are cases.

Political Dynamics

As federal systems become increasingly "marblized," a resultant shift in the powers of state institutions can also be found. The tendency in many systems is for the national government to take the lead in coordinating and directing policies the details of which are developed at the local level. The national government might, for example, establish a single set of standards for the materials, grade allowances, and lane widths for highways, but leave specific routing decisions to local authorities. Combining, as it does, national standards with flexibility in implementation, this kind of decentralization, as noted in chapter 8, is intrinsically appealing but may offer less in practice than meets the eye.

Decision-making power is decentralized in these settings, but decentralized in ways that paradoxically lessen local control. In what Germans call "interlocking politics," there has been "a high degree of bureaucratization . . . restraints on the *Länder's* capacities of separate and distinct agenda-setting, the by-passing of the parliament, especially the *Länder* parliaments, and thus a loss of legitimacy in favor of an executive federalism transcending the tiers of government."[20] Similarly in Switzerland, a seemingly clear distinction between the respective roles of national, canton, and local governments are blurred in practice by substantial overlaps in office holding and what the Swiss call "militia democracy." Local mayors routinely serve in cantonal legislatures, and frequently in Berne as well. The term "militia" stands for a "venerable concept of honorary participation in public office" that is manifest in a corporatized network of quasi-public organizations. Eighty-two percent of the deputies in both houses of parliament serve as paid directors of public organizations "overseeing" various policy areas. "They do their business mainly in the 400 or so hearing commissions that dominate the policy process, and it is perfectly normal that a hearing, say, on banking law will be stacked with representatives of the large banks, or on nuclear reactors with the board members of the energy sector."[21]

Table 10-1

The Constitution of Federalism: Constitutional Institutions in Twenty-Three Federated Democracies

Country	Number of States	Bicameral Legislature?	Dual Court System?	Constitutional Court?	Parliamentary System?
Argentina	23	Yes	Yes	Yes	No
Australia	6	Yes	Yes	Yes	Yes
Austria	9	Yes	No	Yes	Yes
Belgium	3	Weak	No	Yes	Yes
Brazil	27	Yes	Yes	Yes	No
Canada	10	Yes	No	Yes	Yes
Ethiopia	9	Yes	No	No	No
Germany	16	Yes	Yes	Yes	Yes
India	28	Weak	Yes	Yes	Yes
Malaysia	13	Yes	No	Yes	Yes
Mexico	31	Yes	No	Yes	No
Nigeria	21	Yes	Yes	Yes	Yes
St. Kitts/Nevis	2	No	No	No	No
South Africa	9	Yes	No	Yes	Yes
Spain	16	Weak	No	Yes	Yes
Switzerland	26	Yes	No	No	Mixed
United States	50	Yes	Yes	Yes	No
Venezuela	23	No	No	No	No

Source: Most of the material contained in this table can be found under individual country entries in *The Statesman's Yearbook 2004: The Politics, Cultures, and Economies of the World,* ed. Barry Turner (New York: Palgrave-Macmillan, 2003).

Thus no matter how clearly a written constitution may seemingly define the roles of each layer in a federal system, the kinds of overlaps described by the marble cake analogy are increasingly descriptive of political realities, and increasingly likely to displace democratically-controlled local institutions with bureaucracies. The ways in which powers are blended and mixed vary considerably both between countries and between different policy domains within countries. Hooghe and Marks refine Grodzin's concept of marbling by distinguishing systems in which "jurisdictions are defined by durable boundaries" as traditionally federal from newer systems that are intercommunal, specialized, functional associations that may or may not coincide with local, state, or national boundaries. Task driven, these newer organizations are "designed with respect to particular policy problems—not particular communities or constituencies;"[22] and by including non-governmental organizations go beyond the marblizing of institutions described by Grodzins. As with Swiss militias, they often have all the ostensible autonomy of subnational governments. Though hatched by traditional political parents, they frequently develop the capacity to survive and grow outside the nest.

Even where federal-state relations are informal and largely political, federal systems require institutional mechanisms of border control. While some local policies are almost entirely local in impact, many cannot be contained. When New York takes water from the Delaware River, it impacts the water supplies of downstream communities in three other states. Even in federal systems, these problems are frequently resolved at the national level. The Swiss, for example, have some of the world's strongest centrally-imposed environmental policies. Within the federal context, informal meetings between bureaucrats or governors can sometimes provide temporary solutions. Deals are made among higher level bureaucrats or among provincial premiers and then, if taken to the respective legislatures at all, presented in essentially unamendable form. Canadian political scientists call this "executive federalism,"[23] and although it tends to take legislatures out of the loop, it can strengthen the collective powers of the states. In Austria, where there are more than five hundred such conferences a year, "cooperative federalism has been an instrument for consolidating the political power of the states. . . to create a political counterweight against the central government's overwhelming legal powers."[24] Long-term, formal agreements, called interstate compacts in the United States, establishing bodies such as the Delaware River Basin Commission, are common in federal systems.

As with Frankenstein, these interstate agencies tend ultimately to supercede their creators. In 1940, the state of West Virginia entered into a compact with seven other states creating the Ohio River Valley Water Sanitation Commission. Nine years later, the state got into a fight with the commission and voted to stop paying its dues. The other seven states sued. The U.S. Supreme Court upheld them, arguing, in the words of Justice Frankfurter, that the issue was not one of state sovereignty but rather "a conventional grant of legislative power." Once the West Virginia legislature signed its control over water issues to the commission, the bargain was etched in stone: "It requires no elaborate argument," the court held, "to reject the suggestion that an agreement solemnly entered into between States . . . can be unilaterally nullified. . . . A state cannot be its own ultimate judge in a controversy with a sister state."[25]

Courts in the United States have played a particularly important role in defining the contours of federalism. Minor detours aside, the direction of its decisions have supported an expanded national role. The Supreme Court of Canada, in contrast, together with its predecessor, the Judicial Committee of the Provincial Council, "gave a far broader interpretation to provincial jurisdiction over property and civil rights than had been contemplated, and a narrower interpretation of the broad federal powers for peace, order, and good government than had been anticipated."[26] In Latin America, by and large, the role of the courts has been considerably more political with a tendency to ratify executive and central government authority in periods of single-party control, and to act more independently when competition between parties gives them the "political space" to serve as referees.[27]

In most older European federal systems, the courts play a considerably more peripheral role, with direct bargaining between jurisdictions serving in their stead. In Austria, for example, there are actual "treaties" signed between and among provinces, local governments and the states. Switzerland uses an elaborate system of public referendums to resolve jurisdictional conflicts, and some countries have established more-or-less permanent intergovernmental committees to patrol jurisdictional boundaries. A key institution linking regional interests to national policies is often the upper house of a bicameral legislature. Many of the agreements reached between the several Länder and the central government in Germany are negotiated in the halls of the Bundesrat. In most federal systems, representatives in at least one house of the legislature tend to function as guardians of local interests. Even in countries that are not federal in a formal sense, the legislature often serves as a congress of ambassadors as well as a parliament. But the parochialism of legislators is much less a function of which house they sit in than it is of how they are nominated and elected. Where provincial organizations control the nominations of candidates for the legislature, as in Brazil, "the state-based nature of political competition" reaches into both houses of the national legislature.[28] Policy is not necessarily federalized by this kind of parochialism, but it is decentralized. Because states depend so much on such national policies to fund basic services, moreover, they are actually weakened in their capacity to plan their own policy priorities.

Local Governments

In the most centralized countries—the United Kingdom serving as the historic model—local governments are largely as administrative units of the national government. Even in Britain, however, the devolution and decentralization movement has had an impact. One of the Labour Party's first acts in 1997 was to reinstate the London City Council that its predecessors had abolished; but the power of local councils to make significant policy decisions remains limited at best. Local councils remain a force largely at the implementation stage. The United States has a long and strong tradition of local home rule, but the fact is that local government powers are legally derived from the states. State and federal courts have adhered to what is known as "Dillon's Rule," after an 1868 Iowa case which ruled that municipalities are "creatures of the states," having only those powers "granted in express words" or that derive from them.[29] That remains the *legal* status of cities and towns in the United States and most world democracies. In practice, new limits are seldom imposed, and local governments almost never abolished: the tradition of home rule is so firmly established that it is difficult to conceive of circumstances under which it would be significantly cut. But the legal status of local governments in most countries, federal or not, follow the lines of Dillon's Rule, with particularly strict controls on the ability of local governments to borrow and tax.

Many newer constitutions either explicitly require some devolution of power and support for new local units. Extending upon a Hindu tradition of a daily gathering (*panch*) of village wise men, the Indian constitution, for example, says that, "The State shall take steps to organise village panchayats and endow them with such power and authority as may be necessary to enable them to function as units of self-government." The Hungarian local governments act, one of the first passed by the post-Communist legislature, gave 3,200 local councils both the autonomy and electoral bases they had lacked under communism. State grants, particularly to small villages, have not always kept pace with local needs, and controversies over the nature and scope of regional governments have sometimes left these local institutions weak and divided; but the idea of home rule is firmly established.[30] Internationally, a 2001 study estimated that some seventy countries were "implementing political reforms aimed at decentralization and enhancement of municipal governments."[31] Whether devolution actually empowers citizens is not clear. What advocates describe as "new decision frameworks for the processes of negotiation and bargaining between private interests and public authority,"[32] raise the specter of new disparities that narrow rather than broaden the scope of democracy.

> The new metropolis will belong to the managerial and technocratic elite and a new class of very highly paid workers—professionals, middle and lower level managers, brokers, and middlemen of all kinds. The elite will form its own community—a spatially bound, interpersonally networked subculture built around the business center, segregated residential areas, exclusive restaurants, country clubs, arts and culture complexes, and easy access to airports. While it may concede the general administration of the city to democratically elected representatives, the managerial elite will probably resist any interference by the political leadership in strategic decisionmaking that affects business prospects.[33]

Democratic devolution, if it is to avoid this scenario, must be structured around carefully conceived structural reforms that balance resources and autonomy. Local governments that are granted resources but lack democratic institutions or traditions are likely to be oligarchic and strongly constrained by central government bodies; those that have autonomy but lack resources lose credibility.

Local elections have proven "valuable in political systems where competition at the national level is highly constrained or circumscribed by law or in practice."[34] In closed systems, such as China and Saudi Arabia, they may eventually play a role in both pushing demands for democratization and increasing citizen capacities. The sequencing can also proceed in reverse, as in South Africa, where the central government has had to play a more proactive role promoting the capacities of local governments as a means of extending the process of democratization to the more visible and tangible level of towns and villages. Particularly in systems that lack meaningful traditions of democratic rule, citizen trust must sometimes first be built first through institutions to which people can more personally relate.

The Dynamics of Center-Periphery Relations

One of the problems with the marble-cake model of federalism is that it is too static. A more dynamic model that focused more on the process of marbling than the finished cake, would be more expressive of the shifting balances of authority that characterize federal systems. The ultimate question in politics is who has the power to decide the issues that matter. The more complex the society, the more complex and evanescent the answers become. From the perspective of the United States, at least until the 1980s, it was common "to think that federalism was a device to bring about a high degree of political unification, that federations become increasingly centralized over time, and that centralization was an irreversible trend."[35] The logic of economic and demographic change points in that direction; but the past few decades have seen strong political tendencies the other way.

Fiscal Federalism

One way to measure the degree of political decentralization is to follow the money to see which levels of government actually raise and spend it. Central governments in federal systems spend a smaller proportion of government funds than those in unitary systems, and give greater revenue raising powers to states and localities; but the differences are inconsistent, and probably less significant than they might seem. In part the problem is that it is difficult to standardize the ways in which reporting bodies classify revenues and expenditures. Expenditures are particularly difficult to follow because of the many cases in which state agencies are simply acting as payroll clerks for national programs. By these measures, even centralized nations like Denmark can appear "even more decentralized than the United States."[36]

Tax revenue numbers are easier to classify, and, if we assume that revenues and expenditures are in the long run about the same, provide a reasonable index of decentralization. Using tax data compiled in 1997 with his own indicators of federalism and decentralization, Lijphart found a strong correlation, with highly federated countries such as Canada, Germany, and Switzerland among the most fiscally decentralized, and such unitary states as Greece, Portugal, and Great Britain most centralized. Sweden and Japan are interesting exceptions because they are unitary systems that have highly decentralized tax systems.[37] And most Latin American federations, which Lijphart and other pioneering students of the problem did not include, have highly centralized shares of total revenue collected by their central governments. Only in Brazil—which would have ranked somewhere in the middle of Lijphart's federalism ranking—was the state and local share of total revenue more than 20 percent of the total. The central government's share in other Latin federations ranged from 80 percent in Argentina to 100 in Chile.[38] At the same time, Latin America's unitary states are even more centralized on the whole than its federal systems, though the share of spending controlled by subnational governments grew significantly in the 1990s,[39] as it did throughout the world.[40] Few observers are yet prepared to describe the European Union as a national state, yet as McKay points out, "In central controls over fiscal matters, including minimum value added tax rates and control over national borrowing, the EU is actually more centralized than Canada, the U.S., and Switzerland."[41] What probably counts the most in assessing the true extent of fiscal federalism is the ability of subnational governments to predict and/or control their own sources of revenue.

The U.S. founders were firm in their insistence that two sources of potential tax revenue should forever be off-limits to the states. In Article One, they are prohibited either from taxing foreign trade or trade between the states. Even highly decentralized federal systems such as Switzerland have, like the United States, retained national controls over issues of monetary policy and taxing powers that might, in significant ways, put burdens on interstate commerce. There are, however, a number of less direct ways in which state taxing and spending policies can have economic consequences. Much of the attraction of federalism to conservative public choice proponents lies in its putative tendency to promote economic competition. Governments that provide good services and low taxes will attract economic development and force less efficient states to follow their lead. Critics of this approach see it as promoting a "race to the bottom" in which localities cut social welfare costs, reduce environmental standards, cut wages, and so on to attract new business. Based in the overall models of choice theorists like Buchanan and Tiebout,[42] the argument for competition between states is that it achieves important efficiencies by requiring them to control both waste and taxes.

While this position is intuitively sensible, policies designed to attract business don't work very well in practice; and there is some evidence that the effects of interstate competition can be inefficient if not destructive. The differing capacities of local governments to assume the developmental burdens of "the new localism" too often mean "that better-off cities will get richer while poor cities get poorer," and that "past patterns of uneven development will be exacerbated."[43] Because state cutbacks often hit low income groups particularly hard, many national governments mandate their provinces to provide a basic floor level of services. Such "unfunded mandates," as they came to be known in the 1990s, are not popular with subnational politicians who, quite naturally, prefer the federal subsidies to mandated minimums. Subsidies are particularly important to poorer provinces which can otherwise pay for them only by taxing at higher rates and thus hampering economic development. In many of the poorest developing countries, moreover, the very idea of local self-government is dependent upon some form of outside financial help. Without it, "the delegation of new functions to local government . . . makes decentralization meaningless at best and dangerous for democracy at worst. If local governments are responsible for functions they do not have the resources to perform adequately, citizens may become disillusioned not only with their local officials but with the democratic process itself."[44]

Equalization transfers to poorer states, have been typical of budgetary policies in nearly all federations. The scope of such transfers ranges from quite large in Germany and Austria to modest in Canada and Switzerland, and relatively trivial in the contemporary United States and Latin America. Australia, India, and South Africa have independent commissions that exert considerable influence on these redistributive policies, and they are constitutionally set in Austria, Belgium, Malaysia, and Spain; but in most countries the final distribution of funds is a political question in which actual allocations to regions rests on the same combination of real need and political clout that one finds in unitary systems. In federal systems, there is often controversy not just about how much money is given to which regions, but also about the form in which it is given. In the U.S. terminology, the key distinction is between fund transfers known as either "block" or "categorical" grants, with the distinction being essentially about how specific the central government is in saying how its money should be used. The more specific the grants, the more issues of equity are likely to arise. The requirement in the Indian constitution that the budget pay special attention to the needs of tribal peoples and untouchables is typical of the kind of calculation that can complicate these distributions.

The devolution revolution continues to inspire new legislative and constitutional proposals. Clearly, however, "the basic problems of fiscal imbalance in a federation have never been solved satisfactorily." As Hicks concluded:

For federations fiscal adjustment is a much more difficult operation than for unitary countries who have no constitutional obligations to their lower-level governments. Once we leave the (somewhat unreal) Wheare model of strictly coordinate powers of Federal and State Governments, and the Tiebout . . . model where each family realises which community would suit it best and proceeds to move there, there is no easy or general solution to the problem. . . . Established federations will no doubt continue to experiment with adjustments. But if withdrawls (or worse) occur it is unlikely that they will primarily be on fiscal grounds, although fiscal malaise may make an important contribution.[45]

The Politics of Federalism

If the strains that derive from uneven distributions of needs and resources are generally manageable, they often contribute to other sources of malaise and make them more visible. This is especially so in situations where economic disparities and ethnic cleavages coincide. "In Canada," as Richard Simeon notes,

the institutions of federalism parallel and reinforce the historically dominant socioeconomic cleavages; they cut across them in the United States. Nowhere is this more clear than in the most fundamental division in each country: race in the United States, language in Canada. French-speaking Canadiens are concentrated in Quebec, where they constitute the large majority. The rest of the country, with the exception of New Brunswick, is overwhelmingly English-speaking. African-Americans, by contrast, are widely distributed across the country; in no state are they a majority. This difference has profound consequences for federalism, and for the ways in the politics of race and language are played out.[46]

Federalism can contain and alleviate ethnic conflicts through five mechanisms: (1) by compartmentalizing and multiplying the points of power; (2) by softening the lines of inter-ethnic conflicts by generating intra-ethnic conflicts as in struggles for the control of provincial branches of national parties; (3) promoting inter-ethnic cooperation in support of regional needs; (4) encouraging cooperation on other nonethnic issues; and (5) reducing regional disparities by giving ethnic minorities positions of political, bureaucratic, and academic influence.[47] The likelihood of any or all of these processes proving effective is higher the more diverse the units within which they take place. But this kind of ethnically mixed federal unit is increasingly uncommon. In contrast with Horowitz's conflict-reducing mechanisms, a more troubling scenario is one in which a deepening spiral of discontent fuels rather than ameliorates divisions. Gellner has argued that for each potential province or nation in the world there are five potential states which in ethnic and linguistic terms have as good a claim to separate statehood as those that have it.[48] The logic of Balkanization (if Serbia can separate from Yugoslavia, why not Kosovo from Serbia?) can be extended in an almost infinite chain of fragmentation until ethnic and political boundaries are absolutely coincident. "There is," as one Yugoslav observer puts it, "nothing more perilous for a multi-ethnic community of any type (but especially for a federal one), than the systematic narrowing of all relations in the community to relations among ethnic groups."[49]

If federalism is not to "provide the territorial blueprint for future separatism,"[50] it must cultivate dual loyalties, an ability to see oneself as Canadien *and* Québécois, Bavarian *and* German. Such dual loyalties are built more easily in prosperous or growing nations than in poor: loyalty can be bought when resources are sufficient. Immigrants can play an important role too by compounding and thus diffusing bipolar schisms. And the way in which a state manipulates its symbolic order can be important as well. The "ethnically heterogeneous state," as Cairns puts it,

> should transmit a positive symbolic message that constantly reminds citizens of their heterogeneous nationhood. The state's identity should explicitly include citizens who are not part of the natural ethnic/linguistic majority. The . . . well-functioning state incessantly reminds its people of the evolving nature of the political nation by providing a comprehensive answer to the question—"Who are we as a people now?"[51]

Changing the Canadian flag from one derived from the British was a positive step of this sort; but the failure of such symbolism to have any lasting impact in the former Soviet Union is testimony to the importance of more substantive rules.

Two of these seem to be of particular importance. First, the citizens of every territorial unit have viable connections with both the process of representation in, and the process of service delivery from the national government. Symbolic loyalty is lovely, but the sense that there are people in the government who can speak effectively on behalf of your interests, and who can deliver on at least some of their promises is far more important. If the best and brightest of provincial politicians prefer service in local as opposed to national office; if citizens look only to their state governments for roads, clinics, schools, and social services, federalism is in trouble. Second, it is particularly important for federal systems to have strong, enforceable bills of rights. Small or dispersed minorities in particular "need protection from both orders of government, from both country-wide and regional majorities." Even with a sound Bill of Rights, "The resultant wedding of rights and ethnically based federalism should be seen as a difficult but productive balancing act, an attempt to respond to the two faces of modern ethnicity with constitutional instruments directed at very different ethnic situations. The balancing act is difficult because the tension is real."[52] They work, if they do, through politics and through a set of political rules that can make the task easier or more difficult.

The Rules of the Game

The insistence of theorists like Elazar on the existence of a written constitution may be nit-picking; but the notion that some kind of extraordinary steps must be taken before the national government can usurp state powers is quite basic. The ease with which the central government of India can exercise emergency controls over the provinces is troubling in this regard, even as it has generally been used with restraint. A similar, more opaque article in the U.S. Constitution empowers the national government to assure each state a "republican form of government." Based on the argument that the government ought clearly have the "right to insist that the forms of government under which the compact was entered into should be *substantially* maintained,"[53] this clause has never been put to an actual test; but theoretically it raises troubling questions about the nature of the federal bargain: the abuse of similar clauses, particularly in Latin America, should give one pause.

Equally troubling is the question of the right to secede. The United States is not the only country to have fought a civil war over this issue. Sunstein argues that including a right to secession in a constitution is to "increase the risks of ethnic and factional struggle; reduce the prospects for compromise and deliberation in government; raise dramatically the stakes of day-to-day political decisions; create dangers of blackmail, strategic behavior, and exploitation; and, most generally, endanger the prospects of long-term self governance."[54] But although there is considerable appeal to his basic argument that the idea of a "right" to secession is inimical to the pluralistic ideal that problems can be solved through deliberation, I am not convinced. Almost no Slovenian regrets having left Yugoslavia; neither the Czechs nor the Slovaks are pushing to recombine; and the idea of reconstituting all of the Soviet Union has few democratic supporters. With so many nations having their origins in colonial or dictatorial fiat, federalism can provide a temporary home for future partners to test their positions control in a democratic context.

In these systems, as in more firmly constituted federal democracies, the rules of the game that put the question of consolidation to the test primarily involve issues of human rights. Most important are mechanisms for enforcing bills of rights on the states. Although it took the U.S. Supreme Court more than 150 years to get to it, the idea that the most basic constitutional rights were those of *individual citizens* wherever they lived is crucial. In contrast with Canada (and many other federal systems), it has served to ensure that political debate "was more focused on individual rights than it was on the rights and interests of state or regional collectives."[55] The U.S. Supreme Court's growing insistence on applying the bill of rights to the states has recently been matched by a greater likelihood for the high court in Canada to interpret the charter very broadly in the area of human rights, and for the European Union increasingly to play a proactive role as well.

It is also important that there be sufficient coherence between the units of a federal system to permit easy access from one to another. Climate, culture, and perhaps language notwithstanding, the point at which a citizen of province A refuses to travel to or do business with province B is a sign of trouble. Markets for jobs and goods are no longer local, nor are social relations or cultural communications. Nationality still matters, even in the European Union it is not yet easy to change

your country, but, your county, as Gellner puts it, is another matter.[56] Stable federalism requires provincial governments to govern pliantly enough to respect each
other. Weingast and other conservative rational choice theorists prefer putting regulatory powers in the hands of weaker subnational governments, but even under
these decentralized conditions, "market preserving federalism" requires some forms
of centralization. Weingast suggests, at a minimum, that there be assurance of a
common market, that is, mechanisms "preventing lower governments from using
their regulatory authority to erect trade barriers against the goods and services from
other political units;" and monetary stability in which "the lower governments face
a hard budget constraint, that is, they have neither the ability to print money nor
access to unlimited credit."[57]

Some interstate uniformity in nonmarket areas is also important. What U.S.
jurists call "conflict of law" problems arise in all federal systems. The Constitution
requires each state to give "full faith and credit" to each others' laws so that a
driver's license issued in Rhode Island is valid in Connecticut, and a contract
signed in Iowa cannot be escaped by moving to Kansas. Congress has seldom
chosen to give precise meaning to the rule, but a sort of common law has been
developed, particularly with regard to family law: the conditions, for example,
under which a divorce granted in one state is valid in another. Most recently, these
oft-arcane issues have received national political attention over the question of
whether a same-sex marriage performed in one state would have to be accepted in
the other forty-nine.

The attempt to combine the respective virtues of unity and diversity, of small
places and large, will always generate difficult problems of this kind. By empow-
ering citizens to influence public policy at both a general and more localized level,
federalism offers the potential to let a thousand flowers bloom while keeping the
crops under control. Without strong systems of border control that protect the rights
of minorities within minority regions, that allow a relatively free flow of trade and
social customs, and that guarantee the provinces sufficient powers to make diverse
policies that fit local needs, federal systems are probably not worth sustaining.

Federalism versus Decentralization

The point of federalism is to combine the economies of scale, international capacities, and pluralistic potentials of large states with the more communal identities
and politics of smaller places. The more segmented the society, the more such divisions of power makes sense. Even absent the ethnic cleavages that have plagued
attempts at nation building, the appeal of federalism is strong. But the rhetoric of
both academics and politicians that made devolution and decentralization the words
of the day has not always been matched by action. The U.S. government's growing
tendencies to set such once-local standards as the drinking age, school promotion,

and marriage laws call into question the sincerity of decentralist rhetoric, as have failures to redistribute resources. Similar trends can be found throughout the world with the reality of centralization belying the rhetoric of devolution. The problem derives in large part from the different meanings that diverse groups apply to the same term. Many liberals look to federalism as a means of devolving power to local incubators of participation and laboratories of innovation. Conservatives champion federalism as a device adding extra "veto players" to the political mix. What Stepan calls "demos constraining mechanisms," such as malapportioned bicameral legislatures, make "legislation much more difficult to pass and gives minorities great blocking power."[58] Federalism, in this sense, provides added checks on majority rule which "may also bias government responsiveness in favor of the better off. To the extent that business is more mobile than citizens, and wealthier citizens are more mobile than poorer ones, the competition may well be 'downwards' to lower tax rates, weaker environmental rules and the like."[59] Although "the number of cases is too low and too-biased toward older federal systems to be conclusive,"[60] there is empirical confirmation of this perspective.[61]

Whether federalism imparts a conservative bias to policy depends on the nature of the party system and the distribution of resources in society. One cannot escape the impression that there are situations in which the powers of the central government are devolved to weak local units precisely because controls on business will be weakened. "In many cases of apparent decentralization . . . a transfer of power to a local ministry, unelected committee, NGO [non-governmental organization], or similar institution may not bring real empowerment to the local level."[62] A 1998 forestry law in Senegal, for example, while it apparently granted rural councils the power to manage forests, actually left real power with the larger corporations that had access to the central ministry that had the real power.[63] Laws that present more the symbols of decentralization than the substance, devolutions to units without resources, cooperative relationships between bureaucracies and private corporations that bypass elected officials, may satisfy short-term "conservative" agendas of helping corporate interests but have nothing to do with the cases for federalism openly articulated. They represent, as Aaron Wildavsky described them in a twist on Grodzin's marble cake analogy, "fruit cake federalism."[64]

Federalism in constitutional democracies should seek to devolve power in accord with its core principles of limited government and popular sovereignty. The "executive federalism" characteristic of the systems of both Germany and Austria leaves local legislatures with no real role in shaping major policies. "These tendencies may be acceptable to the administration and civil servants of the states, because they have substantial powers with little accountability, but they are dangerous insofar as they reduce the political self-determination and self-reliance of the states. This affects not only the states' parliaments, but also state governments and the whole democratic process."[65] In Latin America, similar transfers have occurred less formally in "a kind of *de facto* disaggregation of the state as various particularistic interest blocs in a sense captured relevant pieces of the state which they manipulated to their own interests."[66] Whatever the etiology of these power transfers—and they vary from one system to another—they are not and should not be confused with federalism.

Notes

1. Leslie Friedman Goldstein, *Constituting Federal Sovereignty: The European Union in Comparative Context* (Baltimore: The Johns Hopkins University Press, 2001), 3.

2. William H. Riker, *Federalism: Origin, Operation, Significance* (Boston: Little, Brown and Company, 1964); Kenneth C. Wheare, *Federal Government* (Oxford: Oxford University Press, 1946); Daniel Elazar, *Exploring Federalism* (Tuscaloosa: University of Alabama Press, 1987).

3. Daniel Elazar, "From Statism to Federalism: A Paradigm Shift," *International Political Science Review* 17 (October 1996), 436.

4. J. Denis Derbyshire and Ian Derbyshire, *Political Systems of the World* (New York: St. Martin's Press, 1996), 21.

5. Josep M. Colomer, *Political Institutions* (New York: Oxford University Press, 2001), 186.

6. *Federalist,* Number 10.

7. Larry Diamond, *Developing Democracy: Toward Consolidation* (Baltimore: The Johns Hopkins University Press, 1999), 155.

8. Richard Gunther and Anthony Mughan, "Political Institutions and Cleavage Management," in *Do Institutions Matter? Government Capabilities in the United States and Abroad,* ed. R. Kent Weaver and Bert A. Rockman (Washington, DC: The Brookings Institution, 1993), 298.

9. Dennis C. Mueller, *Constitutional Democracy* (New York: Oxford University Press, 1996), 86.

10. Ilija G. Vujacic, "The Challenges of Ethnic Federalism: Experiences and Lessons of the Former Yugoslavia," in *Federalism and Decentralization: Perspectives for the Transformation Process in Eastern and Central Europe,* ed. Jürgen Rose and Johannes Ch. Traut (New York: Palgrave-Macmillan, 2002), 267.

11. Vujacic, "Challenges of Ethnic Federalism," 268.

12. Ursula Kathleen Webb Hicks, *Federalism: Failure and Success: A Comparative Study* (New York: Oxford University Press, 1979), 180.

13. Kent Eaton, "Decentralization's Non-democratic Roots: Military Reforms of Subnational Institutions in Latin America," paper presented at the Annual Meeting of the American Political Science Association, Philadelphia, PA, August 28-31, 2003.

14. Iván Illés, "Federalism and Regionalism in Central and Eastern Europe," in Rose and Traut, *Federalism and Decentralization,* 211.

15. Martha Field, "The Differing Federalisms of Canada and the United States," *Law and Contemporary Problems* 55 (Spring 1992), 109.

16. Richard Simeon, "Canada and the United States: Lessons from the North American Experience," in *Rethinking Federalism: Citizens, Markets, and Governments in a Changing World,* ed. Karen Knop et al. (Vancouver: University of British Columbia Press, 1995), 264.

17. Morton Grodzins, "Centralization and Decentralization in the American Federal System," in *A Nation of States,* ed. Robert A Goldwin (Chicago: Rand-McNally, 1973), 4.

18. Robert D. Cooter, *The Strategic Constitution* (Princeton, NJ: Princeton University Press, 2000), 108.

19. William H. Riker, "Federalism: Origins, Operation, Significance," in *American Federalism in Perspective*, ed. Aaron Wildavsky (Boston: Little, Brown and Company, 1979), 56.

20. Martin Grosse Hüttmann, "The Practice of Federalism in Germany," in Rose and Traut, *Federalism and Decentralization,*, 104.

21. Thomas O. Hueglin, "New Wine in Old Bottles? Federalism and Nation States in the Twenty-First Century: A Conceptual Overview," in Knop, *Rethinking Federalism,* 207.

22. Liesbet Hooghe and Gary Marks, "Unraveling the Central State, but How? Types of Multi-Level Governance," *American Political Science Review* 97 (May 2003), 237, 240.

23. Kathy L. Brock, "The End of Executive Federalism?" in *New Trends in Canadian Federalism,* ed. François Rocher and Miriam Smith (Peterborough, Ontario: Broadview Press, 1995), 91-108.

24. Peter Pernthaler, "Austrian Federalism," in Rose and Traut, *Federalism and Decentralization*, 137.

25. *State ex. rel. Dyer v. Sims* (1951) 341 U.S. 22, 27.

26. James Ross Hurley, "Canadian Federalism: Idiosyncratic Characteristics, Evolution, and Lessons Learned," in Rose and Traut, *Federalism and Decentralization,* 149.

27. Jorge I. Dominguez, "Constructing Democratic Governance in Latin America: Taking Stock of the 1990s," in *Constructing Democratic Governance in Latin America,* ed. Jorge I. Dominguez and Michael Shifter (Baltimore: The Johns Hopkins University Press, 2nd ed., 2003), 374-75.

28. David J. Samuels and Scott Mainwaring, "Strong Federalism, Constraints on the Central Government, and Economic Reform in Brazil," in *Federalism and Democracy in Latin America*, ed. Edward L. Gibson (Baltimore: The Johns Hopkins University Press, 2004), 101.

29. *City of Clinton v. Cedar Rapids and Missouri Railroad Company* 24 Iowa 435 (1968), 461.

30. Ilona Pálné Kovács, "The Chances for Regionalism in Hungary," in Rose and Traut, *Federalism and Decentralization,* 217-30.

31. Timothy D. Sisk, *Democracy at the Local Level: The International IDEA Handbook on Participation, Representation, Conflict Management, and Governance* (Stockholm: International Institute for Democracy and Electoral Assistance, 2001), 23.

32. Susan E. Clarke, "The New Localism: Local Politics in a Global Era," in *The New Localism: Comparative Urban Politics in a Global Era,* ed. Edward G. Goetz and Susan E. Clarke (Newbury Park, CA: Sage Publications, 1993), 19.

33. Patha Chatterjee, *The Politics of the Governed: Reflections on Popular Politics in Most of the World* (New York: Columbia University Press, 2004), 144.

34. Sisk, *Democracy at the Local Level,* 118.

35. James Ross Hurley, "Canadian Federalism," 154.

36. Jonathan Rodden, "Comparative Federalism and Decentralization: On Meaning and Measurement," *Comparative Politics* 36 (July 2004), 482.

37. Arend Lijphart, *Patterns of Democracy: Government Forms and Performance in Thirty-Six Countries* (New Haven: Yale University Press, 1999), 193.

38. Samuels and Mainwaring, "Strong Federalism," 95.

39. Maria Escobar-Lehman, "Fiscal Decentralization and Federalism in Latin America," *Publius: The Journal of Federalism* 31 (Fall 2001), 34.

40. Rodden, "Comparative Federalism," 483, found subnational expenditures rising from an average of 20 percent in 1978 to 32 percent in 1995, but leveling off since then.

41. David McKay, *Designing Europe: Comparative Lessons from the Federal Experience* (New York: Oxford University Press, 2001), 3.

42. James M. Buchanan, *Federalism, Liberty, and the Law* (Indianapolis, IN: The Liberty Fund, 2001), and Charles M. Tiebout, "A Pure Theory of Local Expenditure," *Journal of Political Economy* 74 (Fall 1956), 416-25.

43. Clarke, "The New Localism," 14.

44. Diamond, *Developing Democracy,* 140.

45. Hicks, *Federalism: Failure and Success,* 195.

46. Simeon, "Canada and the United States," 253.

47. Donald L. Horowitz, *Ethnic Groups in Conflict* (Berkeley: University of California Press, 1985), 22.

48. Ernest Gellner, *Nations and Nationalism* (Oxford: Basil Blackwell, 1983), 3.

49. Alan C. Cairns, "Constitutional Government and the Two Faces of Ethnicity: Federalism is Not Enough," in Knop et al., *Rethinking Federalism*, 35.

50. Diamond, *Developing Democracy*, 155.

51. Cairns, "Constitutional Government," 35.

52. Cairns, "Constitutional Government," 32.

53. *Federalist ,* Number 43. Italics in original.

54. Cass R. Sunstein, *Designing Democracy: What Constitutions Do* (New York: Oxford University Press, 2001), 96.

55. Simeon, "Canada and the United States," 252.

56. Ernest Gellner, *Conditions of Liberty: Civil Society and Its Rivals* (New York: Penguin Press, 1994), 88,

57. Barry R. Weingast, "The Economic Role of Political Institutions: Market-Preserving Federalism and Economic Development," *Journal of Law, Economics, and Organization* 11 (January 1995), 5.

58. Stepan, "A New Comparative Politics of Federalism," 45.

59. Simeon, "Canada and the United States," 261.

60. Alfred Stepan, "Veto Players in Unitary and Federal Systems," in Gibson, *Federalism and Democracy in Latin America*, 330.

61. World Resources Institute, *World Resources, 2002-2004* (Washington, DC: World Resources Institute, 2003), 96.

62. *World Resources, 2002-2004,* 97.

63. Aaron Wildavsky, *Federalism and Political Culture,* ed. David Schleicher and Brenda Swedlow (New Brunswick, NJ: Transaction Books, 1998), 56.

64. Peter Pernthaler, "Austrian Federalism," in Rose and Traut, *Federalism and Decentralization,* 131.

65. James M. Malloy, "Authoritarianism and Corporatism in Latin America: The Modal Pattern," in *Authoritarianism and Corporatism in Latin America,* ed. James M. Malloy (Pittsburgh, PA: University of Pittsburgh Press, 1977), 65.

Chapter 11

Courts and the Legal System

Law is sometimes cynically described as anything that someone with the power to enforce it says it is. This is the opposite of what constitutional democracy promises in its commitment to *due process*. Its essence is not in "abstract values" so much as in "the character of those processes that make, interpret, and enforce the law."[1] The distinctive role of the legal system in constitutional democracies works backward from this list: it *enforces* the law to be sure; and, in doing so, may *interpret* it; but leaves the process of *making law*, by and large, to the other branches. It does so largely because its power cuts so tellingly close to the everyday lives of every citizen that its powers cry out for restraint. A society founded in rule-of-law ideals must take special steps to keep it under constraint, to bind it by rules that assure fairness.

Hans Kelsan's blunt statement that "the law is a coercive order"[2] makes many uncomfortable; but despite the thousands of pages that have been devoted to more elaborate definitions, most end up depicting law in terms of rewards and sanctions. Social norms often have the strength of law, and church, business, and community leaders often play enforcement roles that resemble those of the legal apparatus to the extent that legal theorists have long been divided on the question of whether law can exist without state backing; or where the line between formal and informal law should be drawn (if at all). But however these questions are answered, the legal systems with which constitutions are concerned are those that are either sanctioned or run by the state. "Law, morality, and religion, all three forbid murder," as Kelsan says,

But the law does this by providing that if a man commits murder, then another man, designated by the legal order, shall apply against the murderer a certain measure of coercion, prescribed by the legal order. Morality limits itself to requiring: though shalt not kill. And if . . . many an individual refrains from murder not so much because he wants to avoid the punishment of law as to avoid the more disapprobation of his fellow men, the great distinction still remains, that the reaction of the law consists in a measure of coercion enacted by the order, and socially organized, whereas the mere reaction against immoral conduct is neither provided by the moral order, nor, if provided, socially organized.[3]

Whether we use the word "law" to apply to social norms and sanctions as well as those of the state is not terribly important here; what is important is that formal laws—the state-sanctioned coercive mechanisms established by constitutions—have expanded in both scope and geographical coverage. State-enforced statutes have supplanted ecclesiastical decrees, social norms, feuds, and individual acts of violence as the accepted ways of resolving disputes and punishing transgressions. The legal arm of the state, moreover, now extends to virtually every corner of the world from the remote settlements of the Inuit in Canada to the deepest jungles of New Guinea.

Legal Systems

It is the proud boast of constitutional democracies not that they divide morality from law, but that they subject it to process. The legal systems of constitutional democracies are not distinguished by being less coercive than those of theocracies or dictatorships (though they may be), but by the careful ways in which they define and constrain state powers. Nor are the legal systems of constitutional democracies particularly distinguished by their content. In most cases new democracies retain the basic laws of the old order with regard to crime, contracts, and so on, adding the particular protections of checks and balances, bills of rights, and the procedural constraints associated with them. While systems may vary in the particular rules they apply,

> The internal morality of the law demands that there be rules, that they be made known, and that they be observed in practice by those charged with their administration. These demands may seem ethically neutral so far as the external aims of law are concerned. Yet just as law is a precondition for good law, so acting by known rule is a precondition for any meaningful appraisal of the justice of law. . . . It is the virtue of a legal order conscientiously constructed and administered that it exposes to public scrutiny the rules by which it acts.[4]

Students of constitutional law in the United States distinguish the "substantive" rights, such as freedom of speech and religion from "procedural rights" which are those that collectively define what the system defends as due process. The basis of the common law concept of due process is "notice and hearing" which means at a minimum that both the general rules of the game and the specific intent to launch legal proceedings must be openly proclaimed. It is on this bedrock principle that the varying legal systems of constitutional democracies are built.

Code and Common Law Traditions

The major concerns of the legal system are strikingly consistent from one country to another. "Every country has criminal laws and uses them to maintain what the authors of the U.S. Constitution termed 'domestic tranquility'.... Roughly the same set of common crimes are outlawed in every country."[5] Courts are also used in most systems to resolve disputes between individuals. The component parts of the system are also similar, commonly including police agencies, legal professionals, and judges. But the differences between systems are also striking both in terms of institutions, the ways they process cases, and even in their attitudes toward the legal system.

Working within the context of local and national cultures, most legal systems have their roots in either a common law or code tradition. With origins largely in the British Isles, common law, adversarial systems predominate in the United Kingdom and its former colonies. Code systems, with their roots in the Roman Empire, dominate in continental Europe as the result of Napoleonic conquest in the early nineteenth century. Through the colonial offices of the French, Spanish, Dutch, German, Portuguese, and Italians, "The importance of the post-revolutionary French penal procedural codes as models for both European and global criminal systems cannot be over-emphasized. Their influence is far more pervasive and extensive than that of the Anglo-American common law and both the intellectual coherence and the practical advantages of the great Napoleonic codification of 1808 have insured its international popularity."[6] Countries such as Canada and South Africa, with mixed colonial roots, tend to mix code and common law system.

In the common law, much as in the tribal councils of traditional systems, precedent rules. Judges, in the course of resolving disputes and punishing miscreants, draw upon the customs and norms of the society to decide particular cases. As these decisions accumulate, they develop the force of law, not so much out of reverence for the past, but because both common sense and justice suggest that similar cases should be similarly decided. Closely associated with the common law tradition is an adversary-based process and what is sometimes described as a "fight theory" of justice which puts judge and jury in the more-or-less neutral role of referee. Courts, in contrast with those in most code countries "are largely passive; they wait for cases to come to them, and, when the cases arrive, they wait for the adversaries to proceed."[7]

Code systems derive legal rules from legislative statutes. The role of the judge is at once far less active in deciding questions of law, far more active in seeking out facts. Rather than wait for the opposing parties, it is the job of the judge to seek out the relevant facts, often before the case even reaches formal trial. Particularly at lower court levels, the atmosphere is informal: instead of questioning by attorneys—with the frequent legal maneuvers familiar to viewers of U.S. courtroom dramas—witnesses are invited simply to describe their perceptions of the facts, often with prodding from the judge.

The differences between common law and code law countries have become more difficult to discern. Recent years have seen code country judges increasingly citing their own decisions, or those of other judges, particularly in cases that involve new social and economic problems not directly accounted for in the older codes. In common law countries, more strikingly, legislatures have become far more active in codifying everything from the rules of conduct governing the police to the fine details of both criminal and civil law. The code movement in the United States, while it did not formally repeal the common law, has for all legal intents and purposes displaced judge-made rules with statutes in trial settings. Criminal law in both Canada and Australia is essentially code-based today, and even in Great Britain, police procedures and a number of centrally important substantive issues are the products more of statutory than of judge-made law.

Until the latter part of the nineteenth century, under the intellectual thrall of Edward Cook, most legal scholars in the United States regarded legislation as little more than a means of filling the gaps in the common law. By 1900, however, virtually every major facet of criminal law in the U.S. states was embodied in or superseded by statutory definitions, and the civil law was soon to follow. New York's penal code of 1891 went so far as to abolish the concept of common law crime, and it has all but done so with civil law as well. Students of comparative law increasingly regard the distinction between common and code law systems as oversimple; but they do continue to distinguish systems that are primarily "adversarial," on the one hand, and "inquisitorial" on the other.

> The adversarial mode of proceeding takes its shape from a contest or dispute: it unfolds as an engagement of two adversaries before a relatively passive decision maker whose principal duty is to reach a verdict. The nonadversarial mode is structured as an official inquiry. Under the first system, the two adversaries take charge of most of the procedural action; under the second, officials perform most of the activities.[8]

Even with this more limited distinction, "there is hardly a country where legal scholars accept their criminal justice system to be purely adversarial or inquisitorial."[9] Hybrids, as in the South African combination of its British common law and Dutch code systems, are more common. The sense that the investigations carried out under judicial supervision sometimes favor the prosecution have given defense lawyers a larger, more adversarial role in many inquisitorial systems. The adversarial system's tendency to depersonalize the fight, conversely, often overlooks mitigating factors and has led to much more proactive court roles in family, juvenile, and drug courts in particular, and in the growing use of mediation in resolving civil disputes.

Criminal Justice and Dispute Resolution

Legal systems have become increasingly fragmented. Although law schools in most countries continue to require a general background in all facets of the basic law, practicing lawyers and courts have become more specialized. In larger, more complex democracies, courts have tended to proliferate and to differentiate themselves from one another. The two most basic functions of the legal system are law enforcement activities in which the state actively seeks to punish and prevent anti-social activities; and conflict resolution, in which the state provides a forum for the settlement of disputes, or for the oversight of privately-negotiated agreements such as contracts and wills. Many systems, especially in common law countries, institutionalize this distinction by distinguishing so-called civil courts which resolve private disputes from criminal courts. Generally, it is these dispute resolution courts that have become more specialized, though criminal courts that deal with special kinds of crimes or offenders are also becoming commonplace. Every U.S. state, for example, now has a distinct system of juvenile courts, and many have special drug courts as well as more traditional traffic and parking courts. Some idea of the kinds of private disputes that civil courts are likely to consider can be gained from a look at the types of cases brought before state courts in the United States in a typical year.

By far the largest proportion of civil cases (33 percent in 1990) were those involving domestic relations.[10] Divorce and child custody cases are the most common in this category, but questions of parental fitness, adoption, foster care, and so on, often require very different kinds of mediation than courts traditionally provide, and are often dealt with by special family courts. The next largest categories of cases in the civil courts of the United States are those involving contracts, torts (or claims of damage), property, and estates. It is the large proportion of cases involving contracts, torts, and property that have given the United States the reputation of being an unusually litigious society. In Japan, conversely, "formal litigation is rarely used to resolve disputes." As Sanders explains, "the government has created a legal system that strongly discourages and even occasionally prohibits private suits to redress grievances. The relative lack of lawyers, court delays, strict standing rules, the unavailability of class actions, and the relative certainty of outcomes all conspire to make litigation an unattractive alternative."[11] Most lawsuits in the United States are also settled out of court, but the very presence of an active judiciary and tradition of litigation means that far more suits are brought than in other countries. These differences are narrowing, with many European countries in particular becoming more litigious.

Economic globalization is spreading the tendency: it requires "a kind of common language—a way for buyers, sellers, traders, dealmakers to communicate with each other."[12] Major law firms now have offices throughout the world. "Legal practice," as Friedman points out, "remains in many ways stubbornly parochial. Most lawyers are as local as barnacles. Yet, on the other hand, there *is* a kind of globalization of law. Something *is* happening. If culture and trade globalize, law will almost inevitably follow. And the emerging global law speaks, more and more, with an American accent."[13] Lawyers are at once proliferating and prospering, with the courts expanding the boundaries of the legal system to bring new issues into their purview. Judges are tightening their grip on the process in both common law and code systems, if only because more aggressive "parties and their lawyers can only be kept at bay by an active judiciary that directs the litigation process and is able to prevent disruptive tactics."[14] An increasing convergence of public and private law has also helped produce a "far-reaching reconceptualization of civil liberties and civil rights" around the world. "Fairness, just compensation, and equality before the law have emerged as persistent themes in modern legal culture."[15]

Courts and Rights

The proliferation of specialized courts, decline of traditional dispute-resolution systems, and globalization have combined to accelerate a convergence of legal systems. If only through increasing contacts with diverse traditions, the world legal community is learning to adapt. More important, formal bills of rights—as noted in earlier chapters—are both more likely to be incorporated into constitutions, and to be enforced. The United Nation's Universal Declaration of Human Rights, once regarded as essentially symbolic, is now embedded to some degree in the constitutions of a majority of democracies, and enforcement has been internationalized. This process is more advanced in the newer democracies where the absence of legal precedents has often led to wholesale borrowing from other systems; but even the U.S. Supreme Court, long fiercely parochial, has begun to take note of certain human, as opposed to national, rights. In 1989, for example, the Court—in ruling that it was not unconstitutional to sentence a sixteen-year-old to death—explicitly denied the relevance of "the sentencing policies of other countries."[16] Just thirteen years later, in holding that executions of the mentally impaired were wrong, the majority specifically cited the thinking of "distinguished jurists" in other countries as a factor in their decision.[17]

Both common and code law systems have been faulted—from different perspectives—for failing to meet the standard of equal justice. The adversary system in particular cries out for rules to guarantee fair fights. In criminal cases, the relative powers of the state are overwhelming: except perhaps for those with great wealth, few individuals can match the investigatory and prosecutorial resources of the state. In civil cases, the very ability of one side to hire better lawyers is often determinative. As modernization forces us to live increasingly among strangers, we rely more on formal rules and less on community ties to protect ourselves from exploitation. The principal of procedural due process, embodied in most world constitutions, attempts to level the playing field for ordinary citizens confronting the state or the elite.

The legal realist movement in the United States, and a variety of other schools deriving from it, argue that such discrepancies can never be overcome. While the realists did not necessarily embrace the Marxist point of view that law is nothing more than a tool of dominant economic forces, their challenge to the ideal of impartiality has proven difficult to refute.[18] Michel Foucault's further suggestion that judicial reform is essentially a mask for more sophisticated forms of repression has been widely debated in intellectual circles, and had considerable influence.[19] With few exceptions, however, all but the most hard-nosed realists have spent at least some time fighting for reforms they hope will help to balance the scales. The most widespread models of change focus on making all sectors of the system—from police and the bar to courts and correctional institutions—work without discriminating on the basis of criteria, such as race, gender, and wealth, that are irrelevant to the case at hand.

Bills of rights provide the parchment guidelines on which these controls are most commonly structured; but the most important forces are those deriving from what could best be described as—if the Americans hadn't appropriated the term for another use—"judicial review." What I mean here is not the ability of a court (as in U.S. usage) to rule a law unconstitutional, but rather the general process of hierarchical review through which various appellate courts are able to impose constitutionally-defined standards of conduct upon other actors in the legal system. It is in the enormous modern expansion of judicial review in this sense that bills of rights have come to play central roles in the process of administering justice. "Constitutional norms," as Favoreau wrote of Europe in 1990, "are progressively impregnating all branches of law, thanks to the increasingly important jurisprudence of fundamental rights. Constitutional law is no longer just institutional law; it is also substantive law whose application has a direct effect on individuals. In this, the European systems increasingly approach the American in breaking with the civil law tradition."[20]

Until recently, most legal systems were organized along parallel as opposed to hierarchical principles. In federal systems, criminal justice procedures, in particular, were seldom reviewed at a national level. In most code law countries, where statutes were supreme, an appellate court might find a lower court in error in its interpretation of a statute; but even if the lower court finding was overruled, the principle used to issue that finding was not *per se* binding on other courts. French appeals (*cassation*) courts, for example, almost never issued written opinions, preferring simply to refer them back to the lower courts for rehearing. In the United States, where virtually all criminal cases were decided in state as opposed to federal courts, the ringing phrases of the Bill of Rights only recently acquired real meaning in the day to day functioning of the legal system. Until the 1960s the Supreme Court remained reluctant to impose the procedural guarantees of the Constitution on state courts. Despite Justice Frankfurter's declaration that "the history of liberty has largely been the history of observance of procedural safeguards,"[21] neither he nor a majority of his colleagues was willing to overrule state procedures in any but the most egregious violations of due process. Within ten years of Frankfurter's retirement, however, "nearly all of the guarantees of the Bill of Rights were applied to the states."[22] The Warren Court, moreover, extended coverage of these rights back into the earliest stages of the legal process, ruling, for example, that the right to counsel applied not just in court but from the moment of arrest, as did the right to remain silent and be apprized of one's rights.

This history—more appropriately told elsewhere[23]—is brought in here because it both portends and exemplifies worldwide tendencies. Except for substantive rights, some major crimes, or crimes against the state such as treason, most modern constitutions focus on procedures. John Finn writes that,

> To my knowledge, every register of constitutional liberties contains a provision substantially like the due process clause. On a particular level, of course, what constitutes due process varies tremendously across political systems, and within political systems over time. At a more general level of abstraction, however, due process clauses of every sort amount to a command that governments act not upon individual rights unless they can articulate publicly a "good reason" on behalf of the proposed action.[24]

Constitutional democracy thus seeks to counter the fear of biased judges by requiring each of them—as well as the police and other actors in the legal system—to be prepared to give a "good reason" for having made a particular decision, a reason that "must somehow transcend the personal, transient beliefs of the judge or the body politic."[25]

Kwasi Prempeh's analysis of African courts distinguishes "a jurisprudence of executive supremacy," in which "the state walks into the courthouse with an almost irrefutable presumption of lawfulness as to its conduct," from a "jurisprudence of constitutionalism," that recognizes and enforces rights.[26] The divergence between the two "is explained not so much by substantive differences in the relevant constitutional texts as by the different strands of jurisprudence at play."[27] Beyond the legal system's willingness and ability to observe due process standards,

> a jurisprudence of constitutionalism imposes on state actors a heavy burden of proof and persuasion before a constitutional right may be lawfully restricted. In this regard, it compels the state to move away from the habit of coercion and self-assertion and to cultivate instead an ethic of restraint and justification. It is this rights-respecting jurisprudence, and not the might-justifying jurisprudence of the past, that must now guide the exercise of judicial review by Africa's courts.[28]

In order to fulfill this role, particularly in less-developed countries, courts and other legal institutions must have the resources to act. Due process, moreover, is not simply measured or tested in the court room, but in the legal system as a whole.

Legal Institutions

Modern proponents of constitutional democracy regard the development of due process and the rule of law as essential to the reduction of official corruption and privilege, and to ultimate public acceptance of the legitimacy of the state. While the realists and most scholars doubt that equal justice can ever fully be obtained, the notion that it is a goal worth striving to achieve has gained widespread currency. Because fair and impartial courts do not guarantee a fair system of law enforcement, a jurisprudence of constitutionalism must embrace all aspects of the legal system from police behavior to systems of punishment and penalty.

The Police

In most criminal cases, and many civil disputes, the citizen's involvement with the legal system begins with the police. It often ends there as well, with the police dispersing a crowd, calming an angry spouse, or issuing a warning to a speeding driver. Most constitutions treat the police much as they treat other bureaucracies, leaving it largely to legislation to define how they work. Given the ubiquity of police forces in modern society, it is interesting how modern they are. Over the objections of those who argued that the methods of prosecuting crime lay in the courts, prosecutors, and "the moral habits and opinion of the people,"[29] it was not until 1819 that British Prime Minister Peel pushed through the creation of a police force. Although it marked the beginning of a worldwide tendency to regard the legal system as an active force in promoting public safety, the idea of controlling crime through "moral habits" and victims taking their antagonists to the local magistrate is not entirely obsolete. Vigilante justice is still common. It can range from spontaneous community attempts to supplement official police activities, to something that resembles a parallel police system run by a political or economic elite unwilling to be constrained by due process. For many years, for example, Costa Rica's business elite sustained the paramilitary *Movimiento Costa Rica Libre* as a check on perceived police failures.[30] And in Brazil, where larger cities such as São Paulo have as few as one policeman for every 3,000 inhabitants (as compared to one for 460 in England), lynchings are common.[31]

If the establishment of a trained police force under legal constraints is generally considered a sign of progress relative to vigilante justice, the line between the two is often ill-defined. Where the courts are perceived to be inefficient, corrupt, or "soft on crime," it is not uncommon for the police to act as judge and jury as well, or to simply hold people in custody without bringing formal charges. In sharply divided societies, the police—or the armed forces acting as domestic police—frequently ignore due process rules entirely to take direct action against perceived terrorists or revolutionaries. Postcolonial and postauthoritarian police forces are often appropriately mistrusted by the populace. It is not just in Latin America that,

> Corruption in the police is endemic. Even when not corrupt, the police do not generally know how to secure convictions by civilized means and resort to brutality in order to extract confessions. . . . Relatively few cases come to trial. . . . This is a process

open to endless abuse. People from poor backgrounds suspected of petty crimes remain in prison for years because they cannot afford bail or bribes while the rich but guilty walk free. As a result of this, crime rates are higher across the region than they have ever been, while there has been an enormous but ineffective increase in imprisonment—not necessarily of the guilty.[32]

The kind of we/they mentality that develops in these situations makes effective law enforcement impossible to achieve. Thus while it is clear that "the policing dimension of state building is closely related to the deepening of democracy, and the reforms needed to develop civilian control over the military apply to the police as well,"[33] few problems of democratization have proven more intractable.

"The tension between the operational consequences of ideas of order, efficiency, and initiative, on the one hand, and legality, on the other, constitutes the principal problem of police as a democratic legal organization."[34] In the European and U.S. traditions, the primary checks work largely through other components of the legal system. In code systems, the active role of magistrates in the process of booking and prosecuting defendants puts the police under the direct control of legally-trained magistrates subject, generally, to hierarchical controls. In the Anglo-American conflict systems, the accused has a right to counsel that provides similar safeguards. And in both systems, there is a basic assumption that abuses which occur at street level can be corrected higher up, so that the police, for example, knowing that a conviction based on tainted evidence will not stand up in court, will eschew such tactics in making arrests. These safeguards, problematic as they can be in mature systems, seldom work in developing ones. But the literature on constitutional democracy is strikingly thin on alternative methods of checking police powers. In the literature on constitutional democracy, the question of how to organize the constabulary receives little attention.

Striking a balance in which the police are at once effective yet controlled is difficult, particularly when resources are limited. Where developed countries spend an average of less than 3 percent of their budgets on crime prevention and criminal justice, the comparable figure for developing countries ranges between 9 and 14.[35] It is rather meaningless to call for "better" police when budgets are so strained. "The task of controlling and directing police efforts becomes all the more difficult when there are multiple police forces that share some overlapping tasks, are directed by different authorities, and tend to compete for the same resources."[36] Multiple agencies, particularly when they include the military, are almost impossible to control through the administrative hierarchy. In modern constitutional democracies, there are few if any areas in which the gap between formal rules and street realities are wider than in policies regarding law enforcement. Civilian control is basic, as is a strong court system; and a variety of experiments with community-based police work show some promise. Civilian review boards can limit some of the worst offenses, but police codes of silence often prove difficult to penetrate. The general tendency has been to check rights-threatening behavior by strengthening those aspects of the legal system that challenge the worst cases of abuse.

Lawyers

The old adage that people who represent themselves in court have fools for clients often rings true. Some lawyers, moreover, are better than others. In adversary systems in particular, disparities in access to competent representation are major barriers to equal justice. States have played increasingly active roles in attempts to level the playing field by guaranteeing the right to effective counsel. The first step is simply one of implementing the right itself. Although Article Six of the U.S. Bill of Rights rather clearly guarantees the accused "the assistance of counsel for his defense," the right applied only in the case of a very few major crimes tried in federal courts. The Supreme Court extended the right to cover all federal crimes in 1938, and to capital crimes and "special cases" in state courts in 1942.[37] Not until the landmark 1963 case of *Gideon v. Wainwright* were defendants in most criminal trials given the right to legal representation whether they could afford it or not.[38] In a series of related decisions, the right to counsel has been held to apply virtually from the moment of arrest, through preliminary hearings, indictments, arraignments, and appeals.

To implement the *Gideon* rule, most of the U.S. states strongly encourage all lawyers to volunteer part time help to indigent criminal defendants. They also provide funds to the Legal Aid Society and similar organizations of lawyers specializing in such cases. Largely because they are chronically underfunded, these agencies are not always able to provide the kinds of legal defenses one might get from private counsel. Public defenders are also far less likely to be provided in civil cases. Absent public funding or the voluntary work of attorneys, the right to counsel is essentially empty. Whatever it says in the constitution, this is the case in many if not most countries, with the resultant reality that the system works better for the rich than the poor. In criminal cases these discrepancies are particularly evident in adversarial systems. In code law countries, an accused party's access to counsel remains very limited. Starting from the premise "that the immediate involvement of an independent judge" combined with "careful regulations for the behavior of police, prosecution and examining judge"[39] are the main barriers to abuse, most European countries continue to downplay the role of counsels for the defense.

The problem in most developing countries is less one of what kind of legal assistance they should provide than of what they can. Simply to provide trained staffing for the courts is problem enough without having also to worry about public defenders. In most cases, new democracies have no realistic alternative to adopting all or most of the previous regimes code or common law rules if only because the few people with legal training were trained according to that system; the law libraries have only those kinds of books. The shortage of trained lawyers in emerging democracies often forces reliance—particularly for the less affluent—on attorneys with little or no formal training. As in the nineteenth century in the United States, standards for admission to the bar tend to be minimal. The emergence of a professional bar in the United States can be quite accurately described as the result of the efforts of a relatively small elite to protect themselves from competition. But it also represented a sincere effort to set minimum levels of competence. Since having a bad lawyer may be worse than having no lawyer at all, state courts, even in the highly competitive U.S. system, have taken an increasingly active role in enforcing standards of conduct; but establishing the standards is not easy: "Judicial scrutiny of counsel's performance," as the Supreme Court has said, "must be highly deferential. It is all too tempting for a defendant to second-guess counsel's assistance after conviction or adverse sentence, and it is all too easy for a court, examining counsel's defense after it has proved unsuccessful, to conclude that a particular act or omission of counsel was unreasonable."[40]

As the rights-oriented view of the legal process reaches across the globe, other systems are becoming increasingly conflictual in style. Particularly in Africa and Asia, it remains a controversial issue as to whether "The western emphasis on civil and political rights" can overcome "an alleged Asian preference for economic well-being and communal goods;"[41] but the consensual modes of decision making said to characterize some cultures, and European preferences for quiet negotiations, seem generally to be yielding to an adverserial, rights-oriented set of institutional dynamics.

Courts

Courts are the central institutions of most legal systems, having the final say in balancing the competing claims of police and the accused, and among lawyers and their clients. To a considerable degree, courts reflect the centralizing tendencies of the government of which they are a part. Federal systems tend to disperse some powers to provincial courts; and complex, pluralistic systems with functionally dispersed bureaucracies have complex networks of specialized courts covering such topics as traffic violations, narcotics, housing, maritime law, workers' compensation, and so on. "With its many distinct court systems, each with its own trial courts, appellate courts, and federal high courts, with the further internal division of the federal high courts into specialized senates, the German judiciary has reached a degree of differentiation unsurpassed by any of its Continental neighbors."[42] Together with the United States it has what is arguably the most complex judiciary in the world; but it is probably less of an anomaly than a harbinger of things to come in other countries, particularly those with federal systems. The more complex the system, the more important it becomes—insofar as equal justice is an important value—to have a well-defined structure of appellate courts, as in the U.S. and German systems, that can impose a degree of uniformity on trial court procedures and rulings.

Appellate courts also play a major role in most newly emerging democracies where trial courts are unreliable and poorly staffed. Lower court judges are often unfamiliar with the changes in law that democratization brings, and this encourages appeals to higher courts. The backlog of cases at the appellate level is generally high, resulting in long delays and still further problems for the system. The legal systems of constitutional democracies strive, in different ways and to varying degrees, to isolate the courts from normal politics. If the core values of constitutionalism and democracy sometimes conflict, the most likely point of contact is in the courts. It is here that the limits constitutions sometimes impose on majorities are most likely to be tested. In a rule-of-law regime, the courts must be independent enough to compel the other branches of the government to act lawfully. When citizens come into conflict with each other, or with their governments, we want "judges whose autonomy or independence gives us reason to believe that they will resolve the issues fairly, according to their understanding of the law, and not out of fear of recrimination or hope of reward."[43] No political actor is ever entirely autonomous, nor would we want them to be; and although we may hope that by donning judicial robes otherwise ordinary human beings will lose all their prejudices and personal beliefs, most of us know better. But if judicial independence is in a sense a myth, most constitutions attempt in various ways to give it substance. Although legislatures are usually empowered to create new courts and redefine the jurisdictions of existing ones, this power, and the vulnerability to which it subjects the courts is usually "moderated by constitutional 'guarantees' that restrict legislative control over the judiciary."[44]

Security of tenure is one cornerstone of these restrictions. Whether judges are granted life tenure, or long, fixed terms, "What is essential for judicial independence is that removal should be very difficult and should be based on a demonstration, judiciously arrived at, that the judge is incapable of discharging the responsibilities of judicial office."[45] The tradition in many U.S. states of directly electing judges has not been widely emulated and is losing ground there as well. The Japanese constitution, together with that of many newer states, models its method of judicial selection on a variant of what has become known in the United States as the Missouri Plan. Its three basic elements include nonpartisan panels that screen and nominate three candidates for each vacancy; appointment by the governor; and ratification, either by the electorate or the legislature. The Japanese supreme court has effectively coopted this procedure: a judicial hierarchy rewards conformity and "discourages individualism on the bench,"[46] and makes the courts captives of the status quo.

Particularly in systems which grant life tenure to judges, some form of consociational politics seems generally desirable. The process of senatorial confirmation in the U.S. Senate has often involved delays, vetoes, and so-called filibusters (which essentially require a 60 percent majority) before a federal judge can be approved, and a growing number of states put judicial nominees through similar hoops. South Africa's judicial service commission, Germany's carefully balanced process, and the roles played by judicial councils in Spain and Portugal play such roles. As Russell cautions, however, "if there is no pluralism in a country's political system, there will be no pluralism in its judicial appointing system."[47] Similarly, it can be argued, if politics is divorced from law, the process of judicial selection is far more likely to be based on merit than it is in countries like the United States where the road to judgeships frequently leads through party politics and running for other offices.

Although it may be a case of locking the barn after the horse has run away, most U.S. states rightly prohibit continued partisan activity once a judge has won election.

In the final analysis, constitutional rules are neither a necessary nor a sufficient condition for judicial independence. Because of their role in protecting basic rights, sometimes in defiance elected officials, the courts often serve as convenient targets of attack. There are times in the histories of most older democracies, where tenured, independent judges have been badly, and sometimes wrongly, out of sync with public opinion and political realities; but the cases in which such independence has persisted, or in which one could characterize the system as "court dominated" are rare. There is rather universal truth to Hamilton's observation that among the branches of government, "the judiciary, from the nature of its functions, will always be the least dangerous to the political rights of the Constitution; because it will be least in a capacity to annoy or injure them."[48] Disputes over the "proper" role of the courts are particularly likely to arise in democracies that give appellate or specially created constitutional courts the power to set aside acts of the other branches as unconstitutional.

Where a 1978 study showed that only twenty-six of the world's democracies had such powers, virtually all subsequent constitutions have created either a special constitutional court or assigned significant powers of judicial review to the appellate courts. In a more recent survey, fifty-six of the eighty-two constitutions studied granted the courts substantial powers of judicial review.[49] The roots of this change are probably to be found largely in the growing emphasis on human rights also found in most of these contemporary documents. To include a bill of rights in a constitution more or less logically suggests creation of an institutional device to enforce it. Ginsburg adds to this the interesting notion that the institutional spread of judicial review may also represent a widespread frustration with the illiberal tendencies of many third wave regimes that are democratic more in form than in substance. The courts are empowered, in this sense, not just to protect rights but to monitor the constitutional elements of democracy more generally.[50] Hamilton, it might be noted, anticipated this function in arguing that "the courts were designed to be an intermediate body between the people and the legislature, in order, among other things, to keep the latter within the limits assigned to their authority."[51]

Equal Justice under the Law

Anatole France's famous observation that the law is equally harsh on both rich and poor people who sleep under the bridges of Paris neatly encapsulates a fundamental irony. "Courts and legal services," as Garro puts it,

> are in theory available to all, just like the Sheraton hotel—anybody can enter, all that is needed is money. The truth of the matter is that justice is an expensive commodity, even in those countries with the highest levels of education and a generous

allocation of expenditure in social welfare. In Latin America, in particular, the sad truth is that the machinery of justice has historically been beyond the reach of the mass of the population, which happens to receive a small proportion of the national income.[52]

Legal theorists increasingly treat the degree to which citizens are treated with equal and fair consideration by the law as a hallmark of constitutional democracy.[53] This does not mean that people are, or should, be equal in any but a rather limited *legal* sense. There is, to be sure, a long and respectable line of argument to the effect that "true" democracy cannot be achieved in the presence of substantial social and economic inequality. The idea that the kind of state intervention required to assure such equality has an equally distinguished set of backers. Somewhere along a continuum of societies that sharply divide the very rich from the very poor, and those that go to great lengths to equalize wealth and status, there are points at both ends of the scale where democracy is problematic. But that is not the issue here, and—except at these extreme points— not the issue in crafting democracies. "The definition," as Guillermo O'Donnell puts it, "that conflates democracy with a substantial degree of social justice or equality is not analytically useful."[54] (Neither, I would argue, is a definition that totally ignores these variables.) What is relevant, and indeed central to the legal systems of con- stitutional democracies, is "the premise that everyone is endowed with a basic degree of autonomy and responsibility, unless there is conclusive and highly elaborate proof to the contrary. This is the presumption that makes every individual a 'legal person,' a carrier of formally equal rights and obligations not only in the political realm but also in contract, tort, criminal, and tax obligations, in dealings with state agencies, and in many other spheres of social life."[55] It is important, and a growing number of constitutional democracies have given explicit recognition to this need, that the legal system and the protections of rights it should afford, be available to the poor as well as the rich. If the state provides a right to divorce, to sue for damages, to have a fair trial, it should provide the means by which these rights are available to all. This is only in part a question of resources. The backlog of cases in many poor countries is so large as to make the concept of accessability virtually irrelevant. But as Jacob points out, "To understand the accessibility of courts, one must examine both the range of options available to those with grievances and the organization of legal advice and assistance."[56] It may require a lawyer, as it does in some countries, to buy a house; but it need not. It may require lawyers and a judge to get a divorce, or the system can be structured to make such "legal" actions largely administrative and inexpensive.

As important as the issue of access is to the concept of equal justice, it is also important that the system be perceived as fair. It is "not only the immense difficulty" the less-privileged "confront for obtaining, if at all, what nominally is their right, but it is also the indifferent, if not disdainful, way in which they are treated and the obvious inequality entailed when the privileged skip these hardships."[57] The ability of members of certain elites to live above the rules that constrain ordinary citizens is as subversive of the legal system as its inaccessability to the poor.

Many of these inequities have their roots in traditional legal cultures in which status hierarchies are deeply embedded in the institutions of the state. Many years ago, Max Weber saw the emergence of an ideal type of law characterized by "formal rationality" that in displacing traditional and feudal concepts of personal laws made possible both the rise of capitalism and the modern state. This concept of law as an abstract, universal set of rules as opposed to the protection of privilege was—when Weber described it nearly a century ago—almost entirely a Western phenomenon that has now spread throughout the world. It has not entirely displaced traditional justice: many legal systems, for example, continue to embrace separate and unequal systems of justice for men and women. And other forms of legal inequality based on economic status continue to flourish. They reflect, from a Weberian perspective, the tendency for a nation's legal system to reflect the political power relations of the societies in which they are embedded.

Weber's ideal types tend actually to blend into one another; but however one writes legal history, the increasingly universal standard for evaluating the legal orders of constitutional democracies emphasizes "the importance of rules and of logical consistency in the application of rules."[58] Equal justice, from this perspective, is justice that derives from the logic of the case rather than from the status of the citizen.

Justice and Democracy

In his ruminations on legal history, Weber speculated about the possible emergence of a fourth system, labeled "substantive rationality," which "accords prominence not to logical consistency but to ethical considerations, utility, expediency and public policy."[59] In recent years, support for this kind of law has emerged in movements to supplement or displace existing systems with community-based, or even "traditional" legal systems that focus less on formal rules and equal justice than on community values, negotiation, and interpersonal communications. A growing number of countries have established special family courts or, in some cases, quasi-legal mediation and conflict resolution agencies which, instead of rendering verdicts, negotiate settlements between the participants. In a number of countries, similar functions are served by traditional community boards or religious courts. Indonesia, for example, has refused to adopt the Islamic rules of *Sharia;* but encourages Moslems to settle a variety of private disputes through state-supported Moslem courts. Papua New Guinea, Kenya, and Zambia have similarly empowered local magistrates to play quasi-legal conflict resolution roles under the supervisory umbrella of district courts. These systems of "developing justice," similar to alternative dispute mechanisms in the U.S. states, provide "traditional means of justice utilising trusted community members as arbitrators, combined with modern considerations involving the standardisation of procedures."[60]

While these courts are often praised for being more accessible, less costly, better attuned to community values, and less likely needlessly to escalate conflicts, some critics of both arbitration and traditional justice argue that it can too easily degenerate into a system of second class justice that runs roughshod over civil liberties, and frequently reinforces the power of traditional elites at the expense of women, the poor, and minorities. Article 15 of the Indian constitution, for example, explicitly prohibits gender discrimination. But Article 25's guarantee of freedom of religion and the absence of a uniform civil code have combined to leave most family law issues to local custom. "The maintenance of different codes of personal law has meant that women of different religions are governed by dramatically different laws; there is, then, discrimination among women."[61]

Complaints about the use of community courts appear to be fairly exceptional. One study of divorce cases in the United States showed that 98 percent of those who succeeded in mediation, and even 57 percent of those who did not, were satisfied with the process, as compared with only 36 percent of those who were satisfied with court processes.[62] Even allowing for the tendency for courts to become involved in the more difficult cases, these figures are quite impressive. Whether the criminal justice system can move toward a similarly less punitive, more personalized form of justice is not as clear. In the face of rising crime rates, for example, initial attempts to develop a community-based, preventative, and participatory system in South Africa have been largely abandoned.[63]

The gap between public attitudes toward criminal justice and professional opinions is wide, with the former far more supportive of a highly punitive model. Even in continental Europe, where fines or community service rather than incarceration are the usual punishments for nonviolent crimes, the general public tends to take a much tougher line. "The growing use of diversion from incarceration and the declining use of prison sentences . . . are the result of the relative professional autonomy of the judiciary rather than of political pressure or popular support."[64] Less developed countries often have even greater disparities. The system of appeals is likely to be poorly funded and inaccessible to most litigants, and is frequently perceived as a vestige of a colonial or authoritarian past that can threaten traditional patterns of community harmony. In Nigeria,

> The formal dispute resolution machinery of the legal system is mostly incompatible with traditional conflict resolution patterns. This incompatibility leads some citizens to regard the legal system as . . . a relic of colonialism unresponsive to society's desire for justice and social harmony. For example, an ardent Moslem will be hard-pressed to understand why the constitutional requirement of freedom of religion makes it perfectly legal for a non-Moslem to openly consume alcohol in a Moslem city. Also, some people cannot relate to the fact that someone who killed his neighbor can escape punishment on technical grounds like self-defense or the prosecution's failure to prove its case beyond a reasonable doubt.[65]

These tensions are not confined to Africa. As legal systems evolve, they tend to become increasingly objective, to treat litigants according to abstract actors bound by regular rules rather than as personalized human beings. Juries in the United States, for example, were once empowered to decide questions of both law and fact; today they must follow increasingly technical instruction on the applicable law as described by the judge, and jury trials are becoming less and less common in the few systems that still retain them.

The Legal System and Constitutional Democracy

There has and always will be a particularly sharp conflict between the legal system and the society of which it is part. It is in the nature of law enforcement to attempt to impose order on disorder; rules and restraints on popular sovereignty. No matter what framework the constitution sets, some tension between courts and other institutions is, quite simply, part of the process. The growth of judicial power, independence, and competence has intensified these tensions producing what Russell describes as the "interesting irony" that,

> As courts, especially the highest courts, become more activist and autonomous in
> their decision making by upholding challenges to the activities of the other branches
> of government and by dealing with hotly contested issues of public law, they attract
> much more political attention and criticism. Thus an increase in judicial autonomy
> and power means that the judiciary becomes more directly connected to a democratic
> society's politics.[66]

Conflicts of this kind between the branches of the government grow in number and importance as more and more systems allow courts to invalidate acts of the other branches. "Prior to 1989, approximately ten countries had effective systems of constitutional review in which a constitutional court or the courts in general *regularly* struck down proposed or validly enacted legislation as contrary to the state's constitution. . . . Now, only ten years since the beginning of this latest constitutional wave, at least seventy states, or approximately thirty-eight percent of all members states of the UNO, have adopted some form of constitutional review."[67]

This role can be given either to a special constitutional court, as it is in roughly forty countries, or to the nation's highest court using its appellate powers to review both lower court rulings and the statutes or administrative acts in question. The latter courts are limited to dealing with actual cases. They cannot, as a rule, offer advisory opinions, and they frequently avoid conflict with the other branches by refusing to take certain kinds of cases. The U.S. Supreme Court, for example, has historically used what is sometimes called the "case or controversy" rule, or the doctrine of "standing" to avoid ruling on challenges to the war powers of the president or the spending policies of the government. Constitutional courts may also have limited jurisdictions; but both judicial activism or restraint are more functions of politics than of formal rule. It does seem, in general, that the judiciary is most likely to be granted, or to assume, an active role in the process of checks and balances when the political forces in society are pluralistic. Ginsburg calls this "the insurance model of judicial review," providing "a form of insurance to losers during constitutional bargaining. Just as the presence of insurance brokers lowers the risks of contracting. . . so the possibility of judicial review lowers the risks of constitution making to those drafters who believe they may not win power. Judicial review thus helps to conclude constitutional bargains that might otherwise fail."[68]

While these balances of political forces are always important, something else has been going on in almost all of the more recent transitions that "reflect common trends that belie their diverse national origins;" and "it is the occurrence of these common elements—including bills of rights, constitutional courts and a host of other provisions—that requires explanation."[69] Klug calls this "a thin, yet significant, international political culture which is shaping the outer parameters of feasible modes of governance."[70] Whatever powers they grant their highest courts, the most important common tendency is the radical yet increasingly routine acceptance of due process, equal justice, and the rule of law. However badly or well they implement these ideals, what is new and dramatically significant in country after country is the recognition and codification of the ways in which the routine activities of the legal system affect the quality of constitutional democracy. Squaring the roles of the institutions of justice with the values of democracy and equality is a continuing challenge. In Sunstein's words,

> It is often said that a constitution, as a form of higher law, must be compatible with the culture and mores of those whom it regulates. Of course there is much truth in this. But in one sense the opposite is true. Constitutions can be understood as *precommitment strategies,* being used as a founding document for practical and concrete purposes, including the provision of protection against the most likely problems in the usual political processes. If this is so, constitutions should be designed to work against those aspects of a country's own most threatening tendencies. We might think of good constitutions as counter-cultural in this respect.[71]

Notes

1. Neil K. Komesar, *Law's Limits: The Rule of Law and the Supply and Demand of Rights* (New York: Cambridge University Press, 2001), 3.

2. Hans Kelsan, *General Theory of Law and the State*, translated by Anders Wedberg (New York: Russell and Russell, 1945), 5.

3. Kelsan, *General Theory,* 17.

4. Lon Fuller, *The Morality of Law* (New Haven: Yale University Press, 1964), 157-58.

5. Herbert Jacob, "Introduction," in *Courts, Law, and Politics in Comparative Perspective,* ed. Jacob et al. (New Haven: Yale University Press, 1996), 12.

6. John Hatchard, Barbara Huber, and Richard Vogler, "Introduction," in *Comparative Criminal Procedure,* ed. Hatchard, Huber, and Vogler (London: British Institute of International and Comparative Law, 1996), 11.

7. Jacob, "Courts and Judges in the United States," in Jacob et al., 22.

8. Mirjan R. Damaška, *The Faces of Justice and State Authority: A Comparative Approach to the Legal Process* (New Haven: Yale University Press, 1986), 3.

9. Francis Pakes, *Comparative Criminal Justice* (Portland, OR: Willan Publishing, 2004), 94.

10. G. Alan Tarr, *Judicial Process and Judicial Policymaking* (St. Paul, MN: West Publishing Co., 1994), 244.

11. Joseph Sanders, "Courts and Law in Japan," in Jacob et al., 385.

12. Lawrence M. Friedman, *American Law in the 20th Century* (New Haven: Yale University Press, 2002), 584.

13. Friedman, *American Law,* 574.

14. Adrian A. S. Zuckerman, "The Myth of Civil Procedure Reform," in *Civil Justice in Crisis: Comparative Perspectives on Civil Procedure,* ed. Adrian A. S. Zuckerman, Sergio Chiarloni, and Peter Gottwald (New York: Oxford University Press, 1999), 47.

15. Kermit L. Hall, *The Magic Mirror: Law in American History* (New York: Oxford University Press, 1989), 334.

16. *Stanford v. Kentucky*, 492 U.S. 361 (1989).

17. *Atkins v. Virginia,* 536 U.S. 304 (2002).

18. The two most widely-read realist books are Karl N. Llewellyn, *The Bramble Bush: On Our Law and Its Study* (New York: Oceana, 1951, originally published in 1931), and Jerome Frank, *Law and the Modern Mind* (Garden City, NY: Anchor Books, 1963, originally published in 1930).

19. Michel Foucault, *Discipline and Punish: The Birth of the Prison*, translated by Ann Sheridan (New York: Vintage Books, 1979).

20. Louis Favoreau, "American and European Models of Constitutional Justice," in *Comparative and Private International Law,* ed. David S. Clark (Berlin: Duncker and Humblot, 1990), 34.

21. *McNabb v. United States*, 318 U.S. 332 (1943), 347.

22. David M. O'Brien, *Constitutional Law and Politics, Volume II: Civil Rights and Civil Liberties* (New York: W. W. Norton, 3rd ed., 1997), 299.

23. Chapter 4 of O'Brien's *Constitutional Law* has a good summary. See also Louis Fisher, *American Constitutional Law: Volume II, Constitutional Rights* (Durham, NC: Carolina Academic Press, 1999), chapter 13.

24. John E. Finn, *Constitutionalism in Crisis: Political Violence and the Rule of Law* (New York: Oxford University Press, 1991), 34.

25. Owen Fiss, as quoted in Finn, *Constitutionalism in Crisis,* 35

26. H. Kwasi Prempeh, "A New Jurisprudence for Africa," in *The Global Divergence of Democracies*, ed. Larry Diamond and Marc F. Plattner (Baltimore: The Johns Hopkins University Press, 2001), 266, 267.

27. Prempeh, "A New Jurisprudence," 267.

28. Prempeh, "A New Jurisprudence," 267.

29. As quoted in Jerome H. Skolnick, *Justice without Trial: Law Enforcement in a Democratic Society* (Englewood Cliffs, NJ: Macmillan, 3rd ed., 1994), 1.

30. H. Jon Rosenbaum and Peter C. Sederberg, eds., *Vigilante Politics* (Philadelphia: University of Pennsylvania Press, 1976), 17 and *passim*.

31. Emilio Dellasoppa, "Brazil," in *Crime and Crime Control: A Global View,* ed. Gregg Barak (Westport, CT: Greenwood Press, 2000), *passim*.

32. George Phillip, *Democracy in Latin America: Surviving Conflict and Crisis?* (Cambridge, UK: Polity Press, 2003), 55.

33. Larry Diamond, *Developing Democracy: Toward Consolidation* (Baltimore: The Johns Hopkins University Press, 1999), 94.

34. Skolnick, *Justice without Trial,* 6.

35. These figures are derived from a 1992 United Nations report cited in Anthony Harriot, *The Police and Crime Control in Jamaica: Problems of Reforming Ex-Colonial Constubularies* (Kingston, Jamaica: University of the West Indies Press, 2000), xv.

36. Hugo Frühling, "Judicial Reform and Democratization in Latin America," in *Fault Lines of Democracy in Post-Transition Latin America,* ed. Felipe Aguero and Jeffrey Stark (Miami, FL: North-South Center Press, 1998), 253.

37. *Johnson v. Zerbst,* 304 U.S. 458 (1938) and *Betts v. Brady,* 316 U.S. 455 (1942).

38. 372 U.S. 335 (1963).

39. Pakes, *Comparative Criminal Justice,* 62.

40. *Strickland v. Washington,* 466 U.S. 668 (1984), 672.

41. Tom Ginsburg, *Judicial Review in New Democracies: Constitutional Courts in Asian Cases* (New York: Cambridge University Press, 2003), 14.

42. Erhard Blankenburg, "Changes in Political Regimes and Continuity of the Rule of Law in Germany," in Jacob et al., 264.

43. Peter H. Russell, "Toward a General Theory of Judicial Independence," in *Judicial Independence in the Age of Democracy: Critical Perspectives from around the World,* ed. Peter H. Russell and David M. O'Brien (Charlottesville: University Press of Virginia, 2001), 10.

44. Russell, "Toward a General Theory," 13.

45. Russell, "Toward a General Theory," 15.

46. David M. O'Brien and Yasuo Ohkoshi, "Stifling Judicial Independence from Within: The Japanese Judiciary," in Russell and O'Brien, *Judicial Independence*, 59.

47. Russell, "Toward a General Theory," 17.

48. *Federalist,* Number 78.

49. Ginsburg, *Judicial Review in New Democracies,* 6-9.

50. Ginsburg, *Judicial Review in New Democracies,* 10.

51. *Federalist,* Number 78.

52. Alejandro M. Garro, "Access to Justice for the Poor in Latin America," in *The (Un)Rule of Law and the Underprivileged in Latin America,* ed. Juan Mendez, Guillermo O'Donnell, and Paulo Sérgio Pinhiero (Notre Dame, IN: University of Notre Dame Press, 1998), 279.

53. See, for example, Ronald Dworkin, *Taking Rights Seriously* (Cambridge, MA: Harvard University Press, 1977).

54. Guillermo O'Donnell, "Polyarchies and the (Un)Rule of Law," in O'Donnell and Pinhiero, 304.

55. O'Donnell, "Polyarchies and the (Un)Rule of Law," 306.

56. Jacob, "Introduction," 7.

57. O'Donnell, "Polyachies and (Un)Rule of Law," 312.

58. Harold J. Berman, *Law and Revolution: The Formation of the Western Legal Tradition* (Cambridge, MA: Harvard University Press, 1983), 551.

59. Berman, *Law and Revolution,* 548.

60. Pakes, *Comparative Criminal Justice*, 88.

61. Leslie J. Calman, *Toward Empowerment: Women and Movement Politics in India* (Boulder, CO: Westview Press, 1992), 151.

62. From a Department of Justice study conducted by Peter McGillis, as cited in Pakes, *Comparative Criminal Justice,* 259.

63. Diana Gordon, *Transformation and Trouble: Confronting Violent Crime in Democratic South Africa* (Ann Arbor: University of Michigan Press, forthcoming).

64. Erhard Blankenburg, "Changes in Political Regimes," 282.

65. Chukwudifu Oputa, retired Justice of the Nigerian Supreme Court, as quoted in Olechukwu Oko, "Consolidating Democracy on a Troubled Continent: A Challenge for Lawyers in Africa," *Vanderbilt Journal of Transnational Law* 33 (Summer 2000), 573.

66. Peter H. Russell, "Conclusion: Judicial Independence in Comparative Perspective," in Russell and O'Brien, *Judicial Independence,* 301.

67. Heinz Klug, *Constituting Democracy: Law, Globalism, and South Africa's Political Reconstruction* (New York: Cambridge University Press, 2000), 13.

68. Ginsburg, *Judicial Review in New Democracies,* 25.

69. Klug, *Constituting Democracy,* 7.

70. Klug, *Constituting Democracy,* 7.

71. Cass R. Sunstein, "Against Positive Rights," in *Western Rights? Post-Communist Application,* ed. András Sajó (Portland, OR: Book News, 1996), 227.

Chapter 12

Constitutional Change

For all the attention given to new constitutions, far less has gone to the continuing relevance and utility of more venerable systems. What happens, or fails to happen, when constitutions no longer work? Virtually all written constitutions include formal procedures for amendment; but it is striking, even in some of the world's older systems, how many of the more significant modifications have taken place through less well-defined procedures or evasions. To return to a theme introduced in earlier chapters, key questions underlying the problem of constitutional change are embodied in the original process of drafting itself: generally speaking, the more detailed and policy-focused the founding document, the more likely it is to become obsolete. Sartori argues that, "Constitutions establish *how* norms are to be created; they do not, and should not, decide *what* is to be established by the norms. That is to say that constitutions are, first and above all, *procedures* designed to ensure a controlled exercise of power. Therefore, and conversely constitutions are required to be *content-neutral.*"[1] In fact, this is seldom the case, and the politics of constitutional change is of growing import.

The Process of Change

While the moment of constitutional creation marks an important milestone in a nation's history, constitutions are living documents that change almost as soon as

they are born. The written texts establishing democracies are in a sense foundations; but Teitel's notion of "transitional constitutionalism" suggests that they are
more markers—important ones to be sure—on a long highway.[2] With the British
common law still in place, for example, the legal rights of Americans were little
changed by the 1789 Constitution: the carry-over legal system provided both continuity and a capacity to adapt to an evolving set of constitutional rights. Constitutional law, seen as living law actually applied, provides both an anchor to pre-
constitutional traditions and a means of adapting constitutions to new challenges.

Formal Amendments

Almost all of the world's constitutions include a special process of formal amendment that makes it more difficult to change the constitution than to pass an ordinary
law. It is characteristic of amending clauses to define themselves as the sole sources
of legitimate constitutional change. But this is not always the way things work:
constitutions evolve; courts, legislatures, and executives frequently work the margins of constitutional rules; and almost every democracy has, at some time or
another, suspended parts of its constitution during national emergencies. While we
know intellectually that such informal "amendments" are fairly common, we know
too that they are, in a sense, subversive. Constitutions derive legitimacy from a
widespread perception that they do in fact constitute and constrain the political
order. If they are to do this effectively, they must combine enduring values with
workable mechanisms for meeting changing conditions. The trick for constitution
makers is to craft documents that generally require respect for the rules of the
game; yet make sure that the rules are flexible enough to accommodate change.

In the extreme case, constitutional amendments are alternatives to revolutions.
By substantially changing the structure of the regime, they are an acknowledgment
that something no longer works. Among academics there is an interesting argument
about just how far such changes can go. Many constitutions prohibit certain kinds
of amendments, thus raising the interesting question of whether an amendment
adopted according to proper procedures can nonetheless be "unconstitutional."
From vague restrictions, like that in Norway, against any amendment that might
"contradict the principles embodied in this constitution," to more explicit prohibitions such as that which forbids any amendment changing state representation in
the U.S. Senate, there are a number of systems in which certain kinds of amendments are, paradoxically, "unconstitutional."[3] This issue has proven particularly
troublesome in practical terms with regard to the extent of protection, if any, a
democratic constitution should guarantee to those political movements that would
destroy such protections. The Latin root of "to amend," Murphy reminds us, means
"to correct," implying that it serves to modify an existing system without changing
its basic nature. Citing a series of cases from India in 1974-1980, he argues that,

A proposal to transform a central aspect of the compact to create another kind of system—for example, to change a constitutional democracy into an authoritarian state, as the Indian Court said Mrs. Gandhi tried to do—would not be an amendment at all, but a re-creation of both the covenant and its people. That deed would lie outside the authority of any set of governmental bodies, for all are creatures of the people's agreement. Insofar as officials destroy that compact, they destroy their own legitimacy.[4]

Table 12-1 summarizes the ways in which 101 world governments amend their constitutions. The table, to be sure, glosses over important nuances, whether, for example, legislative approval is required from one house of a bicameral legislature, both, or—as in Indonesia—a joint meeting of the two. Many constitutions also require different procedures for amendments to different parts of the constitution. But certain basic patterns are quite clear. In only nine countries, five of which are members of the British Commonwealth, is a simple legislative majority sufficient. The modal legislative vote needed is two-thirds, with fifty-nine setting the bar at this fraction. Most systems do not involve the chief executive in the process; but typically some sort of second vote is required: a public referendum, ratification by the states or provinces in a federal system, or simply by a second vote of the legislature following a "cooling off" period of anywhere from thirty days to a year.

Perhaps the most interesting pattern to be found in Table 12-1 is that there are few discernible patterns. Commonwealth countries excepted, the rules seem neither more nor less restrictive in parliamentary as opposed to presidential systems, in older as against newer democracies, or by regions of the world. One might expect that the rules would be restrictive in societies undergoing rapid change where declining elites might try to lock transitional arrangements in place, as with the high barriers in South Africa and Bulgaria. But in fact, some volatile countries of the former Soviet Union, and others where old elites are seriously challenged, such as Paraguay, make the process quite simple. Others have shown that the rules of formal amendment matter much less than the political dynamics of the new order. In Russia, for example, "Constitutional amendments have been used . . . as just another technique for outmaneuvering one's political enemies of the moment." With strong control over major institutions, amendments are used less as a "higher track of lawmaking," than as method of locking powers in place. "And while Russia lies at one extreme of the spectrum, the subordination of constitutional revision to everyday political antics and aims is a trend everywhere in the region."[5]

Informal Amendment

There may be, though experience is limited, some kind of reciprocal relationship between the existence of a strong constitutional court and the relative difficulty of amending the constitution. Courts are, in one sense, profoundly conservative bodies

Table 12-1

Methods of Formal Amendment to One Hundred and One
World Constitutions

Legislative Amendment by Simple Majority Vote with . . .

No further action required   Antigua and Barbuda, Barbados,
                                    Czech Republic, Great Britain, Indo-
                                    nesia, Israel, Jamaica, Mauritius,
                                    New Zealand, Slovakia.
Referendum   Ireland, Malawi, Paraguay, Switz-
                                    erland.
Intervening election or referendum Iceland, Italy.
Intervening election and referendum Denmark.
Referendum or 2/3 vote plus president Armenia, France, Mozambique.
Approval by Provincial Legislatures Australia, Canada,
    or Constitutional Convention   Nicaragua.

Legislative Amendment by 3/5 vote with . . .

Referendum or different majority   Niger (4/5).
                                    Spain (2/3 of one house).
One month to one year delay   Azerbaijan, Brazil, Greece, Estonia,
                                    Turkey.
Constitutional convention   Russia.

Legislature by 65% vote and . . .

Three readings and presidential assent Kenya.

Legislature by 2/3 vote with . . .

Executive approval   Iran (Revolutionary Council),
                                    Kuwait (Emir), Jordan, Nether-
                                    lands, Pakistan, Syria.

Table 12.1 (continued)

Legislature by 2/3 vote with . . .

No further action necessary	Argentina, Belgium, Belize, Cambodia, Chile, Costa Rica, Croatia, Egypt, Estonia, Finland, Germany, Haiti, Hungary, Kuwait, Lebanon, Luxemburg, Macedonia, Malawi, Namibia, Pakistan, Poland, Portugal, Singapore, Sri Lanka, Sudan, Syria, Trinidad and Tobago, Uganda, Ukraine, Vanuatu, Vietnam, Yemen, Zambia.
Referendum	Albania, Austria, Bahamas, Bangladesh, Japan, Kyrgyzstan, Latvia, Malta, Mauritania, Mongolia, Morocco, Philippines, Romania, Slovenia, South Korea.
Majority of Provinces	India, Mexico.
2/3 of Provinces	Ethiopia, Nigeria.
3/4 of States	United States.

Legislature by 3/4 vote with . . .

No further action (or by majority vote plus referendum in Burkina Faso and Sweden)	Bulgaria, Burkina Faso. Dominica, Peru, Rwanda, Sweden, Taiwan.
Majority of Provinces	South Africa.
4/5 majority after one year waiting period.	Eritrea.

Note: Many constitutions provide alternative methods including, most frequently, referendums. This table reflects what I believe to be common practice of the method most frequently used in each country.

with a seeming mandate to protect the written text from contemporary political moves. They are, at the same time, focal points of change. The U.S. Supreme Court, with by far the longest history of judicial review, has certainly played both roles. The tortured reasoning of its "dual federalism" decisions in the late nineteenth century, by which it effectively blocked both state and national attempts to regulate business, represents a classic case of its short-term ability to thwart popular majorities. It did so again in the early 1930s with its brief but decisive rejections of President Roosevelt's New Deal. This time, however, the Court's resistance was short-lived: "When the New Deal court unanimously overruled the case-law of the Republican era, it repudiated the old idea of limited government with all the decisiveness of a formal constitutional amendment."[6] Ackerman has argued, indeed, that two most fundamental changes in the U.S. Constitution—the shift away from the states in the balance of federalism following the Civil War; and the economic powers granted in the New Deal cases—were ratified more by the Supreme Court than by the formal process of constitutional amendment.

The seemingly formidable powers of the courts to interpret the Constitution (and thus "amend" it) has been the subject of considerable debate. In the United States, the issue has been phrased in terms of "activism" and "restraint," words that often conceal more than they reveal. The New Deal rulings, for example, can be classified as "activist" in the sense that they overruled precedent, or "restrained" in upholding the decisions of the elected branches. Some conservatives have also wrapped their ideology in terms of the recondite term "strict-constructionism," a phrase essentially revering the words of the original document. These arguments are almost invariably selective in construing some parts of the Constitution more strictly than others;[7] but they are, at their best, part of a continuing and increasingly global debate particularly in India, and in other democracies where the courts have played a more or less active role in interpreting the constitution. Alternating between periods when it simply acquiesced to whatever the government did, and more activist roles, some "judges in India have asked themselves the question: can judges really escape addressing themselves to substantial questions of social justice? Can they . . . simply follow the legal text when they are aware that their actions will perpetuate inequality and injustice? Can they restrict their inquiry into law and life within the narrow confines of a narrowly defined rule of law?"[8]

Courts are most controversial when they interpret the constitution to protect minorities. The most controversial U.S. cases have been those extending the procedural rights of those accused of crimes, ending racial segregation, privatizing questions of contraception and abortion, and protecting free speech. Court acquiescence in changes in the institutional foundations of the system have, typically, been less controversial, even when they have arguably been of greater long-term significance. The shifts in power to the executive branch, and within it, to the office of the chief executive discussed in chapter 8 have taken place largely without either formal amendment or explicit judicial sanction. The Supreme Court, by refusing to hear cases challenging the legality of wars in Korea, Vietnam, and elsewhere, has in effect repealed Article I, Section 8 of the Constitution giving Congress the sole power to declare war. Its similar willingness to support the dramatic centralization of power in the federal system, discussed in chapter 10, has been noted almost exclusively in academic circles. In general,

> The Court's success in pursuing its agenda makes it appear all powerful, but in reality the modern Court has achieved its power and influence by distancing itself from precisely those issues capable of creating full-scale crises and thereby revealing the limits of its political strength. . . .
>
> The Court's abandonment of its supervision of federal economic policy, combined with its traditional deference to the president and Congress in the formulation and execution of foreign policy, meant that the post-New Deal Court has permitted the political branches to act with almost complete freedom on the most crucial issues on the national agenda. Moreover, the Court permitted Congress to regulate broad areas of social policy, including civil rights, under its power to regulate interstate commerce. As a result, the Court's role in policing the broad contours of federal policy has decreased almost to the vanishing point.[9]

The Indian court has been more aggressive in curbing executive power, and the German more protective of provincial power; but in general, courts have tended to acquiesce in major shifts of power initiated by others. The experience of Indonesia, which, under the same fundamental framework, has had a rich variety of governments is more typical than deviant. Some dictators suspend constitutions, most simply bend them to the needs of the new order. Ideally, it is the role of constitutional courts to sustain the system against the temptations of other actors to consolidate power and require fundamental changes to be effected only through the extraordinary methods set forth in Table 12-1. More difficult to patrol are those changes which evolve over time. "Political institutions are transformed through the mundane processes of everyday life, as well as through the rare metamorpheses at breaking points in history."[10] No one in the older democracies ever sat down and *decided* to have big government; but the difference in the scope of governments a century ago and today are as profound as they were unplanned. Few constitutions contain clauses on the bureaucracy, yet they have become, as argued in chapter 7, the defining institutions of the modern state.

Stress, Seizure, and Subversion

Constitutions can be changed through formal amendment or judicial rulings; but the most dangerous changes are those that sneak in through the consolidation of executive power. "No political system in the world," Larry Diamond says,

> operates strictly according to its formal institutional prescriptions, but what distinguishes most of the democracies in Latin America, Asia, Africa, and the postcommunist states are political institutions too weak to ensure the representation of diverse interests, constitutional supremacy, the rule of law, and the constraint

of executive authority. The terms *low intensity democracy, democracy by default, poor democracy, empty democracy,* and *hybrid regimes* (among others) have been used to describe the institutionally weak and substantively superficial nature of most new and recently restored democracies in Latin America. . . .

Although [such] democracies have the formal constitutional structure of democracy—and may even (barely) meet the empirical standards of liberal democracy, as Argentina does—they are institutionally hollow and fragile.[11]

This fragility represents, in part, a failure to consolidate due to the absence of economic development, the institutions of a viable civic culture, and so on. But underdevelopment is a function of both a failure to develop at the roots and of being deflowered at the top by elites who use the institutions of the new order to reconsolidate the power relations of the old. This is not to denigrate the importance of the growing literature on democratic consolidation: clearly we have much to learn about the process of how democracy develops at the grass roots. Unless a nation's elite is serious about democratization, however, its control over the key levers of economic, military, legal, and executive power is likely to be overwhelming whatever the formal rules. In most democratic transitions, as we have repeatedly shown, the major agencies of the government—including especially the bureaucracy, the military, police, courts, and legal system—continue to be staffed by the same people whose independence is frequently guaranteed in the new constitution itself or, less formally, in the negotiations that produced it. Generally, moreover, new democracies are both philosophically and practically reluctant to confront existing structures of economic power. In both the public and private sectors, it is not simply that the same faces keep showing up; but that they act pretty much as they always have. Democratic consolidation, as Diamond puts it,

> must be reinforced by a political system that works to deliver the political goods of democracy and, eventually, the economic and social goods people expect as well. The normalization of politics and entrenchment of legitimacy that consolidation entails requires the expansion of citizen access, the development of democratic citizenship and culture, the broadening of leadership recruitment and training, and other functions that civil society performs. But it also requires orderly and effective democratic governance, and that is something that civil society cannot in and of itself provide. Political institutions (parties, legislatures, judicial systems, local governments, and the bureaucratic structures of the state more generally) must become more capable, complex, coherent, and responsive.[12]

If constitutional democracy is to be consolidated, it must permeate the system. Enclaves of authoritarianism are not only intrinsically antithetical to consolidation, but they poison the well of constitutionalism by extending citizen mistrust. At best, the old order subverts the new constitution, but not so permanently that it can prevent a new cadre of less-political officers to replace the old military with new; displace the old bureaucracy; and train new cadres of lawyers, judges, politicians, and legislators. Democratic consolidation can take hold through a gradual process of elite displacement and conversion, as it largely has in some parts of Eastern Europe (most notably in Slovenia and the Czech Republic), South Africa, Chile, South Korea, and so on. At worst, however, the enclaves of resistance can worm their way back into control of the formal state (as they have in many parts of the former Soviet Union), co-opt the institutions of constitutional democracy, or so paralyze the system as to lead to authoritarian intervention.

Newly constituted democracies are particularly susceptible to the kinds of real or manufactured crises that provide rationales for the suspension of rights. Virtually all can be destroyed or markedly deflected by the sudden seizure or gradual accretion of powers from the top. Military coups are still the most common instruments of abrupt regime change, and almost all consolidations of executive authority are likely to have at least tacit military support. The first step toward the demise of constitutional governments is often a state of emergency. "When the public safety is seriously threatened," it is argued, "there may be a need for quick and decisive action that cannot, perhaps, wait for the deliberative pace of ordinary constitutional rule."[13] That such threats can be fabricated or blown out of proportion is clear; but the emergency power clauses built into many constitutions are generally temporary in nature and conservative in intent, "aimed at resolving the threat to the system in such a way that the legal/constitutional system is restored to its previous state."[14] The post-September 11 world has renewed interest in the question of emergency powers, with the U.S. debate over the Patriot Act and other measures overriding aspects of the Constitution's due process restrictions, bringing the issue into focus for established systems as well as those in transition.

If truth is the first casualty of war, constitutional democracy is often second. Civil liberties are threatened, executive powers enhanced, and the relations between government and business more firmly intertwined than under normal circumstances. Daniel Franklin's study documents numerous instances in which U.S. "Civilians have been held for military trial, the writ of habeas corpus has been suspended, citizens have been forcibly moved from their homes, and all manner of freedoms 'guaranteed' under the First Amendment have been violated."[15] These deviations have generally been of short duration; but the possibility of a downward spiral is real. Reviewing a depressing saga of a cycle of violence that virtually destroyed the fiber of democracy in Sri Lanka, one recent study concludes that,

Sri Lanka's experiences during emergency rule are especially relevant in the post-September 11 world, where governments have taken renewed interest in stringent, repressive legislation to combat terrorist activity. Although ensuring national security and protection of its citizens is an important state interest, Sri Lanka demonstrates the dangerous potential of such legislation to achieve the opposite effect. Such legislation can lead to a cycle of extremist violence and state repression that threatens the fabric of democratic societies, eroding state legitimacy and international order.[16]

Despite what Franklin calls "an inherent resistance" in the U.S. legal tradition "to the notion that certain powers can be exercised, for whatever purpose, beyond restraint" the checks in emergency situations have not been strong.[17] In times of crisis, neither the Congress nor the courts have hesitated to approve prerogative powers that, in many cases, they have come later to regret. In most cases in the West, such powers have ultimately been rescinded as the country returns to "normal;" but "there is a constant temptation to permit emergency legislation to spill over into the operation of the ordinary legal system. Rights and liberties may be permanently transformed under the threat—real or exaggerated—of terrorist acts."[18] This kind of stretching out of the emergency, in countries as diverse as Uruguay, France, Brazil, Croatia, Canada, and Indonesia, sometimes for as long as twenty or thirty years, should give us pause. There is considerable merit to Ferejohn and Pasquino's suggestion that constitution writers consider "provisions for two legal systems, one that operates in normal circumstances to protect rights and liberties, and another that is suited for dealing with emergency circumstances."[19]

Democracy, Illiberal Democracy, and Good Government

The apparent intractability of authoritarianism in many countries, and the failure of many "third wave" democracies to consolidate has been discouraging. The wave of formal democratization crested, by the widely-cited Freedom House count, at 121 countries in 1995-1996 and fell back to 119 in 2004. Of even greater concern has been the growth of "illiberal democracy," systems in which the quality of democracy falls short of its constitutional aspirations.[20] National emergencies have provided a cover of respectability to some of these regressions; but in the long run the constitution building process has been far more significantly deflected by the persistence of cultural forces that outweigh the aspirations of constitution makers. Before concluding with some of these continuing challenges, it is worth recalling just how far the values of constitutional democracy have spread in the past half century. In the short run of the past decade, undertows from the third wave may have pulled some regimes further from the shores of democratic consolidation; but the number of countries that are either nominally or firmly democratic is of a very different magnitude. The glass that is half empty (or full) is a pint mug compared with a shot glass.

Consolidating Reform

To understand how well-designed constitutions succeed or fail is sometimes a matter of understanding idiosyncratic events and personalities, more often a question of rounding up the usual suspects: poverty, ethnic conflict, underdeveloped civic and political institutions, and so on. Perhaps the best single predictor of success is success: what makes democracies work is a spreading recognition that this is the way things get done. When policy advocates begin to take the legislature seriously, when ambitious lawyers aspire toward judgeships, when the military understands that its professional standards are undermined rather than enhanced by political involvement, and when citizens believe that votes have meaning, the process of true consolidation begins. A "new constitutional framework," as Klug says of South Africa, allows "opposing forces to imagine the possibility of achieving, at least in part, their particular vision within the terms of the Constitution" at the same time as it works to "delegitimize incompatible alternatives or visions."[21] Rustow's argument that democracy is not safe until it has survived a generation, puts this argument in temporal terms.[22] Rustow also argues, as Di Palma summarizes the case, "that habituation only follows a decisional phase in which formal democratic rules are clearly instituted and made operational. It is the concrete operation of these rules that makes habituation possible, indeed likely—not vice versa."[23] The art of crafting constitutional democracies is more a process than an event. Governments are constantly being reinvented, occasionally by formal amendment, more frequently by the creation of new agencies, changes in the statute or case law governing civil and criminal cases, and the changing dynamics of legislative-executive relations. The extent to which these dynamics have changed, in some countries more than others, and with considerable backsliding in many, is the most important story to be told. In 1982, Robert Dahl wrote that, "Of the more than one hundred fifty countries in the world today, the institutions of polyarchy exist in about thirty."[24] There are not only far more today, but far more that meet the standards most citizens and academics would consider acceptable. In its most recent report, Freedom House gives its highest possible scores to forty-six countries, and slightly flawed ratings (four or fewer total points on a scale of two to fourteen) to another thirty-one.[25] It is also a sign of enormous progress, I would argue, that beyond the seventy odd fully functioning constitutional democracies are another thirty whose progress toward consolidation holds enormous promise. Countries such as Indonesia, Nicaragua, Peru, and Turkey are firmly on the path of consolidation.

The clearest indicator of democracy triumphant is in the process of conducting elections. There are, in the first decade of the twenty-first century, more than a hundred countries whose leaders were freely elected in fair contests. An elaborate global system of election monitoring has not only provided important guidance, control, and standards; but it has helped make fair and free elections almost a paradigm of national sovereignty.[26] Also remarkable in the past two decades has been the professionalization and withdrawal from politics of the military. In the 1960s, more than thirty changes in government were engineered by the military in Asia and Africa alone; the last military coup in Asia was in Pakistan in 1999, and the 2003 military takeover in the Central African Republic was more the exception than the rule. In Central and South America—where coups were as common a method of regime change as elections—there has been an almost total inversion of the process. Throughout the region, the poor record of military governments, "often damaging the military institutions," has sharply limited both the "supply" of possible coups by keeping the military in its barracks, and the "demand" for such takeovers from conservative groups that have found in politics a more predictable path to achieving their objectives.[27] More important, perhaps, "the end of the Cold War deprived would be coup-makers of anti-communist 'national security' rationales and U.S. support for possible coups."[28] Rather than the military stepping in to prevent an elected government from taking office, the more common scenario in the twenty-first century has masses of demonstrators pouring into the streets to prevent an entrenched oligarchy from stealing an election.

Progress toward the liberalization of democratic regimes has been less consistent, with marked improvements in the European Community in contrast to the still-problematic records of many other countries in protecting basic rights. While civil societies have become more robust in the renaissance democracies of Latin America, persistently high levels of social inequality and very unequal opportunity structures inhibit consolidation. Here again, there are—particularly from a long-term perspective—a number of encouraging signs. *Every* citizen of Eastern Europe, even those in slow-to-change states like Albania and Romania, enjoys greater freedom than he or she did a generation ago. With few exceptions, though less strikingly, the same can be said of the countries once comprising the Soviet Union. And however much liberal democrats may deplore deficiencies in the rule of law manifest in many parts of Asia, Africa, and Latin America, the "dictablandas" and "democraduras" of today are less repressive than those of such giants of repressive government as Spain's Franco, Pinochet in Chile, or Idi Amin in Uganda. The simple fact that relatively free elections are being held in such a large and growing number of countries intensifies this development. As Plattner puts it, "While many new electoral democracies fall short of liberalism, on the whole, countries that hold free elections are overwhelmingly more liberal than those that do not. . . . This is not simply an accident. It is the result of powerful intrinsic links between electoral democracy and a liberal order."[29]

Failures, Hard Cases, and Danger Signals

To have written more than 200 pages of comparative political analysis without mention of China is like continuing the tea party while ignoring the 2,000-pound gorilla in the corner. As it slowly drags Hong Kong's freedoms down, and continues to liberalize at what can at best be described as a glacial pace, its growing economic, military, and political muscle cannot be ignored. The rising hopes and fast-declining realities of democratization in Russia and such former Soviet republics as Belarus, Turkmenistan, and Uzbekistan combine similarly to remind us that nearly half of the world's people live under regimes that are not constitutional democracies. Together with a bloc of countries in the Middle East, they are also large enough and sufficiently self-sustaining to resist many of the global forces that have been very much a part of the democratization of the rest of the world.

The division of the world into roughly equal numbers of people moving rapidly toward constitutional democracy and standing still or moving the other way is a fact of life. Unlike the bipolarization of the Cold War era, there is no particular competition taking place in which the diverse camps seek inroads into each others' spheres: Western attempts to democratize China, Russia, Pakistan, and Saudi Arabia have been half-hearted and sporadic at best. Hong Kong and perhaps Taiwan aside, the Chinese have shown little interest in how other countries are governed. As China crosses the threshold of affluence which gave partial impetus to political liberalization in Taiwan in the 1970s, and as the information revolution has "demonstration effects" throughout the literate world, "Chinese citizens are becoming more aware of their political and economic rights and more assertive in defending them." And it may be that "economic development is creating a more complex, pluralistic, self-confident, resourceful society, which cannot be managed with the old patterns of monolithic and highly repressive and arbitrary state domination."[30] Still, the situation in China is not encouraging.

Many observers would write off much of the Moslem world as well. The clash of civilizations Huntington describes as pitting Western concepts of individualism, democracy, and the rule of law against a reemerging culture of violence, authoritarianism, and irrational fundamentalism[31] centers on the Islamic world.

> Indeed, Islamic fundamentalists have been described as "religious Stalinists," language that replicates the very Manichaeanism for which fundamentalists are rightly criticized. In its most extreme formulation, this vision has devolved into a caricature of Islam as the "Green peril" (green is the color of Islam) advancing across the world stage, an image that echoes both the "Red Menace" of Cold War discourse and anti-Asian polemics about the "Yellow Peril."[32]

The growth of Christian fundamentalism in the West makes a mockery of attempts to map this dichotomy in strictly geographic or religious terms. Turkey's imperfect democracy, and Indonesia's struggles toward a true new order, are illustrative of the potential that exists for the further development of what Hefner calls "civil Islam." Together with most serious students of Islam, Hefner found a pluralistic culture in Indonesia that had a fundamentalist element, but a much larger group that even in the days of Soeharto's New Order had "learned the language of democracy and constitutionality, and took enthusiastically to its forms. In matters of civic association Muslims found themselves second to no one. None of their rivals could match the breadth and vitality of their associations. Even under the New Order, Muslims [if only because the regime was too weak directly to confront them] were better able than others to resist state controls and nurture alternative ideas of the public good."[33]

Whether this same kind of Islamic culture can be nurtured in the Middle East is problematic in the shadow of many of the world's most closed and repressive regimes. It is ironic that many of those most openly espousing a Western *"jihad"* against Islam have themselves enthusiastically backed the very Arab elites that have closed Middle Eastern society to the winds of change. Most of these countries have gone through a pattern similar to that in Indonesia where "most of the ruling elite who dominated Indonesian society, rather than consolidating precedents for civility and pluralism, ignored or abused them. The colonial policy of divide and conquer had an especially corrosive impact on native civic traditions. The post-colonial state continued this legacy; the Soeharto regime brought it to perfection."[34]

Constitutional Democracy and Good Government

As democracy does emerge in the Moslem world, it is not always going to produce the kinds of government its proponents would prefer. "Suppose the election was declared free and fair," U.S. diplomat Richard Holbrooke pondered on the eve of the 1996 election in Bosnia, and those elected were "racists, fascists, separatists, who are publicly opposed to [peace and reintegration]. That is the dilemma."[35] Since most of us will probably disagree, on the margins at least, as to just what makes for "good" government, the question here is not about issues of health care, mass transit, or tax rates; what I mean by "good" government is one that funda-mentally preserves the procedural rules that enable us peacefully to work out our differences on issues such as these.

There seems little doubt that a democratic Iraq—if such an entity can emerge from conquest—will be less protective of women's rights than was the Saddam dictatorship. Absent pressure from the European Community, Turkey would still have capital punishment. But then, so does the United States. And when slavery was legal, when, in more recent times, lynching went unpunished and segregation was the law, Freedom House would almost certainly have, nonetheless given the United States its highest rating. This is not to say that constitutional democracy is measured simply by mechanics. It is about good government as well; but these values may change. Our insistence in earlier chapters that equality is part of the evaluative equation remains controversial, very much so with regard to economic equality, significantly with regard to gender. These are by no means trivial issues; but they are far less central to the case than those that go to issues of popular sovereignty, civil liberties, checks and balances, pluralism, and the rule of law. The faith of democrats is that once these values are in place, the others will follow. The key to securing minority rights in the long run lies less in constitutional affir-mations of these rights than in guaranteed access to the bargaining table.

It is not typically the result of republican idealists negotiating with the nation's interests foremost in mind. Rather democracy is arrived at through realistic, self-interested calculation and protracted bargaining among hostile actors representing diverse social groups. If the actors remain at the table and hammer out their differences, they can reach democracy. By steadfastly continuing these intense negotiations after the new democratic regime is installed, the actors begin the process of consolidation. Substantive negotiation and hard-won compromise among competing groups in society are, after all, the very core of democracy.[36]

The Future of Constitutional Democracy

The constitution building process has changed dramatically. Second wave constitutions were drafted largely in close consultation with, and often in imitation of, former hegemonic regimes. Regime failure was due in part to underdevelopment and other pathologies, but also to the unsuitability of old constitutions to new circumstances. It is easy to disparage the work of what has become a constitution-building industry, but there is little doubt that the more than seventy states that adopted new constitutions between 1989 and 2004 did so with considerably more sophistication and sensitivity than ever before.

Democratization and Globalization

The constitution-building process in the twenty-first century takes place in the context of what Klug calls "the globalization of the rule of law."[37] *The Federalist Papers* show clearly that the U.S. founders were acutely aware of how other constitutions worked or failed to; but the availability and sophistication of such analyses is of a very different order in 2006 than it was in 1789. Even if the growing deployment of democracy assistance professionals has had only a marginal direct impact, their activity has the more significant "effect of shaping the local imagination, whether posed as the only alternative or as a weight against the local alternatives."[38] When intellectual assistance in the process of democratization is backed by tangible resource deployment, moreover, as efforts of the European Community have shown, the process of defusion is accelerated. By insisting on certain standards of political behavior as a condition for membership, and by backing these demands with economic development funds, the EC's role in promoting civil society and the protection of human rights in Spain, Portugal, Greece, and more recently in Turkey and Eastern Europe has been profound. "European social democratic parties [also] played a considerable role in supporting democracy in Southern Europe from the outside."[39] And organizations like the World Bank and the U.S. Agency for International Development have increasingly made democratization both a focus and condition of economic aid. To the extent that these organizations become increasingly serious in using democratizing efforts as criteria in evaluating programs, so will democratic institutions begin to work.

A number of important caveats are in order. The tendency to conflate the development of democracy with free enterprise is often productive of neither. When the interests of the national industries of donor countries conflict with the goals of democratization, it is the latter that are likely to take second place. Efforts to tighten environmental laws, increase wages, strengthen trade unions, and so on have and will encounter both direct resistance from major multinational corporations and indirect assistance from their home governments. International organizations, both public and private, have played a growing and significant role in sustaining and developing the institutions of civic culture in emerging democracies; but the temptation to bias these efforts on behalf of the sponsoring country's own economic and political agenda often works against democratization. U.S. democracy promotion efforts, for example, have often been sponsored by groups that are allied with the dominant economic groups in the target countries, often in opposition to the elected governments. Civil society strategies, in the extreme case, are used as "an arena for exercising domination" and shoring up these same elites.[40]

While the end of the Cold War has blunted some of the stronger pathologies of support for authoritarian practices, economic and foreign policy objectives will sometimes continue to trump democratization in the day-to-day conduct of governments. Even as established democracies promote reform in the legal process, they may simultaneously work closely with some of the world's most repressive police forces in pursuing the war on terror. And even as economic aid packages are made contingent upon reform, Western investors in countries like Indonesia will continue to be "Happy to invest in what they [know] to be highly corrupt and poorly regulated markets . . . free of the demands of organized labor, social welfare lobbies, environmental protection and progressive taxation."[41]

Charles Beard's economic theory of the U.S. Constitution—that it was drafted by an elite of wealthy property owners protecting their class interests—is correct to an extent: they did protect the institution of slavery and the kind of stable commerical and monetary system that secured their status; but so is the view that the institutions they created deliberately opened the system to progressive democratization and social justice. This is precisely what has been happening in newer democracies, but with the crucial difference that the process has been globalized. Those local elites that tend toward reform have been enormously braced by their superior access to research and argument, by their ability to cite exogenous but relevant examples to publicize their case. In a media age, the reformers, quite simply, look better. On the international stage those who benefit most from, and are most comfortable with corruption and exploitation, are beginning to find it embarrassing as well: is this really the way that Exxon, Nike, and Newmont Mining want to be known? Does the military want to be evaluated on the basis of its professionalism or its brutality? The success of the forces of democratic consolidation depends upon their ability to use the institutional structures crafted in the context of both internal social forces and their relations to the global environment. What counts in addition to the contest at home, as Klug puts it, is "the extent to which participants in postcolonial settings draw upon and interpret legal norms . . . from a variety of jurisdictions to suit their own locally defined ends."[42]

O'Donnell and Schmitter argue that the path of transition from authoritarianism toward something else can go anywhere from violence and stricter rule to democracy. "The outcome can also be simply confusion, that is the rotation in power of successive governments which fail to provide any enduring or predictable solutions to the problem of institutionalizing power."[43] But if institutions matter, they can, when well-constructed, provide road maps through confusion, and the global forces of democratization provide the channels through which they can challenge the old order.

The Marasmus of Western Democracy

I am not, truth be told, quite as confident as I have tried to sound about the ability of well-designed systems to produce good government. And I worry, not a little, and I hope you will too, about the future of constitutional democracy not just in its newer plantings but in its oldest vineyards as well. "All serious democratic thinkers," as Linz and Stepan conclude, understand

> that the much vaunted democratic Third Wave has already produced some dangerous undertows, not only in post-Communist Europe but also in Western Europe. In the United States, influential ideologues of liberty are at times too simplistic and mean spirited for a healthy democratic polity. In this context democratic triumphalism is not only uncalled for but dangerous. Democratic institutions have to be not only created but crafted, nurtured and developed. . . . [T]o create an economic society supportive of democracy requires more than just markets and private property.[44]

These are the tendencies of particular concern: First, it may be time seriously to reexamine the issue of size. Globalization increasingly marginalizes the ability of small countries to govern themselves. Even for the relatively larger countries of the European Union, the logic of political consolidation is inescapable. If the idea that true democracy would only work in very small places was long ago laid to rest, we are talking now about a very different order of magnitude where one member of the European parliament represents five to eight hundred thousand citizens; one U.S. congressman, close to 700,000; a parliamentarian in India well over a million. Is there some point at which the nature of representation changes at these levels?

A closely related concern is with the growing complexity of the issues with which governments and voters must deal. "Most legislative decisions," as I have argued elsewhere, "are made by men and women who have little direct knowledge of the problem at issue." There are institutional means by which "informed decisions can be made by uninformed human beings," but a graduate of the finest course in speed reading could not read, much less understand, all the bills introduced in a single session of a modern legislature.[45] The problem for citizens is even more frustrating. Combine this gap with the question of size and the vision of representative democracy as involving a dialogue between citizens and their representatives recedes. We move (inevitably?) toward what Sartori calls "video politics" in which "the public is fed with affect-based information, with images that stir compassion or anger, but which 'warm up' problems far beyond our capacity for solving them."[46] And it is not just "that video politics produces increasing affect-mobilized participation under conditions of decreasing and impoverished information,"[47] but that politicians and their advisors, understanding how they can manipulate the visual symbols displayed, feel safe in ignoring the public and its elected representatives in making key decisions.

The rise of video democracy is facilitated by the declining numbers and role of the institutions of civil society discussed in chapter 5. And it may be at the base of the depressingly low voter turnout figures for many of the mature democracies. The decline of the middle class—the share in national income of the lowest 40 percent of U.S. families fell by almost a fifth between 1973 and 2001[48]—threatens further to diminish the base from which the participating strata have historically been drawn. There has, and always will be, a tension between the limits imposed by constitutionalism and the forces of democratization. As basic a role as constitutions play in protecting the rights upon which real democracy depends, we need to be alert to the growing democratic deficits that these trends reflect. And this is true for many newer democracies as well.

> It must be noted that the failure of democracy in most Third World countries, and in others as well, is not often brought about by the reckless behavior of political majorities acting through legislative bodies. On the contrary, the histories of these countries suggest that more often than not, it is the majority of citizens who need protection from political elites who consistently frustrate democratic demands in order to protect their interests. Sadly, the negative conception of constitutionalism is often used as ideological cover to legitimize such behavior.[49]

Constitutions are, in too many cases, overdesigned. For all the praise appropriately lavished on South Africa, it is not clear whether "the Constitution will enable the newly enfranchised majority to achieve a significant democratic shift in the balances of both public and private power." For the same constitution can also be viewed from the perspective of the old elites, who see it "as a protection against the redistributive demands of the new democratic majority and view judicial review as the last bastion protecting their property and freedom against threats they perceive to be implicit in the notion of an unrestrained democratic will with access to the levers of public power."[50]

Finally, established democracies increasingly face the problem of excessive rules. Children often develop wonderfully spontaneous games with one point for this bounce of a ball, two points for that. Gradually, exceptions—when the ball hits a stair or is dropped—are added to the point at which the rules become so complex that the game is no longer fun. Do low voter turnout rates in countries like Switzerland and the United States suggest that their citizens feel that the game, if not rigged, has become too complicated to be worth playing? The complex "thickening" of bureaucracy discussed in chapter 7, in which more and more time and money is spent checking and monitoring and less and less in delivering services increases the democratic deficit. If democratic consolidation is to progress around the world, it must find ways of refreshing itself at its Western core. In the final analysis it may lie in the ability of the older democracies "to adjust their well-entrenched rules and practices to accommodate the growing disaffection of their citizens [that] will determine the prospects for democracy worldwide."[51]

Once a constitution is in place it tends to acquire an often-undeserved sanctity that locks in political deals as well as philosophical ideals. Robert Dahl has trenchantly summarized the most glaring deficiencies of the U.S. Constitution as they relate to contemporary standards of evaluation. There is no need here to rehash his arguments concerning the absurdity of the electoral college or problems with the Senate, judicial review, federalism, and so on. But we do need to take to heart his plea that, "it is time—long past time—to invigorate and greatly widen the critical examination of the Constitution and its shortcomings. Public discussion that penetrates beyond the Constitution as a national icon is virtually nonexistent. Even when in-depth analysis does occur . . . the Constitution as a whole is rarely tested against democratic standards or against the performance of constitutional systems in other advanced democratic countries."[52] It is my hope that his book can help stimulate that dialogue.

Notes

1. Giovanni Sartori, *Comparative Constitutional Engineering: An Inquiry into Structures, Incentives, and Outcomes* (New York: New York University Press, 2nd ed., 1997), 200.

2. Ruti Teitel, "Transitional Justice: The Role of Law in Political Transformation," *Yale Law Journal* 106 (1997), 2009.

3. See the differing opinions on this in John R. Vile, "The Case against Implicit Limits on the Constitutional Amending Process" and Walter F. Murphy, "Merlin's Memory: The Past and Future Imperfect of the Once and Future Polity," both in *Responding to Imper-*

fection: The Theory and Practice of Constitutional Amendment, ed. Sanford V. Levinson (Princeton, NJ: Princeton University Press, 1995).

4. Walter F. Murphy, "Constitutions, Constitutionalism, and Democracy," in *Constitutionalism and Democracy: Transitions in the Contemporary World,* ed. Douglas Greenberg et al. (New York: Oxford University Press, 1993), 14.

5. Stephen Holmes and Cass R. Sunstein, "The Politics of Constitutional Revision in Eastern Europe," in *Responding to Imperfection,* 282.

6. Bruce Akerman, "Liberating Abstraction," in *The Bill of Rights in the Modern State,* ed. Geoffrey R. Stone, Richard A. Epstein, and Cass R. Sunstein (Chicago: University of Chicago Press, 1992), 322.

7. For a spirited critique of the New Right's attacks on the court, see Satirious Barber, *The Constitution of Judicial Power* (Baltimore: The Johns Hopkins University Press, 1993).

8. Jamie Cassels, "Judicial Activism and Public Interest Litigation in India: Attempting the Impossible?" *American Journal of Comparative Law* 37 (1989), 499.

9. William Lasser, *The Limits of Judicial Power: The Supreme Court in American Politics* (Chapel Hill: University of North Carolina Press, 1988), 263-64.

10. James G. March and Johan P. Olsen, *Democratic Governance* (New York: The Free Press, 1995), 184.

11. Larry Diamond, *Developing Democracy: Toward Consolidation* (Baltimore: The Johns Hopkins University Press, 1999), 34.

12. Diamond, *Developing Democracy,* 259.

13. John Ferejohn and Pasquale Pasquino, "The Law of Exception: A Typology of Emergency Powers," *International Journal of Constitutional Law* 2 (April 2004), 210.

14. Ferejohn and Pasquino, "The Law of Exception," 210.

15. Daniel P. Franklin, *Extraordinary Measures: The Exercise of Prerogative Powers in the United States* (Pittsburgh, PA: University of Pittsburgh Press, 1991), 135.

16. Radhika Coomaraswamy and Charmaine de los Reyes, "Rule by Emergency: Sri Lanka's Postcolonial Constitutional Experience," *International Journal of Constitutional Law* 2 (April 2004), 295.

17. Franklin, *Extraordinary Measures,* 7.

18. Ferejohn and Pasquino, "The Law of Exception," 235.

19. Ferejohn and Pasquino, "The Law of Exception," 234.

20. Larry Diamond, "Is the Third Wave Over?" *Journal of Democracy* 7 (1996), 1.

21. Heinz Klug, *Constituting Democracy: Law, Globalism, and South Africa's Political Reconstruction* (New York: Cambridge University Press, 2000), 177.

22. Dunkwart Rustow, "Transitions to Democracy," *Comparative Politics* 2 (April 1970), 337-63.

23. Giuseppe Di Palma, *To Craft Democracies: An Essay on Democratic Transitions* (Berkeley: University of California Press, 1990), 222-23.

24. Robert A. Dahl, *Dilemmas of Pluralist Democracy: Autonomy vs. Control* (New Haven: Yale University Press, 1982), 29.

25. Arch Puddington and Aili Piano, "Worrisome Signs, Modest Shifts," *Journal of Democracy* 16 (January 2005), 106-7.

26. Eric C. Bjornlund, *Beyond Free and Fair: Monitoring Elections and Building Democracy* (Baltimore: The Johns Hopkins University Press, 2004).

27. Jorge I. Donimguez, "Constructing Democratic Governance in Latin America: Taking Stock of the 1990s," in *Constructing Democratic Governance in Latin America,* ed. Jorge I. Dominguez and Michael Shifter (Baltimore: The Johns Hopkins University Press, 2nd ed., 2003), 355-56.

28. Dominguez, "Constructing Democratic Governance," 356.

29. Marc E. Plattner, "Liberalism and Democracy: Can't Have One without the Other," *Foreign Affairs* 76 (November/December 1997), 31.

30. Diamond, *Developing Democracy*, 265-66.

31. Samuel Huntington, *The Clash of Civilizations and the Remaking of World Order* (New York: Simon and Schuster, 1996).

32. Roxanne L. Euben, *Enemy in the Mirror: Islamic Fundamentalism and the Limits of Modern Rationalism* (Princeton, NJ: Princeton University Press, 1999), 6.

33. Robert W. Hefner, *Civil Islam: Muslims and Democratization in Indonesia* (Princeton, NJ: Princeton University Press, 2000), 217.

34. Hefner, *Civil Islam*, 25.

35. As quoted in Fareed Zakaria, "The Rise of Illiberal Democracy," *Foreign Affairs* 76 (November/December 1997), 22.

36. Gretchen Casper and Michelle M. Taylor, *Negotiating Democracy: Transitions from Authoritarian Rule* (Pittsburgh: University of Pittsburgh Press, 1996), 244.

37. Hans Klug, "Hybrid(ity) Rules: Creating Local Law in a Globalized World," in *Global Prescriptions: The Production, Exportation and Importation of a New Legal Order,* ed. Yves Dezalay and Bryant G. Garth (Ann Arbor: University of Michigan Press, 2002), 277.

38. Klug, "Hybrid(ity) Rules," 277.

39. Jean Grugel, *Democratization: A Critical Introduction* (New York: Palgrave-Macmillan, 2002), 162.

40. William I. Robinson, "Venezuela," in *Promoting Polyarchy: Globalization, U. S. Intervention, and Hegemony,* ed. William I Robinson et al. (New York: Cambridge University Press, 1996), 19.

41. Richard Robinson and Vedi R. Hadiz, *Reorganizing Power in Indonesia: The Politics of Oligarchy in an Age of Markets* (New York: Routledge Curzon, 2004), 34-35.

42. Klug, "Hybrid(ity) Rules," 280.

43. Guillermo O'Donnell, Philippe C. Schmitter, "Tentative Conclusions about Uncertain Democracy," in Guillermo O'Donnell, Philippe C. Schmitter, and Laurence Whitehead, eds. *Transitions from Authoritarian Rule: Prospects for Democracy* (Baltimore: The Johns Hopkins University Press, 1986), 71.

44. Juan J. Linz and Alfred Stepan, *Problems of Democratic Transition and Consolidation: Southern Europe, South Africa, and Post-Communist Europe* (Baltimore: The Johns Hopkins University Press, 1996), 457.

45. See chapter 5, "Legislative Intelligence," in Edward V. Schneier and Bertram Gross, *Legislative Strategy: Shaping Public Policy* (New York: St. Martin's Press, 1993), 73.

46. Sartori, *Comparative Constitutional Engineering,* 149.

47. Sartori, *Comparative Constitutional Engineering,* 150.

48. Lawrence Mishel, Jared Bernstein, and Heather Boushey, *The State of Working America 2002/2003* (Ithaca, NY: Cornell University Press, 2003).

49. Julio Faundez, "Constitutionalism: A Timely Revival," in Greenberg et al., *Constitutionalism and Democracy*, 358.

50. Klug, *Constituting Democracy,* 181.

51. Philippe C. Schmitter, "Democracy's Future: More Liberal, Preliberal, or Post-liberal?" *Journal of Democracy* 6 (January 1995), 21.

52. Robert A. Dahl, *How Democratic Is the American Constitution?* (New Haven: Yale University Press, 2001), 156.

Appendix

Average Voter Turnout, Election System, and Vote Requirements for Lower House of the Legislature in Countries Holding At Least Two Relatively Free Elections, 1945-2002

Country and Governing System	Number of Elections	Seats/terms in Lower House	Percentage of VAP Voting Mean	Latest	Election System # of Parties
Italy (Parliamentary)	15	630 / 5V	91.7	81.3[c-w]	MMP/5
Seychelles (Presidential)	3	34 / 5F	90.3	84.5	FPTP+/2
Iceland (Parliamentary)	17	63 / 4V	89.4	86.2	LPR/5
Indonesia (Mixed)	7	425 / 5F	87.6	81.3	LPR/8
Malawi (Presidential)	2	193 / 5F	86.2	92.3	FPTP/3
New Zealand (Parl.)	19	120 / 3V	85.6	75.4	MMP[a]/7
Belgium (Parliamentary)	18	150 / 4V	84.9	85.2[c-e]	LPR/10
Netherlands (Parl.)	16	150 / 4V	84.5	79.9	LPR/9
Australia (Parliamentary)	23	183 / 3V	84.4	83.9[c-e]	AV/3
Albania (Parliamentary)	5	140 / 4V	84.3	80.2	PTRS/11
Austria (Mixed)	17	183 / 4V	84.3	72.6[c-p]	LPR/4
Denmark (Parliamentary)	23	179 / 4V	83.8	89.3	LPR/8
Sweden (Parliamentary)	18	349 / 4V	83.1	80.1	LPR/7
Mauritius (Parliamentary)	7	66 / 5V	82.5	80.9	FPTP/3
Mongolia (Parliamentary)	4	76 / 4V	82.5	83.2	FPTP/3
Guyana (Parliamentary)	7	65 / 5V	81.5	89.1	LPR/3
Portugal (Mixed)	10	230 / 4V	81.4	62.3	LPR/5
Andorra (Parliamentary)	3	28 / 4V	81.4	81.6	FPTP+/3
Aruba (Parliamentary)	4	21 / 4V	81.4	84.5.	FPTP/4
Tuvalu (Parliamentary)	3	12 / 4V	81.3	80.0	FPTP/0[b]
South Africa (Presidential)	2	400 / 5F	81.1	76.7	LPR/6
Germany (Parliamentary)	14	603 / 4V	80.4	79.1	MMP/4
Slovakia (Parliamentary)	5	150 / 4V	80.3	70.1	LPR/7
Samoa (Parliamentary)	3	49 / 5F	80.1	82.4	FPTP-B/3
Greece (Parliamentary)	18	300 / 4V	80.0	75.7[c-w]	LPR/4
Kuwait (Monarchy)	6	50 / 4F	79.6	80.0	BV/0[b]
Norway (Parliamentary)	15	165 / 4F	79.2	74.5	LPR/6

Israel (Parliamentary)	15	120 / 4V	79.1	67.8	LPR/10
Malta (Parliamentary)	14	65 / 5V	78.8	95.4	STV/2
Finland (Mixed)	16	200 / 4V	78.2	66.6	LPR/7
Czech Republic (Parl.)	5	200 / 4V	77.9	58.0	LPR/5
Slovenia (Parliamentary)	3	90 / 4V	77.0	69.9	LPR/8
Spain (Parliamentary)	8	350 / 4V	76.2	70.6	LPR/6
Bulgaria (Parliamentary)	5	240 / 4V	75.1	66.7	LPR/4
Suriname (Parliamentary)	6	51 / 5V	74.9	51.0	LPR/8
Namibia (Presidential)	3	72 / 5F	74.6	62.8	LPR/3
United Kingdom (Parl.)	16	659 / 5V	74.5	59.4	FPTP/3
Ireland (Parliamentary)	17	166 / 4V	74.2	63.0	STV/6
Turkey (Parliamentary)	10	550 / 5V	74.0	78.9[c-w]	LPR/2
Belize (Parliamentary)	6	29 / 5V	73.2	78.9	FPTP/2
South Korea (Mixed)	10	273 / 4V	73.0	57.2	FPTP+/3
Croatia (Mixed)	5	151 / 4V	72.9	70.5	FPTP+/4
Romania (Parliamentary)	4	346 / 4V	72.8	65.1	LPR/5
Iran (Mixed)	3	290 / 4F	72.7	83.0	PM2/3
Macedonia (Parliamentary)	2	120 / 4V	72.4	73.5	P-TRS/4
St.Vincent/Grenadines(Pa)	13	15 / 5V	72.1	68.7	FPTP/2
Cyprus (Presidential)	7	59 / 5F	71.4	90.5[c-c]	LPR/8
Uruguay (Presidential)	10	99 / 5F	71.4	92.3[c-e]	LPR/4
Philippines (Presidential)	7	460 / 3F	71.0	81.1[c-n]	BV/5
Argentina (Presidential)	17	257 / 4F	70.8	73.7[c-w]	LPR/5
Venezuela (Presidential)	10	165 / 5F	70.6	56.4	MMP/8
Dominica (Parliamentary)	12	32 / 5V	70.3	60.2	FPTP/3
Vanuatu (Parliamentary)	4	52 / 4V	70.2	NA[d]	SNTV/7
Cape Verde Islands (Pres.)	3	72 / 5V	69.7	57.8	LPR/3
Taiwan (Presidential)	5	164 / 3F	69.3	66.2	SNV+/4
Papua New Guinea (Parl.)	6	109 / 5V	69.1	NA[d]	FPTP+/6
Togo (Parliamentary)	4	81 / 5V	68.9	67.4	PM2/4
Japan (Parliamentary)	22	500 / 4V	68.7	62.4	FPTP+/9
Liechtenstein (Mixed)	17	25 / 4V	68.3	86.7[c-w]	LPR/3
Costa Rica (Presidential)	13	57 / 4F	68.2	66.6[c-n]	LPR/4
Canada (Parliamentary)	18	301 / 5V	68.1	62.9	FPTP/5
Dominican Republic (Pr.)	12	150 / 4F	67.3	51.4[c-n]	LPR/3
France (Mixed)	16	577 / 5V	67.1	64.4	PM2/
Ukraine (Presidential)	4	450 / 4F	66.9	69.4	PM2/6
Trinidad and Tobago(Pa.)	12	36 / 5V	66.4	68.0	FPTP/2
Madagascar (Presidential)	6	138 / 4F	66.4	67.9	LPR/3
Fiji (Parliamentary)	3	71 / 5V	66.2	78.9[c-c]	BV/6
Bahamas (Parliamentary)	11	40 / 5V	65.9	82.4	FPTP/2
Luxembourg (Parl.)	13	60 / 5V	65.9	86.5[c-c]	LPR/5

Hungary (Parliamentary)	4	386 / 4V	65.7	70.5	MMP/3
Lesotho (Mixed)	4	120 / 5V	64.3	68.1	MMP/6
Grenada (Parliamentary)	12	15 / 5/V	64.2	56.7	FPTP/1
Nepal (Mixed)	6	205 / 5V	64.1	65.8	FPTP/4
Moldova (Parliamentary)	3	101 / 4V	63.7	70.0	TRS/3
Mozambique (Presidential)	2	250 / 5F	63.6	62.8	LPR/3
Barbados (Parliamentary)	11	28 / 5V	63.5	63.1	FPTP/2
Nicaragua (Presidential)	11	93 / 6F	63.1	75.0	LPR/3
Georgia (Presidential)	3	235 / 4F	62.9	67.6	PR2/3
Benin (Presidential)	3	83 / 4F	62.0	65.8	LPR/2
Sri Lanka (Parliamentary)	11	225 / 6V	61.9	75.8	LPR/5
Bolivia (Mixed)	14	130 / 5F	61.8	66.7[c-n]	MMP/7
Latvia (Parliamentary)	4	100 / 4V	61.1	55.0	LPR/6
Lithuania (Parliamentary)	3	141 / 4V	60.7	63.0	PR2/6
India (Parliamentary)	13	543 / 5V	60.7	59.7	FPTP/10
St. Lucia (Parliamentary)	14	17 / 5V	59.7	52.5	FPTP/2
Solomon Islands (Parl.)	6	50 / 4V	59.3	61.9	FPTP/4
Malaysia (Parliamentary)	8	193 / 5V	59.0	?[d]	FPTP/3
Bangladesh (Parl.)	7	300 / 5V	58.7	74.9	FPTP/4
St. Kitts and Nevis (Parl.)	10	11 / 5V	58.7	64.2	FPTP/3
Jamaica (Parliamentary)	13	60 / 5V	58.4	56.8	FPTP/2
Panama (Presidential)	5	72 / 5F	57.9	75.9	LPR/3
Russia (Presidential)	3	450 / 4F	57.3	61.8	PR2/6
Paraguay (Presidential)	12	80 / 5F	57.2	80.0[c-w]	LPR/2
Sao Tome/Principe(Parl.)	4	55 / 4V	56.7	59.9	LPR/3
Morocco (Monarchy)	6	325 / 5V	56.6	51.6	FPTP/11
Estonia (Parliamentary)	4	101 / 4V	56.5	58.2	LPR/6
Honduras (Presidential)	13	128 / 4F	56.2	66.3[c-n]	LPR/4
Guinea-Bissau (Mixed)	2	102 / 4F	56.1	80.0	LPR/6
The Gambia (Presidential)	6	53 / 4F	55.8	56.4	FPTP/3
Bosnia/Herz'venia(Mixed)	4	42 / 4V	53.7	55.4	LPR/13
Antigua/Barbuda (Parl.)	11	17 / 5V	51.3	63.6	FPTP/3
Poland (Parliamentary)	5	460 / 4V	51.2	46.3	LPR/6
Sierra Leone(Presidential)	4	112 / 4F	51.1	60.0	LPR/2
Botswana (Mixed)	8	47 / 5F	50.1	77.3	FPTP/3
Brazil (Presidential)	15	513 / 4F	50.0	68.9[c-w]	LPR/11
Peru (Presidential)	8	120 / 5F	49.9	63.2[c-w]	LPR/5
Chile (Presidential)	12	117 / 4F	49.4	86.3[c-w]	LPR/2
Switzerland (Parl.)	14	200 / 4V	48.9	43.4[c-p]	LPR/5
Mexico (Presidential)	19	500 / 6F	48.9	64.0	MMP/3
Thailand (Parliamentary)	15	393 / 4V	48.9	69.8[c-n]	BV-PR/6
Haiti (Presidential)	3	83 / 4F	48.8	60.0	PM2/4

Armenia (Presidential)	3	131 / 4V	48.0	45.5	P-FPTP/16
Kenya (Presidential)	3	224 / 5F	47.9	56.1	FPTP/3
United States (Presidential)	29	435 / 2F	47.4	39.0	FPTP/2
Zambia (Presidential)	5	159 / 5F	46.1	68.5	FPTP/5
Ghana (Presidential)	6	200 / 4F	46.0	62.0	FPTP/2
Micronesia (Mixed)	14	14 / 2-4F	45.7	29.5	FPTP/2
Ecuador (Presidential)	19	100 / 5F	45.7	63.5[c-w]	PR2/9
Senegal (Presidential)	7	120 / 5F	44.7	67.4	PR2/4
El Salvador (Presidential)	17	84 / 3F	43.4	38.5	LPR/5
Burkina Faso (Presidential)	5	111 / 5F	43.1	64.1	LPR
Pakistan (Parliamentary)	7	342 / 5F	41.8	41.8	FPTP/6
Nauru (Parliamentary)	9	18 / 3V	37.3	?[c-n/d]	AV/NP[b]
Niger (Presidential)	3	83 / 5F	36.8	39.4	P-FPTP/5
Colombia (Presidential)	21	161 / 4F	36.5	42.4	LPR/7
Djibouti (Presidential)	3	65 / 5F	33.2	48.4	PB/1
Guatemala (Presidential)	16	113 / 4F	31.4	53.8	P-FPTP/3
Mali (Presidential)	2	160 / 5F	21.7	24.0	TRS/4
Monaco (Parliamentary)	8	24 / 5V	13.5	17.1	TRS/2

Key: Terms in the lower house of each nation's parliament are either fixed (F) at a set number of years, or variable (V) where there are maximum limits but where parliament may be dissolved at any time and new elections ordered.

Voter turnout figures are calculated as the percentage of the voting age population actually casting ballots (whether valid or not). The assumption is that most spoiled ballots are cast as acts of deliberate protest rather than inadvertent error. Mean turnout is the arithmetic mean of all elections since 1945. The latest election, depending on the cycles of each country, reflects the results of elections held between 1997 and 2002.

Voting systems are abbreviated as follows: FPTP = First Past the Post with Single Member districts; BV = Block Voting, or plurality systems with more than one candidate per district; TRS = Two-Round Systems in which runoff elections are required where no candidate receives a majority; AV = Alternative Voting systems, which count voters' second preferences to manufacture majorities; LPR = List Proportional Representation, where votes are cast for party lists of candidates; MMP = Mixed Member Proportional, where party lists are used to adjust district returns to assure partisan proportionality; STV = Single Transferable Votes where ranked voter choices are used to achieve proportionality; SNTV = Single, Non-Transferable Vote, where there are multimember districts but voters can choose only one candidate; and P or Parallel Systems which have separate FPTP and proportional components. The number of parties column counts any party holding at least 2 percent of overall membership in the lower house as of the end of 2002.

Sources: The classification of election systems used here, and much of the data on voting systems and turnout, is derived from the website and various publications of the International Institute of Democracy and Electoral Assistance (www.idea.int). Equally useful are the annual editions of the Inter-Parliamentary Union, *Chronicle of Parliamentary Elections*

(Geneva: Inter-Parliamentary Union, various years); their website (www.ipu.org.parline); and the very accessible website of www.electionworld.org. Electionworld also includes links to other useful sites, such as psephos.adam-carr.net, and to the national websites of more than one hundred world parliaments. A number of newspapers, academic specialists, and embassy information offices were also contacted for missing data and to help resolve the many discrepancies found in these sources.

Notes

a. New Zealand changed its electoral system from first-past-the-post in 1993.

b. Elections are conducted on a nonpartisan basis.

c-e. Compulsory voting laws in effect and enforced.

c-w. Compulsory voting laws in effect, but only weakly enforced.

c-p. Compulsory voting laws in effect in some provinces or cantons only.

c-n. Compulsory voting laws in effect but not enforced.

d. Reliable returns are not available.

Selected Bibliography

Abizadeh, Arash. "Does Liberal Democracy Presuppose a Cultural Nation? Four Arguments." *American Political Science Review* 96 (September 2002): 495-510.

Ackerman, Bruce A. "Neo-Federalism?" In *Constitutionalism and Democracy*, ed. Jon Elster and Rune Slagstad, 153-94. New York: Cambridge University Press, 1993.

Aguero, Felipe, and Jeffrey Stark, eds. *Fault Lines of Democracy in Post-Transition Latin America*. Miami: North-South Center Press, 1998.

Anckar, Carsten. "Effects of Electoral Systems: A Study of 80 Countries." Paper presented at the Swedish Center for Business and Policy Studies Seminar in Stockholm, September 28-29, 2001.

Anderson, Benedict. *Imagined Communities*. New York: Verso Books, rev. ed., 1991.

————. *The Spectre of Comparisons: Nationalism, Southeast Asia, and the World*. New York: Verso Books, 2000.

Anderson, Lisa, ed. *Transitions to Democracy*. New York: Columbia University Press, 1999.

Baker, Randall, ed. *Transitions from Authoritarianism: The Role of the Bureaucracy*. Westport, CT: Praeger, 2002.

Bastian, Sunil, and Robin Luckham, eds. *Can Democracy Be Designed? The Politics of Institutional Choice in Conflict-Torn Societies*. New York: Zed Books, 2003.

Beard, Charles A. *An Economic Interpretation of the Constitution of the United States*. New York: Macmillan, 1913.

Bendix, Reinhard. *Kings or People: Power and the Mandate to Rule*. Berkeley: University of California Press, 1978.

Bjornlund, Eric C. *Beyond Free and Fair: Monitoring Elections and Building Democracy*. Baltimore: The Johns Hopkins University Press, 2004.

Blondel, J. *Comparative Legislatures*. Englewood Cliffs, NJ: Prentice-Hall, 1977.

Boone, Catherine. "Decentralization as a Political Strategy in West Africa." *Comparative Political Studies* 36 (May 2003): 370-85.

Bowler, Shaun, David M. Farrell, and Richard S. Katz. *Party Discipline and Parliamentary Government*. Columbus: Ohio State University Press, 1999.

Buchanan, James M. *Federalism, Liberty, and the Law*. Indianapolis, IN: The Liberty Fund, 2001.

Burnham, Walter Dean. "The Turnout Problem." In *Elections American Style*, ed. A. James Reichley, 97-133. Washington, DC: The Brookings Institution, 1987.

Butler, David and Austin Ranney. *Referendums: A Comparative Study of Practice and Theory*. Washington, DC: American Enterprise Institute, 1978.

Casper, Gretchen, and Michelle M. Taylor. *Negotiating Democracy: Transitions from Authoritarian Rule*. Pittsburgh: University of Pittsburgh Press, 1996.

Chatterjee, Patha. *The Politics of the Governed: Reflections on Popular Politics in Most of the World*. New York: Columbia University Press, 2004.

Clark, David S., ed. *Comparative and Private International Law*. Berlin: Duncker and Humblot, 1990.

Cohen, Carl. *Democracy*. New York: The Free Press, 1973.

Colomer, Josep M. *Political Institutions*. New York: Oxford University Press, 2001.

Connor, Walker. "Nation-Building or Nation Destroying." *World Politics* 24 (1972): 314-28.

Coomaraswamy, Radhika. "The Politics of Institutional Design: An Overview of the Case of Sri Lanka." In *Can Democracy Be Designed? The Politics of Institutional Choice in Conflict-Torn Societies*, ed. Sunil Bastian and Robin Luckham. New York: Zed Books, 2003.

Coomaraswamy, Radhika, and Charmaine de los Reyes. "Rule by Emergency: Sri Lanka's Postcolonial Constitutional Experience." *International Journal of Constitutional Law* 2 (April 2004): 295-312.

Cooter, Robert D. *The Strategic Constitution*. Princeton, NJ: Princeton University Press, 2000.

Cox, Gary W. *Making Votes Count: Strategic Coordination in the World's Electoral Systems*. New York: Cambridge University Press, 1997.

Crouch, Arnold. "Patrimonialism and Military Rule in Indonesia." *World Politics* 31 (1979): 571-87.

Crozier, Michael, Samuel P. Huntington, and Joji Watanuki. *The Crisis of Democracy*. New York: New York University Press, 1975.

Dahl, Robert A. *A Preface to Democratic Theory*. Chicago: University of Chicago Press, 1956.

———. *After the Revolution*. New Haven: Yale University Press, 1970.

———. *Democracy and Its Critics* New Haven: Yale University Press, 1989.

———. *Dilemmas of Pluralist Democracy: Autonomy vs. Control*. New Haven: Yale University Press, 1982.

———. *How Democratic Is the American Constitution?* New Haven: Yale University Press, 2001.

———. *Polyarchy: Participation and Opposition*. New Haven: Yale University Press, 1971

Dahl, Robert A., and Edward R. Tufte. *Size and Democracy*. Stanford, CA: Stanford University Press, 1977.

Derbyshire, J. Denis and Ian. *Political Systems of the World*. New York: St. Martin's Press, 1996.

Dezalay, Yves, and Bryant G. Garth, eds. *Global Prescriptions: The Production, Exportation, and Importation of a New Legal Order*. Ann Arbor: University of Michigan Press, 2002.

Diamond, Larry. *Developing Democracy: Toward Consolidation*. Baltimore: The Johns Hopkins University Press, 1999.

———. "Is the Third Wave Over?" *Journal of Democracy* 7 (1996): 1-12.

Diamond, Larry, and Marc F. Plattner. *The Global Divergence of Democracies*. Baltimore: The Johns Hopkins University Press, 2001.

Diggins, John P. *The Lost Soul of American Politics: Virtue, Self-Interest, and the Foundations of Liberalism*. Chicago: University of Chicago Press, 1984.

Di Palma, Giuseppe. *To Craft Democracies: An Essay on Democratic Transitions*. Berkeley: University of California Press, 1990.

Dominguez, Jorge I., and Michael Shifter, eds. *Constructing Democratic Governance in Latin America*. Baltimore: The Johns Hopkins University Press, 2nd ed., 2003.

Döring, Herbert. "Parliamentary Agenda Control and Legislative Outcomes in Western Europe." *Legislative Studies Quarterly* 26 (February 2001): 145-66.

————. *Parliaments and Majority Rule in Western Europe.* New York: St. Martin's Press, 1995.

Dovi, Suzanne. "Preferable Descriptive Representatives: Will Just Any Woman, Black, or Latino Do?" *American Political Science Review* 96 (December 2002): 745-54.

Duverger, Maurice. "'Duverger's Law': Forty Years Later." In *Electoral Laws and Their Political Consequences*, ed. Bernard Grofman and Arend Lijphart. New York: Agathon Press, 1986.

————. *Political Parties: Their Organization and Activity in the Modern State.* New York: John Wiley and Sons, 1954.

Eckstein, Harry. *Division and Cohesion in Democracy: A Study of Norway.* Princeton, NJ: Princeton University Press, 1966.

Elazar, Daniel. *Exploring Federalism.* Tuscaloosa: University of Alabama Press, 1987.

Elgie, Robert. *Political Leadership in Liberal Democracies.* New York: St. Martin's Press, 1995

Elster, Jon. "Constitutional Courts and Central Banks: Suicide Prevention or Suicide Pact." *East European Constitutional Review* 3 (Summer-Fall 1994): 57-69.

————. "The Necessity and Impossibility of Simultaneous Economic and Political Reform." In *Constitutionalism and Democracy: Transitions in the Contemporary World*, ed. Douglas Greenberg et al. New York: Oxford University Press, 1993.

Elster, Jon, and Rune Slagstad, eds. *Constitutionalism and Democracy.* New York: Cambridge University Press, 1993.

Esaiasson, Peter, and Knut Heidar, eds. *Beyond Westminster and Congress: The Nordic Experience.* Columbus: Ohio State University Press, 2000.

Evans, Peter B. *Embedded Autonomy: States and Industrial Transformation.* Princeton, NJ: Princeton University Press, 1995.

Evans, Peter B., Dietrich Rueschmeyer, and Theda Skocpol, eds. *Bringing the State Back In.* New York: Cambridge University Press, 1985.

Ferejohn, John, and Pasquale Pasquino. "The Law of Exception: A Typology of Emergency Powers." *International Journal of Constitutional Law* 2 (April 2004): 207-36.

Finn, John E. *Constitutionalism in Crisis: Political Violence and the Rule of Law.* New York: Oxford University Press, 1991.

Fraenkel, Jon. "The Alternative Vote System in Fiji: Electoral Engineering or Ballot-Rigging?" *Journal of Commonwealth and Comparative Politics* 39 (July 2001): 1-13.

Franklin, Daniel P. *Extraordinary Measures: The Exercise of Prerogative Powers in the United States.* Pittsburgh: University of Pittsburgh Press, 1991.

Friedman, Lawrence M. *American Law in the 20th Century.* New Haven: Yale University Press, 2002.

Gellner, Ernest. *Conditions of Liberty: Civil Society and Its Rivals.* New York: Penguin Press, 1994.

Gibson, Edward L., ed. *Federalism and Democracy in Latin America.* Baltimore: The Johns Hopkins University Press, 2004.

Ginsburg, Tom. *Judicial Review in New Democracies: Constitutional Courts in Asian Cases.* New York: Cambridge University Press, 2003.

Goetz, Edward G., and Susan E. Clarke, eds. *The New Localism: Comparative Urban Politics in a Global Era.* Newbury Park, CA: Sage Publications, 1993.

Goldstein, Leslie Friedman. *Constituting Federal Sovereignty: The European Union in Comparative Context.* Baltimore: The Johns Hopkins University Press, 2001.

Gordon, Scott. *Controlling the State: Constitutionalism from Ancient Athens to Today.* Cambridge, MA: Harvard University Press, 1999.

Greenberg, Douglas, Stanley N. Katz, Melanie Beth Oliveiro, and Steven C. Wheatley, eds. *Constitutionalism and Democracy: Transitions in the Contemporary World.* New York: Cambridge University Press, 1993.

Grodzins, Morton. "Centralization and Decentralization in the American Federal System." In *A Nation of States*, ed. Robert A. Goldwin. Chicago: Rand-McNally, 1973.

Hadenius, Axel. *Institutions and Democratic Citizenship.* New York: Oxford University Press, 2001.

Hammons, Christopher W. "Was James Madison Wrong? Rethinking the American Preference for Short, Framework-Oriented Constitutions." *American Political Science Review* 93 (December 1999): 837-50.

Hassall, Graham, and Cheryl Saunders. *Asia-Pacific Constitutional Systems* New York: Cambridge University Press, 2002.

Hatchard, John, Barbara Huber, and Richard Vogler, eds. *Comparative Criminal Procedure.* London: British Institute of International and Comparative Law, 1996.

Haynes, Jeff. *Democracy in the Developing World: Africa, Asia, Latin America, and the Middle East.* Malden, MA: Blackwell Publishers, 2001.

Haysom, Nicholas. *Negotiating a Political Settlement in South Africa: Are There Lessons for Burma?* Stockholm: International Institute for Democracy and Electoral Assistance, 2001.

Hazan, Reuven Y. *Reforming Parliamentary Committees: Israel in Comparative Perspective.* Columbus: Ohio State University Press, 2001.

Hefner, Robert W. *Civil Islam: Muslims and Democratization in Indonesia.* Princeton, NJ: Princeton University Press, 2000.

————, ed. *The Politics of Multiculturalism: Pluralism and Citizenship in Malaysia, Singapore, and Indonesia.* Honolulu: University of Hawaii Press, 2001.

Held, David. *Democracy and the Global Order: From the Modern State to Cosmopolitan Governance.* Stanford, CA: Stanford University Press, 1995

Hicks, Ursula Kathleen Webb. *Federalism: Failure and Success: A Comparative Study.* New York: Oxford University Press, 1979.

Hooghe, Liesbet, and Gary Marks. "Unraveling the Central State, but How? Types of Multilevel Governance." *American Political Science Review* 97 (May 2003): 233-44.

Horowitz, David L. *Ethnic Groups in Conflict.* Berkeley: University of California Press, 1985.

Holmes, Stephen. "Constitutionalism, Democracy, and State Decay." In *Deliberative Democracy and Human Rights*, ed. Harold Hongju Koh and Ronald C. Slye. New Haven: Yale University Press, 1999.

————. "The End of Decommunization." In *Transitional Justice: How Emerging Democracies Reckon with Former Regimes*, ed. Neil J. Kritz, Washington, DC: United States Institute of Peace, 1995.

————. "Precommitment and the Paradox of Democracy." In *Constitutionalism and Democracy*, ed. Jon Elster and Rune Slagstad. New York: Cambridge University Press, 1993.

Howard, Dick. "The Indeterminacy of Constitutions." *Wake Forest Law Review* 31 (1996): 367-403.

Huber, Evelyne, Dietrich Rueschemeyer, and John D. Stephens. "Economic Development and Democracy." In *Classes and Elites in Democracy and Democratization*, ed. Eva Etzioni-Halevy. New York: Garland, 1997.

Huntington, Samuel P. *The Third Wave: Democratization in the Late Twentieth Century*. Norman: University of Oklahoma Press, 1991.

Hutchcroft, Paul D. *Booty Capitalism: The Politics of Banking in the Philippines*. Ithaca, NY: Cornell University Press, 1998.

Inglehart, Ronald. "How Solid Is Mass Support for Democracy—And How Can We Measure It?" *PS: Political Science and Politics* 36 (January 2003): 51-59.

International Institute for Democracy and Electoral Assistance. *Conference Report: Towards Sustainable Democratic Institutions in Southern Africa*. Stockholm: International IDEA, 2000.

Jackson, Vicki C., and Mark Tushnet. *Comparative Constitutional Law*. New York: Foundation Press, 1999.

Jacob, Herbert et al., eds. *Courts, Law, and Politics in Comparative Perspective*. New Haven: Yale University Press, 1996.

Jacoby, Henry. *The Bureaucratization of the World*. Translated by Eveline Kanes. Berkeley: University of California Press, 1973.

Johnson, James. "Inventing Constitutional Traditions: The Poverty of Fatalism." In *Constitutional Culture and Democratic Rule*, ed. John Ferejohn, Jack N. Rakove, and Jonathan Riley. New York: Cambridge University Press, 2001.

Jones, Mark P. "Electoral Laws in Latin America and the Caribbean." *Electoral Studies* 12 (1993): 59-75.

Joseph, Richard. "Democratization in Africa after 1989: Comparative and Theoretical Perspectives." In *Transitions to Democracy*, ed. Lisa Anderson. New York: Columbia University Press, 1999.

Judge, David. "Legislative Institutionalization: A Bent Analytic Arrow?" *Government and Opposition* 38 (Autumn 2003): 513-32.

———. *The Parliamentary State*. London: Sage Publications, 1993.

Jurgens, Erik. "Parliaments and Treaty-Making." *Journal of Legislative Studies* 1 (Summer 1995): 178-91.

Kelsan, Hans. *General Theory of Law and the State*. Translated by Anders Wedberg. New York: Russell and Russell, 1945.

Kersh, Rogan. *Dreams of a More Perfect Union*. Ithaca, NY: Cornell University Press, 2001.

King, Anthony. "How to Strengthen Legislatures—Assuming That We Want To." In *The Role of Legislatures in Western Democracies*, ed. Norman J. Ornstein. Washington, DC: American Enterprise Institute, 1981.

———. "Modes of Executive-legislative Relations: Great Britain, France, and West Germany." *Legislative Studies Quarterly* 1 (February 1976): 37-65.

Kleppner, Paul. *Who Voted?: The Dynamics of Electoral Turnout, 1870-1980*. New York: Praeger, 1982.

Klug, Heinz. *Constituting Democracy: Globalism and South Africa's Political Reconstruction*. New York: Cambridge University Press, 2000.

Knop, Karen, ed., *Rethinking Federalism: Citizens, Markets, and Governments in a Changing World*. Vancouver: University of British Columbia Press, 1995.

Kohn, Richard H. "How Democracies Control the Military." In *The Global Divergence of Democracies*, ed. Larry Diamond and Marc F. Plattner. Baltimore: The Johns Hopkins

University Press, 2001.

Kolarska-Bobinska, Lena. "The Role of the State: Contradictions in the Transition to Democracy." In *Constitutionalism and Democracy*, ed. Douglas Greenberg et al. New York: Oxford University Press, 1993.

Komesar, Neil K. *Law's Limits: The Rule of Law and the Supply and Demand of Rights.* New York: Cambridge University Press, 2001.

Krehbiel, Keith. *Information and Legislative Organization.* Ann Arbor: University of Michigan Press, 1991.

Kurian, George Thomas, ed. *World Encyclopedia of Parliaments and Legislatures.* Washington, DC: Congressional Quarterly Press, 1998.

Lasswell, Harold. "The Garrison State." *American Journal of Sociology* 46 (1941): 110-24.

Laver, Michael, and Norman Schofield. *Multiparty Government: The Politics of Coalition in Europe.* Ann Arbor: University of Michigan Press, 1998.

Laver, Michael, and Kenneth A. Shepsle. *Making and Breaking Governments: Cabinets and Legislatures in Parliamentary Democracies.* New York: Cambridge University Press, 1996.

Lees, John D., and Malcolm Shaw, eds. *Committees in Legislatures: A Comparative Analysis.* Durham, NC: Duke University Press, 1979.

Lev, Daniel S. "Social Movements, Constitutionalism, and Human Rights: Comments from the Malaysian and Indonesian Experiences." In *Constitutionalism and Democracy: Transitions in the Contemporary World*, ed. Douglas Greenberg et al. New York: Oxford University Press, 1993.

Levinson, Sanford V. *Responding to Imperfection: The Theory and Practice of Constitutional Amendment.* Princeton, NJ: Princeton University Press, 1995.

Light, Paul C. *Thickening Government: Federal Hierarchy and the Diffusion of Accountability.* Washington, DC: The Brookings Institution, 1995.

Lijphart, Arend. *Democracies: Patterns of Majoritarian and Consensus Government in Twenty-One Countries.* New Haven: Yale University Press, 1984.

———. *Democracy in Plural Societies: A Comparative Exploration.* New Haven: Yale University Press, 1977.

———. *Patterns of Democracy: Government Forms and Performance in Thirty-Six Countries.* New Haven: Yale University Press, 1999.

———. "The Alternative Vote: A Realistic Alternative for South Africa?" *Politikon* 18 (June 1991): 83-92.

Lindblom, Charles E. "The Science of Muddling Through," *Public Administration Review* 14 (Spring 1959): 79-88.

Linz, Juan J., and Alfred Stepan. *Problems of Democratic Transition and Consolidation: Southern Europe, South America, and Post-Communist Europe.* Baltimore: The Johns Hopkins University Press, 1996.

Lipset, Seymour Martin. *Political Man: The Social Bases of Politics.* New York: Doubleday, 1960.

Longley, Lawrence D., ed. *The Role of Legislatures and Parliaments in Democratizing and Newly Democratic Regimes.* Appleton, WI: Research Committee of Legislative Specialists, 1994.

Longley, Lawrence D., and Attila Ágh, eds. *The Changing Role of Parliamentary Committees.* Appleton, WI: Research Committee of Legislative Specialists, 1997.

Longley, Lawrence D., Attila Ágh, and Drago Zajc, eds. *Parliamentary Members and Leaders: The Delicate Balance.* Appleton, WI: Research Committee of Legislative Specialists, 2000.

Longley, Lawrence D., and Drago Zajc, eds. *The New Democratic Parliaments: The First Years.* Lawrence, WI: Research Committee of Legislative Specialists, 1998.

Luckham, Robert, Anne Marie Goetz, and Mary Kaldor. "Democratic Institutions and Democratic Politics." In *Can Democracy Be Designed? The Politics of Institutional Choice in Conflict-Torn Societies*, ed. Sunil Bastian and Robin Luckman. New York: Zed Books, 2003.

Lutz, Donald S. "Toward a Theory of Constitutional Amendment." *American Political Science Review* 88 (June 1994): 355-68.

Mainwaring, Scott. "Presidentialism, Multi-Party Systems, and Democracy: The Difficult Equation." *Comparative Politics* 25 (October 1992): 21-43.

————. *Rethinking Party Systems in the Third Wave of Democratization: The Case of Brazil.* Stanford, CA: Stanford University Press, 1999.

Maltzman, Forrest. *Competing Principles: Committees, Parties, and the Organization of Congress.* Ann Arbor: University of Michigan Press, 1998.

Mansbridge, Jane. *Beyond Adversary Democracy.* Chicago: University of Chicago Press, 1983.

March, James G., and Johan P. Olsen. *Democratic Governance.* New York: The Free Press, 1995.

McCubbins, Matthew, and Thomas Schwartz. "Congressional Oversight Overlooked: Police Patrol Versus Fire Alarm." *American Journal of Political Science* 41 (1984): 165-77.

McKay, David. *Designing Europe: Comparative Lessons from the Federal Experience.* New York: Oxford University Press, 2001.

Mendez, Juan, Guillermo O'Donnell, and Paulo Sérgio Pinhiero, eds. *The (Un)Rule of Law and the Underprivileged in Latin America.* Notre Dame, IN: University of Notre Dame Press, 1998.

Mezey, Micahel L. "Legislatures: Individual Purpose and Institutional Performance." In *Political Science: The State of the Discipline II*, ed. Ada W. Finifter. Washington, DC: American Political Science Association, 1993.

Miller, William Ian. *Bloodtaking and Peacemaking: Feud, Law, and Society in Saga Iceland.* Chicago: University of Chicago Press, 1990.

Moore, Barrington. *The Social Origins of Dictatorship and Democracy.* Boston: Beacon Press, 1966.

Morgenstern, Scott, and Benito Nacif, eds. *Legislative Politics in Latin America.* New York: Cambridge University Press, 2002.

Mueller, Dennis C. *Constitutional Democracy.* New York: Oxford University Press, 1996.

Müller, Wolfgang C., and Kaare Strøm, eds. *Coalition Governments in Western Europe.* New York: Oxford University Press, 2000

Murphy, Walter F. "Civil Law, Common Law, and Constitutional Democracy." *Louisiana Law Review* 91 (1991): 171-94.

————. "Constitutions, Constitutionalism, and Democracy." In *Constitutionalism and Democracy: Transitions in the Contemporary World*, ed. Douglas Greenberg et al. New York: Oxford University Press, 1993.

National Democratic Institute for International Affairs. *Legislatures and the Budget Process: An International Survey.* Washington, DC: National Democratic Institute, 2003.

Nedelsky, Jennifer. "American Constitutionalism and the Paradox of Private Property." In

Constitutionalism and Democracy, ed. John Elster and Rune Slagstad. New York: Cambridge University Press, 1993.

Nino, Carlos Santiago. *The Constitution of Deliberative Democracy*. New Haven: Yale University Press, 1996.

Norris, Pippa. *Electoral Engineering*. New York: Cambridge University Press, 2004.

Norton, Phillip, ed. *Legislatures*. New York: Oxford University Press, 1970.

————, ed. *Parliaments and Governments in Western Europe*. Portland, OR: Frank Cass Publishers, 1998.

Olson, David M. *Democratic Legislative Institutions: A Comparative View*. Armonk, NY: M. E. Sharpe, 1994.

Organization for Economic Cooperation and Development. *Results of the Survey on Budget Practices and Procedures*. Paris: OECD, 2004.

Pabottingi, Mochtar. "In the Absence of Autocentricity: The Case of Historical Preclusion of Democracy in Indonesia." In *Crafting Indonesian Democracy*, ed. R. William Liddle. Bandung: Penerbit Mizan, 2001.

Pakes, Francis. *Comparative Criminal Justice*. Portland, OR: Willan Publishing, 2004.

Peeler, John. *Building Democracy in Latin America*. Boulder, CO: Lynne Reiner, 1998.

Pennock, J. R., and R. W. Chapman, eds., *Nomos XXV: Liberal Democracy*. New York: New York University Press, 1983.

Pharr, Susan J., Robert D. Putnam, and Russell J. Dalton. "A Quarter Century of Declining Confidence." In *The Global Divergence of Democracies*, ed. Larry Diamond and Marc C. Plattner. Baltimore: The Johns Hopkins University Press, 2001.

Pickus, Noah M. J. "'Hearken Not to the Unnatural Voice': Publius and the Artifice of Attachment." In *Diversity and Citizenship: Rediscovering American Nationhood*, ed. Gary J. Jacobson and Susan Dunn. Lanham, MD: Rowman and Littlefield, 1996.

Polsby, Nelson W. "The Institutionalization of the U.S. House of Representatives." *American Political Science Review* 62 (March 1968): 144-68.

Przeworski, Adam. "Democracy as a Contingent Outcome of Conflicts." In *Constitutionalism and Democracy*, ed. Jon Elster and Rune Slagstad. New York: Cambridge University Press, 1988.

Przeworski, Adam et al. *Democracy and Development: Political Institutions and Well-Being in the World, 1950-1990*. New York: Cambridge University Press, 2000

Putnam, Robert. *Bowling Alone: The Collapse and Revival of American Community*. New York: Simon and Schuster, 2000.

————. *Making Democracy Work: Civic Traditions in Modern Italy*. Princeton, NJ: Princeton University Press, 1993.

Rakove, Jack N. *Original Meanings: Politics and Ideas in the Making of the Constitution*. New York: Vintage Books, 1997.

Ramaswamy, Sunder, and Jeffrey W. Cason, eds. *Development and Democracy: New Perspectives on an Old Debate*. Lebanon, NH: Middlebury College Press, 2003.

Rasch, Bjørn Erik. "Parliamentary Floor Voting Procedures and Agenda Setting in Europe." *Legislative Studies Quarterly* 25 (February 2000): 3-23.

Reilly, Benjamin. *Democracy in Divided Societies: Electoral Engineering for Conflict Management*. Cambridge: Cambridge University Press, 2001.

Reynolds, Andrew. "Designing Electoral Systems." In Richard Rose, ed. *International Encclopedia of Elections*. Washington, DC: Congressional Quarterly Press, 2000, 58-66.

Reynolds, Andrew, and Benjamin Reilly. *The International IDEA Handbook of Electoral System Design*. Stockholm: International Institute for Democracy and Electoral

Assistance, 1997.

Riggs, Fred W. "The Survival of Presidentialism in America: Para-constitutional Practices." *International Political Science Review* 9 (1988): 247-63.

————. *Thailand: The Modernization of a Bureaucratic Polity.* Honolulu: East-West Center Press, 1966.

Riker, William. *The Theory of Political Coalitions.* New Haven: Yale University Press, 1962.

————. *Federalism: Origin, Operation, Significance.* Boston: Little, Brown, 1964.

Rocher, François, and Miriam Smith, eds. *New Trends in Canadian Federalism.* Peterborough, Ontario: Broadview Press, 1995.

Rodden, Jonathan. "Comparative Federalism and Decentralization: On Meaning and Measurement." *Comparative Politics* 36 (July 2004): 481-96.

Rogers, James R. "The Impact of Bicameralism on Legislative Production." *Legislative Studies Quarterly* 28 (November 2003): 509-28.

Rohr, John A. *Civil Servants and Their Constitutions.* Lawrence: University Press of Kansas, 2002.

Rose, Jürgen, and Johannes Ch. Traut, eds. *Federealism and Decentralization: Perspectives for the Transformation Process in Eastern and Central Europe.* New York: Palgrave-Macmillan, 2002.

Russell, Peter H. *Constitutional Odyssey: Can Canadians Become a Sovereign People?* Toronto: University of Toronto Press, 2nd ed., 1993.

Russell, Peter H., and David M. O'Brien. *Judicial Independence in the Age of Democracy: Critical Perspectives from around the World.* Charlottesville: University Press of Virginia, 2001.

Rustow, Dankwart. "Transitions to Democracy." *Comparative Politics* 2 (April 1970): 337-63.

Sajo, Andras, and Vera Losonci, "Rule by Law in East Central Europe: Is the Emperor's New Suit a Straightjacket?" In *Constitutionalism and Democracy: Transitions in the Contemporary World*, ed. Douglas Greenberg et al. New York: Oxford University Press, 1993.

Sartori, Giovanni. *Comparative Constitutional Engineering: An Inquiry into Structures, Incentives, and Outcomes.* New York: New York University Press, 2nd ed., 1997.

Schattschneider, E. E. *The Semisovereign People: A Realist's View of Democracy in America.* New York: Holt, Rinehart and Winston, 1960.

Schneider, Ben Ross, and Blanca Heredia, eds. *Reinventing Leviathan: The Politics of Administrative Reform in Developing Countries.* Miami: North-South Center Press, 2003.

Schneier, Edward, and Bertram Gross. *Legislative Strategy: Shaping Public Policy.* New York: St. Martin's Press, 1993.

Schneier, Edward, and John Brian Murtaugh. *New York Politics: A Tale of Two States.* Armonk, NY: M. E. Sharpe, 2001.

Schwarz, Adam. *A Nation in Waiting: Indonesia's Search for Stability.* Boulder, CO: Westview Press, 2nd ed., 2000.

Schwarz, Herman. "Lustration in Eastern Europe." In *Transitional Justice: How Emerging Democracies Reckon with Former Regimes*, ed. Neil J. Kritz. Washington, DC: United States Institute of Peace, 1995.

Shapiro, Ian. *Democracy's Place.* Ithaca, NY: Cornell University Press, 1996.

Sharoff, Alan. "Women's Representation in Legislatures and Cabinets in Industrial

Democracies." *International Political Science Review* 21 (April 2000): 203-16.

Shugart, Matthew Soberg, and John M. Carey. *Presidents and Assemblies: Constitutional Design and Electoral Dynamics.* New York: Cambridge University Press, 1992.

Sisk, Timothy D. *Democracy at the Local Level: The International IDEA Handbook on Participation, Representation, Conflict Management, and Governance.* Stockholm: International Institute for Democracy and Electoral Assistance, 2001.

Sklar, Richard L. "Democracy in Africa." *African Studies Review* 26 (1983): 1-14.

Skolnick, Jerome H. *Justice without Trial: Law Enforcement in a Democratic Society.* Englewood Cliffs, NJ: Macmillan, 3rd ed., 1994.

Squire, Peverill. "Career Opportunities and Membership Stability in Legislatures." *Legislative Studies Quarterly* 13 (February 1988): 65-82.

Stepan, Alfred. *Arguing Comparative Politics.* New York: Oxford, 2001.

Stone, Geoffrey R., Richard A. Epstein, and Cass R. Sunstein, eds. *The Bill of Rights in the Modern State.* Chicago: University of Chicago Press, 1992.

Suleiman, Ezra. "Bureaucracy and Democratic Consolidation: Lessons from Eastern Europe." In *Transitions to Democracy*, ed. Lisa Anderson. New York: Columbia University Press, 1999.

———. *Dismantling Democratic States.* Princeton, N.J.: Princeton University Press, 2003.

Sunstein, Cass R. "Constitutionalism and Secession." *University of Chicago Law Review* 58 (1991): 633-70.

———. *Designing Democracy: What Constitutions Do.* New York: Oxford University Press, 2001.

Teitel, Ruti. "Transitional Justice: The Role of Law in Political Transformation." *Yale Law Journal* 106 (1997): 2009-51.

Tiebout, Charles M. "A Pure Theory of Local Expenditure." *Journal of Political Economy* 74 (Fall 1956): 416-25.

Tilly, Charles. "The Top-down and Bottom-up Construction of Democracy." In *Classes and Elites in Democracy and Democratization*, ed. Eva Etzioni-Halevy. New York: Garland, 1997.

Tocqueville, Alexis de. *Democracy in America.* New York: Alfred A. Knopf, 1945.

Tsebelis, George. *Veto Players: How Political Institutions Work.* Princeton, NJ: Princeton University Press, 2002.

Tsebelis, George, and Jeanette Money. *Bicameralism.* New York: Cambridge University Press, 1997.

Vanhanen, Tatu. *The Process of Democratization: A Comparative Study of 147 States, 1980-88.* New York: Crane Russak, 1990.

Warren, Mark E. *Democracy and Association.* Princeton, NJ: Princeton University Press, 2001.

Weaver, R. Kent, and Bert A. Rockman, eds. *Do Institutions Matter? Government Capabilities in the United States and Abroad.* Washington, DC: The Brookings Institution, 1993.

Weber, Max. *The Theory of Social and Economic Organization.* Translated by A. M. Henderson and Talcott Parsons. New York: Oxford University Press, 1947.

Wheare, Kenneth C. *Federal Government.* Oxford: Oxford University Press, 1946.

Wildavsky, Aaron. *Federalism and Political Culture.* Edited by David Schleicher and Brenda Swedlow. New Brunswick, NJ: Transaction Books, 1998.

Wood, B. Dan, and Richard W. Waterman. *Bureaucratic Dynamics: The Role of Bureaucracy in a Democracy.* Boulder, CO: Westview Press, 1994.

Zagarri, Rosemarie. *The Politics of Size: Representation in the United States, 1776-1850.* Ithaca, NY: Cornell University Press, 1987.

Ziolkowski, Theodore. *The Mirror of Justice: Literary Reflections of Legal Crises.* Princeton, NJ: Princeton University Press, 1997.

Zuckerman, Adrian A. S., Sergio Chiarloni, and Peter Gottwald, eds. *Civil Justice in Crisis: Comparative Perspectives on Civil Procedure.* New York: Oxford University Press, 1999.

Index

About the Author

Edward ("Ned") Schneier is professor emeritus of political science at The City College of the City University of New York. He has also taught at Johns Hopkins, Princeton, and Columbia universities; most recently as the Charles Evans Hughes Visiting Professor of Jurisprudence at Colgate University. He has twice worked as a research fellow at the Brookings Institution, won fellowships from the National Endowment for the Humanities, and was a Fulbright fellow in Iceland in 1989 and Indonesia in 2001. He has authored or coauthored eight other books, including *Legislative Strategy: Shaping Public Policy* and *New York Politics: A Tale of Two States*. A recent monograph on the constitution-building process in Indonesia is available from the International Institute for Democracy and Electoral Assistance in Stockholm. Dr. Schneier, who was educated at Oberlin College and Claremont University, is twice a father and grandfather and lives with his wife Margrit in Copake, New York. He is president of the Board of Trustees of the Roe-Jan Library, president of the Copake Democratic Club, and executive director of the Fund for Higher Education Research. He has also run unsuccessfully for Congress, worked as legislative assistant to Senator Birch Bayh, served as professor-in-residence for the New York State Assembly Internship Committee, worked as a lobbyist in Albany, and is a partner in Grassroots, a neighborhood bar in New York's East Village.